ABOUT THE EDITORS

ILYA KAMINSKY was born in Odessa, in the former Soviet Union, and arrived in the United States in 1993, when his family was granted asylum by the American government. He is the author of *Dancing in Odessa*, which won the American Academy of Arts and Letters' Metcalf Award, a Whiting Writers Award, and a Lannan Fellowship, among other honors. He teaches at San Diego State University.

SUSAN HARRIS is the Editorial Director of Words Without Borders. She is the former director and editor in chief of Northwestern University Press and the founding editor of its Hydra imprint of literature in translation.

WORDS WITHOUT BORDERS is a partner of PEN American Center and the Center for Literary Translation at Columbia University, and is hosted by Bard College in Annandale-on-Hudson, New York. It serves as an online haven for international literature and as an advocate for writers around the world.

THE ECCO ANTHOLOGY
OF INTERNATIONAL POETRY

THIS BOOK DWELLS
ANTIOCH
THE ANTA LIBRARY

ALSO BY

ILYA KAMINSKY

POETRY

Dancing in Odessa
Musica Humana

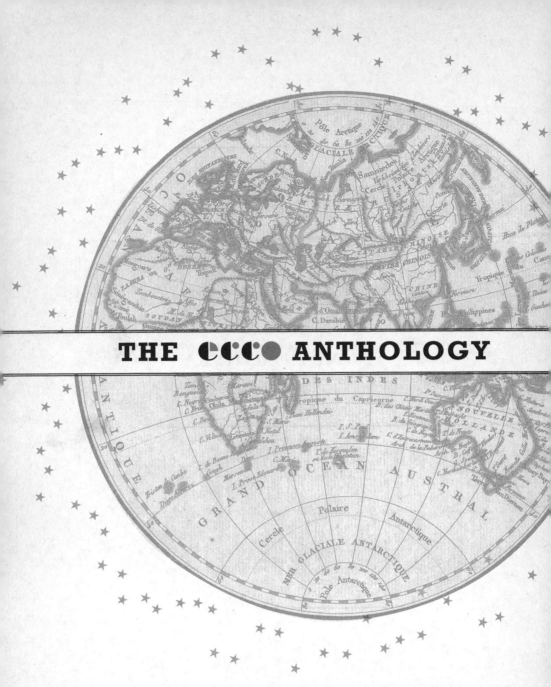

THE ECCO ANTHOLOGY

An Imprint of HarperCollinsPublishers

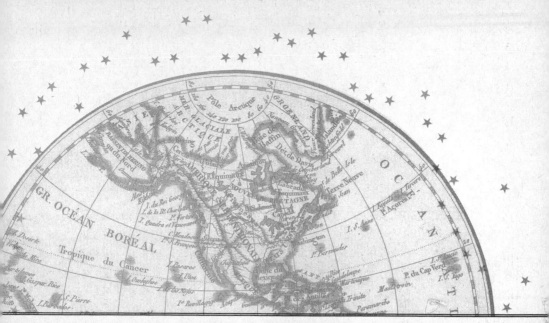

ᴼᶠ INTERNATIONAL POETRY

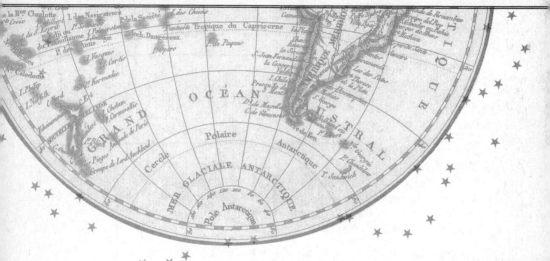

EDITED BY

ILYA KAMINSKY
ᴬᴺᴰ **SUSAN HARRIS**

ᴼᶠ WORDS WITHOUT BORDERS

THE ECCO ANTHOLOGY OF INTERNATIONAL POETRY. Copyright © 2010 by Words Without Borders. All rights reserved. Printed in the United States of America. No part of this book may be used or reproduced in any manner whatsoever without written permission except in the case of brief quotations embodied in critical articles and reviews. For information, address HarperCollins Publishers, 10 East 53rd Street, New York, NY 10022.

HarperCollins books may be purchased for educational, business, or sales promotional use. For information, please write: Special Markets Department, HarperCollins Publishers, 10 East 53rd Street, New York, NY 10022.

FIRST EDITION

Designed by Mary Austin Speaker

Library of Congress Cataloging-in-Publication Data is available upon request.

ISBN 978-0-06-158324-7

10 11 12 13 14   DIX/RRD   10 9 8 7 6 5 4 3 2

CONTENTS

ACKNOWLEDGMENTS

We thank Daniel Halpern, Michael Signorelli, and Alane Salierno Mason for their support of this project, David Stanford Burr for his meticulous copy editing, and Liz Cali, Christy Call, Vincent Francone, and Anne McPeak for editorial and permissions assistance. Ilya Kaminsky thanks Eleanor Wilner, Carolyn Forché, Edward Hirsch, Arthur Sze, and Jerome Rothenberg for advice; the Lannan Foundation for financial support while editing the book and MacDowell Colony for the time and place to do so; his teachers and students for the world of poetry they have daily shared with him; and Katie Farris for ten years of joy.

All royalties from the sales of this book will be donated to Words Without Borders.

INTRODUCTION

CORRESPONDENCES IN THE AIR

Octavio Paz once wrote that the modern poet "extracts his visions from within himself." It is my hope that a comprehensive, aesthetically varied anthology of poetry from around the globe will allow American poets and readers a chance to extract such visions not just from "within themselves" but in conversation with a global poetic tradition. Reading an anthology of world poetry gives one a chance to overhear similarities, or what Anna Akhmatova once called "correspondences in the air"—that is, moments when authors of different geographical and historical circumstances, languages, and traditions, seem to address each other in their works. I hope that these voices brought from outside our borders will allow us, in this somewhat unsettling time in Anglo American political history, to find the voice within that is strong and compelling, an instrument of poetry that—to rephrase Auden—is our chief means of breaking bread with the world.

Such "correspondences in the air" abound in this collection. Open this book to any page and you may discover a poem by Szymborska in conversation with a line by Akhmatova, who in turn was responding to Szymborska's countryman Mitskevich's allusion to Shakespeare's echoing a moment in the Old Testament. Perhaps the most important lesson we can glean from these correspondences is how necessary it is for poets to dialogue, to return to their poetic origins in order to create something new. After all, the word "originality" in English has its roots in "origin." Or, as American poet Frank Bidart suggests, we fill preexisting forms, and in filling them we change them, and are ourselves changed.

Let's consider one such set of "correspondences" by going back to Ecclesiastes, which had a strong influence on twentieth-century world poetry, as is evident throughout this anthology. Here is the original biblical text:

> To every thing there is a season,
> And a time to every purpose under the heaven:
> A time to be born, and a time to die;
> A time to plant, and a time to pluck up that which is planted;
> A time to kill, and a time to heal;
> A time to break down, and a time to build up;
> A time to weep, and a time to laugh;
> A time to mourn, and a time to dance;
> A time to cast away stones, and a time to gather stones together;
> A time to embrace, and a time to refrain from embracing;
> A time to get, and a time to lose;
> A time to keep, and a time to cast away;
> A time to rend, and a time to sew;
> A time to keep silence, and a time to speak;
> A time to love, and a time to hate;
> A time of war, and a time of peace.

In the Bible, the narrator of the above verses speaks in a voice of authority to the community. The voice is declarative, aware that it speaks wisdom. Look what happened when Polish poet Tymoteusz Karpowicz borrowed this "list poem" format with its anaphorical repetition of the word "time," and transformed it into a post–World War II landscape:

Ecclesiastes

there is a time of opening the eyes and closing the bed
time for donning a shirt and shedding sleep
time for drowsy soap and half-awakened skin
time for the hair-brush and for the sparks in the hair
time for trouser-legs time for shoe-laces time for buttons
for laddered stockings for the slipper's blindness
time for the fork and for the knife time for sausages and boiled eggs
time for the tram time for the conductress time for the policeman
time for good morning and time for goodbye
time for carrots peas and parsley
for tomato soup and shepherd's pie
time for trussing chicken and releasing forbidden speeds of thought
time for a cinema ticket or a ticket to nowhere
to a river perhaps perhaps to a cloud
there is finally a time of closed eyelids and the open bed
time for past present and future
praesens historicum and plusquamperfectum
time perfect and imperfect
time from wall to wall

While Karpowicz announces from the start—the very title of the piece—his intent to correspond with the older text, the images, tone, and use of detail do a great deal to transform the tone of the canonical litany. This onslaught of detail in Karpowicz's version—a cinema ticket, tomato soup, a hair-brush—offers its own metaphysics, homelier in comparison to the ecclesiastical narrator's grand proclamations. Writing in postwar Europe, having witnessed the great acts of destruction and survival, Karpowicz makes use of a tone that is both ironic and tender. His response is multilingual, multivocal; it refuses to console, and yet consoles. It allows the canonical form to enter into our world.

Another poet writing in the post–World War II landscape, Paul Celan, offers us a very different take on what a "correspondence" with a canonical text may accomplish:

Corona

Autumn eats its leaf out of my hand: we are friends.
From the nuts we shell time and we teach it to walk:
then time returns to the shell.

In the mirror it's Sunday,
in dream there is room for sleeping,
our mouths speak the truth.

My eye moves down to the sex of my loved one:
we look at each other,
we exchange dark words,
we love each other like poppy and recollection,
we sleep like wine in the conches,
like the sea in the moon's blood ray.

We stand by the window embracing, and people look up from the street:
it is time they knew!
It is time the stone made an effort to flower,
time unrest had a beating heart.
It is time it were time

It is time

Celan's poem is a very private, personal address. "It is time they knew!" he exclaims, as his repetition of "time" in the last five lines of the poem echoes the old text, giving it a chance to enter a twentieth-century love lyric. If the speaker is addressing the public (as in Ecclesiastes), it is by standing with his lover by the window, embracing.

Yet another twentieth-century poet who echoed this biblical litany in a very personal way is Carlos Drummond de Andrade. In his poem "Your Shoulders Hold Up the World," he offers intense self-examination:

A time comes when you no longer can say: my God.
A time of total cleaning up.

A time when you no longer can say: my love.
Because love proved useless.
And the eyes don't cry.
And the hands do only rough work.
And the heart is dry.

Women knock at your door in vain, you won't open.
You remain alone, the light turned off,
and your enormous eyes shine in the dark.
It is obvious you no longer know how to suffer.
And you want nothing from your friends.

Who cares if old age comes, what is old age?
Your shoulders are holding up the world
and it's lighter than a child's hand.
Wars, famine, family fights inside buildings
prove only that life goes on
and not everybody has freed himself yet.
Some (the delicate ones) judging the spectacle cruel
will prefer to die.
A time comes when death doesn't help.
A time comes when life is an order.
Just life, without any escapes.

The wisdom of Ecclesiastes is updated here to the twentieth-century voice in a similar way as in the previous poems—the proclamatory public tone is replaced by the utterance of an individual, in this case, one persuading himself against suicide. This voice, although at times public, is not so interested in teaching others how to live—it is interested in voicing one human's need to survive. The struggle here is not so much with the community as it is with one's self. This, of course, reminds us of Yeats's great twentieth-century statement that "argument with another is a rhetoric, argument with one's self is poetry."

Finally, Yehuda Amichai's poem "A Man in His Life" enters into confrontation with Ecclesiastes:

A Man in His Life

A man doesn't have time in his life
to have time for everything.
He doesn't have seasons enough to have
a season for every purpose. Ecclesiastes
Was wrong about that.

A man needs to love and to hate at the same moment,
to laugh and cry with the same eyes,
with the same hands to throw stones and to gather them,
to make love in war and war in love.
And to hate and forgive and remember and forget,
to arrange and confuse, to eat and to digest
what history
takes years and years to do.

A man doesn't have time.
When he loses he seeks, when he finds
he forgets, when he forgets he loves,
when he loves he begins to forget.

And his soul is seasoned, his soul
is very professional.
Only his body remains forever
an amateur. It tries and it misses,
gets muddled, doesn't learn a thing,
drunk and blind in its pleasures
and its pains.

He will die as figs die in autumn,
Shriveled and full of himself and sweet,
the leaves growing dry on the ground,
the bare branches pointing to the place
where there's time for everything.

This ability to hate and love at once, in the same line, in the same mo-
ment, is perhaps one of the more characteristic attributes of many

great poems from this era, whose "confusion" is not for the sake of mere linguistic fireworks, but to describe the joyfulness and terror of a human being in the twentieth century. Amichai, like the other poets before him, is able to go back to the origin of the biblical text, but he does not merely update it for our own moment in time—he confronts it. His confrontation is personal, intimate just as much as it is public; the argument with the tradition becomes more powerful in its intimacy of address.

The above group of twentieth-century poets echoing the same origin could of course be much larger, and could make up an anthology in its own right. Such cases are not at all unusual. Thus, Faiz Ahmed Faiz of Pakistan was strongly influenced by the formal Persian tradition, and García Lorca "corresponded" with traditions as various as *romanceros*, Arabic *qasidas* of medieval Spain, Góngora's metaphors, and the poetic expanse of Walt Whitman. Whitman, our American forebear, also deeply affected numerous twentieth-century poets worldwide: Mayakovsky, Apollinaire, Pessoa, Neruda, Césaire, Miłosz, and many others come to mind. Languages are many, says Voznesensky, poetry is one. If this is true, then perhaps an avid reader of poetry from around the globe may have a chance to glimpse into the heart of the art of poetry itself—of that which exists between languages. Poets, of course, create their own communities of influence, and this anthology has used the idea of a poetic, rather than geopolitical, community as a guiding principle.

If poets can speak to one another over time, space, and cultural difference, it is translation that provides the conduit.

TRANSLATION

Translation should be similar [to the original] but not the very same; and the similarity should not be like that of a painting or a statue to the person represented, but rather like that of a son to a father, where there is a shadowy something—akin to what painters call one's air—hovering about the face, and especially in the eyes, out of which there grows a likeness that immediately, upon our beholding the child, calls the father up before us.

—PETRARCH

According to George Steiner, an original poem exists in an ideal, static state, and the translator attempts to transmigrate this ideal totality into a second language. Since two languages never mesh perfectly, a translation can never be completely successful; something is always lost. If translation can never serve as a perfect mirror, we could hypothesize that it works instead as an evidence or trace of a great voice. Sometimes such traces are enough—García Lorca and Anna Akhmatova even in their English translations have influenced American poets of the twentieth century. Like a phoenix, the poems of great masters are reborn from the ashes of translation.

However, watching the magic of this rebirth in a new language teaches us about not only the genius of the poet translated but also the genius of what is possible in English, as it bends each single one of its own rules to accommodate various new forms. We learn something new about the English language each time we confront another syntax, another grammar, another musical way of organizing silences in a mouth. By translating, we learn how the limits of our English-speaking minds can be stretched to accommodate the foreign, and how thereby we are able to make our own language more beautiful—to awaken it.

To realize that some of the more successful translations done in twentieth-century English do not serve as mirrors, one needs only to look at John Felstiner's version of Paul Celan's "Deathfugue" included in this volume. While one appreciates Felstiner's powerful use of German words interspersed with English, readers should know that this striking and powerful juxtaposition of languages (which also occurs in Jerome Rothenberg's earlier translation) does not happen in Celan's poem in German. The poem is made more powerful as we learn the tragic meaning of the foreign words without needing to know German ourselves—it gives English readers the experience of being other, alienated, from language, from power. To realize this is to see clearly that the successful translation, even a very "faithful" one, has no need to hold up the mirror to the original. In a successful translation we observe the renewal of the living tissue; the original undergoes the process of transformation. Celan himself understood the complexity of this process: "The language with which I make my poems has nothing to do with one spoken here or elsewhere." Translation should, Mahmoud Darwish suggested, become more than a new poem in another language. It should expend into that language new vastness.

+ + +

John Dryden, writing his seventeenth-century preface to *Ovid's Epistles*, suggested that translations could be divided into three categories. The first one Dryden called "metaphrase," which translates the poem word by word, line by line, from one language to another. The second is "paraphrase," or what Dryden called "translation with latitude," which permits the translator to keep the author in view while changing words of the original. Dryden's third category is closer to "imitation"— a translation in which the poet works with the original text but allows the departure from its meaning and words where necessary to produce the best final result in a new language.

What, then, is a faithful translation? What is not? And what, precisely, is the moment one becomes more interesting than the other, and why? Here is an example of how in a formal, word-by-word translation the meanings of another language are brought into English. The language here is Hebrew, and it requires us to read the passage from right to left:

צֶרָאֶה ת אֶן, סִיַמֶּשׁה תֵא, סֵיהֹלֶא ארְבֿ, תִישׁאֶרְבֿ.
[and the earth] [the earth] [and] [the heavens] [God] [created] [in the beginning]

חוּרְ ו; סוֹהֹת יַנֿפֿ-לַע, רֶשֹׁחֹו, וּהֹבֿן וּהֹת
[God] [and the spirit of] [deep] [upon the face of] [and darkness] [and void] [waste] [was]

סִיַמַה יַנֿפֿ-לַע תֶפֶחֶרְמ, סֵיהֹלֶא הֶתֶיָה, צֶרָאֶהֹו.
[and there was] [light] [let there be] [God] [and said] [the waters] [upon the face of] [moved]

רוֹא-יהְיַו; רוֹא יהְי, סֵיהֹלֶא רֶמאֹיַו.
[between] [God] [and divided] [that good] [the light] [God] [and saw light]

These opening verses of Genesis are of course well known. But what if we, in a moment of intercultural confusion, read them from left to right, the way we are accustomed to read in English:

> And the earth, the earth and the heavens God created in the
>   beginning
> God and the spirit of deep upon the face of and darkness and void
>   waste was
> And there was light let there be God and said the waters . . .

What sort of poetry is found in this way of willful misreading? And, what does it teach us about the new possibilities translation can bring to our reading of even the most canonical texts?

Fascination with what could be "found" in translation, with structures of other languages and their relationships to poetic impulse in English, has long intrigued poets and translators alike, sometimes producing famous blunders, such as the case of Ezra Pound's and Ernest Fenollosa's cultural misreadings in their attempts to draw parallels between their appropriation of classical Chinese texts, and their emphasis on "ideogrammic" poetry as a classical example of imagism. While the Anglo American Imagist movement, which Pound helped to create in 1909 (along with H.D., Amy Lowell, William Carlos Williams, and others), to a large extent misunderstood the Chinese traditions they claimed to appropriate, their scholarly blunders resulted in new ways of seeing what poetry can do in the English language.

The scandals of classical scholars need not detain us, for any version in the end lives or dies on the strength of its own readability. Here is an example of the Chinese language. Observe the characters, their similarities, and how they change visually with new meanings:

Here is the word for Man:

人

And what happens to it when we write Fire:

火

And what happens to it when we write Autumn:

秋

And here is the word for Heart/Mind:

心

Now, see what happens when we want to convey Sorrow:

秋
心

When many Westerners encounter these ideograms, they are quick to suggest that an element of poetry exists in their very appearance. But how to bring that effect across into English? This question is relevant to many Asian American poets at work today. Here are a few lines from "A Table in the Wilderness" by a contemporary Asian American poet, Li-Young Lee:

> I draw a window
> And a man sitting inside it.
>
> I draw a bird in flight above the lintel.
>
> That is my picture of thinking.
>
> If I put a woman there instead
> Of the man, it is a picture of speaking.
>
> If I draw a second bird
> In the woman's lap, it's ministering.
>
> A third flying below her feet.
> Now it's singing.
>
> Or erase the birds,
> Make ivy branching

Around the woman's ankles, clinging
To her knees, and it becomes remembering.

You will have to find your own
Pictures, whoever you are,
Whatever your need [. . .]

The challenges of translation from Asian languages are formidable. Here is an example of a brief poem by Kancho translated by various hands. First, how it sounds in the original:

kara-oto mo sukoshi iitaki botan kana.

And in word-by-word translation:

Chinese-sound even, a little-say-want, peony 'tis!

Now, here are five different versions done by several translators, each claiming to be authentic:

the peony blooms: / I feel like making some / Chinese sounds

I'd like to say / some thing in Chinese / to the peony

my peony: / I'd like to treat it to / some Chinese

the peonies bloom: / I wish I could speak / a little Chinese

is that rustling / the peony saying something / in Chinese?

The multiplicity of meanings in the above versions of the same text is somewhat comic. Yet when we put all these versions together we also see how many different poems can be written with the same number of words; this shows us what a rich variety of possibilities the English language offers to its poets. One wants to encourage the readers of this book to look for such possibilities, to see how poetry in translation can expand the limits of their own language.

+   +   +

Paul Celan called works of translation "encounters." All are encounters, he wrote of his translations: "here, too, I have gone with my very being towards language."

Celan's own translations of Emily Dickinson's work into German, translated back into English by John Felstiner, offer perhaps the most interesting case study for our discussion. Here are Emily Dickinson's own words:

> Let down the board, Oh Death—
> The tired Flocks come in
> Whose bleating ceases to repeat
> Whose wandering is done—

And, here is what Celan's German translation does to this text, when rendered back into English:

> Off with the barrier, Death!
> The flock comes in, there comes
> who bleated and now never bleats,
> who no more wanders, comes.

What is lost in translation? The famous dashes, of course. The "tired flock" is also a clear loss, and we miss it. But what is gained? Certainly, many will find "wanders, comes" to be an elegant, appealing addition. But the question of "lost" and "found" is less interesting than the chance itself of our watching two great minds at work on the same stanza.

Perhaps this approach to discussing the art of translation is not very different from the tradition of midrash, in which the holy book is revised again and again, so the years bring only more richness and variety. By admitting that no poem can truly be translated, but that a new poetics can flow from the originals, a literary tradition is established in that midrash-like handshake between the author of the original and her translators. In this mode of translation, we allow ourselves to shake hands with Ovid and Shakespeare, Anna Swir, Paul Celan, Marina Tsvetaeva, and Mahmoud Darwish. The music of the original is almost always lost when the meaning of the poem is transported into another language (imagine translating Blake's "The Tiger" into Japanese). On the other side, the inherent strangeness of the true poem, its use of images and details to convey ideas, can certainly be carried across into a different tongue. After all, followers of numerous world religions read their sacred texts in third- or fourth-hand translation. The magic of image, litany, rhythm, and incantation does survive linguistic boundaries. We enter the company of great poets not by ruthlessly rewriting their work, shoving it into our language, but instead by honoring them in the medium we possess, giving them a second voice.

The bottom line is not in the play of "gains" and "losses" of translation but in our ability to observe how great poets approach language—and the lessons we ourselves may learn from such observations. "We sleep in language," writes Robert Kelly; "We sleep in language, if language does not come to wake us with its strangeness."

+   +   +

Finally, one must mention the influence of translation on recent poetry in English, which has been enormous. It is difficult to imagine the work of most contemporary poets, from Robert Bly to Anne Carson, without the influence of global literature. And, in fact, major transformations in English literature are often associated with translation, as noted by Ezra Pound: "English literature lives on translations, it is fed by translations, every new exuberance, every new heave is stimulated by translations, every allegedly great age is an age of translations, beginning with Geoffrey Chaucer." One needs only to cite such works as Chaucer's *Troilus and Criseyde*, the King James version of the Bible, Sydney's translations from Petrarch, and Pound's translations from Anglo-Saxon and from Li Po, to see the key roles translation has played in shaping and reshaping English poetry, much as American nationhood and politics have changed through our interaction with the world.

It is nearly impossible to write about translation in the twentieth century without mentioning history and politics. Although the poet Joseph Brodsky, himself a political prisoner and an exile, movingly claimed that the realms of poetry and politics share only a few things: "the letter p and the letter o—and not much more than that," it could also be observed that twentieth-century poetics were deeply affected by numerous geopolitical changes. For instance, the aftermath of colonial policies in France dramatically changed the poetics of the French language. Léopold Sédar Senghor, the first president of Senegal, and Augustinho Neto, the first president of independent Angola, both wrote powerful poetry in French. These poets, along with many others such as Aimé Césaire, the genius of the Négritude movement, widened the scope of French poetics by blending it with the oral tradition of precolonial languages. This work, "hurt" into history (to paraphrase Auden), had a volcanic influence in the life of the Francophone intellectual world.

Then, there is a question of minority languages, such as Belorussian, Catalan, Gaelic, Yiddish, and numerous others. I tried to include in this volume a selection from many such languages, paying particular attention to lesser known but excellent poets such as the Yiddish writer Israel Emiot, or younger poets trying to preserve and revive the poetics endangered by their current political regimes, such as Belorussian poet Valzhyna Mort. Then, there are colonial languages such as Afrikaans, which was as central to the identity of many "colored" South Africans as it was to the white Boers—and is a tragic reminder for many black South Africans of a language that served as a medium of the apartheid regime. The history that surrounds this language is torturous and oppressive, and yet the work of poets writing in it—such as Breyten Breytenbach—is resonant, moving, rehabilitating.

Another welcome development translation has undertaken in the mid- to late twentieth century is the recognition of the importance of translation as an act of civic responsibility. It is not unusual these days to hear an American translator say that she translates partly because she lives in an empire and sees translation work as a chance to educate the American readers about the voices of the larger world. The expansion of languages of colonial power continues. Marilyn Hacker's brilliant translations of Vénus Khoury-Ghata, published several years ago, were a revelation to many of her English-speaking contemporaries. Khoury-Ghata, born in Lebanon in 1937, has been a resident of France since 1973, though Lebanon continues to inspire her, becoming now an imaginary landscape seen through the lens of French verse—and changing the perspective from which many of us have seen poetics of that language. This transformation is not entirely different from the one inspired by Edmond Jabès, a great Egypt-born Jewish poet of the earlier generation, who was exiled to Paris and there wrote the powerful *The Book of Questions*, his response to the political and dramatic events of his time. Jabès's multivocal perspective deeply affected—and expanded—late twentieth-century French poetry. Masterfully translated into English by Rosmarie Waldrop, this text had a similar effect on English-speaking poets of a new generation. In his book of essays, *A Faithful Existence*, Forrest Gander writes: "I may hope that my own translations are less colonial raids into other languages than subversions of English, injections of new poetic forms, ideas, images and rhythms into the muscular arm of the language of power."

So, here is our attempt to present an American audience with the poems of the larger world, poems of perversion and praise and lament from a century of destroyed cities, molten borders between states and nations, apartheid, Hiroshima, Auschwitz, totalitarianism, racism, world wars, massive destruction, torture, epidemics, struggle, resistance. Here are love songs and songs of protest depicting private life, tenderness, eroticism, passion, kindness, forgiveness, spiritual life, exploration of new forms of demotic language and consciousness, experiments with dream-work, intersections of poetry and prose. Here are voices of a century of witness in art, and of ecstatic address, of manifestoes and declarations, and quiet lyricisms on the joys of private existence—not unlike our own. A real book, W. H. Auden suggested, is not the one that we read, but the one that reads us.

A NOTE ON THIS BOOK'S SELECTION PROCESS

All anthologies are unfinished and very private attempts to compose a song in many tongues. The anthologist begins her or his work already knowing that the final selection will in the end displease many and that no one—herself or himself least of all—will be satisfied with the final choices. Contemporary poetries are thankfully so diverse and varied that limitations had to be imposed, much to my own displeasure. But one must persist. This book does not pretend or claim to be a representative anthology of contemporary world poetry. I had a single criterion for my selection: the quality of the poem in English. Of course I do not mean "perfect" English—many poems in this anthology sound strange, even at times awkwardly alien, not because they are poorly written in English, but because they express something new in it. This collection attempts to reflect and honor the tradition of the rich, varied, and diverse anthologies of international poetry published in the past few decades, as well adding many new names, translations, and approaches to the mix.

Any selection process includes numerous frustrations. Inability to publish poets due to the expenses of permissions or failure to find appropriate copyright holders ranks very high on that list of frustrations. Several important poets whose work I love are not in this book or are represented by only one poem because we could not afford their copyright-holders' fees.

Perhaps the most frustrating part of editing this collection was the unfortunate scarcity of quality translation from contemporary Asian and African poetries. While European, and to some extent Latin American, poets are available to us in quality translation, there have been some glaring and shameful omissions in making available work from other parts of the world. While it is easy to name dozens of influential contemporary American poets involved in the work of translation from a region like Paris, France, it is not easy at all to name any who translate from the wonderfully rich tradition of the French-language poetries of Africa. Furthermore, I am the first to lament that there are far fewer women poets than I would have liked to include here who are found in English in quality translations. To encourage the future translations of such poets, Words Without Borders (www .wordswithoutborders.org) will open a forum on the Web site for discussion of poets whose work we did not include here, but who should be more known and anthologized in the United States. We welcome readers and critics to visit us and to give us your suggestions for the future.

On a more technical note, we decided against accompanying poetry with lengthy biographical and critical information (only very brief notes are available at the end of the book), because those materials often affect the way poetry is read, and we feel that information ranging from awards to world wars has little to do with a "soul's search for a release in language," which is what Joseph Brodsky claimed our best poems enact. Or to put it another way, "It really matters that great poems get written," Ezra Pound said, "and it doesn't matter a damn who writes them." We know very little, after all, of the biography of one of the greatest English poets who ever lived, William Shakespeare. As William Hazlitt suggested, Shakespeare was "the least of an egotist that it was possible to be," but instead embodied "all that others were, or that they could become." Keats, in his letter to Richard Woodhouse in 1818, agreed:

> A Poet is the most unpoetical of any thing in existence; because he has no Identity—he is continually in for—and filling some other Body—The Sun, the Moon, the Sea, and Men and Women who are creatures of impulse are poetical and have about them an unchangeable attribute—the poet has none; no identity—he is certainly the most unpoetical of all God's creatures.

The sentiments expressed in Keats's letter are echoed in the work of many poets included in this book. Borges's prose poem "Everything and Nothing" is perhaps the most powerful and overt response.

Along these same lines, I hoped to disregard the influences of history as much as possible. We divided poets not by countries of birth (what, then, of hundreds of Hindi poets writing in Pakistan, Yiddish poets writing around the globe, or cases like the Lithuanian-born Polish poet Czesław Miłosz, or Edmond Jabès?) or by their languages (numerous poets, such as Tristan Tzara, wrote in more than one language), but collected their works in chronological order of one hundred years—a period they all shared. For many of them—displaced, exiled, dislocated between languages and geographies—time alone was their dwelling. A poet's relation to time is never simple; some in this book argue that poets should speak for their time, others say that poets should speak as if time does not exist. Still, all voiced their poems in the same one hundred years we know as the twentieth century.

+   +   +

Finally, my deepest gratitude goes to my collaborator, Susan Harris, editorial director of Words Without Borders, for her amazing ability to deal with the complex world of permissions, copyrights, and the publishing industry, and for her grace, wisdom, passion, and enormous patience. This project would never have been possible without her formidable gifts. However, all the mistakes and omissions in selecting the work of the poets included here are mine only.

In the end, it was hard to resist certain thematic, formal, or stylistic themes. There are poems of eros and lament and praise. There are prayers, erotic poems, protest, moments of meditation, elegies, litanies. There are pages from novels (which some argue were in fact prose poem sequences). There are poets of surrealism, futurism, Acmeism, Négritude, and numerous other movements—but my hope is that you will leave all those labels aside and read these poems for what they do to our language, our emotional and spiritual lives. Perhaps you will want to share them with friends, to call friends on the phone and recite a stanza or a couplet to them. I know: I have done it myself.

—Ilya Kaminsky
San Diego, California, 2009

RABINDRANATH TAGORE

(BENGAL, 1861–1941)

On My Birthday

Today I imagine the words of countless
Languages to be suddenly fetterless—
After long incarceration
In the fortress of grammar, suddenly up in rebellion.
Maddened by the stamp-stamping
Of unmitigated regimented drilling.
They have jumped the constraints of sentence
To seek free expression in a world rid of intelligence,
Snapping the chains of sense in sarcasm
And ridicule of literary decorum.
Liberated thus, their queer
Postures and cries appeal only to the ear.
They say, "We who were born of the gusty tuning
Of the earth's first outbreathing
Came into our own as soon as the blood's beat
Impelled man's mindless vitality to break into dance in his throat.
We swelled his infant voice with the babble
Of the world's first poem, the original prattle
Of existence. We are kin to the wild torrents
That pour from the mountains to announce
The month of Śrāban: we bring to human habitations
Nature's incantations—"
The festive sound of leaves rustling in forests,
The sound that measures the rhythm of approaching tempests,
The great night-ending sound of daybreak—
From these sound-fields man has captured words, curbed them like a
                                                      breakneck
Stallion in complex webs of order
To enable him to pass on his messages to the distant lands of the
                                                      future.
By riding words that are bridled and reined
Man has quickened
The pace of time's slow clocks:

The speed of his reason has cut through material blocks,
Explored recalcitrant mysteries;
With word-armies
Drawn into battle-lines he resists the perpetual assault of imbecility.
But sometimes they slip like robbers into realms of fantasy,
Float on ebbing waters
Of sleep, free of barriers,
Lashing any sort of flotsam and jetsam into metre.
From them, the free-roving mind fashions
Artistic creations
Of a kind that do not conform to an orderly
Universe—whose threads are tenuous, loose, arbitrary,
Like a dozen puppies brawling,
Scrambling at each other's necks to no purpose or meaning:
Each bites another—
They squeal and yelp blue murder,
But their bites and yelps carry no true import of enmity,
Their violence is bombast, empty fury.
In my mind I imagine words thus shot of their meaning,
Hordes of them running amuck all day,
As if the sky there were nonsense nursery syllables booming—
Horselum, bridelum, ridelum, into the fray.

Translated from the Bengali by William Radice

CONSTANTINE P. CAVAFY
(GREECE, 1863–1933)

The City

You said: "I'll go to another country, go to another shore,
find another city better than this one.
Whatever I try to do is fated to turn out wrong
and my heart lies buried as though it were something dead.
How long can I let my mind moulder in this place?
Wherever I turn, wherever I happen to look,

I see the black ruins of my life, here,
where I've spent so many years, wasted them, destroyed them totally."

You won't find a new country, won't find another shore.
This city will always pursue you. You will walk
the same streets, grow old in the same neighborhoods,
will turn gray in these same houses.
You will always end up in this city. Don't hope for things elsewhere:
there is no ship for you, there is no road.
As you've wasted your life here, in this small corner,
you've destroyed it everywhere else in the world.

Translated from the Greek by Edmund Keeley and Philip Sherrard

Body, Remember

Body, remember not only how much you were loved,
not only the beds you lay on,
but also those desires that glowed openly
in eyes that looked at you,
trembled for you in the voices—
only some chance obstacle frustrated them.
Now that it's all finally in the past,
it seems almost as if you gave yourself
to those desires too—how they glowed,
remember, in eyes that looked at you,
remember, body, how they trembled for you in those voices.

Translated from the Greek by Edmund Keeley and Philip Sherrard

Waiting for the Barbarians

What are we waiting for, assembled in the forum?

    The barbarians are due here today.

Why isn't anything happening in the senate?
Why do the senators sit there without legislating?

Because the barbarians are coming today.
What laws can the senators make now?
Once the barbarians are here, they'll do the legislating.

Why did our emperor get up so early,
and why is he sitting at the city's main gate
on his throne, in state, wearing the crown?

Because the barbarians are coming today
and the emperor is waiting to receive their leader.
He has even prepared a scroll to give him,
replete with titles, with imposing names.

Why have our two consuls and praetors come out today
wearing their embroidered, their scarlet togas?
Why have they put on bracelets with so many amethysts,
and rings sparkling with magnificent emeralds?
Why are they carrying elegant canes
beautifully worked in silver and gold?

Because the barbarians are coming today
and things like that dazzle the barbarians.

Why don't our distinguished orators come forward as usual
to make their speeches, say what they have to say?

Because the barbarians are coming today
and they're bored by rhetoric and public speaking.

Why this sudden restlessness, this confusion?
(How serious people's faces have become.)

Why are the streets and squares emptying so rapidly,
everyone going home so lost in thought?

Because night has fallen and the barbarians have not come.
And some who have just returned from the border say
there are no barbarians any longer.

And now, what's going to happen to us without barbarians?
They were, those people, a kind of solution.

Translated from the Greek by Edmund Keeley and Philip Sherrard

Ithaka

As you set out for Ithaka
hope the voyage is a long one,
full of adventure, full of discovery.
Laistrygonians and Cyclops,
angry Poseidon—don't be afraid of them:
you'll never find things like that on your way
as long as you keep your thoughts raised high,
as long as a rare excitement
stirs your spirit and your body.
Laistrygonians and Cyclops,
wild Poseidon—you won't encounter them
unless you bring them along inside your soul,
unless your soul sets them up in front of you.

Hope the voyage is a long one.
May there be many a summer morning when,
with what pleasure, what joy,
you come into harbors seen for the first time;
may you stop at Phoenician trading stations
to buy fine things,
mother of pearl and coral, amber and ebony,
sensual perfume of every kind—
as many sensual perfumes as you can;
and may you visit many Egyptian cities
to gather stores of knowledge from their scholars.

Keep Ithaka always in your mind.
Arriving there is what you are destined for.
But do not hurry the journey at all.
Better if it lasts for years,
so you are old by the time you reach the island,

wealthy with all you have gained on the way,
not expecting Ithaka to make you rich.

Ithaka gave you the marvelous journey.
Without her you would not have set out.
She has nothing left to give you now.
And if you find her poor, Ithaka won't have fooled you.
Wise as you will have become, so full of experience,
you will have understood by then what these Ithakas mean.

Translated from the Greek by Edmund Keeley and Philip Sherrard

RUBÉN DARÍO
(NICARAGUA, 1867–1916)

The Wandering Song

A singer goes all over the world
impassioned or bored

In a little train or a white train
by the gulls or through the grain

A singer walks into wars and peaces
into civil wars, trench wars, trade wars
through discord or concord
a singer goes to all these places

A poet moves in the world

On the ridge spine of the elephant
into the narrows of the Hellespont

On a palanquin, in gemmy silks
she crosses glaciers in the Alps

On a cloud backed and glinting jet
into Buddhist and bright Tibet

In a car into St. Lucia
On a dark train through Galicia

Over the pampas and the flats
on American colts

She goes by river in a canoe
or props herself in the banging prow

of a pelagic freighter
or she simply rides an escalator

She brings her nose to archipelagoes
And carts her ears into Tangiers

On a dromedary across the sands
by jiggling boats, she visits lands

She goes to the tundra's edge
on an expeditious sledge

And far from the equator's flora
she thrills to the boreal aurora

The singer strolls through hissing crops
across the rows and by the cows

She enters her London on a bus
her Jerusalem on an ass

She goes with mailbags and pouches of the State
to open doors to eternal things

To salve the sores of human beings
is why she sings.

Translated from the Spanish by Gabriel Gudding

ELSE LASKER-SCHÜLER
(GERMANY, 1869–1945)

In the Evening

I had to do it—suddenly, I had to sing.
I had no idea why—
But when the evening came I wept. I wept bitterly.

Pain was everywhere. Sprang out of everything—
Spread everywhere. Into everything—
And then lay on top of me.

Translated from the German by Eavan Boland

PAUL VALÉRY
(FRANCE, 1871–1945)

The Angel Handed Me a Book

Placing a book in my hands, the angel said, "It holds all you would
wish to know." And he vanished.

So I opened the book, which wasn't thick.

It was written in an unknown alphabet.

Scholars translated it, but produced very different versions.

They disagreed even about their own readings, agreeing neither
upon the tops or bottoms of them, nor the beginnings, nor the ends.

Toward the close of this vision, it seemed to me that the book

melted, until it could not longer be told apart from the world that sur-
rounds us.

Translated from the French by Carolyn Forché

ANTONIO MACHADO
(SPAIN, 1875–1939)

I Never Sought the Glory

I never sought the glory
nor to leave in memory
of men my song;
I love subtle worlds,
Weightless and graceful
like bubbles of soap.
I like to see them painted
In sunlight and scarlet, wafting
under the blue sky, trembling
suddenly and pop.

Translated from the Spanish by Katie King

Last Night, as I Was Sleeping

Last night, as I was sleeping,
I dreamt—marvelous error!—
that a spring was breaking
out in my heart.
I said: Along which secret aqueduct,
Oh water, are you coming to me,
water of a new life
that I have never drunk?
Last night, as I was sleeping,
I dreamt—marvelous error!—
that I had a beehive
here inside my heart.

And the golden bees
were making white combs
and sweet honey
from my old failures.
Last night, as I was sleeping,
I dreamt—marvelous error!—
that a fiery sun was giving
light inside my heart.
It was fiery because I felt
warmth as from a hearth,
and sun because it gave light
and brought tears to my eyes.
Last night, as I slept,
I dreamt—marvelous error!—
that it was God I had
here inside my heart.

Translated from the Spanish by Robert Bly

from Moral Proverbs and Folksongs

The best of the good people
know that in this life
it's all a question of proportion;
a little more, a little less . . .

Don't be surprised, dear friends,
that my forehead is furrowed.
With men I live at peace, but with my insides
I am at war.

The cricket in his cage
by his tomato
sings, sings, sings.

Pay attention:
a solitary heart
is no heart at all.

In my solitude
I have seen very clearly
things that are not true.

Translated from the Spanish by Mary G. Berg and Dennis Maloney

Eyes

I

When his lover died
he decided to grow old
in the closed mansion
with his memory and the mirror
in which she saw herself one clear day.
Like the gold in the miser's coffer,
he thought he would save
all of yesterday in the clear mirror.
Time for him would not run out.

II

And after the first year—
"How were they," he asked, "brown or black,
her eyes? Light green? . . . Gray?
How were they, good God, that I don't remember?"

III

He went out to the street one day
of Spring, and silently strolled
his double mourning, the heart locked . . .
From a window, in the hollow shade
he saw flashing eyes. He lowered his
and walked on . . . Like those!

Translated from the Spanish by Rosa Berumen

RAINER MARIA RILKE
(AUSTRO-HUNGARIAN EMPIRE, 1875–1926)

Autumn Day

Lord: it is time. The summer was immense.
Stretch out your shadow on the sundial's face,
and on the meadows let the winds go loose.

Command the last fruits to be full in time;
grant them even two more southerly days,
press them toward fulfillment soon and chase
the last sweetness into the heavy wine.

Whoever has no house now, will build none.
Who is alone now, will stay long alone,
will lie awake, read, get long letters written,
and through the streets that follow up and down
will wander restless, when the leaves are driven.

Translated from the German by John Felstiner

Sometimes a Man Stands Up During Supper

Sometimes a man stands up during supper
and walks outdoors, and keeps on walking,
because of a church that stands somewhere in the East.

And his children say blessings on him as if he were dead.

And another man, who remains inside his own house,
dies there, inside the dishes and in the glasses,
so that his children have to go far out into the world
toward that same church, which he forgot.

Translated from the German by Robert Bly

The Eighth Duino Elegy

With all their eyes, all creatures see
the open. Only our eyes are
turned around, and surround it
with pitfalls, all round the way to be free.
What *is* outside, we know from animal
eyes alone; since even the youngest child
we turn round, force it backwards
to see conformity, not the openness that's
so deep in an animal's face. Free from death.
Which is what only we see; the free animal
has its perishing always behind it,
and God in front; and when it moves, it moves
in eternity, the way springs run.
We never, not even one single day, have
pure space in front of us, into which the flowers
endlessly arise. Always it is world
and never nothing without no:
the pure, unsupervised, that one breathes
and endlessly knows and craves nothing. As a child
you sometimes get lost there in silence and then
somebody shakes you. Or someone dies and *is* it.

Since close to death one doesn't see death any more,
just stares ahead, perhaps with big animal gaze.

Lovers, if the other weren't there to
block the view, lovers are near it and wonder . . .
As if by oversight it's disclosed to them
behind the other . . . But beyond that
no one gets any further, and the world happens to him again.
Always turned towards creation, we see
only a mirroring of the free
dimmed by our breath. Or an animal,
wordless, looks up quietly and sees right through us.
That's what destiny means; to be opposite
and nothing but that, and always opposite.

If consciousness of our sort existed
in the sure animal that draws close to us
on his own other path, he would change our course
with his kind of life. Since for him, being is
unending, ungrasped and without glimpse
of his condition, pure, just like his gaze.
And where we see the future, he sees everything
and himself in everything and healed for ever.

And yet in the watchful warm animal
is the weight and care of a great sadness.
Since he too is always in touch with
what often overpowers us too—remembrance
as if once upon a time what we're striving for
had been closer, truer and its connection
infinitely tender. Here all is being apart,
there it was breath. After the first homeland
the second seems to him doubtful and vague.

Oh bliss of the *littlest* creatures
that remain forever in the womb that bore them;
happiness of little gnats that still leap within
even when they marry—for womb is all.
Look at the half-certainty of the bird
who from his origin is almost aware of both,
as if he were the soul of an Etruscan
and came from the dead man welcomed inside a space
that bears his image in repose for a lid.
And how dismayed anything is that has to fly
if it comes from a womb. As if from its very self
it shrinks back in fear, zigzags through the air as a crack
runs through a cup. The way the track of a bat
tears through the porcelain of evening.

And we: spectators, always, everywhere,
devoted to everything and never free of it!
It fills us to the brim. We arrange it. It perishes.
We arrange it again and perish ourselves.

Who turned us around this way, so that we,
whatever we may do, always are in the posture
of someone who's going away? As he on
the last hill, that will show him his whole
valley one last time, turns round, pauses, lingers—
we live that way forever saying goodbye.

Translated from the German by Robert Kelly

Orpheus. Eurydice. Hermes.

That was the so unfathomed mine of souls.
And they, like silent veins of silver ore,
were winding through its darkness. Between roots
welled up the blood that flows on to mankind,
like blocks of heavy porphyry in the darkness.
Else there was nothing red.

But here were rocks
and ghostly forests. Bridges over voidness
and that immense, gray, unreflecting pool
that hung above its so far distant bed
like a gray rainy sky above a landscape.
And between meadows, soft and full of patience,
appeared the pale strip of the single pathway,
like a long line of linen laid to bleach.

And on this single pathway they approached.

In front the slender man in the blue mantle,
gazing in dumb impatience straight before him.
His steps devoured the way in mighty chunks
they did not pause to chew; his hands were hanging,
heavy and clenched, out of the falling folds,
no longer conscious of the lightsome lyre,
the lyre which had grown into his left
like twines of rose into a branch of olive.
It seemed as though his senses were divided:

for, while his sight ran like a dog before him,
turned round, came back, and stood, time and again,
distant and waiting, at the path's next turn,
his hearing lagged behind him like a smell.
It seemed to him at times as though it stretched
back to the progress of those other two
who should be following up this whole ascent.
Then once more there was nothing else behind him
but his climb's echo and his mantle's wind.
He, though, assured himself they still were coming;
said it aloud and heard it die away.
They still were coming, only they were two
that trod with fearful lightness. If he durst
but once look back (if only looking back
were not undoing of this whole enterprise
still to be done), he could not fail to see them,
the two light-footers, following him in silence:

The god of faring and distant message,
the traveling-hood over his shining eyes,
the slender wand held out before his body,
the wings around his ankles lightly beating,
and in his left hand, as entrusted, *her.*

She, so belov'd, that from a single lyre
more mourning rose than from all women-mourners—
that a whole world of mourning rose, wherein
all things were once more present: wood and vale
and road and hamlet, field and stream and beast—
and that around this world of mourning turned,
even as around the other earth, a sun
and a whole silent heaven full of stars,
a heaven of mourning with disfigured stars—
she, so beloved.

But hand in hand now with that god she walked,
her paces circumscribed by lengthy shroudings,

uncertain, gentle, and without impatience.
Wrapt in herself, like one whose time is near,
she thought not of the man who went before them,
nor of the road ascending into life.
Wrapt in herself she wandered. And her deadness
was filling her like fullness.
Full as a fruit with sweetness and with darkness
was she with her great death, which was so new
that for the time she could take nothing in.

She had attained a new virginity
and was intangible; her sex had closed
like a young flower at the approach of evening,
and her pale hands had grown so disaccustomed
to being a wife, that even the slim god's
endlessly gentle contact as he led her
disturbed her like a too great intimacy.

Even now she was no longer that blond woman
who'd sometimes echoed in the poet's poems,
no longer the broad couch's scent and island,
nor yonder man's possession any longer.

She was already loosened like long hair,
and given far and wide like fallen rain,
and dealt out like a manifold supply.

She was already root.

And when, abruptly,
the god had halted her and, with an anguished
outcry, outspoke the words: He has turned round!—
she took in nothing, and said softly: Who?

But in the distance, dark in the bright exit,
someone or other stood, whose countenance
was indistinguishable. Stood and saw

how, on a strip of pathway between meadows,
with sorrow in his look, the god of message
turned silently to go behind the figure
already going back by that same pathway,
its paces circumscribed by lengthy shroudings,
uncertain, gentle, and without impatience.

Translated from the German by J. B. Leishman

MAX JACOB
(FRANCE, 1876–1944)

Mystery of the Sky

Coming back from the ball, I sat down at the window and gazed at
the sky: it seemed to me the clouds were the huge heads of old men
sitting at the table and someone brought them a white bird all decked
out. A big river crossed the sky. One of the old men looked down at
me, he was even going to speak when the spell was broken, leaving
the pure twinkling stars.

Translated from the French by William T. Kulik

GUILLAUME APOLLINAIRE
(FRANCE, 1880–1918)

The Little Car

On the 31st day of August in the year 1914
I left Deauville shortly before midnight
In Rouveyre's little car

Including his chauffeur there were three of us

We said goodbye to a whole epoch
Furious giants were looming over Europe

The eagles were leaving their eyries expecting the sun
Voracious fishes were swimming up from the abysses
Nations were rushing together to know each other through
    and through
The dead were trembling with fear in their dark dwellings

The dogs were barking in the direction of the frontiers
As I went I carried within me all the armies that were fighting
I felt them rising within me and spreading out over the regions
    through which their columns wound
With the forests the happy villages of Belgium
Francorchamps and Eau Rouge and the *pouhons*
A region through which invasions are always taking place
And the railway arteries along which those who were going away
    to die
Saluted one more time a life full of colours
The deep oceans where monsters were stirring
In old carcasses of wrecks
The unimaginable heights where men fight
Higher than the eagle soars
Man fights there against man
And falls suddenly like a shooting star
I felt within me new beings full of dexterity
Building a new universe and running it as well
A merchant of unheard-of opulence and of prodigious
    stature
Was setting out an extraordinary display of stock
And gigantic shepherds were driving forward
Great dumb flocks grazing on words as they went
And at them barked all the dogs along the road

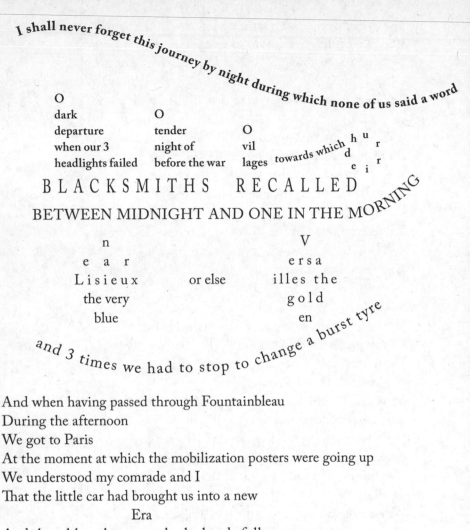

I shall never forget this journey by night during which none of us said a word

O
dark   O
departure   tender   O
when our 3   night of   vil
headlights failed before the war   lages towards which h u r
                                              d   r
                                               e i

BLACKSMITHS   RECALLED
BETWEEN MIDNIGHT AND ONE IN THE MORNING

        n   V
      e   a   r   e r s a
      L i s i e u x   or else i l l e s   t h e
        the very   g o l d
        blue   en

and 3 times we had to stop to change a burst tyre

And when having passed through Fountainbleau
During the afternoon
We got to Paris
At the moment at which the mobilization posters were going up
We understood my comrade and I
That the little car had brought us into a new
                    Era
And that although we were both already fully grown men
We had nevertheless just been born

Translated from the French by Oliver Bernard

Hotel

My room has the dismal shape of a cage
But the sun slips its arm in at the window
And I thinking of a cigarette's mirage

I have this sunbeam for a light
I don't want to work I want to smoke

Translated from the French by Roger Shattuck

Zone

You are tired at last of this old world

O shepherd Eiffel Tower the flock of bridges bleats at the morning

You have had enough of life in this Greek and Roman antiquity

Even the automobiles here seem to be ancient
Religion alone has remained entirely fresh religion
Has remained simple like the hangars at the airfield

You alone in all Europe are not antique O Christian faith
The most modern European is you Pope Pius X
And you whom the windows look down at shame prevents you
From entering a church and confessing this morning
You read prospectuses catalogues and posters which shout aloud
Here is poetry this morning and for prose there are the newspapers
There are volumes for 25 centimes full of detective stories
Portraits of famous men and a thousand assorted titles

This morning I saw a pretty street whose name I have forgotten
Shining and clean it was the sun's bugle
Executives and workers and lovely secretaries
From Monday morning to Saturday evening pass here four times a day
In the morning the siren wails three times
A surly bell barks around noon
Inscriptions on signs and walls
Plaques and notices cried out like parrots
I love the charm of this industrial street
Located in Paris somewhere between the rue Aunont-Thiéville and the
    avenue des Ternes

Here is the young street and you are once again a little child
Your mother dresses you only in blue and white
You are very pious and with your oldest friend Rene Dalize
You like nothing so well as the ceremonies of church
It is nine o'clock the gas is down to the blue you come secretly out of
    the dormitory
You pray the whole night in the college chapel
While eternal and adorable an amethyst profundity
The flaming glory of Christ turns forever
It is the beautiful lily we all cultivate
It is the red-headed torch which the wind cannot blow out
It is the pale and ruddy son of a sorrowful mother
It is the tree always thick with prayers
It is the double gallows of honor and of eternity
It is a six-pointed star
It is God who died on Friday and rose again on Sunday
It is Christ who soars in the sky better than any aviator
He breaks the world's altitude record
Christ the pupil of the eye
Twentieth pupil of the centuries he knows how
And turned into a bird this century rises in the air like Jesus
The devils in their abysses lift their heads to look at it
They say it is imitating Simon Magus in Judea
They shout that if it knows how to fly it should be called a flyer
Angels hover about the lovely aerialist
Icarus Enoch Elijah Apollonius of Tyana
Flutter around the original airplane
They separate occasionally to give passage to those whom the Holy
    Eucharist carries up
Those priests who rise eternally in lifting the host
The airplane lands at last without folding its wings
The sky fills up then with millions of swallows
In a flash crows falcons and owls arrive
Ibis flamingoes and marabous arrive from Africa
The great Roc celebrated by storytellers and poets
Glides down holding in its claws Adam's scull the first head
The eagle rushes out of the horizon giving a great cry
From America comes the tiny hummingbird

From China have come long supple pihis
Which only have one wing and fly tandem
Then the dove immaculate spirit
Escorted by the lyre bird and the ocellated peacock
The phoenix that pyre which re-creates itself
Veils everything for an instant with its glowing coals
Sirens leaving their perilous straits
Arrive all three of them singing beautifully
And everything eagle phoenix and Chinese pihis
Fraternize with the flying machine

Now you walk through Paris all alone in the crowd
Herds of bellowing busses roll by near you
The agony of love tightens your throat
As if you could never be loved again
If you were living in olden days you would enter a monastery
You are ashamed when you catch yourself saving a prayer
You ridicule yourself and your laughter bursts out like hellfire
The sparks of your laughter gild the depths of your life
It is a picture hung in a somber museum
And sometimes you go to look at it closely

Today you walk through Paris the women are bloodstained
It was and I would prefer not to remember it was during beauty's decline
Surrounded by fervent flames Notre Dame looked at me in Chartres
The blood of your Sacred Heart flooded me in the Montmartre
I am ill from hearing happy words
The love from which I suffer is a shameful sickness
And the image which possesses you makes you survive in sleeplessness
    and anguish
It is always near you this passing image

Now you are on the shore of the Mediterranean
Under the lemon trees which blossom all year
With your friends you take a boat ride
One is a Nissard there is a Mentonasque and two Turbiasques
We look down in fear at the octopodes on the bottom
And amid the algae swim fish images of our Saviour

You are in the garden of an inn on the outskirts of Prague
You feel completely happy a rose is on the table
And instead of writing your story in prose you watch
The rosebug which is sleeping in the heart of the rose

Astonished you see yourself outlined in the agates of Saint Vitus
You were sad enough to die the day you saw yourself in them
You looked like Lazarus bewildered by the light
The hands of the clock in the Jewish quarter turn backwards
And you go slowly backwards in your life
Climbing up to Hradchin and listening at night
In taverns to the singing of Czech songs

Here you are in Marseilles amid the watermelons

Here you are in Coblenz at the Hotel of the Giant

Here you are in Rome sitting under a Japanese medlar tree

Here you are in Amsterdam with a girl you find pretty and who is ugly
She is to marry a student from Leyden
There are rooms for rent in Latin Cubicula locanda
I remember I stayed three days there and as many at Gouda

You are in Paris at the *juge d'instruction*
Like a criminal you are placed under arrest
You have made sorrowful and happy trips
Before noticing that the world lies and grows old
You suffered from love at twenty and thirty
I have lived like a fool and wasted my time
You no longer dare look at your hands and at every moment I want to
    burst out sobbing
For you for her I love for everything that has frightened you

With tear-filled eyes you look at those poor emigrants
They believe in God they pray the women nurse their children
Their odor fills the waiting room of the gare Saint-Lazare
They have faith in their star like the Magi

They hope to make money in Argentina
And come back to their countries having made their fortunes
One family carries a red quilt as one carries one's heart
That quilt and our dream are both unreal
Some of these emigrants stay here and find lodging
In hovels in the rue des Rosiers or the rue des Écouffes
I have often seen them in the evening they take a stroll in the street
And rarely travel far like men on a checker board
There are mostly Jews their wives wear wigs
They sit bloodlessly in the backs of little shops

You are standing at the counter of a dirty bar
You have a nickel coffee with the rest of the riffraff

At night you are in a big restaurant

These women are not wicked however they have no worries
All of them even the ugliest has made her lover suffer
She is the daughter of a Jersey City policeman

Her hands which I have not seen are hard and chapped
I have an immense pity for the scars on her belly

I humble my mouth by offering it to a poor slut with a horrible laugh

You are alone the morning is almost here
The milkmen rattle their cans in the street

The night departs like a beautiful Métive
It is Ferdine the false or Leah the waiting one

And you drink this burning liquor like your life
Your life which you drink like an eau-de-vie

You walk toward Auteuil you want to walk home on foot
To sleep among your fetishes from Oceania and Guinea
They are all Christ in another form and of another faith

They are inferior Christs obscure hopes

Adieu adieu

The sun a severed neck

Translated from the French by Roger Shattuck

ALEXANDER BLOK
(RUSSIA, 1880–1921)

[Night. Street. Lamp. Drugstore.]

Night. Street. Lamp. Drugstore.
Dull and sleazy light.
Live twenty-five years more—
It will be as now. No way out.

You die—and again you begin.
All is repeated as before:
Night. The canal's icy ripples.
Drugstore. Lamp. Street.

Translated from the Russian by Ilya Kaminsky

JUAN RAMÓN JIMÉNEZ
(SPAIN, 1881–1958)

Oceans

   I have a feeling that my boat
has struck, down there in the depths,
against a great thing.
                 And nothing
happens! Nothing . . . Silence . . . Waves . . .

—Nothing happens? Or has everything happened,
and are we standing now, quietly, in the new life?

Translated from the Spanish by Robert Bly

FRANZ KAFKA
(AUSTRO-HUNGARIAN EMPIRE, 1883–1924)

On Parables

Many complain that the words of the wise are always merely parables
and of no use in daily life, which is the only life we have. When the sage
says: "Go over," he does not mean that we should cross to some actual
place, which we could do anyhow if the labor were worth it; he means
some fabulous yonder, something unknown to us, something too that he
cannot designate more precisely, and therefore cannot help us here in
the very least. All these parables really set out to say merely that the
incomprehensible is incomprehensible, and we know that already. But
the cares we have to struggle with every day: that is a different matter.

Concerning this a man once said: Why such reluctance? If you
only followed the parables you yourselves would become parables and
with that rid of all your daily cares.

Another said: I bet that is also a parable.

The first said: You have won.

The second said: But unfortunately only in parable.

The first said: No, in reality: in parable you have lost.

Translated from the German by Willa Muir and Edwin Muir

UMBERTO SABA
(ITALY, 1883–1957)

The Goat

I had a conversation with a goat.
She was tied up, alone, in a field.

Full up with grass, wet
with rain, she was bleating.

That monotonous bleat was brother
to my own pain. And I replied in kind, at first
in jest, and then because pain is eternal
and speaks with one voice, unchanging.
This was the voice I heard
wailing in a lonely goat.

In a goat with a Semitic face
I heard the cry of every woe on earth,
every life on earth.

Translated from the Italian by Stephen Sartarelli

VELIMIR KHLEBNIKOV
(RUSSIA, 1885–1922)

Incantation by Laughter

Hlahla! Uthlofan, lauflings!
Hlahla! Uflofan, lauflings!
Who lawghen with lafe, who hlaegen lewchly,
Hlahla! Uflofan hlouly!
Hlahla! Hloufish lauflings lafe uf beloght lauchalorum!
Hlahla! Loufenish lauflings lafe, hlohan utlaufly!
Lawfen, lawfen,
Hloh, hlouh, hlou! luifekin, luifekin,
Hlofeningum, hlofeningum.
Hlahla! Utlofan, lauflings!
Hlahla! Utlofan, lauflings!

Translated from the Russian by Paul Schmidt

DINO CAMPANA
(ITALY, 1885–1932)

Journey to Montevideo

From the deck of the ship I saw
The hills of Spain
Disappear, the golden twilight
Hiding the brown earth in the green
Like a song:
Like a blue song
Of a lonely girl from an unknown place,
A violet still trembling on the bank of the hills. . . .
The azure evening languished on the sea:
Even the golden silences of wings
Crossed slowly minute by minute in blueness. . . .
Distant golden birds tinged
In varicolored hues crossed the heavenly evening
From more distant silences: the ship
Already blind crossing battering the darkness
With our shipwrecked hearts
Battering the darkness, its azure wings on the sea.
But one day
The solemn matrons from Spain climbed aboard the ship
With turbid and angelic eyes
And breasts heavy with vertigo. When
In a deep bay of an equatorial island
In a quiet bay much more profound than the nocturnal sky
We saw rising in the bewitching light
A white city asleep
At the foot of the highest peaks of the dead volcanoes
In the equator's turbid breath: till
After much screaming and many shadows in an unknown country
After much clattering of chains and much inflamed fervor
We left the equatorial city
For the restless nocturnal sea.
We went on and on for days and days: the ships
Heavy with sails limp in the hot gusts of wind passed opposite us slowly:

Nearby on the upper deck there appeared a bronzed
Girl of a new race,
Eyes shining, her clothes to the wind! and here: wild at day's end
There appeared the wild shore down there next to the endless sea:
And I saw the dunes
Like dizzy horses that dissolved
Into limitless grassland
Deserted without houses for anyone
And we turned flying from the dunes and there appeared
On a yellow floodtide of the miraculous abundance of the river
The marine capital of the new continent.
Limpid fresh and electric was the light
Of evening and there the tall houses seemed deserted
Down below on the pirate's sea
Of the abandoned city
Between the yellow sea and the dunes

Translated from the Italian by I. L. Salomon

GOTTFRIED BENN
(GERMANY, 1886–1956)

This Is Bad

Someone hands you an English thriller,
highly recommended.
You don't read English.

You've worked up a thirst
for something you can't afford.

You have deep insights,
brand new, and they sound
like an academic glossing Hölderlin.

You hear the waves at night
ramping against the shore
and you think: that's what waves do.

Worse: you're asked out
when at home you get better coffee,
silence, and you don't expect to be amused.

Awful: not to die in summer
under a bright sky
when the rich dirt
falls easily from the shovel.

Translated from the German by Harvey Shapiro

Chopin

Not much of a conversationalist,
ideas weren't his strong suit,
ideas miss the point,
when Delacroix expounded his theories
it made him nervous, he for his part
could offer no explanation of the Nocturnes.

A poor lover;
mere shadow in Nohant
where George Sand's children
rejected his attempts
at discipline.

His tuberculosis
took the chronic form,
with repeated bleeding and scarring;
a creeping death,
as opposed to one
in convulsions of agony
or by firing squad:
the piano (Erard) was pushed back against the door

and Delphine Potocka
sang him
a violet song in his last hour.

He took three pianos with him to England:
Pleyel, Erard, Broadwood,
for twenty guineas
he would give fifteen-minute recitals in the evenings
at the Rothschilds' and the Wellingtons', in Strafford House
to the assembled cummerbunds;
then, dark with fatigue and imminent death,
he went home
to the Square d'Orleans.

Then he burned his sketches
and manuscripts,
didn't want any leftover scraps
betraying him—
at the end he said:
"I have taken my experiment
as far as it was possible for me to go."

Each finger was to play
to no more than its natural strength,
the fourth being the weakest
(twinned with the middle finger).
At the start, they occupied the keys
of E, F sharp, G sharp, B and C.

Anyone hearing
certain of his Preludes
in country seats or
at altitude,
through open French windows
on the terrace, say, of a sanatorium,
will not easily forget it.

He composed no operas,
no symphonies,
only those tragic progressions
from artistic conviction
and with a small hand.

Translated from the German by Michael Hofmann

MOISHE LEIB HALPERN
(SPAIN, 1886–1932)

Man, That Ape

Man, that ape, the first time in his life
He sees an elephant at night,
In all that darkness, the elephant's
Wearing, it seems, a pair of pants.
He broods about this for a while,
Then from some fig leaves, constructs a pair
Of pants, a pull-over, and underwear,
A shirt and shoes and then a hat,
And a skullcap for wearing under that.
Man, that ape.

That's nothing—the first time in his life
He sees the risen moon on high,
He locks his wife in an embrace
To singe the hair from off her face;
And after that, to make her gleam,
First he smears on a chalky cream,
Then sticks on all the gold he's got.
She doesn't emanate one beam.
He howls and bays and starts to scream.
Man, that ape.

That's nothing—the first time in his life
He sees the sun ascending where

The mountaintop and heaven meet,
He raises his right fist to swear
That he will follow it up there;
Since when, too short of time, he's run
From east to west, just like the sun.
The sun comes up, the sun descends:
He climbs, and falls—it never ends.
Man, that ape.

Translated from the Yiddish by John Hollander

BLAISE CENDRARS

(FRANCE, 1887–1961)

White Suit

I walk on the bridge in my white suit that I bought in Dakar
On my feet my rope sandals bought at Villa Garcia
In my hand my Basque cap brought back from Biarritz
My pockets are full of Caporals Ordinaires
From time to time I sniff my little wooden box from Russia
I jingle the small change in my pocket and a pound sterling in gold
I have my big Calabrian handkerchief and these wax matches of a
     size you don't find anywhere but in London
I am clean washed scrubbed more than the deck
Happy as a king
Rich as a millionaire
Free as a man

Translated from the French by Peter Hoida

GEORG TRAKL
(AUSTRIA, 1887–1914)

A Romance to Night

Under a tent of stars a lonely man
Walks through the silence of midnight.
A boy wakes, bewildered by his dreams,
His gray face wasting away into the moon.

At a barred window
A half-witted woman with loose hair is weeping.
Lovers float by on the pond
Continuing their sweet journey.

The murderer laughs until he grows pale in the wine,
Horror of death consumes the afflicted.
Naked and wounded, a nun prays
Before the Savior's agony on the cross.

A mother sings softly in her sleep.
Content, her child
Gazes into the night.
Laughter fades in from the whorehouse.

Below, in the alley next to the tavern, by lamplight,
The dead paint a sneering silence on the walls
With their white hands.
The one sleeping continues to whisper.

Translated from the German by Daniel Simko

Grodek

Second Version

In the evening, the autumn woods ring
With deadly weapons, the sun rolls somberly

Over the golden plains and blue lakes,
And night embraces
The dying warriors, the wild lament
Of their broken mouths.
Red clouds, spilled blood, gather silently over the meadow,
Where an angry God lives, a cold moon;
All roads end in black decay.
Under the golden branches of night and stars,
A sister's shadow staggers through the silent grove
To greet the ghosts of heroes, the bloodied heads,
And the dark flutes of autumn keep playing softly in the reeds.
O prouder grief! You, brass altars,
Today the hot flame of the spirit is fed by a more violent pain—
The grandsons still unborn.

Translated from the German by Daniel Simko

GIUSEPPE UNGARETTI

(ITALY, 1888–1970)

In Memoriam

He was called
Mohammed Sheab
Descendant of nomad emirs
a suicide
because he no longer had
a country

He loved France
and changed his name

Became Marcel
but was not French
and had forgotten how
to live
in his own people's tent

where they listen to the sing-song
of the Koran
as they sip coffee

He did not know
how to release
the song
of his unconstraint

I followed his coffin
I and the manageress of the hotel
where we lived
in Paris
number 5 rue des Carmes
steep decrepit alleyway

He rests
in the cemetery at Ivry
a suburb that always
looks
like the day
they dismantle a fairground

And perhaps only I
still know
he lived

Translated from the Italian by Patrick Creagh

FERNANDO PESSOA
(PORTUGAL, 1888–1935)

If they want me to be a mystic, fine. I'm a mystic.

If they want me to be a mystic, fine. I'm a mystic.
I'm a mystic, but only of the body.
My soul is simple and it doesn't think.

My mysticism is not wanting to know.
It's living without thinking about it.

I don't know what Nature is. I sing it.
I live on a hilltop
In a solitary whitewashed cabin.
And that's my definition.

Translated from the Portuguese by Edwin Honig and Susan M. Brown

GABRIELA MISTRAL
(CHILE, 1889–1957)

The Footprint

Of the fleeing man I have
only the footprint,
the weight of his body,
and the wind that blows him.
No signs, no name,
no country or town,
only the damp
shell of his footprint,
only this syllable
absorbed by the sand
and the earth, Veronica
who murmured it to me.

Only the anguish
that hurries his flight:
hammering pulse,
gasping breath,
glistening sweat,
teeth on edge,
and the hard dry wind
that hits his back.

And the thorn he leaps,
the marsh he crosses,
the bush that hides him
and the sun that reveals him,
the hill that helps him,
and the one that betrays him,
the root that trips him
and God who gets him to his feet.

And his daughter, the blood
that calls out through him:
the footprint, Lord,
the bright footprint,
the mouthless cry,
the footprint, the footprint!

Holy sands
eat up his sign.
Dogs of mist,
cover his track.
Falling night,
swallow in one gulp
the great, sweet
mark of a man.

I see, I count
the two thousand footprints.
I go running, running
across old Earth,
mixing up his
poor tracks with mine,
or I stop and erase them
with my wild hair,
or facedown I lick
away the footprints.

But the white Earth
turns eternal,
stretches endless
as a chain,
lengthens out into a snake,
and the Lord God does not break its back.
And the footprints go on
to the end of the world.

Translated from the Spanish by Ursula K. Le Guin

ANNA AKHMATOVA
(RUSSIA, 1889–1966)

A Land Not Mine

A land not mine, still
forever memorable,
the waters of its ocean
chill and fresh.

Sand on the bottom whiter than chalk,
and the air drunk, like wine,
late sun lays bare
the rosy limbs of the pinetrees.

Sunset in the ethereal waves:
I cannot tell if the day
is ending, or the world, or if
the secret of secrets is inside me again.

Translated from the Russian by Jane Kenyon

Requiem

1935–1940

No foreign sky protected me,
no stranger's wing shielded my face.
I stand as witness to the common lot,
survivor of that time, that place.

—1961

INSTEAD OF A PREFACE

In the terrible years of the Yezhov terror I spent seventeen months
waiting in line outside the prison in Leningrad. One day somebody in
the crowd identified me. Standing behind me was a woman, with lips
blue from the cold, who had, of course, never heard me called by
name before. Now she started out of the torpor common to us all and
asked me in a whisper (everyone whispered there):

"Can you describe this?"

And I said: "I can."

Then something like a smile passed fleetingly over what had once
been her face.

—Leningrad, 1 April 1957

DEDICATION

Such grief might make the mountains stoop,
reverse the waters where they flow,
but cannot burst these ponderous bolts
that block us from the prison cells
crowded with mortal woe. . . .
For some the wind can freshly blow,
for some the sunlight fade at ease,
but we, made partners in our dread,
hear but the grating of the keys,
and heavy-booted soldiers' tread.
As if for early mass, we rose
and each day walked the wilderness,

trudging through silent street and square,
to congregate, less live than dead
The sun declined, the Neva blurred,
and hope sang always from afar.
Whose sentence is decreed? . . . That moan,
that sudden spurt of woman's tears,
shows one distinguished from the rest,
as if they'd knocked her to the ground
and wrenched the heart out of her breast,
then let her go, reeling, alone.
Where are they now, my nameless friends
from those two years I spent in hell?
What specters mock them now, amid
the fury of Siberian snows,
or in the blighted circle of the moon?
To them I cry, Hail and Farewell!

      —March 1940

PROLOGUE

That was a time when only the dead
could smile, delivered from their wars,
and the sign, the soul, of Leningrad
dangled outside its prison-house;
and the regiments of the condemned,
herded in the railroad-yards,
shrank from the engine's whistle-song
whose burden went, "Away, pariahs!"
The stars of death stood over us.
And Russia, guiltless, beloved, writhed
under the crunch of bloodstained boots,
under the wheels of Black Marias.

1

At dawn they came and took you away.
You were my dead: I walked behind.

In the dark room children cried,
the holy candle gasped for air.
Your lips were chill from the ikon's kiss,
sweat bloomed on your brow—those deathly flowers!
Like the wives of Peter's troopers in Red Square
I'll stand and howl under the Kremlin towers.
                              —1935

2

Quietly flows the quiet Don;
into my house slips the yellow moon.

It leaps the sill, with its cap askew,
and balks at a shadow, that yellow moon.

This woman is sick to her marrow-bone,
this woman is utterly alone,

with husband dead, with son away
in jail. Pray for me. Pray.

3

Not, not mine: it's somebody else's wound.
I could never have borne it. So take the thing
that happened, hide it, stick it in the ground.
Whisk the lamps away . . .
                              Night.

4

They should have shown you—mocker,
delight of your friends, hearts' thief,
naughtiest girl of Pushkin's town—
this picture of your fated years,
as under the glowering wall you stand,

shabby, three hundredth in the line,
clutching a parcel in your hand,
and the New Year's ice scorched by your tears.
see there the prison poplar bending!
no sound. No sound. Yet how many
innocent lives are ending. . . .

5

For seventeen months I have cried aloud,
calling you back to your lair.
I hurled myself at the hangman's foot.
You are my son, changed into nightmare.
Confusion occupies the world,
and I am powerless to tell
somebody brute from something human,
or on what day the word spells, "Kill!"
Nothing is left but dusty flowers,
the tinkling thurible, and tracks
that lead to nowhere. Night of stone,
whose bright enormous star
stares me straight in the eyes,
promising death, ah soon!

6

The weeks fly out of mind,
I doubt that it occurred:
how into your prison, child,
the white nights, blazing, stared;
and still, as I draw breath,
they fix their buzzard eyes
on what the high cross shows,
this body of your death.

7

THE SENTENCE

The word dropped like a stone
on my still living breast.
Confess: I was prepared,
am somehow ready for the test.

So much to do today:
kill memory, kill pain,
turn heart into a stone,
and yet prepare to live again.

Not quite. Hot summer's feast
brings rumors of carouse.
How long have I foreseen
this brilliant day, this empty house?

—Summer, 1939

8

TO DEATH

You will come in any case—so why not now?
How long I wait and wait. The bad times fall.
I have put out the light and opened the door
for you, because you are simple and magical.
Assume, then, any form that suits your wish,
take aim, and blast at me with poisoned shot,
or strangle me like an efficient mugger,
or else infect me—typhus be my lot—
or spring out of the fairy tale you wrote,
the one we're sick of hearing, day and night,
where the blue hatband marches up the stairs,
led by the janitor, pale with fright.
It's all the same to me. The Yenisei swirls,
the North Star shines, as it will shine forever;

and the blue lustre of my loved one's eyes
is clouded over by the final horror.

—The House on the Fontanka,
19 August 1939

9

Already madness lifts its wing
to cover half my soul.
That taste of opiate wine!
Lure of the dark valley!

Now everything is clear.
I admit my defeat. The tongue
of my ravings in my ear
is the tongue of a stranger.

No use to fall down on my knees
and beg for mercy's sake.
Nothing I counted mine, out of my life,
is mine to take:

not my son's terrible eyes,
not the elaborate stone flower
of grief, not the day of the storm,
not the trial of the visiting hour,

not the dear coolness of his hands,
not the lime trees' agitated shade,
not the thin cricket-sound
of consolation's parting word.

—4 May 1940

10

CRUCIFIXION

*"Do not weep for me, Mother,
when I am in my grave."*

I

A choir of angels glorified the hour,
the vault of heaven was dissolved in fire.
"Father, why hast Thou forsaken me?
Mother, I beg you, do not weep for me. . . ."

II

Mary Magdalene beat her breasts and sobbed,
His dear disciple, stone-faced, stared.
His mother stood apart. No other looked
into her secret eyes. Nobody dared.
                                    —1940–1943

EPILOGUE
I

I have learned how faces fall to bone,
how under the eyelids terror lurks,
how suffering inscribes on cheeks
the hard lines of its cuneiform texts,
how glossy black or ash-fair locks
turn overnight to tarnished silver,
how smiles fade on submissive lips,
and fear quavers in a dry titter.
And I pray not for myself alone . . .
for all who stood outside the jail,
in bitter cold or summer's blaze,
with me under that blind red wall.

II

Remembrance hour returns with the turning year.
I see, I hear, I touch you drawing near:

the one we tried to help to the sentry's booth,
and who no longer walks this precious earth,

and that one who would toss her pretty mane
and say, "It's just like coming home again."

I want to name the names of all that host,
but they snatched up the list, and now it's lost.

I've woven them a garment that's prepared
out of poor words, those that I overheard,

and will hold fast to every word and glance
all of my days, even in new mischance,

and if a gag should blind my tortured mouth,
through which a hundred million people shout,

then let them pray for me, as I do pray
for them, this eve of my remembrance day.

And if my country ever should assent
to casting in my name a monument,

I should be proud to have my memory graced,
but only if the monument be placed

not near the sea on which my eyes first opened—
my last link with the sea has long been broken—

nor in the Tsar's garden near the sacred stump,
where a grieved shadow hunts my body's warmth,

but here, where I endured three hundred hours
in line before the implacable iron bars.

Because even in blissful death I fear
to lose the clangor of the Black Marias,

to lose the banging of that odious gate
and the old crone howling like a wounded beast.

And from my motionless bronze-lidded sockets
may the melting snow, like teardrops, slowly trickle,

and a prison dove coo somewhere, over and over,
as the ships sail softly down the flowing Neva.

—March 1940

Translated from the Russian by Stanley Kunitz and Max Hayward

Northern Elegies #4

> *The last key—is the cold key of oblivion. It gives sweeter
> satisfaction than all the ardors of the heart.*
>
> —PUSHKIN

There are three ages to memories,
And the first—is like just yesterday.
The soul is under their blissful arch,
And the body basks in their blissful shade.
Laughter has not yet died, tears flow,
The ink blot on the desk has not faded—
And, like a seal on the heart, the kiss,
Unique, valedictory, unforgettable . . .
But this does not long endure . . .
Already there is no arch overhead, but somewhere
In a remote suburb, a solitary house,
Where it is cold in winter, hot in summer,
Where there are spiders, and dust on everything,
Where ardent letters are decomposing,
Portraits are stealthily changing.
People walk to this house as if to their grave,
And wash their hands with soap—when they return,
And blink away a facile tear
From weary eyes—and breathe out heavy sighs . . .
But the clock ticks, one springtime is superseded
By another, the sky glows pink,

Names of cities change
And there are no remaining witnesses to the events,
And no one to weep with, no one to remember with.
And slowly the shades withdraw from us,
Shades we no longer call back,
Whose return would be too terrible for us.
And waking one morning we realize that we have forgotten
Even the path to that solitary house,
And, choking with anger and shame,
We run there, but (as it happens in dreams),
Everything has changed: the people, the objects, the walls,
And nobody knows us—we are strangers.
We don't find ourselves there . . . My God!
And then it is that bitterness wells up:
We realize that we couldn't have fit
That past into the boundaries of our life,
And that it is almost as foreign to us
As to our next-door neighbor,
That those who died we wouldn't recognize,
And those from whom God separated us
Got along perfectly well without us—and even
That everything turned out for the best . . .

Translated from the Russian by Judith Hemschemeyer

Our Own Land

*There is no one in the world more tearless,
more proud, more simple than us.*

—1922

We don't wear it in sacred amulets on our chests.
We don't compose hysterical poems about it.
It does not disturb our bitter dream-sleep.
It doesn't seem to be the promised paradise.
We don't make of it a soul
object for sale and barter,
and we being sick, poverty-stricken, unable to utter a word
don't even remember about it.

Yes, for us it's mud on galoshes,
   for us it's crunch on teeth,
   and we mill, mess and crush
   that dust and ashes
   that is not mixed up in anything.
But we'll lie in it and be it,
that's why, so freely, we call it our own.

Translated from the Russian by Richard McKane

PIERRE REVERDY
(FRANCE, 1889–1960)

The Book

The white paper leaf new-grown on the fence. One climbs up and climbs down.

The mountain is a book whose heroes travel the wind. The pages turn. Words often fall.

The sound of thunder rolls over the paving stones. That's where the accident happens. The book is done. Men climb up, one section of it under each arm.

Leaning against the wall, the anxious author watches the world live and does not follow.

Fruit Bowl

A hand reaches toward the arrangement of fruit and, like a bee, hovers over it. The circle where the fingers glide is drawn tight as a trap—then they resume their flight, leaving at the bottom of the dish a bright red scar. A drop of blood, of honey, on the fingertips.

Between light and teeth, the web of desire weaves the bowlful of lips.

Bottle

The bottle in the middle of the fire, at arm's length or on the table. In the shape of hands, in the source of pockets—there is silver and

there's a spirit up the sleeve. When color runs freely, when air
   ...gled in branches. The heart goes farther than the eyes, flame is
reborn from ash. Between the flowing thread and the stroke of light,
words stop making sense.

   No more need of words to make ourselves understood.

Translated from the French by Dan Bellm

BORIS PASTERNAK

(RUSSIA, 1890–1960)

Wild Vines

Beneath a willow entwined with ivy,
we look for shelter from the bad weather;
one raincoat covers both our shoulders—
my fingers rustle like the wild vine around your breasts.

I am wrong. The rain's stopped.
Not ivy, but the hair of Dionysus
hangs from these willows. What am I to do?
Throw the raincoat under us!

Translated from the Russian by Robert Lowell

Sparrow Hills

Like water pouring from a pitcher, my mouth on your nipples.
Not always. The summer well runs dry.
Not for long the dust of our stamping feet, encore on encore
from the saxes in the casino's midnight gazebo.

I've heard of age—its obese warbling!
When no wave will clap hands to the stars.
If they speak, you doubt it. No face in the meadows,
no heart in the pools, no god among the pines.

Split your soul like wood. Let today froth from your mouth.
It's the world's noontide. Have you no eyes for it?
Look, conception bubbles from the bleached fallows;
fir-cones, woodpeckers, clouds, pine-needles, heat.

Here the city's trolley tracks give out.
Further, you must put up with peeled pine. The trolley poles are
    detached.
Further, it's Sunday. Boughs screwed loose for the picnic bonfire,
playing tag in your bra.

"The world is always like this," say the woods,
as they mix the midday glare, Whitsunday, and walking.
All's planned with checkerberry couches, inspired with clearings—
the piebald clouds spill down on us like a country woman's housedress.

Translated from the Russian by Robert Lowell

For Anna Akhmatova

It seems I am choosing words that will stand,
and you are in them,
but if I blunder, it doesn't matter—
I must persist in my errors.

I hear the soiled, dripping small talk of the roofs;
the students' black boots drum eclogues on the boardwalks,
the undefined city takes on personality,
is alive in each sound.

Although it's spring, there's no leaving the city.
The sharp customers overlook nothing.
You bend to your sewing until you weep;
sunrise and sunset redden your swollen eyes.

You ache for the calm reaches of Ladoga,
then hurry off to the lake for a change

of fatigue. You gain nothing,
the shallows smell like closets full of last summer's clothes.

The dry wind dances like a dried-out walnut
across the waves, across your stung eyelids—
stars, branches, milestones, lamps. A white
seamstress on the bridge is always washing clothes.

I know that objects and eyesight vary greatly
in singleness and sharpness, but the iron
heart's vodka is the sky
under the northern lights.

That's how I see your face and expression.
This, not the pillar of salt, the *Lot's Wife* you pinned down
in rhyme five years ago to show up our fear,
limping forward in blinders, afraid of looking back.

How early your first dogged, unremitting idiom
hardened—no unassembled crumbs!
In all our affairs, your lines throb
with the high charge of our passing world. Each wire is a conductor.

Translated from the Russian by Robert Lowell

A Wedding

Into the enormous sky flew
a whirlwind of blue-gray patches—
a flock of doves spiraling up
suddenly from the dovecotes.

And to see them makes you wish,
just as the wedding-feast is ending,
years of happiness for this couple,
flung onto the wind like doves.

Life too is only an instant,
only a dissolving of ourselves
into everyone,
as if we gave ourselves as gifts.

Only a wedding, only the depths
of a window and the sound rushing in,
only a song, or a dream,
only a blue-gray dove.

Translated from the Russian by Robert Hass and Stephen Mitchell

NELLY SACHS
(GERMANY, 1891–1970)

Chorus of the Rescued

We, the rescued,
From whose hollow bones death had begun to whittle his flutes,
And on whose sinews he had already stroked his bow—
Our bodies continue to lament
With their mutilated music.
We, the rescued,
The nooses wound for our necks still dangle
Before us in the blue air—
Hourglasses still fill with our dripping blood.
We, the rescued,
The worms of fear still feed on us.
Our constellation is buried in dust.
We, the rescued,
Beg you:
Show us your sun, but gradually.
Lead us from star to star, step by step.
Be gentle when you teach us to live again.
Lest the song of a bird,
Or a pail being filled at the well,
Let our badly sealed pain burst forth again

And carry us away—
We beg you:
Do not show us an angry dog, not yet—
It could be, it could be
That we will dissolve into dust—
Dissolve into dust before your eyes.
For what binds our fabric together?
We whose breath vacated us,
Whose soul fled to Him out of that midnight
Long before our bodies were rescued
Into the arc of the moment.
We, the rescued,
We press your hand
We look into your eye—
But all that binds us together now is leave-taking.
The leave-taking in the dust
Binds us together with you

Translated from the German by Michael Roloff

OSIP MANDELSTAM
(RUSSIA, 1891–1938)

O Lord, help me to live through this night—

O Lord, help me to live through this night—
I'm in terror for my life, your slave:
to live in Petersburg is to sleep in a grave.

Translated from the Russian by Clarence Brown and W. S. Merwin

Take from my palms, to soothe your heart

Take from my palms, to soothe your heart
a little honey, a little sun,
in obedience to Persephone's bees.

You can't untie a boat that was never moored,
nor hear a shadow in its furs,
nor move through thick life without fear.

For us, all that's left is kisses
tattered as the little bees
that die when they leave the hive.

Deep in the transparent night they're still humming,
at home in the dark wood on the mountain,
in the mint and lungwort and the past.

But lay to your heart my rough gift,
this unlovely dry necklace of dead bees
that once made a sun out of honey.

Translated from the Russian by Clarence Brown and W. S. Merwin

Leningrad

I've come back to my city. These are my own old tears,
my own little veins, the swollen glands of my childhood.

So you're back. Open wide. Swallow
the fish-oil from the river lamps of Leningrad.

Open your eyes. Do you know this December day,
the egg-yolk with the deadly tar beaten into it?

Petersburg! I don't want to die yet!
You know my telephone numbers.

Petersburg! I've still got the addresses:
I can look up dead voices.

I live on back stairs, and the bell,
torn out nerves and all, jangles in my temples.

And I wait till morning for guests that I love,
and rattle the door in its chains.

Leningrad. December 1930

Translated from the Russian by Clarence Brown and
W. S. Merwin

Pear blossom and cherry blossom aim at me

Pear blossom and cherry blossom aim at me.
Their strength is crumbling but they never miss.

Stars in clusters of blossoms, leaves with stars—
what twin power is there? On what branch does truth blossom?

It fires into the air with flower or strength.
Its air-white full blossom-bludgeons put it to death.

And the twin scent's sweetness is unwelcoming.
It contends, it reaches out, it is mingled, it is sudden.

Translated from the Russian by Clarence Brown and
W. S. Merwin

Through Kiev, through the streets of the monster

Through Kiev, through the streets of the monster
some wife's trying to find her husband.
One time we knew that wife,
the wax cheeks, dry eyes.

Gypsies won't tell fortunes for beauties.
Here the concert hall has forgotten the instruments.
Dead horses along the main street.
The morgue smells in the nice part of town.

The Red Army trundled its wounded
out of town on the last streetcar,

one bloodstained overcoat calling,
"Don't worry, we'll be back!"

Voronezh. May 1937

Translated from the Russian by Clarence Brown and W. S. Merwin

Your thin shoulders are for turning red under whips

Your thin shoulders are for turning red under whips,
turning red under whips, and flaming in the raw cold.

Your child's fingers are for lifting flatirons,
for lifting flatirons, and for knotting cords.

Your tender soles are for walking on broken glass,
walking on broken glass, across bloody sand.

And I'm for burning like a black candle lit for you,
for burning like a black candle that dare not pray.

Translated from the Russian by Clarence Brown and W. S. Merwin

The Stalin Epigram

Our lives no longer feel ground under them.
At ten paces you can't hear our words.

But whenever there's a snatch of talk
it turns to the Kremlin mountaineer,

the ten thick worms his fingers,
his words like measures of weight,

the huge laughing cockroaches on his top lip,
the glitter of his boot-rims.

Ringed with a scum of chicken-necked bosses
he toys with the tributes of half-men.

One whistles, another meouws, a third snivels.
He pokes out his finger and he alone goes boom.

He forges decrees in a line like horseshoes,
One for the groin, one the forehead, temple, eye.

He rolls the executions on his tongue like berries.
He wishes he could hug them like big friends from home.

Translated from the Russian by Clarence Brown and W. S. Merwin

MARINA TSVETAEVA
(RUSSIA, 1892–1941)

from Poems for Moscow

2

From my hands—take this city not made by hands,
my strange, my beautiful brother.

Take it, church by church—all forty times forty churches,
and flying up over them, the small pigeons;

And Spassky Gates—in their flower—
where the Orthodox take off their hats;

And the Chapel of Stars—refuge chapel—
where the floor is—polished by tears;

Take the circle of the five cathedrals,
my soul, my holy friend.

And here, the Mary of Inadvertent Joy,
her garden, my beloved stranger.

The domes shine out their darkgold,
the sleepless bells thunder,

And down onto your shoulders, from the red clouds,
the Mother of God will drop her own thin coat,

And you will rise, happened of wonder powers . . .
—never ashamed you loved me.

March 31, 1916

Translated from the Russian by Jean Valentine and Ilya Kaminsky

from Poems to Czechia

8

A black mountain
has blocked out the light of the Earth.
Time—time—time
to give back to God his ticket.

I refuse to—be. In
the madhouse of the inhumans
I refuse to—live. To swim
with the current of human spines.

I have no need for holes
in my ears, no need for seeing eyes.
To your mad world—
one answer—to refuse.

1938

Translated from the Russian by Jean Valentine and Ilya Kaminsky

from Poems to Czechia

They took—suddenly—and took—openly—
took mountains—and took their entrails,
they took coal and took steel,
from us, lead they took—and crystal.

They took the sugar, and took the clover,
they took the North and took the West,
they took the beehive, and took the haystack,
they took the South from us, and the East.

Vari—they took and Tatras—they took,
they took our fingers—took our friends—
but we're not done for—
as long as there's spit in our mouths!
                                        1938

Translated from the Russian by Jean Valentine and Ilya Kaminsky

from Poems for Blok

1

Your name is a—bird in my hand,
a piece of ice on my tongue.
The lips' quick opening.
Your name—five letters.
A ball caught in flight,
a silver bell in my mouth.

A stone thrown into a silent lake
is—the sound of your name.
The light click of hooves at night
—your name.
Your name at my temple
—shrill click of a cocked gun.

Your name—impossible—
kiss on my eyes,
the chill of closed eyelids.
Your name—a kiss of snow.
Blue gulp of icy spring water.
With your name—sleep deepens.

Translated from the Russian by Jean Valentine and
Ilya Kaminsky

from Poems for Akhmatova

I won't fall behind you. I'm the guard.
You—the prisoner. Our fate is the same.
And here in the same open emptiness
they command us the same—Go away.

So—I lean against nothing.
I see it.
Let me go, my prisoner,
to walk over towards that pine tree.

June 1916

Translated from the Russian by Jean Valentine and
Ilya Kaminsky

To Kiss a Forehead

To kiss a forehead is to erase worry.
I kiss your forehead.

To kiss the eyes is to lift sleeplessness.
I kiss your eyes.

To kiss the lips is to drink water.
I kiss your lips.

To kiss a forehead is to erase memory.
I kiss your forehead.

Translated from the Russian by Ilya Kaminsky

EDITH SÖDERGRAN
(FINLAND, 1892–1923)

On Foot I Wandered Through the Solar Systems

On foot
I wandered through the solar systems,
before I found the first thread of my red dress.
Already I have a sense of myself.
Somewhere in space my heart hangs,
emitting sparks, shaking the air,
to other immeasurable hearts.

Translated from the Swedish by Malena Mörling and Jonas Ellerström

The Trees of My Childhood

The trees of my childhood stand tall in the grass
and shake their heads: what has become of you?
Rows of pillars stand like accusations: unworthy you walk beneath us!
You're a child and should know everything,
why are you caught in the trap of illness?
You've become a human being, strange, hateful.
When you were a child, you conducted long conversations with us,
your gaze was wise.
Now we'd like to tell you your life's secret:
the key to all secrets is in the grass on the hill of raspberries.
Sleeper, we wanted to rattle you,
we wanted to wake you, you dead one, from your sleep.

Translated from the Swedish by Malena Mörling and Jonas Ellerström

CÉSAR VALLEJO
(PERU, 1892–1938)

The Black Riders

There are blows in life so violent—I can't answer!
Blows as if from the hatred of God; as if before them,
the deep waters of everything lived through
were backed up in the soul . . . I can't answer!

Not many; but they exist . . . They open dark ravines
in the most ferocious face and in the most bull-like back.
Perhaps they are the horses of that heathen Attila,
or the black riders sent to us by Death.

They are the slips backward made by the Christs of the soul,
away from some holy faith that is sneered at by Events.
These blows that are bloody are the crackling sounds
from some bread that burns at the oven door.

And man . . . poor man! . . . poor man! He swings his eyes, as
when a man behind us calls us by clapping his hands;
swings his crazy eyes, and everything alive
is backed up, like a pool of guilt, in that glance.

There are blows in life so violent . . . I can't answer!

Translated from the Spanish by Robert Bly

The anger that breaks a man down into boys

The anger that breaks a man down into boys,
that breaks the boy down into equal birds,
and the bird, then, into tiny eggs;
the anger of the poor
owns one smooth oil against two vinegars.

The anger that breaks the tree down into leaves,
and the leaf down into different-sized buds,
and the buds into infinitely fine grooves;
the anger of the poor
owns two rivers against a number of seas.

The anger that breaks the good down into doubts,
and doubt down into three matching arcs,
and the arc, then, into unimaginable tombs;
the anger of the poor
owns one piece of steel against two daggers.

The anger that breaks the soul down into bodies;
the body down into different organs,
and the organ into reverberating octaves of thoughts;
the anger of the poor
owns one deep fire against two craters.

Translated from the Spanish by Robert Bly

Masses

When the battle was over,
and the fighter was dead, a man came toward him
and said to him: "Do not die; I love you so!"
But the corpse, it was sad! went on dying.

And two came near, and told him again and again:
"Do not leave us! Courage! Return to life!"
But the corpse, it was sad! went on dying.

Twenty arrived, a hundred, a thousand, five hundred thousand,
shouting: "So much love, and it can do nothing against death!"
But the corpse, it was sad! went on dying.

Millions of persons stood around him,
all speaking the same thing: "Stay here, brother!"
But the corpse, it was sad! went on dying.

Then all the men on the earth
stood around him; the corpse looked at them sadly, deeply moved;
he sat up slowly,
put his arms around the first man; started to walk . . .

Translated from the Spanish by Robert Bly

There are days, there comes to me an exuberant, political hunger

There are days, there comes to me an exuberant, political hunger
to desire, to kiss tenderness on both cheeks,
and there comes to me from afar a demonstrative
desire, another desire to love, willingly or by force,
whoever hates me, whoever tears up his paper, a little boy,
the woman who weeps for the man who was weeping,
the king of wine, the slave of water,
whoever hid in his wrath,
whoever sweats, whoever passes, whoever shakes his person in my soul.
And I desire, therefore, to adjust
the braid of whoever talks to me; the soldier's hair;
the light of the great; the greatness of the child.
I desire to iron directly
a handkerchief for whoever is unable to cry
and, when I am sad or happiness aches me,
to mend the children and the geniuses.

I desire to help the good one become a little bit bad
and I have an urge to be seated
to the right of the left-handed, and to respond to the mute,
trying to be useful to him as
I can, and likewise I desire very much
to wash the cripple's foot,
and to help my one-eyed neighbor sleep.

Ah to desire, this one, mine, this one, the world's,
interhuman and parochial, mature!
It comes perfectly timed,
from the foundation, from the public groin,

and, coming from afar, makes me hunger to kiss
the singer's muffler,
and whoever suffers, to kiss him on his frying pan,
the deaf man, fearlessly, on his cranial murmur;
whoever gives me what I forgot in my breast,
on his Dante, on his Chaplin, on his shoulders.

I desire, finally,
when I'm at the celebrated end of violence
or my heart full of chest, I would like
to help whoever smiles laugh,
to put a little bird right on the evil man's nape,
to take care of the sick annoying them,
to buy from the vendor,
to help the killer kill—a terrible thing—
and I would desire to be good to myself
in everything.

Translated from the Spanish by Clayton Eshleman

A man walks by with a baguette on his shoulder

A man walks by with a baguette on his shoulder.
Am I going to write, after that, about my double?

Another sits, scratches, extracts a louse from his armpit, kills it.
How dare one speak about psychoanalysis?

Another has entered my chest with a stick in hand.
To talk then about Socrates with the doctor?

A cripple passes by holding a child's hand.
After that I'm going to read André Breton?

Another trembles from cold, coughs, spits blood.
Will it ever be possible to allude to the deep Self?

Another searches in the muck for bones, rinds
How to write, after that, about the infinite?

A bricklayer falls from a roof, dies and no longer eats lunch.
To innovate, then, the trope, the metaphor?

A merchant cheats a customer out of a gram.
To speak, after that, about the fourth dimension?

A banker falsifies his balance sheet.
With what face to cry in the theater?

An outcast sleeps with his foot behind his back.
To speak, after that, to anyone about Picasso?

Someone goes to a burial sobbing.
How then become a member of the Academy?

Someone cleans a rifle in his kitchen.
How dare one speak about the beyond?

Someone passes by counting with his fingers.
How speak of the non-self without screaming?

Translated from the Spanish by Clayton Eshleman

from The Nine Monsters

The pain grabs us, brother men,
from behind, in profile,
and drives us wild in the movies,
nails us into gramophones,
unnails us in bed, falls perpendicularly
onto our tickets, our letters,
and it is very serious to suffer, one might pray . . .
For as a result
of the pain, there are some
who are born, others grow, others die,

and others who are born and do not die, others
who die without having been born, and others
who neither are born nor die (the majority).
And likewise as a result
of suffering, I am sad
up to my head, and sadder down to my ankle,
from seeing bread, crucified, the turnip,
bloodied,
the onion, crying,
cereal, in general, flour,
salt, made dust, water, fleeing,
wine, an *ecce homo*,
such pallid snow, such an ardent sun!
How, human brothers,
not to tell you that I can no longer stand it and
can no longer stand so much drawer,
so much minute, so much
lizard and so much
inversion, so much distance and so much thirst for thirst!
Mr. Minister of Health: what to do?
Ah, unfortunately, human men,
there is, brothers, much too much to do.

Translated from the Spanish by Clayton Eshleman

Today I like life much less

Today I like life much less,
but I always like to live: I've often said it.
I almost touched the part of my whole and restrained myself
with a shot in the tongue behind my word.

Today I touch my chin in retreat
and in these momentary trousers I tell myself:
So much life and never!
So many years and always my weeks! . . .
My parents buried with their stone
and their sad stiffening that has not ended;

full-length brothers, my brothers,
and finally, my being standing and in a vest.

I like life enormously,
but, of course,
with my beloved death and my café
and looking at the leafy chestnut trees of Paris
and saying:
This is an eye, that one too, this a forehead, that one too . . . And repeating:
So much life and never does the tune fail me!
So many years and always, always, always!

I said vest, said
whole, part, yearning, said almost, to avoid crying.
For it is true that I suffered in that hospital close by
and it has is good and it is bad to have watched
from below up my organism.

I would like to live always, even flat on my belly,
because, as I was saying and I say it again,
so much life and never! And so many years,
and always, much always, always always!

Translated from the Spanish by Clayton Eshleman

Black Stone Lying on a White Stone

I will die in Paris, on a rainy day,
on some day I can already remember.
I will die in Paris—and I don't step aside—
perhaps on a Thursday, as today is Thursday, in autumn.

It will be a Thursday, because today, Thursday, setting down
these lines, I have put my upper arm bones on
wrong, and never so much as today have I found myself
with all the road ahead of me, alone.

César Vallejo is dead. Everyone beat him,
although he never does anything to them;
they beat him hard with a stick and hard also

with a rope. These are the witnesses:
the Thursdays, and the bones of my arms,
the solitude, and the rain, and the roads . . .

Translated from the Spanish by Robert Bly

VLADIMIR MAYAKOVSKY
(RUSSIA, 1893–1930)

Past One O'Clock

Past one o'clock. You must have gone to bed.
The Milky Way streams silver through the night.
I'm in no hurry; with lightning telegrams
I have no cause to wake or trouble you.
And, as they say, the incident is closed.
Love's boat has smashed against the daily grind.
Now you and I are quits. Why bother then
To balance mutual sorrows, pains, and hurts.
Behold what quiet settles on the world.
Night wraps the sky in tribute from the stars.
In hours like these, one rises to address
The ages, history, and all creation.

Translated from the Russian by Max Hayward and George Reavey

from The Cloud in Trousers

A Tetraptych

Your thought,
musing on a sodden brain
like a boated lackey on a greasy couch,

I'll taunt with a bloody morsel of heart;
and satiate my insolent, caustic contempt.

No gray hairs streak my soul,
no grandfatherly fondness there!
I shake the world with the might of my voice,
and walk—handsome,
twentytwoyearold.

Tender souls!
You play your love on a fiddle,
and the crude club their love on a drum.
But you cannot turn yourselves inside out,
like me, and be just bare lips!

Come and be lessoned—
prim officiates of the angelic league,
lisping in drawing-room cambric.

You, too, who leaf your lips like a cook
turns the pages of a cookery book.

If you wish,
I shall rage on raw meat;
or, as the sky changes its hue,
if you wish,
I shall grow irreproachably tender:
not a man, but a cloud in trousers!

I deny the existence of blossoming Nice!
Again in song I glorify
men as crumpled as hospital beds,
and women as battered as proverbs.

Translated from the Russian by Max Hayward and George Reavey

JORGE DE LIMA
(BRAZIL, 1893–1953)

Distribution of Poetry

I took wild honey from the plants,
I took salt from the waters, I took light from the sky.
Listen, my brothers: I took poetry from everything
To offer it to the Lord.
I did not dig gold from the earth
Or leech blood from my brothers.
Inn-keepers: let me alone.
Peddlers and bankers:
I can fabricate distances
To keep you away from me.
Life is a failure,
I believe in the magic of God.
The roosters are not crowing,
The day has not dawned.
I saw the ships go and return.
I saw misery go and return.
I saw the fat man in the fire.
I saw zig-zags in the darkness.
Captain, where is the Congo?
Where is the Isle of Saint Brandon?
Captain, what a black night!
Mastiffs howl in the darkness.
O Untouchables, which is the country,
Which is the country that you desire?
I took wild honey from the plants.
I took salt from the waters, I took light from the sky.
I have only poetry to give you.
Sit down, my brothers.

Translated from the Portuguese by John Nist

MITSUHARU KANEKO

(JAPAN, 1895–1975)

Opposition

In my youth
I was opposed to school.
And now, again,
I'm opposed to work.

Above all it is health
And righteousness that I hate the most.
There's nothing so cruel to man
As health and honesty.

Of course I'm opposed to "the Japanese spirit"
And duty and human feeling make me vomit.
I'm against any government anywhere
And show my bum to authors' and artists' circles.

When I'm asked for what I was born,
Without scruple, I'll reply, "To oppose."
When I'm in the east
I want to go to the west.

I fasten my coat at the left, my shoes right and left.
My hakama I wear back to front and I ride a horse facing its buttocks.
What everyone else hates I like
And my greatest hate of all is people feeling the same.

This I believe: to oppose
Is the only fine thing in life.
To oppose is to live.
To oppose is to get a grip on the very self.

Translated from the Japanese by Geoffrey Bownas and Anthony Thwaite

YANKEV GLATSHTEYN
(POLAND, 1896–1971)

Mozart

I dreamed that
the gentiles crucified Mozart
and buried him in a pauper's grave.
But the Jews made him a man of God
and blessed his memory.

I, his apostle, ran all over the world,
convening everyone I met,
and wherever I caught a Christian
I made him a Mozartian.

How wonderful is the musical testament
of this divine man!
How nailed through with song
his shining hands!
In his greatest need
all the fingers of this crucified
singer were laughing.
And in his most crying grief
he loved his neighbor's ear
more than himself.

How poor and stingy—
compared with Mozart's legacy—
is the Sermon on the Mount.

Translated from the Yiddish by Ruth Whitman

A Song

In the Jewish parliament
The walls are burning.
People are learning Talmud,

arguing over commentaries.
Suddenly—quiet, please!
A gentile comes in
And says in gentile-ese:
Gentlemen,
That's the kind of world this is.

The learners split into equal parties
Forbidding, permitting, and deriving.
What did the gentile mean when he said
"The kind of world it is"? They grab their heads.
Oh, dearest God, the kind of world this is!

The right says:
It may not suit the gentile
But let's start shooting in a little while.
From the center aisle:
Yes, we agree, a little bit.
Right then the left shouts:
Let's get out of here
And not do it shoot-'em-up style.

Shouts the gentile: Gentlemen, please,
That's the kind of world this is.
And all sing: Dearest God, the kind of world this is.

Translated from the Yiddish by Zachary Sholem Berger

TRISTAN TZARA
(FRANCE/ROMANIA, 1896–1963)

Metal Coughdrops

her bare feet tell the neurasthenic: fake moustaches on that ostrich
made in u.s.a.
the cold bird tells the monocle: mouth got no lips I'll kill myself
but the cubist tells the cubist: i have invented the chief-of-scratch & I am

his boss
the boss tells the boss: boss

Translated from the French by Jerome Rothenberg

ANDRÉ BRETON
(FRANCE, 1896–1966)

Free Union

My wife whose hair is a brush fire
Whose thoughts are summer lightning
Whose waist is an hourglass
Whose waist is the waist of an otter caught in the teeth of a tiger
Whose mouth is a bright cockade with the fragrance of a star of the
    first magnitude
Whose teeth leave prints like the tracks of white mice over snow
Whose tongue is made out of amber and polished glass
Whose tongue is a stabbed wafer
The tongue of a doll with eyes that open and shut
Whose tongue is incredible stone
My wife whose eyelashes are strokes in the handwriting of a child
Whose eyebrows are nests of swallow
My wife whose temples are the slate of greenhouse roofs
With steam on the windows
My wife whose shoulders are champagne
Are fountains that curl from the heads of dolphins under the ice
My wife whose wrists are matches
Whose fingers are raffles holding the ace of hearts
Whose fingers are fresh cut hay
My wife with the armpits of martens and beech fruit
And Midsummer night
That are hedges of privet and nesting places for sea snails
Whose arms are of sea foam and a landlocked sea
And a fusion of wheat and a mill
Whose legs are spindles
In the delicate movements of watches and despair

My wife whose calves are sweet with the sap of elders
Whose feet are carved initials
Keyrings and the feet of steeplejacks who drink
My wife whose neck is fine milled barley
Whose throat contains the Valley of Gold
And encounters in the bed of the maelstrom
My wife whose breasts are of the night
And are undersea molehills
And crucibles of rubies
My wife whose breasts are haunted by the ghosts of dew-moistened
    roses
Whose belly is a fan unfolded in the sunlight
Is a giant talon
My wife with the back of a bird in vertical flight
With a back of quicksilver
And bright lights
My wife whose nape is of smooth worn stone and wet chalk
And of a glass slipped through the fingers of someone who has just
    drunk
My wife with the thighs of a skiff
That are lustrous and feathered like arrows
Stemmed with the light tailbones of a white peacock
And imperceptible balance
My wife whose rump is sandstone and flax
Whose rump is the back of a swan and the spring
My wife with the sex of an iris
A mine and a platypus
With the sex of an alga and old-fashioned candies
My wife with the sex of a mirror
My wife with the eyes full of tears
With eyes that are purple armor and a magnetized needle
With eyes of savannahs
With eyes full of water to drink in prisons
My wife with eyes that are forests forever under the ax
My wife with eyes that are the equal of water and air
    and earth and fire

Translated from the French by David Antin

GERARDO DIEGO
(SPAIN, 1896–1987)

Julio Campal

We were walking to your funeral, eleven friends.
And the twenty-eight letters of your alphabet,
your letters, Julio, all set free
that were once so gladly bound together.

Throw letters into the air, like dice:
always a poem turns up.
Sow the scattered fragments of bone
in this or that
or in the remotest grave:
they will be made whole again, down
to the least fingerbone.

Your Mar del Plata or native land,
Julio Campal.
Twenty-eight letters hiding your secret.

Translated from the Spanish by Robert Mezey

EUGENIO MONTALE
(ITALY, 1896–1981)

Lemon Trees

Listen:
the poets laureate live in a world
of plants whose names we're not likely to say.
But the roads I love
lead to weed-thronged gullies where a boy
can catch an eel sometimes
in a shrinking puddle:
narrow paths that wind around the hills,

drop through clumps of cattails
and enter an orchard, the rows of lemon trees.

It's best when even bird-song
evaporates into the blue sky;
then we can hear the friendly boughs
whisper in air that's just stirring
and we catch
the thick earth odor
that can pour an unsettling sweetness through us.
This is where all the passions fighting each other
miraculously stop:
this is where everyone's allowed a share of riches—
the fragrance of the lemon trees.

Look:
in these silences in which everything
loosens its hold on itself and seems
about to betray its last secret
we're almost sure
we're going to discover some flaw in nature—
the world's dead point, the weak link that gives,
the unraveling thread that finally leads us
into the presence of what is really true.
Carefully I look around,
my mind is trying all the possibilities,
it holds them one by one and then breaks them
in the thickening lemon-scent
as the late slow day begins to die.
These are the silences when
every retreating man-shadow
Can look like the figure of some god who's lost his way.

That momentary illusion doesn't last, though—
time turns us back
to our clamoring cities where the blue gleams
only in high patches, between roof peaks.
The rain pools in the tired streets, a winter tedium

lies heavily on all the houses,
the light won't give us enough of itself, our souls grow bitter.
Yet one day through a gate that someone has left half open
there are yellow lemons shining at us
and our heart's ice melts
and into our empty being
again these golden horns of sunlight
can pour their songs.

Translated by Reginald Gibbons

Xenia I

1

Dear little Mosca,
so they called you, I don't know why,
this evening almost in the dark,
while I was reading Deutero-Isaiah
you reappeared beside me,
but without your glasses,
so that you could not see me,
nor could I recognize you in the haze
without that glitter.

2

Poor Mosca without glasses or antennae,
who had wings only in imagination,
a worn-out and dismantled Bible,
and not very dependable either,
night's black, a flash, a peal of thunder
and then not even the storm.
Could you have left so soon
even without talking?
But it's ridiculous to think
you still had lips.

3

At the Saint James in Paris
I shall have to ask for a "single" room
(and they don't like single guests).
And so also in the fake Byzantium
of your hotel in Venice; then immediately
to look for the girls at the switchboard,
always your friends, and leave again
the moment the automatic charge
is spent—
the desire to have you with me again,
if only through a gesture or a habit.

4

We had studied for the hereafter
a token of recognition, a whistle;
I'm now trying to modulate it in the hope
that we're all already dead without knowing it.

5

I've never understood if it was I
who was your faithful and distempered dog,
or if you were that for me.
For them you were only a myopic
insect lost in the babble
of high society. How ingenuous
of those clever people not to know
it was they who were your laughingstock,
that you could see them even in the dark,
and unmask them with your infallible flair
and your bat's radar.

6

It never occurred to you
to leave any trace of yourself
in prose or verse, which was
your charm—and then my self-disgust.
It was also what terrified me:
that you might cast me back
into the croaking mire of the neòteroi.

7

Self-pity, infinite pain and anguish
his who worships what's *here below*
and hopes and despairs of something else . . .
(and who dares say another world?)
. . .
"Strange pity . . ." (Azucena, Act II).

8

Your speech so halting and unguarded
is the only thing left
with which to content myself.
But the accent is changed, the colour is different.
I'm getting used to listening to you
in the tick-tack of the teletype,
or in the voluble smoke rings of
my cigars from Brissago.

9

Listening was your only way of seeing.
The telephone bill now amounts to very little.

10

"Did she pray?" "Yes, she prayed to St. Anthony
who helps one find lost umbrellas
and other things of St. Hermes' wardrobe."
"Only for this?" "Also for her dead
and for me."
"It's enough," said the priest.

11

To recall your tears (and mine were double)
is not enough to suppress your bursts of laughter.
These were like the foretaste of your private Last Judgment
which unfortunately never took place.

12

Spring comes out at the pace of a mole.
I shall hear you talk no more
of the poisonous antibiotics,
the rivet in your thighbone, or
the patrimony that shrewd unnamed rat
nibbled away.

Spring advances with its thick mists,
its long light days and unbearable hours.
No longer shall I hear you struggle
with the regurgitation of time
or of phantoms
or of the logistic problems of summer.

13

Your brother died young; you were
the dishevelled child who now watches me,
formally posed, from the oval of a portrait.
He wrote music but it was unpublished,

unheard, and today lies buried
in a trunk or is gone to dust.
Perhaps someone's reinventing it without knowing,
if what is written is written.
I loved him without having known him
and no one remembered him except you.
I asked no questions; and now it's useless.
I'm the only one after you
for whom he ever existed.
But it's possible, you know, to love a shadow,
we ourselves being shadows.

14

They say that mine
is a poetry of non-belonging.
But if it was yours, it was someone's:
not your form any more but your essence.
They say that poetry at its highest
glorifies the Whole in its flight,
and deny
that the tortoise is swifter than lightning.
You alone knew
that motion is not different from stillness,
that the void is the same as fullness,
that the clearest sky is but
the most diffused of clouds.
Thus I understand better your long journey
imprisoned among bandages and plasters.
Yet it gives me no rest to know
that alone or together
we are one.

Translated from the Italian by G. Singh

To Conclude

I charge my descendants (if I have
any) on the literary plane
which is rather improbable, to make
a big bonfire of all that concerns
my life, my actions, my non-actions.
I'm no Leopardi, I leave
little behind me to be burnt,
and it's already too much to live
by percentages. I lived at the rate
of five per cent; don't increase
the dose. And yet
it never rains but it pours.

Translated from the Italian by G. Singh

In the Smoke

How often I waited for you
at the station in the cold and fog,
trolled up and down, coughing, buying papers
not even worth the name,
smoking Giuba, later banned by the minister
of tobacco, what a fool!
Perhaps a wrong train, or an extra section,
or one that was simply cancelled.
I'd peer at the trolleys of the porters
to see if your luggage was there,
and you coming late, behind it.
And there you were at last!
One memory this among many.
It pursues me in my dreams.

Translated from the Italian by G. Singh

FEDERICO GARCÍA LORCA
(SPAIN, 1898–1936)

The Little Mute Boy

The little boy was looking for his voice.
(The king of the crickets had it.)
In a drop of water
the little boy was looking for his voice.

I do not want it for speaking with;
I will make a ring of it
so that he may wear my silence
on his little finger

In a drop of water
the little boy was looking for his voice.

(The captive voice, far away,
put on a cricket's clothes.)

Translated from the Spanish by W. S. Merwin

Farewell

If I die,
leave the balcony open.

The little boy is eating oranges.
(From my balcony I can see him.)

The reaper is harvesting the wheat.
(From my balcony I can hear him.)

If I die,
leave the balcony open!

Translated from the Spanish by W. S. Merwin

Lament for Ignacio Sanchez Mejias

1. COGIDA AND DEATH

At five in the afternoon.
It was exactly five in the afternoon.
A boy brought the white sheet
at five in the afternoon.
A frail of lime ready prepared
at five in the afternoon.
The rest was death, and death alone
at five in the afternoon.

The wind carried away the cottonwool
at five in the afternoon.
And the oxide scattered crystal and nickel
at five in the afternoon.
Now the dove and the leopard wrestle
at five in the afternoon.
And a thigh with a desolate horn
at five in the afternoon.
The bass-string struck up
at five in the afternoon.
Arsenic bells and smoke
at five in the afternoon.
Groups of silence in the corners
at five in the afternoon.
And the bull alone with a high heart!
At five in the afternoon.
When the sweat of snow was coming
at five in the afternoon,
when the bull ring was covered with iodine
at five in the afternoon.
Death laid eggs in the wound
at five in the afternoon.
At five in the afternoon.
Exactly at five o'clock in the afternoon.

A coffin on wheels is his bed
at five in the afternoon.
Bones and flutes resound in his ears
at five in the afternoon.
Now the bull was bellowing through his forehead
at five in the afternoon.
The room was iridiscent with agony
at five in the afternoon.
In the distance the gangrene now comes
at five in the afternoon.
Horn of the lily through green groins
at five in the afternoon.
The wounds were burning like suns
at five in the afternoon,
and the crowd was breaking the windows
at five in the afternoon.
At five in the afternoon.
Ah, that fatal five in the afternoon!
It was five by all the clocks!
It was five in the shade of the afternoon!

2. THE SPILLED BLOOD

I will not see it!

Tell the moon to come
for I do not want to see the blood
of Ignacio on the sand.

I will not see it!

The moon wide open.
Horse of still clouds,
and the grey bull ring of dreams
with willows in the barreras.

I will not see it!

Let my memory kindle!
Warm the jasmines
of such minute whiteness!

I will not see it!

The cow of the ancient world
passed her sad tongue
over a snout of blood
spilled on the sand,
and the bulls of Guisando,
partly death and partly stone,
bellowed like two centuries
sated with threading the earth.
No.
I do not want to see it!
I will not see it!

Ignacio goes up the tiers
with all his death on his shoulders.
He sought for the dawn
but the dawn was no more.
He seeks for his confident profile
and the dream bewilders him
He sought for his beautiful body
and encountered his opened blood
I will not see it!
I do not want to hear it spurt
each time with less strength:
that spurt that illuminates
the tiers of seats, and spills
over the corduroy and the leather
of a thirsty multitude.
Who shouts that I should come near!
Do not ask me to see it!

His eyes did not close
when he saw the horns near,

but the terrible mothers
lifted their heads.
And across the ranches,
an air of secret voices rose,
shouting to celestial bulls,
herdsmen of pale mist.
There was no prince in Seville
who could compare with him,
nor sword like his sword
nor heart so true.
Like a river of lions
was his marvellous strength,
and like a marble torso
his firm drawn moderation.
The air of Andalusian Rome
gilded his head
where his smile was a spikenard
of wit and intelligence.
What a great torero in the ring!
What a good peasant in the sierra!
How gentle with the sheaves!
How hard with the spurs!
How tender with the dew!
How dazzling the fiesta!
How tremendous with the final
banderillas of darkness!

But now he sleeps without end.
Now the moss and the grass
open with sure fingers
the flower of his skull.
And now his blood comes out singing;
singing along marshes and meadows,
sliding on frozen horns,
faltering soulless in the mist,
stumbling over a thousand hoofs
like a long, dark, sad tongue,
to form a pool of agony

close to the starry Guadalquivir.
Oh, white wall of Spain!
Oh, black bull of sorrow!
Oh, hard blood of Ignacio!
Oh, nightingale of his veins!
No.
I will not see it!
No chalice can contain it,
no swallows can drink it,
no frost of light can cool it,
nor song nor deluge of white lilies,
no glass can cover it with silver.
No.
I will not see it!

3. THE LAID OUT BODY

Stone is a forehead where dreams grieve
without curving waters and frozen cypresses.
Stone is a shoulder on which to bear Time
with trees formed of tears and ribbons and planets.

I have seen grey showers move towards the waves
raising their tender riddled arms,
to avoid being caught by the lying stone
which loosens their limbs without soaking the blood.

For stone gathers seed and clouds,
skeleton larks and wolves of penumbra:
but yields not sounds nor crystals nor fire,
only bull rings and bull rings and more bull rings without walls.

Now, Ignacio the well born lies on the stone.
All is finished. What is happening? Contemplate his face:
death has covered him with pale sulphur
and has placed on him the head of a dark minotaur.

All is finished. The rain penetrates his mouth.
The air, as if mad, leaves his sunken chest,
and Love, soaked through with tears of snow,
warms itself on the peak of the herd.

What are they saying? A stenching silence settles down.
We are here with a body laid out which fades away,
with a pure shape which had nightingales
and we see it being filled with depthless holes.

Who creases the shroud? What he says is not true!
Nobody sings here, nobody weeps in the corner,
nobody pricks the spurs, nor terrifies the serpent.
Here I want nothing else but the round eyes
to see this body without a chance of rest.

Here I want to see those men of hard voice.
Those that break horses and dominate rivers;
those men of sonorous skeleton who sing
with a mouth full of sun and flint.

Here I want to see them. Before the stone.
Before this body with broken reins.
I want to know from them the way out
for this captain strapped down by death.

I want them to show me a lament like a river
which will have sweet mists and deep shores,
to take the body of Ignacio where it loses itself
without hearing the double panting of the bulls.

Loses itself in the round bull ring of the moon
which feigns in its youth a sad quiet bull:
loses itself in the night without song of fishes
and in the white thicket of frozen smoke.

I don't want them to cover his face with handkerchiefs
that he may get used to the death he carries.

Go, Ignacio; feel not the hot bellowing.
Sleep, fly, rest: even the sea dies!

4. ABSENT SOUL

The bull does not know you, nor the fig tree,
nor the horses, nor the ants in your own house.
The child and the afternoon do not know you
because you have died for ever.

The back of the stone does not know you,
nor the black satin in which you crumble.
Your silent memory does not know you
because you have died for ever.

The autumn will come with small white snails,
misty grapes and with clustered hills,
but no one will look into your eyes
because you have died for ever.

Because you have died for ever,
like all the dead of the Earth,
like all the dead who are forgotten
in a heap of lifeless dogs.

Nobody knows you. No. But I sing of you.
For posterity I sing of your profile and grace.
Of the signal maturity of your understanding.
Of your appetite for death and the taste of its mouth.
Of the sadness of your once valiant gaiety.

It will be a long time, if ever, before there is born
an Andalusian so true, so rich in adventure.
I sing of his elegance with words that groan,
and I remember a sad breeze through the olive trees.

Translated from the Spanish by Stephen Spender and J. L. Gili

City That Does Not Sleep

(*Nightsong of Brooklyn Bridge*)

In the sky there is nobody asleep. Nobody, nobody.
Nobody is asleep.
The creatures of the moon sniff and prowl about their cabins.
The living iguanas will come to bite the men who do not dream,
and the man who rushes out with his spirit broken will meet on
        the streetcorner
the unbelievable alligator quiet beneath the tender protest of
        the stars.

Nobody is asleep on earth. Nobody, nobody.
Nobody is asleep.
In the graveyard far off there is a corpse
who has moaned for three years
because of a dry countryside in his knee;
and that boy they buried this morning cried so much
it was necessary to call out the dogs to keep him quiet.

Life is not a dream. Careful! Careful! Careful!
We fall down the stairs in order to eat the moist earth
or we climb to the knife-edge of the snow with the voices of
        the dead dahlias.
But forgetfulness does not exist, dreams do not exist;
flesh exists. Kisses tie our mouths
in a thicket of new veins,
and whoever his pain pains will feel that pain forever
and whoever is afraid of death will carry it on his shoulders.

One day
the horses will live in the saloons
and the enraged ants
will throw themselves on the yellow skies that take refuge in the
        eyes of cows.
Another day
we will watch the preserved butterflies rise from the dead

and still walking through a country of gray sponges and silent
	boats
we will watch our ring flash and roses spring from our tongue.
Careful! Be careful! Be careful!
The men who still have marks of the claw and the thunderstorm,
and that boy who cries because he has never heard of the
	invention of the bridge,
or that dead man who only possesses now his head and a shoe,
we must carry them to the wall where the iguanas and the snakes
	are waiting,
where the bear's teeth are waiting,
where the mummified hand of the boy is waiting,
and the hair of the camel stands on end with a violent blue
	shudder.

    Nobody is sleeping in the sky. Nobody, nobody.
Nobody is sleeping.
If someone does close his eyes,
a whip, boys, a whip!
Let there be a landscape of open eyes
and bitter wounds on fire.
No one is sleeping in this world. No one, no one.
I have said it before.
No one is sleeping.
But if someone grows too much moss on his temples during the
	night,
open the stage trapdoors so he can see in the moonlight
the lying goblets, and the poison, and the skull of the theaters.

Translated from the Spanish by Robert Bly

Rundown Church

(*Ballad of the First World War*)

I had a son and his name was John.
I had a son.
He disappeared into the arches one Friday of All Souls.

I saw him playing on the highest steps of the Mass
throwing a little tin pail at the heart of the priest.
I knocked on the coffin. My son! My son! My son!
I drew out a chicken foot from behind the moon and then
I understood that my daughter was a fish
down which the carts vanish.
I had a daughter.
I had a fish dead under the ashes of the incense burner.
I had an ocean. Of what? Good Lord! An ocean!
I went up to ring the bells but the fruit was all wormy
and the blackened match-ends
were eating the spring wheat.
I saw a stork of alcohol you could see through
shaving the black heads of the dying soldiers
and I saw the rubber booths
where the goblets full of tears were whirling.
In the anemones of the offertory I will find you, my love!
when the priest with his strong arms raises up the mule and the ox
to scare the nighttime toads that roam in the icy landscapes of the chalice.
I had a son who was a giant,
but the dead are stronger and know how to gobble down pieces of the sky.
If my son had only been a bear,
I wouldn't fear the secrecy of the crocodiles
and I wouldn't have seen the ocean roped to the trees
to be raped and wounded by the mobs from the regiment.
If my son had only been a bear!
I'll roll myself in this rough canvas so as not to feel the chill of the mosses.
I know very well they will give me a sleeve or a necktie,
but in the innermost part of the Mass I'll smash the rudder and then
the insanity of the penguins and seagulls will come to the rock
and they will make the people sleeping and the people singing on the
    streetcorners say:
he had a son.
A son! A son! A son
and it was no one else's, because it was his son!
His son! His son! His son!

Translated from the Spanish by Robert Bly

Little Infinite Poem

For Luis Cardoza y Aragón

To take the wrong road
is to arrive at the snow,
and to arrive at the snow
is to get down on all fours for twenty centuries and eat the grasses of
    the cemeteries.

To take the wrong road
is to arrive at woman,
woman who isn't afraid of light,
woman who murders two roosters in one second,
light which isn't afraid of roosters,
and roosters who don't know how to sing on top of the snow.

But if the snow truly takes the wrong road,
then it might meet the southern wind,
and since the air cares nothing for groans,
we will have to get down on all fours again and eat the grasses of the
    cemeteries.

I saw two mournful wheatheads made of wax
burying a countryside of volcanoes;
and I saw two insane little boys who wept as they leaned on a
    murderer's eyeballs.

Translated from the Spanish by Robert Bly

Song of the Cuban Blacks

When the full moon comes
I'll go to Santiago in Cuba.
I'll go to Santiago
in a carriage of black water.
I'll go to Santiago.

Palm-thatching will start to sing.
I'll go to Santiago.
When the palm trees want to turn into storks,
I'll go to Santiago.
When the banana trees want to turn into jellyfish,
I'll go to Santiago.
With the golden head of Fonseca
I'll go to Santiago.
And with the rose of Romeo and Juliet
I'll go to Santiago.
Oh Cuba! Oh rhythm of dry seeds!
I'll go to Santiago.
Oh warm waist, and a drop of wood!
I'll go to Santiago.
Harp of living trees. Crocodile. Tobacco blossom!
I'll go to Santiago.
I always said I would go to Santiago
in a carriage of black water.
I'll go to Santiago.
Wind and alcohol in the wheels,
I'll go to Santiago.
My coral in the darkness,
I'll go to Santiago.
The ocean drowned in the sand,
I'll go to Santiago.
White head and dead fruit,
I'll go to Santiago.
Oh wonderful freshness of the cane fields!
Oh Cuba! Arc of sights and mud!
I'll go to Santiago.

Translated from the Spanish by Robert Bly

GIACOMO NOVENTA

(ITALY, 1898–1960)

What's Beyond

What's beyond
the sky, father?
Sky, my son.
And beyond that?
More sky.
And beyond that?
Worse luck,
God.

Translated from the Italian by Pearse Hutchinson

BERTOLT BRECHT

(GERMANY, 1898–1956)

I, the Survivor

I know of course: it's simply luck
That I've survived so many friends. But last night in a dream
I heard those friends say of me: "Survival of the fittest"
And I hated myself.

Translated from the German by John Willett

Motto

In the dark times,
Will there also be singing?
Yes, there will also be singing
About the dark times.

Translated from the German by John Willett

HENRI MICHAUX

(BELGIUM, 1899–1984)

from I Am Writing to You from a Far-off Country

I

We have here, she said, only one sun in the month, and for only
a little while. We rub our eyes days ahead. But to no purpose.
Inexorable weather. Sunlight arrives only at its proper hour.

Then we have a world of things to do, so long as there is light, in fact
we hardly have time to look at one another a bit.

The trouble is that nighttime is when we must work, and we really
must: dwarfs are born constantly.

II

When you walk in the country, she further confided to him, you may
chance to meet with substantial masses on your road. These are
mountains and sooner or later you must bend the knee to them.
Resisting will do no good, you could go no farther, even by hurting
yourself.

I do not say this in order to wound. I could say other things if I really
wanted to wound.

III

The dawn is grey here, she went on to tell him. It was not always like
this. We do not know whom to accuse.

At night the cattle make a great bellowing, long and flutelike at the
end. We feel compassionate, but what can we do?

The smell of eucalyptus surrounds us: a blessing—serenity, but it cannot protect us from everything, or else do you think that it really can protect us from everything?

IV

I add one further word to you, a question rather.

Does water flow in your country too? (I don't remember whether you've told me so) and it gives chills too, if it is the real thing.

Do I love it? I don't know. One feels so alone when it is cold. But quite otherwise when it is warm. Well then? How can I decide? How do you others decide, tell me, when you speak of it without disguise, with open heart?

V

I am writing to you from the end of the world. You must realize this. The trees often tremble. We collect the leaves. They have a ridiculous number of veins. But what for? There's nothing between them and the tree any more, and we go off troubled.

Could not life continue on earth without wind? Or must everything tremble, always, always?

There are subterranean disturbances, too, in the house as well, like angers which might come to face you, like stern beings who would like to wrest confessions.

We see nothing, except what is so unimportant to see. Nothing, and yet we tremble. Why?

Translated from the French by Richard Ellman

FRANCIS PONGE
(FRANCE, 1899–1988)

The Pleasures of the Door

Kings do not touch doors.

They do not know that happiness: to push before them with kindness or rudeness one of these great familiar panels, to turn around towards it to put it back in place—to hold it in one's arms.

The happiness of grabbing by the porcelain knot of its belly one of these huge single obstacles; this quick grappling by which, for a moment, progress is hindered, as the eye opens and the entire body fits into its new environment.

With a friendly hand he holds it a while longer before pushing it back decidedly thus shutting himself in—of which, he, by the click of the powerful and well-oiled spring, is pleasantly assured . . .

Translated from the French by Raymond Federman

JORGE LUIS BORGES
(ARGENTINA, 1899–1986)

Borges and I

The other one, the one called Borges, is the one things happen to. I walk through the streets of Buenos Aires and stop for a moment, perhaps mechanically now, to look at the arch of an entrance hall and the grillwork on the gate; I know of Borges from the mail and see his name on a list of professors or in a biographical dictionary. I like hourglasses, maps, eighteenth-century typography, the taste of coffee and the prose of Stevenson; he shares these preferences, but in a vain way that turns them into the attributes of an actor. It would be an exaggeration to say that ours is a hostile relationship; I live, let myself go on living, so that Borges may contrive his literature, and this literature justifies me. It is no effort for me to confess that he has achieved some valid pages, but those pages cannot save me, perhaps because what is good belongs to no one, not even to him, but rather to the language and to tradition. Besides, I am destined to perish, definitively, and only some instant of myself can survive in him. Little by little, I am giving over everything to him, though I am quite aware of his perverse custom of falsifying and magnifying things. Spinoza knew that all things long to persist in their being; the stone eternally wants to be a stone and the tiger a tiger. I shall remain in Borges, not in myself (if it is true that I am someone), but I recognize myself less in his books than in many others or in the laborious strumming of a guitar. Years ago I tried to free myself from him and went from the mythologies of the suburbs to the games with time and infinity, but those games belong to Borges now and I shall have to imagine other things. Thus my life is a flight and I lose everything and everything belongs to oblivion, or to him.

I do not know which of us has written this page.

Translated from the Spanish by James E. Irby

Everything and Nothing

There was no one in him; behind his face (which even through the bad paintings of those times resembles no other) and his words, which were copious, fantastic and stormy, there was only a bit of cold-ness, a dream dreamt by no one. At first he thought that all people were like him, but the astonishment of a friend to whom he had begun to speak of this emptiness showed him his error and made him feel always that an individual should not differ in outward appear-ance. Once he thought that in books he would find a cure for his ills and thus he learned the small Latin and less Greek a contemporary would speak of; later he considered that what he sought might well be found in an elemental rite of humanity, and let himself be initiated by Anne Hathaway one long June afternoon. At the age of twenty-odd years he went to London. Instinctively he had already become proficient in the habit of simulating that he was someone, so that others would not discover his condition as no one; in London he found the profession to which he was predestined, that of the actor, who on a stage plays at being another before a gathering of people who play at taking him for that other person. His histrionic tasks brought him a singular satisfaction, perhaps the first he had ever known; but once the last verse had been acclaimed and the last dead man withdrawn from the stage, the hated flavor of unreality returned to him. He ceased to be Ferrex or Tamerlane and became no one again. Thus hounded, he took to imagining other heroes and other tragic fables. And so, while his flesh fulfilled its destiny as flesh in the taverns and brothels of London, the soul that inhabited him was Caesar, who disregards the augur's admonition, and Juliet, who abhors the lark, and Macbeth, who converses on the plain with the witches who are also Fates. No one has ever been so many men as this man, who like the Egyptian Proteus could exhaust all the guises of reality. At times he would leave a confession hidden away in some corner of his work, certain that it would not be deciphered; Richard affirms that in his person he plays the part of many and Iago claims with curious words "I am not what I am." The fundamental identity of existing, dreaming and acting inspired famous passages of his.

For twenty years he persisted in that controlled hallucination, but one morning he was suddenly gripped by the tedium and the terror of being so many kings who die by the sword and so many suffering lovers who converge, diverge and melodiously expire. That very day he arranged to sell his theater. Within a week he had returned to his native village, where he recovered the trees and rivers of his childhood and did not relate them to the others his muse had celebrated, illustrious with mythological allusions and Latin terms. He had to be someone; he was a retired impresario who had made his fortune and concerned himself with loans, lawsuits and petty usury. It was in this character that he dictated the arid will and testament known to us, from which he deliberately excluded all traces of pathos or literature. His friends from London would visit his retreat and for them he would take up again his role as poet.

History adds that before or after dying he found himself in the presence of God and told Him: "I who have been so many men in vain want to be one and myself." The voice of the Lord answered from a whirlwind: "Neither am I anyone; I have dreamt the world as you dreamt your work, my Shakespeare, and among the forms in my dream are you, who like myself are many and no one."

Translated from the Spanish by James E. Irby

WEN I-TO

(CHINA, 1899–1946)

Perhaps

Perhaps you have wept and wept, and can weep no more.
Perhaps. Perhaps you ought to sleep a bit;
then don't let the nighthawk cough, the frogs
croak, or the bats fly.

Don't let the sunlight open the curtain onto your eyes.
Don't let a cool breeze brush your eyebrows.
Ah, no one will be able to startle you awake:
I will open an umbrella of dark pines to shelter your sleep.

Perhaps you hear earthworms digging in the mud,
or listen to the root hairs of small grasses sucking up water.
Perhaps this music you are listening to is lovelier
than the swearing and cursing noises of men.

Then close your eyelids, and shut them tight.
I will let you sleep, I will let you sleep.
I will cover you lightly, lightly with yellow earth.
I will slowly, slowly let the ashes of paper money fly.

Translated from the Chinese by Arthur Sze

JACQUES PRÉVERT

(FRANCE, 1900–1977)

Barbara

Remember Barbara
It rained all day on Brest that day
And you walked smiling
Flushed enraptured streaming-wet
In the rain

Remember Barbara
It rained all day on Brest that day
And I ran into you in Siam Street
You were smiling
And I smiled too
Remember Barbara
You whom I didn't know
You who didn't know me
Remember
Remember that day still
Don't forget
A man was taking cover on a porch
And he cried your name
Barbara
And you ran to him in the rain
Streaming-wet enraptured flushed
And you threw yourself in his arms
Remember that Barbara
And don't be mad if I speak familiarly
I speak familiarly to everyone I love
Even if I've seen them only once
I speak familiarly to all who are in love
Even if I don't know them
Remember Barbara
Don't forget
That good and happy rain
On your happy face
On that happy town
That rain upon the sea
Upon the arsenal
Upon the Ushant boat
Oh Barbara
What shitstupidity the war
Now what's become of you
Under this iron rain
Of fire and steel and blood
And he who held you in his arms
Amorously

Is he dead and gone or still so much alive
Oh Barbara
It's rained all day on Brest today
As it was raining before
But it isn't the same anymore
And everything is wrecked
It's a rain of mourning terrible and desolate
Nor is it still a storm
Of iron and steel and blood
But simply clouds
That die like dogs
Dogs that disappear
In the downpour drowning Brest
And float away to rot
A long way off
A long long way from Brest
Of which there's nothing left.

Translated from the French by Lawrence Ferlinghetti

ROBERT DESNOS
(FRANCE, 1900–1945)

I've Dreamed of You So Much

I've dreamed of you so much you're losing your reality.
Is there still time to reach that living body and kiss
onto that mouth the birth of the voice so dear to me?
I've dreamed of you so much that my arms, accustomed
to being crossed on my breast while hugging your shadow
would perhaps not bend to the shape of your body.
And, faced with the real appearance of what has haunted
and ruled me for days and years, I would probably
become a shadow.
O sentimental balances.
I've dreamed of you so much it's no longer right
for me to awaken. I sleep standing up, my body exposed

to all signs of life and love, and you
the only one who matters to me now, I'd be less able
to touch your face and your lips than the face and the lips
of the first woman who came along.

       I've dreamed of you so much, walked so much, spoken
and lain with your phantom that perhaps nothing more is left me
than to be a phantom among phantoms and a hundred times more
       shadow
than the shadow that walks and will joyfully walk
on the sundial of your life.

Translated from the French by Carolyn Forché and William Kulik

ALEKSANDER WAT
(POLAND, 1900–1967)

Before Breughel the Elder

Work is a blessing.
I tell you that, I—professional sluggard!
Who slobbered in so many prisons! Fourteen!
And in so many hospitals! Ten! And innumerable inns!
Work is a blessing.
How else could we deal with the lava of fratricidal love towards fellow men?
With those storms of extermination of all by all?
With brutality, bottomless and measureless?
With the black and white era which does not want to end
endlessly repeating itself da capo like a record
forgotten on a turntable
spinning by itself?
Or perhaps someone invisible watches over the phonograph? Horror!
How, if not for work, could we live in the paradise of social hygienists
who never soak their hands in blood without aseptic gloves?
Horror!
How else could we cope with death?
That Siamese sister of life
who grows together with it—in us, and is extinguished with it

and surely for that reason is ineffective.
And so we have to live without end,
without end. Horror!
How, if not for work, could we cope with ineffective death
(Do not scoff!)
which is like a sea,
where everyone is an Icarus, one of nearly three billion,
while besides, so many things happen
and everything is equally unimportant, precisely, unimportant
although so difficult, so inhumanly difficult, so painful!
How then could we cope with all that?
Work is our rescue.
I tell you that—I, Breughel, the Elder (and I, for one,
your modest servant, Wat, Aleksander)—work is our rescue.

Translated from the Polish by Czesław Miłosz

GEORGE SEFERIS
(GREECE, 1900–1971)

from Mythistorema

Argonauts

And a soul
if it is to know itself
must look
into its own soul:
the stranger and enemy, we've seen him in the mirror.

They were good, the companions, they didn't complain
about the work or the thirst or the frost,
they had the bearing of trees and waves
that accept the wind and the rain
accept the night and the sun
without changing in the midst of change.

They were fine, whole days
they sweated at the oars with lowered eyes
breathing in rhythm
and their blood reddened a submissive skin.
Sometimes they sang, with lowered eyes
as we were passing the deserted island with the Barbary figs
to the west, beyond the cape of the dogs
that bark.
If it is to know itself, they said
it must look into its own soul, they said
and the oars struck the sea's gold
in the sunset.
We went past many capes many islands the sea
leading to another sea, gulls and seals.
Sometimes disconsolate women wept
lamenting their lost children
and others frantic sought Alexander the Great
and glories buried in the depths of Asia.
We moored on shores full of night-scents,
the birds singing, with waters that left on the hands,
the memory of a great happiness.
But the voyages did not end.
Their souls became one with the oars and the oarlocks
with the solemn face of the prow
with the rudder's wake
with the water that shattered their image.
The companions died one by one,
with lowered eyes. Their oars
mark the place where they sleep on the shore.

No one remembers them. Justice.

Translated from the Greek by Edmund Keeley and Philip Sherrard

Interlude of Joy

That whole morning we were full of joy,
my God, how full of joy.

First, stones leaves and flowers shone
then the sun
a huge sun all thorns and so high in the sky.
A nymph collected our cares and hung them on the trees
a forest of Judas trees.
Young loves and satyrs played there and sang
and you could see pink limbs among the black laurels
flesh of little children.
The whole morning long we were full of joy;
the abyss a closed well
tapped by the tender hoof of a young faun.
Do you remember its laugh—how full of joy!
Then clouds rain and the wet earth.
you stopped laughing when you lay down in the hut
and opened your large eyes as you watched
the archangel practicing with a fiery sword—
"Inexplicable," you said, "inexplicable.
I don't understand people:
no matter how much they play with colors
they all remain pitch-black."

Translated from the Greek by Edmund Keeley and Philip Sherrard

TATSUJI MIYOSHI
(JAPAN, 1900–1964)

The Ground

Ants
are dragging a wing of a butterfly—
See!
it is like a yacht.

Translated from the Japanese by Ichiro Kôno and Rikutaro Fukuda

Great Aso

Horses are standing in rain.
A herd of horses with one or two foals is standing in rain.
In hushed silence rain is falling.
The horses are eating grass.
With tails, and backs too, and manes too, completely soaking wet
they are eating grass,
eating grass.
Some of them are standing with necks bowed over absentmindedly
and not eating grass.
Rain is falling and falling in hushed silence.
The mountain is sending up smoke.
The peak of Nakadake is sending up dimly yellowish and heavily
oppressive volcanic smoke, densely, densely.
And rain clouds too all over the sky.
Still they continue without ending.
Horses are eating grass.
On one of the hills of the Thousand-Mile-Shore-of-Grass
they are absorbedly eating blue-green grass.
Eating.
They are all standing there quietly.
They are quietly gathered in one place forever, dripping and soaked
with rain.
If a hundred years go by in this single moment, there would be
no wonder.
Rain is falling. Rain is falling.
In hushed silence rain is falling.

Translated from the Japanese by Edith Marcombe Shiffert and Yuki Sawa

VITESLAV NEZVAL
(AUSTRO-HUNGARIAN EMPIRE, 1900–1958)

Woman in Plural

The windmill of her hands that signal a good morning
The coffee mill the spinning wheel of so much talk they draw me on
                                       now lulls me into sleep
They are like everything & nothing like the augury of wrinkled
    tablecloths
The body of a woman loved like heavily starched linen
They walk & walk like walking ferns their steps so sprightly
The midnight perfumes cover them, the beechwood cabins
Over those streets a bearskin splattered with the dregs of evening
Their faces smeared with rain the cold air of their wardrobes
                                       makes me whine
They are walking disassembling & assembling in my dream
A cardfile like a deck of cards of aces hearts & spades & clubs
From every side down by the crossroads where their outcry
        like black mullein
            fills the eyes of these machines with fear
They block the flow of traffic silly manikins there in their tearooms
Lighting the long fuses of those anarchists in torment
One of them so small a question mark as such a cockscomb
                walking quietly
      with whip poised in her hand
As if commanding a whole riding school a row of red-striped trousers
in hot pursuit of some chess-playing flea
The miracle as such of wicker laced with hemp
Another darker than a spool of oakum black & strung with coral
She whose will breaks thru whose heel cracks dynamite a hidden cache
A teletypist who only transmits the news in code
Who drops a red carnation on each step a honeycomb a wire brush
How I adore her neck with soap & lavender
Smell wafted down a stable's corridors that takes you by surprise
Fanned by a hand of sandalwood that plucks at the bouquet
              of her own nape a lathered dandelion
So as to wipe away the last most searing spark of daylight

Her breasts are purring like a cat
Caught in that chill a waterfall that cascades over her
                              a marble staircase
And which she only now feels in her belly pure like a white camphor
    bandage
Or with her eyelids under which an icy wafer plays
                              will be her gaze in chocolate
The third one a strawberry blond a nest of salamanders
With her thighs of ground wheat coarsened by a kiss
She lifts an arm to dupe the crested lark
Her head two sapphire knobs have buttoned up a reliquary
                              for my two invaluable medallions
What a storage house for excavations where I squeeze thru to accost her
                              woman changed into a chair
And neither dressed nor naked in a scrap of netting she will not affirm
    some other
                                        way of life
Forever this desire like the sheep of certain beasts & as convulsive as
                              a sofa's springs
This one devoted to the fall of dominos & dice & checkers
                    something forever changing
          or like the shuttle in a sewing machine
A woman made from sponges I will never find again
As from her wig of nettles sweat comes trickling down she doesn't wait
    to be addressed
But on a moonlit night her shadow sinks into the quicklime
                    in the court behind the brickyard
And you can chew her mouth like gelatin
Tall lamps or rusty shreds of oakum
When on steamy days the young girls wash their shoulders on the
    high banks
                         among the fly specks of a vanished summer
The young pearlike mothers & the fainting spells at midnight
                    widowed hens with cockscombs
How my desire to lift them from that burning building eats me up
                    that & the blaze of their straw hair

                    Translated from the Czech by Jerome Rothenberg

MARIE LUISE KASCHNITZ
(GERMANY, 1901–1974)

Hiroshima

The man who dropped death on Hiroshima
Rings bells in the cloister, has taken vows.
The man who dropped death on Hiroshima
Put his head in a noose and hanged himself.
The man who dropped death on Hiroshima
Is out of his mind, is battling with risen souls
Made of atomic dust who are out to attack him.
Every night. Hundreds and thousands of them.

None of it's true.
In fact, I saw him the other day
In his front garden, there in the suburb—
With immature hedges and dainty roses.
You need time to make a Forest of Forgetting
Where someone can hide. Plainly on view
Was the naked, suburban house and the young wife
Standing beside him in her floral dress
And the little girl attached to her hand
And the boy hoisted up on his back
And cracking a whip over his head.
And he was easy to pick out
On all fours there on the lawn, his face
Contorted with laughter, because the photographer stood
Behind the hedge, the seeing eye of the world.

Translated from the German by Eavan Boland

SALVATORE QUASIMODO
(ITALY, 1901–1968)

Only If Love Should Pierce You

Do not forget that you live in the midst of the animals,
horses, cats, sewer rats
brown as Solomon's woman, terrible
camp with colours flying,
do not forget the dog with harmonies of the unreal
in tongue and tail, nor the green lizard, the blackbird,
the nightingale, viper, drone. Or you are pleased to think
that you live among pure men and virtuous
women who do not touch
the howl of the frog in love, green
as the greenest branch of the blood.
Birds watch you from trees, and the leaves
are aware that the Mind is dead
forever, its remnant savours of burnt
cartilage, rotten plastic; do not forget
to be animal, fit and sinuous,
torrid in violence, wanting everything here
on earth, before the final cry
when the body is cadence of shrivelled memories
and the spirit hastens to the eternal end;
remember that you can be the being of being
only if love should pierce you deep inside.

Translated from the Italian by Jack Bevan

And Suddenly It's Evening

Each of us is alone on the heart of the earth
pierced by a ray of sun:
and suddenly it's evening.

Translated from the Italian by Jack Bevan

ROSE AUSLANDER
(GERMANY, 1901–1988)

Motherland

My Fatherland is dead.
They buried it
in fire

I live
in my Motherland—
Word

Translated from the German by Eavan Boland

NÂZIM HIKMET
(TURKEY, 1902–1963)

Things I Didn't Know I Loved

the year is 1962 March 28
I'm next to the window on the Prague-Berlin train
evening is falling
I didn't know I loved how evening descends like a tired bird upon the
    smoky wet plain
I didn't like the comparison of evening's descent with that of a tired bird

I didn't know I loved the earth
can one say he loves the earth when one has never ploughed it
I've never ploughed it
so this is my one and only platonic love

I didn't know I loved rivers
whether they twist motionless like this one towards the foot of the hills
the European hills with castles on their peaks
or stretch straight ahead as far as the eye can see

I know one can't wash in the same river more than once
I know the river will bring new lights you'll never see
I know our lives are slightly longer than the workhorse's and much
        shorter than the raven's
I know people have felt this sorrow before
                            and will feel this sorrow after
all of this has been said a thousand times before me
                        and will be said after

I didn't know I loved the sky
whether it's sunny or cloudy
the firmament that Andrey watched lying on his back in the
        battlefields of Borodino
in prison I translated two volumes of *War and Peace* into Turkish
voices reach my ears
not from the firmament but from the yard
the guards are beating someone up again

I didn't know I loved trees
in winter outside Moscow in Peredelkino the beech trees appear stark
        naked before me humble and courteous
beeches are Russian in the same way poplars are Turkish
Izmir's poplars
whose leaves fall
who call us the Knife-makers
                    my tall beloved sapling
we shall burn the villas
in the forests of Ilgaz in the year 1920 I hung a linen handkerchief
        from a pine branch with embroidered edges

I didn't know I loved roads
and their asphalt
Vera is driving we're going from Moscow to Crimea to Koktebel
                            whose real name is Göktepe County
the two of us in a closed box
the world flows by on either side distant and silent

I've never been so close to anyone before
bandits crossed my path as I came down the red road from Bolu to
    Gerede I was eighteen
there was nothing in the carriage for them to take but my life
and at eighteen our lives are what we value least
I wrote this once before
I'm stumbling across a dark muddy street to go see Karagöz one
    Ramadan night
a paper lantern before me
maybe this never happened
maybe I read somewhere about an eight-year-old boy going to see
    Karagöz one Ramadan night in Istanbul holding his
    grandfather's hand
his grandfather wearing a fez and a sable-collared fur coat over his robe
    and a lantern in the eunuch's hand
        and I can't contain my joy

I suddenly thought of flowers
poppies cacti daffodils
In Istanbul in Kadiköy in a daffodil field I kissed Marika
her breath smelled of almonds
I was seventeen
my heart was a swing moving in and out of the clouds
I didn't know I loved flowers
comrades sent me three red carnations in prison 1948
I just remembered the stars
I didn't know I loved them
whether I'm watching them bewildered from below
or flying among them

I have some questions for the cosmonauts
did the stars appear much bigger
in the black velvet were they gigantic jewels
        or orange-colored apricots
does one feel proud as one approaches the stars
I saw their color photographs in *Ogonyok* magazine
don't get angry friends but shall we call it nonfigurative or abstract
    but they looked like those old oil paintings figurative and concrete

one's heart stops before them
they represent the endlessness of our yearning our minds our hands
I could look at them and think
I could think about death without feeling the slightest sorrow
I didn't know I loved the stars

Snowfall appears before my eyes
both the slow silent flakes and the whirling blizzards
I didn't know I loved the snow

I didn't know I loved the sun
even now as it sets full of cherry jam
sometimes in Istanbul too the sun sets just like those color postcards
but that's not how you'll portray it

I didn't know I loved the sea
                              and how
but Aivazovsky's seas are another matter

I didn't know I loved the clouds
whether I'm below them or above
whether they resemble mammoths or white-feathered creatures

moonlight comes to mind at its most languid most illusory most
    bourgeois
turns out I love it
I didn't know I loved the rain
whether it tumbles down upon me like a net or drips across the
    window my heart leaves me behind tangled in the net or inside a
    raindrop and journeys to a country that doesn't exist on maps
I didn't know I loved the rain

but why did I suddenly discover these loves on the Prague-Berlin
    train next to the window
is it because I've lit my sixth cigarette
a single one means death for me
is it because I can't stop thinking about someone who stayed in Moscow
with sandy blonde hair and blue eyelashes

The train moves in the pitch black
I didn't know I loved pitch black
sparks fly from the locomotive
I didn't know I loved sparks
so many things I only realized I loved at sixty years old
on the Prague-Berlin train next to the window beholding the earth as though
    I'd embarked upon a journey from which there was no return

Translated from the Turkish by Deniz Perin

Angina Pectoris

If half my heart is here,
                    half of it is in China, doctor,
in the army streaming
                    toward the Yellow River.

And, every morning, doctor,
                    every morning my heart
                                is shot by a firing squad in Greece.

And, when the prisoners have fallen asleep
                    and abandoned the infirmary
            my heart is in a dilapidated villa in Çamlıca.
                                        Every night,
                                                    doctor.

And, after ten years,
all I have to offer my poor people
        is a single apple, doctor,
                            one red apple:
                                    my heart.

It's not arteriosclerosis, or nicotine, or prison
but this, my sweet doctor, this
                    has caused my angina pectoris.

I watch the night through the bars
and despite the squeezing of my chest
my heart still beats with the most distant stars.

Translated from the Turkish by Deniz Perin

Since I Was Thrown Inside

Since I was thrown inside,
                the earth has orbited the sun ten times.
If you ask it:
      "Not even worth mentioning,
           a microscopic time."
If you ask me:
      "Ten years of my life."

I had a pencil
                the year I was thrown inside.
I used it all up in a week.
If you ask it:
      "A whole life."
If you ask me:
      "Come on now, just one week."

Since I was thrown inside,
                Osman, doing time for murder,
                    finished his seven and a half years and left,
                    drifted around for a while,
                    was thrown back inside for smuggling,
                    did six months and was re-released,
                    his letter came yesterday, he's married,
                    his child will be born in the spring.

They're ten years old now,
          the children who were conceived
              the year I was thrown inside.
And that year's trembling, long-legged colts
          have long turned into confident, wide-rumped mares.

But the olive seeds are still olive seeds,
             they're still children.

New squares have cropped up in my far-away city
                    since I was thrown inside.
And my loved ones
       are living on a street I don't know
                    in a house I've never seen.

Bread was white, fluffy as cotton
                    the year I was thrown inside.
Then it was rationed
and here, inside, the people beat each other
       for a pitch-black, fist-sized piece.
Now it flows freely again,
but dark and tasteless.

The year I was thrown inside,
       the second war hadn't started yet,
the ovens at Dachau weren't lit,
the atom bomb hadn't dropped on Hiroshima.

Time flowed like the blood of a child whose throat's been slit.
Then that chapter officially ended,
and now the U.S. dollar speaks of a third.

Yet, in spite of everything, the days have shone
                    since I was thrown inside,
and from the edges of darkness,
       the people, pressing their heavy hands to the pavement,
                    have begun to rise.

Since I was thrown inside
             the earth has orbited the sun ten times
and just as passionately I repeat
             what I wrote
                    the year I was thrown inside:

"The people, who are plentiful as ants on the ground
                        as fish in the sea
                                as birds in the sky,
who are cowardly, courageous,
                ignorant, supreme
                                and childlike,
it is they who crush
        and create,
it is but their exploits sung in songs."
                And as for the rest,
                        my ten-year incarceration, for instance,
                                it's all meaningless words.

Translated from the Turkish by Deniz Perin

On Living

1

Living is no joke.
You must live with great seriousness
                like a squirrel, for example,
I mean, expecting nothing above and beyond living,
                I mean your entire purpose should be living.
You must take living seriously,
I mean so much so, so terribly
that, for example, your hands tied behind your back, your back
    to the wall,
or in your fat goggles
                and white laboratory coat
                        you can die for people,
                even for people whose faces you have not seen,
                without anyone forcing you,
                even though you know the most beautiful, the most
                        real thing is living.

I mean, you must take living so seriously
that, even when you're seventy, for example, you'll plant olive seeds,
         and not so the trees will remain for the children,
            but because though you fear death you don't believe in it,
                        I mean because living is more important.

2

Let's say we're due for serious surgery,
I mean there's a chance
                  we might not get up from the white table.
Even if it's impossible not to feel sorrow at leaving a little too early
we'll still laugh at the Bektashi joke,
we'll look out the window to see if it's raining,
or impatiently await
                  the latest news.

Let's say we're on the front,
                        for something worth fighting for, let's say.
At the very first assault, on that very day
            we could keel over and die.
We'll know this with a strange resentment,
            but we'll still wonder madly
            about how this war, which could last years, will end.

Let's say we're in prison
and nearly 50,
and let's imagine we have 18 more years before the opening of the
      iron doors.
We'll still live with the outside,
with its people, its animals, its toil and wind,
                  I mean with the outside beyond the walls.

I mean, however and wherever we are
      we must live as if we will never die.

3

This earth will grow cold,
a star among stars,
                    and one of the smallest too,
a gilded granule in blue velvet, I mean,
                    I mean this tremendous world of ours.

This earth will grow cold one day,
and not like a chunk of ice
or a dead cloud—
it'll roll like an empty walnut shell
                    endlessly in the pitch black.

One must lament this now,
must feel this pain now.
This is how you must love this earth
                    so you can say "I've lived" . . .

Translated from the Turkish by Deniz Perin

RAFAEL ALBERTI
(SPAIN, 1902–1999)

Song 35

I think now—at midnight—
that I never slept in my life,
that when from time to time I closed
my eyes and submerged all I saw
in the semblance of sleep,
I didn't sleep.

Translated from the Spanish by José A. Elgorriaga and Martin Paul

CARLOS DRUMMOND DE ANDRADE
(BRAZIL, 1902–1987)

Seven-Sided Poem

When I was born, one of the crooked
angels who live in shadow, said:
Carlos, go on! Be *gauche* in life.

The houses watch the men,
men who run after women.
If the afternoon had been blue,
there might have been less desire.

The trolley goes by full of legs:
white legs, black legs, yellow legs.
My God, why all the legs?
my heart asks. But my eyes
ask nothing at all.

The man behind the moustache
is serious, simple, and strong.
He hardly ever speaks.
He has a few, choice friends,
the man behind the spectacles and the moustache.

My God, why hast Thou forsaken me
if Thou knew'st I was not God,
if Thou knew'st that I was weak?

Universe, vast universe,
if I had been named Eugene
that would not be what I mean
but it would go into verse
faster.
Universe, vast universe,
my heart is vaster.

I oughtn't to tell you,
but this moon
and this brandy
play the devil with one's emotions.

Translated from the Portuguese by Elizabeth Bishop

Don't Kill Yourself

Carlos, keep calm, love
is what you're seeing now:
today a kiss, tomorrow no kiss,
day after tomorrow's Sunday
and nobody knows what will happen
Monday.

It's useless to resist
or to commit suicide.
Don't kill yourself. Don't kill yourself!
Keep all of yourself for the nuptials
coming nobody knows when,
that is, if they ever come.

Love, Carlos, tellurian,
spent the night with you,
and now your insides are raising
an ineffable racket,
prayers,
Victrolas,
saints crossing themselves,
ads for a better soap,
a racket of which nobody
knows the why or wherefore.

In the meantime you go on your way
vertical, melancholy.
You're the palm tree, you're the cry
nobody heard in the theatre

and all the lights went out.
Love in the dark, no, love
in the daylight, is always sad,
sad, Carlos, my boy,
but tell it to nobody,
nobody knows nor shall know.

Translated from the Portuguese by Elizabeth Bishop

Infancy

My father got on his horse and went to the field.
My mother stayed sitting and sewing.
My little brother slept.
A small boy alone under the mango trees,
I read the story of Robinson Crusoe,
the long story that never comes to an end.

At noon, white with light, a voice that had learned
lullabies long ago in the slave-quarters—and never forgot—
called us for coffee.
Coffee blacker than the black old woman
delicious coffee
good coffee.

My mother stayed sitting and sewing
watching me:
Shh—don't wake the boy.
She stopped the cradle when a mosquito had lit
and gave a sigh . . . how deep!
Away off there my father went riding
through the farm's endless wastes.

And I didn't know that my story
was prettier than that of Robinson Crusoe.

Translated from the Portuguese by Elizabeth Bishop

Your Shoulders Hold Up the World

A time comes when you can no longer say: my God.
A time of total cleaning up.
A time when you no longer can say: my love.
Because love proved useless.
And the eyes don't cry.
And the hands do only rough work.
And the heart is dry.

Women knock at your door in vain, you won't open.
You remain alone, the light turned off,
and your enormous eyes shine in the dark.
It is obvious you no longer know how to suffer.
And you want nothing from your friends.

Who cares if old age comes, what is old age?
Your shoulders are holding up the world
and it's lighter than a child's hand.
Wars, famine, family fights inside buildings
prove only that life goes on
and not everybody has freed himself yet.
Some (the delicate ones) judging the spectacle cruel
will prefer to die.
A time comes when death doesn't help.
A time comes when life is an order.
Just life, without any escapes.

Translated from the Portuguese by Mark Strand

Family Portrait

Yes, this family portrait
is a little dusty.
The father's face doesn't show
how much money he earned.

The uncles' hands don't reveal
the voyages both of them made.
The grandmother's smoothed and yellowed;
she's forgotten the monarchy.

The children, how they've changed.
Peter's face is tranquil,
that wore the best dreams.
And John's no longer a liar.

The garden's become fantastic.
The flowers are gray badges.
And the sand, beneath dead feet,
is an ocean of fog.

In the semicircle of armchairs
a certain movement is noticed.
The children are changing places,
but noiselessly! it's a picture.

Twenty years is a long time.
It can form any image.
If one face starts to wither,
another presents itself, smiling.

All these seated strangers,
my relations? I don't believe it.
They're guests amusing themselves
in a rarely opened parlor.

Family features remain
lost in the play of bodies.
But there's enough to suggest
that a body is full of surprises.

The frame of this family portrait
holds its personages in vain.

They're there voluntarily,
they'd know how—if need be—to fly.

They could refine themselves
in the room's chiaroscuro,
live inside the furniture
or the pockets of old waistcoats.

The house has many drawers,
papers, long staircases.
When matter becomes annoyed,
who knows the malice of things?

The portrait does not reply,
it stares; in my dusty eyes
it contemplates itself.
The living and dead relations

multiply in the glass.
I don't distinguish those
that went away from those
that stay. I only perceive
the strange idea of family

travelling through the flesh.

Translated from the Portuguese by Elizabeth Bishop

In the Middle of the Road There Was a Stone

In the middle of the road there was a stone
there was a stone in the middle of the road
there was a stone
in the middle of the road there was a stone.

Never should I forget this event
in the life of my fatigued retinas.
Never should I forget that in the middle of the road

there was a stone
there was a stone in the middle of the road
in the middle of the road there was a stone.

Translated from the Portuguese by Elizabeth Bishop

JORGE CARRERA ANDRADE
(ECUADOR, 1902–1978)

The Guest

Against the huge black door of the night
twelve knocks resound.

Men sit up in their beds;
fear glides over them with icy scales.

Who can it be? Through the houses
fear slips unsandalled.

Men see the flames of their lamps
blown out by the clamorous knocking:

The unknown guest is calling,
and a thin blue flame runs along their eyelids.

Translated from the Spanish by Muna Lee de Muñoz Marin

NICOLAS GUILLEN
(CUBA, 1902–1989)

Sensemayá (Chant for Killing a Snake)

Mayombe—bombe—mayombé!
Mayombe—bombe—mayombé!
Mayombe—bombe—mayombé!

The snake's got eyes made of glass;
The snake he comes and wraps around a stick;
With his eyes made of glass, he wraps around a stick,
With his eyes made of glass.
The snake he travels without feet;
The snake he hides in the grass,
He travels and he hides in the grass,
Walking without feet.

Mayombe—bombe—mayombé!
Mayombe—bombe—mayombé!
Mayombe—bombe—mayombé!

Let him have it with the hatchet and he's dead:
Let him have it!
Don't do it with your foot or he'll bite you,
Don't do it with your foot or he'll get clean away!

Sensemayá, see that snake now,
Sensemayá.
Sensemayá, with those eyes of his,
Sensemayá.
Sensemayá, with that tongue of his,
Sensemayá.
Sensemayá, with that mouth of his,
Sensemayá!

That snake when he's dead can't eat any more;
That snake when he's dead can't hiss any more:
Can't travel any more,
Can't run any more!
That snake when he's dead can't look any more;
That snake when he's dead can't drink any more:
Can't breathe any more,
Can't bite any more!

Mayombe—bombe—mayombé!
SENSEMAYÁ, SEE THAT SNAKE NOW

Mayombe—bombe—mayombé!
SENSEMAYÁ, HE LIES QUIET
Mayombe—bombe—mayombé!
SENSEMAYÁ, SEE THAT SNAKE NOW
Mayombe—bombe—mayombé!
SENSEMAYÁ, HE'S DEAD . . . !

Translated from the Spanish by H. R. Hays

RAYMOND QUENEAU
(FRANCE, 1903–1976)

The Human Species

The human species has given me
the right to be mortal
the duty to be civilized
a conscience
2 eyes that don't always function very well
a nose in the middle of my face
2 feet 2 hands
speech

the human species has given me
my father and mother
some brothers maybe who knows
a whole mess of cousins
and some great-grandfathers
the human species has given me
its 3 faculties
feeling intellect and will
each in moderation
32 teeth and 10 fingers a liver
a heart and some other viscera

the human species has given me
what I'm supposed to be satisfied with

Translated from the French by Teo Savory

If You Imagine

If you imagine
if you imagine
little sweetie little sweetie
if you imagine
this will this will this
will last forever
this season of
this season of
season of love
you're fooling yourself
little sweetie little sweetie
you're fooling yourself

If you think little one
if you think ah ah
that that rosy complexion
that waspy waist
those lovely muscles
the enamel nails
nymph thigh
and your light foot
if you think little one
that will that will that
will last forever
you're fooling yourself
little sweetie little sweetie
you're fooling yourself

The lovely days disappear
the lovely holidays
suns and planets

go round in circles
but you my little one
you go straight
towards you know not what
very slowly draw near
the sudden wrinkle
the weighty fat
the triple chin
the flabby muscle
come gather gather
the roses the roses
roses of life
and may their petals
be a calm sea
of happinesses
come gather gather
if you don't do it
you're fooling yourself
little sweetie little sweetie
you're fooling yourself

Translated from the French by Michael Benedikt

JEAN FOLLAIN
(FRANCE, 1903–1971)

Face the Animal

It's not always easy
to face the animal
even if it looks at you
without fear or hate
it does so fixedly
and seems to disdain
the subtle secret it carries
it seems better to feel
the obviousness of the world

that noisily day and night
drills and damages
the silence of the soul.

Translated from the French by Heather McHugh

Music of Spheres

He was walking a frozen road
in his pocket iron keys were jingling
and with his pointed shoe absentmindedly
he kicked the cylinder
of an old can
which for a few seconds rolled its cold emptiness
wobbled for a while and stopped
under a sky studded with stars.

Translated from the French by Czesław Miłosz and Robert Hass

A Mirror

Having gone upstairs
on steps of dark oak
she finds herself before
a mirror with worm-eaten frame
she contemplates in it her virgin torso
all the countryside is ablaze
and gently arrives at her feet
a domestic beast
as if to remind her
of the animal life
which conceals in itself also
the body of a woman.

Translated from the French by Czesław Miłosz and Robert Hass

EDVARD KOCBEK

(SLOVENIA, 1904–1981)

Longing for Jail

I was late for the most important
spiritual exercises of my life,
I am left without proof
of my true value.
Each jail is a treasury,
a secret drawer, a jealous
torture chamber, the most important stage
of an executioner's asceticism before he is
corrupted by a naked woman holding a knife.
I miss the delight of that love,
I would die easier if I had counted out
the squares on the floor of my solitary cell
and in my thoughts completed the transparent frescoes
on the dusty pane,
and gazed through the walls
at the frontier posts of mankind.
Now, my cell, you have collapsed,
disintegrated to openness,
the world is no longer a world of redeeming cruelty,
it's only a sabbath yard.
You can test me no more,
I am no longer a figure for the Christmas crib,
for a puppet show or display of robots.
I am preparing myself for a different game—
look, I am turning into a little gray mouse,
my hiding places are all around,
tonight I shall sleep in the sleeve of a child
with no right hand, tomorrow I shall dream
in the echo of a shadow that sleeps after its voyage
through a fairy tale that has no end.

Translated from the Slovenian by Michael Scammell and Veno Taufer

PABLO NERUDA

(CHILE, 1904–1973)

Body of a Woman

Body of a woman, white hills, white thighs,
you look like a world, lying in surrender.
My rough peasant's body digs in you
and makes the son leap from the depth of the earth.

I was alone like a tunnel. The birds fled from me,
and night swamped me with its crushing invasion.
To survive myself I forged you like a weapon,
like an arrow in my bow, a stone in my sling.

But the hour of vengeance falls, and I love you.
Body of skin, of moss, of eager and firm milk.
Oh the goblets of the breast! Oh the eyes of absence!
Oh the roses of the pubis! Oh your voice, slow and sad!

Body of my woman, I will persist in your grace.
My thirst, my boundless desire, my shifting road!
Dark riverbeds where the eternal thirst flows
and weariness follows, and the infinite ache.

Translated from the Spanish by W. S. Merwin

I Remember You as You Were

I remember you as you were in the last autumn
You were the gray beret and the still heart.
In your eyes the flames of the twilight fought on.
And the leaves fell in the water of your soul.

Clasping my arms like a climbing plant
the leaves garnered your voice, that was slow and at peace.
Bonfire of awe in which my thirst was burning.
Sweet blue hyacinth twisted over my soul.

I feel your eyes traveling, and the autumn is far off:
gray beret, voice of a bird, heart like a house
towards which my deep longings migrated
and my kisses fell, happy as embers.

Sky from a ship. Field from the hills.
Your memory is made of light, of smoke, of a still pond!
Beyond your eyes, farther on, the evenings were blazing.
Dry autumn leaves revolved in your soul.

Translated from the Spanish by W. S. Merwin

Tonight I Can Write

Tonight I can write the saddest lines.

Write, for example, "The night is starry
and the stars are blue and shiver in the distance."

The night wind revolves in the sky and sings.

Tonight I can write the saddest lines.
I loved her, and sometimes she loved me too.

Through nights like this one I held her in my arms.
I kissed her again and again under the endless sky.

She loved me, sometimes I loved her too.
How could one not have loved her great still eyes.

Tonight I can write the saddest lines.
To think that I do not have her. To feel that I have lost her.

To hear the immense night, still more immense without her.
And the verse falls to the soul like dew to the pasture.

What does it matter that my love could not keep her.
The night is starry and she is not with me.

This is all. In the distance someone is singing. In the distance.
My soul is not satisfied that it has lost her.

My sight tries to find her as though to bring her closer.
My heart looks for her, and she is not with me.

The same night whitening the same trees.
We, of that time, are no longer the same.

I no longer love her, that's certain, but how I loved her.
My voice tried to find the wind to touch her hearing.

Another's. She will be another's. As she was before my kisses.
Her voice, her bright body. Her infinite eyes.

I no longer love her, that's certain, but maybe I love her.
Love is so short, forgetting is so long.

Because through nights like this one I held her in my arms
my soul is not satisfied that it has lost her.

Though this be the last pain that she makes me suffer
and these the last verses that I write for her.

Translated from the Spanish by W. S. Merwin

Nothing but Death

There are cemeteries that are lonely,
graves full of bones that do not make a sound,
the heart moving through a tunnel,
in it darkness, darkness, darkness,
like a shipwreck we die going into ourselves,
as though we were drowning inside our hearts,
as though we lived falling out of the skin into the soul.

And there are corpses,
feet made of cold and sticky clay,

death is inside the bones,
like a barking where there are no dogs,
coming out from bells somewhere, from graves somewhere,
growing in the damp air like tears or rain.

Sometimes I see alone
coffins under sail,
embarking with the pale dead, with women that have dead hair,
with bakers who are as white as angels,
and pensive young girls married to notary publics,
caskets sailing up the vertical river of the dead,
the river of dark purple,
moving upstream with sails filled out by the sound of death,
filled by the sound of death which is silence.

Death arrives among all that sound
like a shoe with no foot in it, like a suit with no man in it,
comes and knocks, using a ring with no stone in it, with no
        finger in it,
comes and shouts with no mouth, with no tongue, with no
            throat.
Nevertheless its steps can be heard
and its clothing makes a hushed sound. Like a tree.

I'm not sure, I understand only a little, I can hardly see,
but it seems to me that its singing has the color of damp violets,
of violets that are at home in the earth,
because the face of death is green,
and the look death gives is green,
with the penetrating dampness of a violet leaf
and the somber color of embittered winter.

But death also goes through the world dressed as a broom,
lapping the floor, looking for dead bodies,
death is inside the broom,
the broom is the tongue of death looking for corpses,
it is the needle of death looking for thread.

Death is inside the folding cots:
it spends its life sleeping on the slow mattresses,
in the black blankets, and suddenly breathes out:
it blows out a mournful sound that swells the sheets,
and the beds go sailing toward a port
where death is waiting, dressed like an admiral.

Translated from the Spanish by Robert Bly

Walking Around

It happens that I am tired of being a man.
It happens that I go into the tailors' shops and the movies
all shriveled up, impenetrable, like a felt swan
navigating on a water of origin and ash.

The smell of barber shops makes me sob out loud.
I want nothing but the repose either of stones or of wool,
I want to see no more establishments, no more gardens,
nor merchandise, nor glasses, nor elevators.

It happens that I am sick of my feet and my nails
and my hair and my shadow.
It happens that I am tired of being a man.

Just the same it would be delicious
to scare a notary with a cut lily
or knock a nun stone dead with one blow of an ear.
It would be beautiful
to go through the streets with a green knife
shouting until I died of cold.

I do not want to go on being a root in the dark,
hesitating, stretched out, shivering with dreams,
downwards, in the wet tripe of the earth,
soaking it up and thinking, eating every day.

I do not want to be the inheritor of so many misfortunes.
I do not want to continue as a root and as a tomb,
as a solitary tunnel, as a cellar full of corpses,
stiff with cold, dying with pain.

For this reason Monday burns like oil
at the sight of me arriving with my jail-face,
and it howls in passing like a wounded wheel,
and its footsteps towards nightfall are filled with hot blood.

And it shoves me along to certain corners, to certain damp houses,
to hospitals where the bones come out of the windows,
to certain cobblers' shops smelling of vinegar,
to certain streets horrendous as crevices.

There are birds the color of sulphur, and horrible intestines
hanging from the doors of houses which I hate,
there are forgotten sets of teeth in a coffeepot,
there are mirrors
which should have wept with shame and horror,
there are umbrellas all over the place, and poisons, and navels.

I stride along with calm, with eyes, with shoes,
with fury, with forgetfulness,
I pass, I cross offices and stores full of orthopedic appliances,
and courtyards hung with clothes on wires,
underpants, towels and shirts which weep
slow dirty tears.

Translated from the Spanish by W. S. Merwin

Ode to My Socks

Maru Mori brought me
a pair
of socks
which she knitted herself

with her sheepherder's hands,
two socks as soft
as rabbits.
I slipped my feet
into them
as though into
two
cases
knitted
with threads of
twilight
and goatskin.
Violent socks,
my feet were
two fish made
of wool,
two long sharks
sea-blue, shot
through
by one golden thread,
two immense blackbirds,
two cannons:
my feet
were honored
in this way
by
these
heavenly
socks.
They were
so handsome
for the first time
my feet seemed to me
unacceptable,
like two decrepit
firemen,
firemen

unworthy
of that woven
fire,
of those glowing
socks.

Nevertheless
I resisted
the sharp temptation
to save them somewhere
as schoolboys
keep
fireflies,
as learned men
collect
sacred texts,
I resisted
the mad impulse
to put them
into a golden
cage
and each day give them
birdseed
and pieces of pink melon.
Like explorers
in the jungle who hand
over the very rare
green deer
to the spit
and eat it
with remorse,
I stretched out
my feet
and pulled on
the magnificent
socks
and then my shoes.

The moral
of my ode is this:
beauty is twice
beauty
and what is good is doubly
good
when it is a matter of two socks
made of wool
in winter.

Translated from the Spanish by Robert Bly

Nothing More

I made my contract with the truth
to restore light to the earth.

I wished to be like bread.
The struggle never found me wanting.

But here I am with what I loved,
with the solitude I lost.
In the shadow of that stone, I do not rest.

The sea is working, working in my silence.

Translated from the Spanish by Alastair Reid

Too Many Names

Mondays are meshed with Tuesdays
and the week with the whole year.
Time cannot be cut
with your weary scissors,
and all the names of the day
are washed out by the waters of night.

No one can claim the name of Pedro,
nobody is Rosa or Maria,
all of us are dust or sand,
all of us are rain under rain.
They have spoken to me of Venezuelas,
of Chiles and of Paraguays,
I have no idea what they are saying,
I know only the skin of the earth
and I know it is without a name.

When I lived amongst the roots
they pleased me more than flowers did,
and when I spoke to a stone
it rang like a bell.

It is so long, the spring
which goes on all winter.
Time lost its shoes.
A year is four centuries.

When I sleep every night,
what am I called or not called?
And when I wake, who am I
if I was not I while I slept?

This means to say that scarcely
have we landed into life
than we come as if newborn;
let us not fill our mouths
with so many faltering names,
with so many sad formalities,
with so many pompous letters,
with so much of yours and mine,
with so much signing of papers.

I have a mind to confuse things,
unite them, bring them to birth,

mix them up, undress them,
until the light of the world
has the oneness of the ocean,
a generous, vast wholeness,
a crepitant fragrance.

Translated from the Spanish by Alastair Reid

Keeping Still

Now we will count to twelve
and let's keep quiet.

For once on earth
let's not talk in any language;
let's stop for one second,
and not move our arms so much.

A moment like that would smell sweet,
no hurry, no engines,
all of us at the same time
in need of rest.

Fishermen in the cold sea
would stop harming whales
and the gatherer of salt
would look at his hurt hands.

Those who prepare green wars,
wars with gas, wars with fire,
victories with no survivors,
would put on clean clothes
and go for a walk with their brothers
out in the shade, doing nothing.

Just don't confuse what I want
with total inaction;

it's life and life only;
I'm not talking about death.

If we weren't so single-minded
about keeping our lives moving
and could maybe do nothing for once,
a huge silence might interrupt this sadness
of never understanding ourselves,
of threatening ourselves with death;
perhaps the earth could teach us;
everything would seem dead
and then be alive.

Now I will count up to twelve
and you keep quiet
and I will go.

Translated from the Spanish by Dan Bellm

VLADIMIR HOLAN
(AUSTRO-HUNGARIAN EMPIRE/CZECHOSLOVAKIA, 1905–1980)

May, 1945

I

I can still hear it: it was Saturday and the whistles of all locomotives
announced to us, the Hopeful from Hopetown,
the departure for freedom from all stations of revolt.
The explosive atmosphere, which for months had been carrying and
　　expecting in a corner,
gave birth to cannons and deranged machine guns
that perforated bodies,
so easily severed from souls at the post office of death.
And it didn't take long and Prague with all its torn-up paving stones,

sand, puddles, and felled trees
looked as if a new city were about to be founded, the City of Extinction.

II

I'm not going to sing about heroes . . . Their manly being
lies in their silence and in our wordless shame.
But there were children, the same children who for several years,
upon hearing the wailing sirens, quickly packed their favorite things
into "air raid bags"—
the same children who in May were driven
in front of the German butchers' tanks.
Those and others who had not been slaughtered and mutilated,
those who went sobbing from door to door
and at last found their defenseless loved ones,
who still wake up from nightmares and scream:
"Mummy, where's my leg!"

III

And I saw a man shooting
at a German plane with a popgun . . .
And I saw two trucks passing each other at Smichov:
one carried the dead from Zbraslav
and the other live calves and a large inscription: Gift for Prague.
It's insane, what I'm saying, but that's what life was like.

IV

And I know a painter . . . Knife in hand, he guarded a poorhouse.
On the ninth day at dawn he heard a banging on the door.
He opened the door and saw a dust-covered human being spreading
      gigantic arms
and in Russian saying, simply and with a smile: "You know me!"

V

And who could ever forget an old man,
who, enraptured, skipped in front of the enormous Soviet tanks
and removed every tiny pebble in their way!

Translated from the Czech by C. G. Hanzlicek and Dana Hábová

June, July, and August, 1945

Do you remember? No! Let me help you:
they were months of scorching heat, ruins, and dust
moistened only in places where women watered flowers
at hastily built little memorials,
but children already played at being barricade fighters and generals in
    bunkers,
and shrilled like the recently silenced alarm sirens,
and yelled loudly that an air raid is reported,
while street loudspeakers called: "Relatives of the missing
should visit the *Collecting Center for Corpses* in such-and-such district,
or else the dead will be buried in a common grave!"—
It was freedom, yes, it was freedom,
but with all its still murky massive features,
there was some wind here and there, and it blew loathingly,
as if it had found a German hair between two pages of a brand-new book,
every large square was sick at heart,
scabby buses from concentration camps arrived there:
"Kadel, my love! . . . Annie! . . . All right, Mary,
stop crying! You're back home, you know? . . . One more, one more
    kiss, Jenda!"
I'm telling you, they were months of scorching heat, ruins, and dust
moistened only by the tears of the returned ones, the welcoming ones,
they all stood there, absolutely free, like at a time
when we don't want anything else,
after a brief sorrowful moment
the memory of the dead began searching in pockets
for tangible keepsakes: a woman's lock of hair,
and a man's red censor's pencil of shame

deleting the carved wrinkles on the face of a tragedy
and transforming it into a smile of self-denial.
They were standing there, in a brotherhood so unanimous
you could hardly grasp that they could return to their sentimental homes,
return with the desire to catch up on all the missed Christmas Eyes,
yes, and when a streetcar moved jerkily,
and some girls grabbed the handrails,
their sleeves pulled up and you could see, just above their wrists,
prisoners' tattooed numbers . . .
They hunted for wide bracelets to cover them,
but it isn't easy to find such a bracelet, my dear!
And even now, the gates in a Prague street are wide open, May-like,
with scribbled words: DO NOT ENTER! SHOOTING GOING ON!
Do you remember? No! I don't want to remember any more, either,
but I can still see the splendid Red Army girls,
who at the crossroads of our new destiny
started signaling with their flags
the safe life that's allowed to keep its spontaneity,
the spontaneity of a miracle and love . . .
And I can see a little boy and girl.
She said: "Show me! You got blue teeth?"
But he didn't, he took out another paper bag
and they both dug into more blueberries . . .

Translated from the Czech by C. G. Hanzlicek and Dana Hábová

Resurrection

After this life here, we're to be awakened one day
by the terrible screams of trumpets and bugles?
Forgive me, Lord, but I trust
that the beginning and the resurrection of us, the dead,
will be announced by the crowing of a rooster . . .

We'll lie on for a little longer . . .
The first one to rise
will be mother . . . We'll hear her
quietly making the fire,

quietly putting the kettle on,
and cozily taking the coffee grinder out of the cupboard.
We'll be at home again.

Translated from the Czech by C. G. Hanzlicek and Dana Hábová

DANIIL KHARMS
(RUSSIA, 1905–1942)

The Beginning of a Beautiful Day (A Symphony)

The rooster had hardly crowed when Timofey jumped out of the window onto the roof and frightened all the passersby who were on the street at that hour. The peasant Khariton stopped, picked up a stone, and threw it at Timofey. Timofey disappeared somewhere. "That is a clever one!" the herd of people shouted, and Zubov ran full speed and rammed his head into a wall. "Oh!" a woman with a swollen cheek shouted. But Komarov beat up the woman, and the woman ran howling through the doorway. Fetelyushin walked past and laughed at them. Komarov walked up to him and said, "Hey, you greaseball," and hit Fetelyushin in the stomach. Fetelyushin leaned against the wall and started to hiccup. Romashkin spat from the top-story window, trying to hit Fetelyushin. At that moment, not far from there, a big-nosed woman was beating up her kid with a trough. A fattish young mother rubbed a pretty little girl's face against the brick wall. A little dog broke its thin leg and rolled around on the pavement. A little boy ate some kind of loathsome thing out of a spittoon. At the grocery store there was a long line for sugar. The women swore loudly and pushed one another with bags. The peasant Khariton got drunk on denatured alcohol and stood in front of the women with unbuttoned trousers and said bad words.

Thus began a beautiful summer day.

Translated from the Russian by George Gibian

ATTILA JÓZSEF
(HUNGARY, 1905–1937)

The Seventh

If you set foot on this earth,
you must go through seven births.
Once, in a house that's burning,
once, among ice floes churning,
once, amidst madmen raving,
once, in a field of wheat swaying,
once, in a cloister, bells ringing,
once, in a pigsty a-squealing.
Six babes crying, not enough, son.
Let yourself be the seventh one!

If foes confront you, that is when
Your enemies must see seven men.
One, who's off on a holiday,
one, who goes to work on Monday,
one, who teaches unpaid on a whim,
one, who has learned to sink or swim,
one, who will seed a whole forest,
one, whom wild forefathers protect.
But all their tricks are not enough, son.
Let yourself be the seventh one!

If you want to find a lover,
Let seven men go look for her.
One, whose words contain his heart,
one, who can pay his part,
one, pretending to be a dreamer,
one, who will be a skirt-peeler,
one, who knows the snaps and hooks,
one who can put down his foot—
buzz like flies around her, son.
And you yourself be the seventh one.

Be a poet if you can afford it,
but seven men make up one poet.
One, a marble-village builder,
one, who was born a sleeper,
one, an adept sky-charter,
one, whom words befriend and favor,
one, who is his own soul-maker,
and one who dissects a rat's liver.
Two are brave and four are wise, son—
let yourself be the seventh one.

And if all went as was written,
You will be buried as seven men.
One, nursed on a soft milky breast,
one, who likes tough titties best,
one, who flips empty plates in the bin,
one, who helps the poor to win,
one, who labors, falling apart,
one, who stares at the Moon all night.
The world will be your tombstone, son:
if you yourself are the seventh one.

Translated from the Hungarian by John Bátki

SANDRO PENNA

(ITALY, 1906–1977)

Maybe I'm getting old, staying seated

Maybe I'm getting old, staying seated
the whole long journey, seeing nothing outside
but the rain, and tired sunbeam
of silent life . . . (workmen
climbed on and off my train,
carrying their sleep with their tools
from a small town to a quiet lake).

When I reached my bed I too cried out:
We're men, we are tired, not wretched.

Translated from the Italian by W. S. Di Piero

A glass of milk and a piazza

A glass of milk and a piazza
with a statue. A glass of milk
from your sweet, new, dirty hands.

Translated from the Italian by W. S. Di Piero

Look at the workers on the green field

Look at the workers on the green field
eating. Aren't they beautiful?
Cars drive by on every side,
people pass, clutching newspapers.

But the workers, aren't they beautiful?

Translated from the Italian by W. S. Di Piero

The accused has only words

The accused has only words.
And sometimes he doesn't have, or even want,
only sunlit words in sunlight.

Translated from the Italian by W. S. Di Piero

LÉOPOLD SÉDAR SENGHOR

(SENEGAL, 1906–2001)

To New York, 3

New York! I say New York, let black blood flow into your blood.
Let it wash the rust from your steel joints, like an oil of life
Let it give your bridges the curve of hips and supple vines.
Now the ancient age returns, unity is restored,
The reconciliation of Lion and Bull and Tree
Idea links to action, the ear to the heart, sign to meaning.
See your rivers stirring with musk alligators
And sea cows with mirage eyes. No need to invent the Sirens.
Just open your eyes to the April rainbow
And your ears, especially your ears, to God
Who in one burst of saxophone laughter
Created heaven and earth in six days,
And on the seventh slept a deep Negro sleep.

Translated from the French by Melvin Dixon

Taga for Mbaye Dyôb

(for one tama*)*

Mbaye Dyôb! I want to say your name and your honor.

Dyôb! I want to hoist your name to the tall returning mast,
Sound your name like the bell clanging victory
I want to praise your name Dyôbène! You who called me
Your master and warmed me with your fervor those winter nights
Around the red stewpot growing cold.
Dyôb! You may not know how to recite your genealogy
Or tame the darkness, you whose ancestors do not keep time
To the *tama* drums. You who never killed a rabbit,
Who lay down under the bombs of the giant vultures, Dyôb!
Who was neither captain, nor pilot, nor firing horseman,

Nor working only in the supply wagon,
But a private second-class in the 4th regiment
Of Senegalese soldiers
Dyôb!—I want to praise your white honor.

The Gandyol virgins will make you a triumphal arch
With their rounded arms and a veil of glory
With their arms of silver and red gold
And rare *pagnes* from the Southern Rivers.
Then they will make you an ivory necklace from their mouths,
Prettier than a royal cloak, then they will cradle your step,
Their voices will merge with the ocean waves and sing:
"You have braved more than death, more than the tanks
And planes that defied our sorcery.
You have braved hunger, cold, and the slave's humiliation.
Daredevil, you were the stepping stone of *griots*, of buffoons
Oh, you who added more nails to your cross
To remain with your companions and to keep your promise
Not to leave your burden for others to carry, whose backs
Break with each departure, whose arms droop each evening
With one less hand to hold, and whose brow
Darkens from light from fewer eyes,
Whose eyes grow dim with one less smile to reflect."
Dyôb! From Ngâbu to Walo, from Ngalam to the Sea
The songs of amber virgins will rise
To the music of *kora* strings! to the music of wind-and-wave
Dyôb! I say your name and your honor.

Translated from the French by Melvin Dixon

GÜNTER EICH
(GERMANY, 1907–1972)

Inventory

This is my cap,
this is my coat,

here's my shaving gear
in a linen sack.

A can of rations:
my plate, my cup,
I've scratched my name
in the tin.

Scratched it with this
valuable nail
which I hide
from avid eyes.

In the foodsack is
a pair of wool socks
and something else that I
show to no one,

it all serves as a pillow
for my head at night.
The cardboard here lies
between me and the earth.

The lead in my pencil
I love most of all:
in the daytime it writes down
the verses I make at night.

This is my notebook,
this is my tarpaulin,
this is my towel,
this is my thread.

Translated from the German by David Young

RENÉ CHAR

(FRANCE, 1907–1988)

The Gods Are Back

The gods are back, companions. Right now they have just entered this life; but the words that revoke them, whispered underneath the words that reveal them, have also appeared that we might suffer together.

Translated from the French by Peter Boyle

CESARE PAVESE

(ITALY, 1908–1950)

Death will come and will have your eyes

Death will come and will have your eyes—
this death that accompanies us
from morning till evening, unsleeping,
deaf, like an old remorse
or an absurd vice. Your eyes
will be a useless word,
a suppressed cry, a silence.
That's what you see each morning
when alone with yourself you lean
toward the mirror. O precious hope,
that day we too will know
that you are life and you are nothingness.

Death has a look for everyone.
Death will come and will have your eyes.
It will be like renouncing a vice,
like seeing a dead face
reappear in the mirror,

like listening to a lip that's shut.
We'll go down into the maelstrom mute.

Translated from the Italian by Geoffrey Brock

Words from Confinement

Bright and early we went down to the fishmarket
To wash stale eyes alive. The fish were
Scarlet, green, silver, color of the sea.
The sea was shining, all scales of silver,
But the fish were brighter. We thought of home.

Beautiful too the women, with jars on their heads,
Olive green, and molded like their hips,
Softly rounded. We thought of our women,
How they talk and laugh and walk down the street.
We all laughed. Out at sea, it was raining.

In vineyards, along ravines, grapes and leaves
Glisten with rain. The sky is ruddy
With scattered clouds, colored with sun
And pleasure. On earth, smells; in the sky,
Colors. We were on our own; unguarded.

We thought of home, the way a man thinks
Of morning after a sleepless night. The sea
Smelled musty, and we reveled in freshness,
In the moistness of the fruit and the colors of the fish.
We were drunk on the news: we were going home!

Translated from the Italian by William Arrowsmith

LEONARDO SINISGALLI

(ITALY, 1908–1981)

Dog Flies

Fido has fat buttocks.
He's an old church dog
who loafs under the altar.
He's lost his sense of smell, his fangs
are loose and he's given up
scratching himself with his muzzle.
Even cats scare him
but he's here at the requiem mass
for my mother's bones.
His head stretched out between his paws,
he's stuck out his tongue: suddenly
he swallows a big fly that was bothering him.

Translated from the Italian by Jamie McKendrick

Old Grief

Grief comes easily to old people.
At midday
sitting in a corner of an empty house
they burst into tears.
Infinite despair
catches them by surprise.
They lift a withered slice of pear
to their lips, or the pulp of a fig
baked on the roof tiles.
Even a sip of water
or a visit by a snail
helps to ease a crisis.

Translated from the Italian by W. S. Di Piero

Via Velasca

Years of pounding have nearly
Caved it in, and it's hard to believe
The street's gotten narrower.
This is my hour, my favorite hour.
I remember one night all noise died
In the fading light, a voice
Cried my name as if in a dream
Then stopped.
The street bends, the day
Drips from the rooftops,
The sweet hour sings in me.
The light is only a stubborn
Ghost, a glow: a fish
Gleams in the glass bottle.

Translated from the Italian by W. S. Di Piero

YANNIS RITSOS
(GREECE, 1909–1990)

The Meaning of Simplicity

I hide behind simple things so you'll find me;
if you don't find me, you'll find the things,
you'll touch what my hand has touched,
our hand-prints will merge.

The August moon glitters in the kitchen
like a tin-plated pot (it gets that way because of what I'm saying to you),
it lights up the empty house and the house's kneeling silence—
always the silence remains kneeling.

Every word is a doorway
to a meeting, one often cancelled,
and that's when a word is true: when it insists on the meeting.

Translated from the Greek by Edmund Keeley

Wonder

Before going to bed, he placed his watch under his pillow.
Then he went to sleep. The wind outside was blowing.
You, who know the wondrous succession of the slightest movements,
you will understand. A man, his watch, the wind. Nothing more.

Translated from the Greek by Minas Savvas

Beauty

Naked, she took the red handkerchief
and covered her eyes so as not to be seen
in case fear would force them to look.
Silent and arrogant—maybe even afraid,
within the darkness of her concealed eyes,
she may have even touched or even mixed
    the light
Then she did not wake.

Under the straw-chair of the garden, her shoes remained
with the bare form of her feet. On the tree—
    the branch
her white dress streamed, unfastening all
    her nudity.

She had hoped for this after death. The light
    of the garden
fluttered—I don't know how—like mocking,
    like applause.

Translated from the Greek by Minas Savvas

Audible and Inaudible

A sudden, unexpected movement; his hand
clutched the wound to stop the bleeding,
though we had not heard the gunburst at all
or the whistling of a bullet. A short time later
he lowered his hand and smiled;
but again slowly he placed his palm
on that same spot, pulled out his wallet,
paid the waiter politely, and went out.
Just then the small coffee cup cracked by itself.
That at least we heard clearly.

Translated from the Greek by Minas Savvas

MIKLÓS RADNÓTI
(HUNGARY, 1909–1944)

Postcard

I fell next to him. His body rolled over.
It was tight as a string about to snap.
Shot in the back of the head—"This is how
you'll end." "Just lie quietly," I said to myself.
Patience flowers into death now.
"Der springt noch auf," I heard above me.
Dark filthy blood was drying on my ear.

Translated from the Hungarian by Steven Polgar,
Stephen Berg, and S. J. Marks

ISRAEL EMIOT
(POLAND/RUSSIA, 1909–1978)

A Prayer in Nineteen Forty-Three

for H. Lang

Good God, look I am poor, and trip over myself,
and my child wears shoes three times his size,
plays with children, falls, and runs crying to me,
as I to you—with and without a reason.

I know, all prayers crown you in gold,
and address the most exquisite words to you;
still, don't insult the prayer of a child, who just wants
his own bed, and has to sleep fourth on the ground.

Your song—the day—I read and admire daily;
I still marvel at your last verse—the sunset,
but when I want to praise you my hands fail me!
Oh do not punish me, even my shirt is borrowed.

Wisdom tells me man is insignificant,
and earth the least of all your spheres;
still, do not punish me: listen to the lament
of a child who sleeps fourth on the ground.

[Kazakhstan, war years]

Translated from the Yiddish by Leah Zazulyer and
Brina Menachovsky Rose

ANNA SWIR
(POLAND, 1909–1984)

She Does Not Remember

She was an evil stepmother.
In her old age she is slowly dying
in an empty hovel.

She shudders
like a clutch of burnt paper.
She does not remember that she was evil.
But she knows
that she feels cold.

Translated from the Polish by Czesław Miłosz

The First Madrigal

That night of love was pure
as an antique musical instrument
and the air around it.

Rich
as a ceremony of coronation.
It was fleshy as a belly of a woman in labor
and spiritual
as a number.

It was only a moment of life
and it wanted to be a conclusion drawn from life.
By dying
it wanted to comprehend the principle of the world.

That night of love
had ambitions.

Translated from the Polish by Czesław Miłosz

The Second Madrigal

A night of love
exquisite as a
concert from old Venice
played on exquisite instruments.
Healthy as a
buttock of a little angel.
Wise as an
anthill.
Garish as air
blown into a trumpet.
Abundant as the reign
of a royal Negro couple
seated on two thrones
cast in gold.

A night of love with you,
a big baroque battle
and two victories.

Translated from the Polish by Czesław Miłosz

A Woman Talks to Her Thigh

It is only thanks to your good looks
I can take part
in the rites of love.

Mystical ecstasies,
Treasons delightful
as a crimson lipstick,
a perverse rococo
of psychological involutions,
sweetness of carnal longings
that take your breath,
pits of despair

sinking to the very bottom of the world:
all this I owe to you.

How tenderly I should every day
lash you with a whip of cold water,
if you alone allow me to possess
beauty and wisdom
irreplaceable.

The souls of my lovers
open to me in a moment of love
and I have them in my dominion.

I look as does a sculptor
at his work
at their faces snapped shut with eyelids,
martyred by ecstasy,
made dense by happiness.
I read as does an angel
thoughts in their skulls,
I feel in my hand
a beating human heart,
I listen to the words
which are whispered by one human to another
in the frankest moments of one's life.

I enter their souls,
I wander
by a road of delight or of horror
to lands as inconceivable
as the bottoms of the oceans.
Later on, heavy with treasures
I am coming slowly back
to myself.

Oh, many riches,
many precious truths
growing immense in a metaphysical echo,

many initiations
delicate and startling
I owe to you, my thigh.

The most exquisite refinement of my soul
would not give me any of those treasures
if not for the clear, smooth charm
of an amoral little animal.

Translated from the Polish by Czesław Miłosz

A Conversation Through the Door

At five in the morning
I knock on his door.
I say through the door:
in the hospital at Sliska Street
your son, a soldier, is dying.

He half-opens the door,
does not remove the chain.
Behind him his wife
shakes.

I say: your son asks his mother
to come.
He says: the mother won't come.
Behind him the wife
shakes.

I say: the doctor allowed us
to give him wine.
He says: please wait.

He hands me a bottle through the door,
locks the door,
locks the door with a second key.

Behind the door his wife
begins to scream as if she were in labor.

Translated from the Polish by Czesław Miłosz and Leonard Nathan

from *Building the Barricade*

Building the Barricade

We were afraid as we built the barricade
under fire.

The tavern-keeper, the jeweler's mistress, the barber,
all of us cowards.
The servant-girl fell to the ground
as she lugged a paving stone, we were terribly afraid
all of us cowards—
the janitor, the market-woman, the pensioner.

The pharmacist fell to the ground
as he dragged the door of a toilet,
we were even more afraid, the smuggler-woman,
the dressmaker, the streetcar driver,
all of us cowards.

A kid from reform school fell
as he dragged a sandbag,
you see we were really
afraid.

Though no one forced us,
we did build the barricade
under fire.

Translated from the Polish by Magnus Jan Krynski and
Robert A. Maguire

He Steals Furs

A shell tears apart the door
of the furrier's shop.

A man leaps in,
grabs an armful of furs,
lugs them to the gateway at a run.

At the gateway another shell
tears apart the man.

Translated from the Polish by Magnus Jan Krynski and
Robert A. Maguire

A Woman Said to Her Neighbor

A woman said to her neighbor:
"Since my husband was killed I can't sleep,
when there's shooting I dive under the blanket,
I tremble all night long under the blanket.
I'll go crazy if I have to be alone today,
I have some cigarettes my husband left, please
do drop in tonight."

Translated from the Polish by Magnus Jan Krynski and
Robert A. Maguire

Two Hunchbacks

"I can't afford to die, ma'm,
what would my sister do without me.
She's a hunchback, she's lying there by the window."

"I can't afford to die, ma'm,
what would my sister do without me,
She's a hunchback, she's lying there by the door."

Each of them died
of the wound of her sister
died the death of her hunchbacked sister.

Translated from the Polish by Magnus Jan Krynski and
Robert A. Maguire

He Was Lucky

The old man
leaves his house, carries books.
A German soldier snatches his books
flings them in the mud.

The old man picks them up,
the soldier hits him in the face.
The old man falls,
the soldier kicks him and walks away.

The old man
lies in mud and blood.
Under him he feels
the books.

Translated from the Polish by Magnus Jan Krynski and
Robert A. Maguire

MIGUEL HERNÁNDEZ
(SPAIN, 1910–1942)

Lullabies of the Onion

Dedicated to his son, after receiving a letter from his wife saying that all
she had to eat was bread and onion

The onion is frost
shut in and poor.

Frost of your days
and of my nights.
Hunger and onion,
black ice and frost
large and round.

My little boy was
in hunger's cradle
He suckled on
onion blood.
But your blood is
frosted with sugar,
onions and hunger.

A dark woman dissolved
into moonlight
spills, thread by thread,
over the cradle.
Laugh, child,
You can drink moonlight
if you have to.

Lark of my house,
laugh freely.
Your laughter in your eyes
is the world's light.
Laugh so much
that hearing you, my soul
will beat through space.

Your laughter frees me,
gives me wings.
It banishes loneliness,
tears down these walls.
Mouth that flies,
heart that flashes
on your lips.

Your laughter is
the supreme sword,
conqueror of flowers
and larks.
Rival of the sun.
Future of my bones
and of my love.

The flesh flutters
as sudden as an eyelid;
life, as never before,
takes on new color.
How many linnets,
wings beating, take off
from your body!

I woke from childhood:
don't you ever.
I wear my mouth sadly:
always laugh.
Stay always in your cradle
defending laughter
feather by feather.

You are a flight
so high, so wide,
that your flesh is heaven
just born.
If only I could climb
to the origin
of your flight!

For eight months you laugh
with five orange blossoms.
With five little
ferocities,
with five teeth

like five young
jasmine buds.

They will be the frontier
of kisses tomorrow
when you feel a gun
in your mouth.
When you feel a burning
past the teeth
searching for the center.

Fly, child, on the double moon
of her breast:
it is saddened by onions,
you are satisfied.
Never let go.
Don't ever know what's coming,
what goes on.

Translated from the Spanish by Philip Levine

CZESŁAW MIŁOSZ
(LITHUANIA/POLAND, 1911–2004)

Dedication

You whom I could not save
Listen to me.
Try to understand this simple speech as I would be ashamed of another.
I swear, there is in me no wizardry of words.
I speak to you with silence like a cloud or a tree.

What strengthened me, for you was lethal.
You mixed up farewell to an epoch with the beginning of a new one,
Inspiration of hatred with lyrical beauty,
Blind force with accomplished shape.

Here is the valley of shallow Polish rivers. And an immense bridge
Going into white fog. Here is a broken city,
And the wind throws the screams of gulls on your grave
When I am talking with you.

What is poetry which does not save
Nations or people?
A connivance with official lies,
A song of drunkards whose throats will be cut in a moment,
Readings for sophomore girls.

That I wanted good poetry without knowing it,
That I discovered, late, its salutary aim,
In this and only this I find salvation.

They used to pour millet on graves or poppy seeds
To feed the dead who would come disguised as birds.
I put this book here for you, who once lived
So that you should visit us no more.

Translated from the Polish by the author

A Song on the End of the World

On the day the world ends
A bee circles a clover,
A fisherman mends a glimmering net.
Happy porpoises jump in the sea,
By the rainspout young sparrows are playing
And the snake is gold-skinned as it should always be.

On the day the world ends
Women walk through the fields under their umbrellas,
A drunkard grows sleepy at the edge of a lawn,
Vegetable peddlers shout in the street
And a yellow-sailed boat comes nearer the island,
The voice of a violin lasts in the air
And leads into a starry night.

And those who expected lightning and thunder
Are disappointed.
And those who expected signs and archangels' trumps
Do not believe it is happening now.
As long as the sun and the moon are above,
As long as the bumblebee visits a rose,
As long as rosy infants are born
No one believes it is happening now.

Only a white-haired old man, who would be a prophet
Yet is not a prophet, for he's much too busy,
Repeats while he binds his tomatoes:
There will be no other end of the world,
There will be no other end of the world.

Translated from the Polish by the author

A Poor Christian Looks at the Ghetto

Bees build around red liver,
Ants build around black bone.
It has begun: the tearing, the trampling on silks,
It has begun: the breaking of glass, wood, copper, nickel, silver, foam
Of gypsum, iron sheets, violin strings, trumpets, leaves, balls, crystals.
Poof! Phosphorescent Ore from yellow walls
Engulfs animal and human hair.

Bees build around the honeycomb of lungs,
Ants build around white bone.
Torn is paper, rubber, linen, leather, flax,
Fiber, fabrics, cellulose, snakeskin, wire.
The roof and the wall collapse in flame and heat seizes the foundations.
Now there is only the earth, sandy, trodden down,
With one leafless tree.

Slowly, boring a tunnel, a guardian mole makes his way,
With a small red lamp fastened to his forehead.
He touches buried bodies, counts them, pushes on,

He distinguishes human ashes by their luminous vapor,
The ashes of each man by a different part of the spectrum.
Bees build around a red trace.
Ants build around the place left by my body.

I am afraid, so afraid of the guardian mole.
He has swollen eyelids, like a Patriarch
Who has sat much in the light of candles
Reading the great book of the species.

What will I tell him, I, a Jew of the New Testament,
Waiting two thousand years for the second coming of Jesus?
My broken body will deliver me to his sight
And he will count me among the helpers of death:
The uncircumcised.

Translated from the Polish by the author

Mittelbergheim

Wine sleeps in casks of Rhine oak.
I am wakened by the bell of a chapel in the vineyards
Of Mittelbergheim. I hear a small spring
Trickling into a well in the yard, a clatter
Of sabots in the street. Tobacco drying
Under the eaves, and ploughs and wooden wheels
And mountain slopes and autumn are with me.

I keep my eyes closed. Do not rush me,
You, fire, power, might, for it is too early.
I have lived through many years and, as in this half-dream,
I felt I was attaining the moving frontier
Beyond which color and sound come true
And the things of this earth are united.
Do not yet force me to open my lips,
Let me trust and believe I will attain.
Let me linger here in Mittelbergheim.

I know I should. They are with me,
Autumn and wooden wheels and tobacco hung
Under the eaves. Here and everywhere
Is my homeland, wherever I turn
And in whatever language I would hear
The song of a child, the conversation of lovers.
Happier than anyone, I am to receive
A glance, a smile, a star, silk creased
At the knee. Serene, beholding,
I am to walk on hills in the soft glow of day
Over waters, cities, roads, human customs.

Fire, power, might, you who hold me
In the palm of your hand whose furrows
Are like immense gorges combed
By southern wind. You who grant certainty
In the hour of fear, in the week of doubt,
It is too early, let the wine mature,
Let the travelers sleep in Mittelbergheim.

Translated from the Polish by the author

Café

Of those at the table in the café
where on winter noons a garden of frost glittered on windowpanes
I alone survived.
I could go in there if I wanted to
and drumming my fingers in a chilly void
convoke shadows.

With disbelief I touch the cold marble,
with disbelief I touch my own hand,
It—is, and I—am in ever novel becoming,
while they are locked forever and ever
in their last word, their last glance,
and as remote as Emperor Valentinian

or the chiefs of the Massagetes, about whom I know nothing,
though hardly one year has passed, or two or three.

I may still cut trees in the woods of the far north,
I may speak from a platform or shoot a film
using techniques they never heard of.
I may learn the taste of fruits from ocean islands
and be photographed in attire from the second half of the century.
But they are forever like busts in frock coats and jabots
in some monstrous encyclopedia.

Sometimes when the evening aurora paints the roofs in a poor street
and I contemplate the sky, I see in the white clouds
a table wobbling. The waiter whirls with his tray
and they look at me with a burst of laughter
for I still don't know what it is to die at the hand of man,
they know—they know it well.

Translated from the Polish by the author

A Gift

A day so happy.
Fog lifted early, I worked in the garden.
Hummingbirds were stopping over honeysuckle flowers.
There was no thing on earth I wanted to possess.
I knew no one worth my envying him.
Whatever evil I had suffered, I forgot.
To think that once I was the same man did not embarrass me.
In my body I felt no pain.
When straightening up, I saw the blue sea and sails.

Translated from the Polish by the author

Winter

The pungent smells of a California winter,
Grayness and rosiness, an almost transparent full moon.
I add logs to the fire, I drink and I ponder.

"In Ilawa," the news item said, "at age 70
Died Aleksander Ryrnkiewicz, poet."

He was the youngest in our group. I patronized him slightly,
Just as I patronized others for their inferior minds
Though they had many virtues I couldn't touch.

And so I am here, approaching the end
Of the century and of my life. Proud of my strength
Yet embarrassed by the clearness of the view.

Avant-gardes mixed with blood.
The ashes of inconceivable arts.
An omnium-gatherum of chaos.

I passed judgment on that. Though marked myself.
This hasn't been the age for the righteous and the decent.
I know what it means to beget monsters
And to recognize in them myself.

You, moon, You, Aleksander, fire of cedar logs.
Waters close over us, a name lasts but an instant.
Not important whether the generations hold us in memory.
Great was that chase with the hounds for the unattainable meaning
    of the world.

And now I am ready to keep running
When the sun rises beyond the borderlands of death.

I already see mountain ridges in the heavenly forest
Where, beyond every essence, a new essence waits.

You, music of my late years, I am called
By a sound and a color which are more and more perfect.

Do not die out, fire. Enter my dreams, love,
Be young forever, seasons of the earth.

Translated from the Polish by the author

And the City Stood in Its Brightness

And the city stood in its brightness when years later I returned.
And life was running out, Ruteboeuf's or Villon's.
Descendants, already born, were dancing their dances.
Women looked in their mirrors made from a new metal.
What was it all for if I cannot speak.
She stood above me, heavy; like the earth on its axis.
My ashes were laid in a can under the bistro counter.

And the city stood in its brightness when years later I returned
To my home in the display case of a granite museum,
Beside eyelash mascara, alabaster vials,
And menstruation girdles of an Egyptian princess.
There was only a sun forged out of gold plate,
On darkening parquetry the creak of unhurried steps.

And the city stood in its brightness when years later I returned,
My face covered with a coat though now no one was left
Of those who could have remembered my debts never paid,
My shames not forever, base deeds to be forgiven.
And the city stood in its brightness when years later I returned.

Translated from the Polish by the author

from Throughout Our Lands

1

When I pass'd through a populous city
(as Walt Whitman says, in the Polish version)
When I pass'd through a populous city;
for instance near San Francisco harbor, counting gulls,
I thought that between men, women, and children there is
something, neither happiness nor unhappiness.

3

I had to tell what the world is for me
I would take a hamster or a hedgehog or a mole
and place him in a theater seat one evening
and, bringing my ear close to his humid snout,
would listen to what he says about the spotlights,
sounds of the music, and movements of the dance.

11

Paulina, her room behind the servants' quarters, with one window on
    the orchard
where I gather the best apples near the pigsty
squishing with my big toe the warm muck of the dunghill,
and the other window on the well (I love to drop the bucket down
and scare its inhabitants, the green frogs).
Paulina, a geranium, the chill of a dirt floor,
a hard bed with three pillows,
an iron crucifix and images of the saints,
decorated with palms and paper roses.
Paulina died long ago, but is.
And, I am somehow convinced, not just in my consciousness.

14

Cabeza, if anyone knew all about civilization, it was you.
A bookkeeper from Castile, what a fix you were in
to have to wander about, where no notion,
no cipher, no stroke of a pen dipped in sepia,
only a boat thrown up on the sand by surf,
crawling naked on all fours, under the eye of immobile Indians,
and suddenly their wail in the void of sky and sea,
their lament: that even the gods are unhappy.
For seven years you were their predicted god,
bearded, white-skinned, beaten if you couldn't work a miracle.
Seven years' march from the Mexican Gulf to California,
the hu-hu-hu of tribes, hot bramble of the continent.
But afterward? Who am I, the lace of cuffs
not mine, the table carved with lions not mine, Doña Clara's
fin, the slipper from under her gown—hell, no.
On all fours! On all fours!
Smear our thighs with war paint.
Lick the ground. Wha wha, hu hu.

Translated from the Polish by Peter Dale Scott and the author

A Felicitous Life

His old age fell on years of abundant harvest.
There were no earthquakes, droughts, or floods.
It seemed as if the turning of the seasons gained in constancy,
Stars waxed strong and the sun increased its might.
Even in remote provinces no war was waged.
Generations grew up friendly to fellow men.
The rational nature of man was not a subject of derision.

It was bitter to say farewell to the earth so renewed.
He was envious and ashamed of his doubt,
Content that his lacerated memory would vanish with him.

Two days after his death a hurricane razed the coasts.
Smoke came from volcanoes inactive for a hundred years.
Lava sprawled over forests, vineyards, and towns.
And war began with a battle on the islands.

Translated from the Polish by Peter Dale Scott and the author

from Bobo's Metamorphosis

V

I liked him as he did not look for an ideal object.
When he heard: "Only the object which does not exist
Is perfect and pure," he blushed and turned away.

In every pocket he carried pencils, pads of paper
Together with crumbs of bread, the accidents of life.

Year after year he circled a thick tree
Shading his eyes with his hand and muttering in amazement.

How much he envied those who draw a tree with one line!
But metaphor seemed to him something indecent.

He would leave symbols to the proud busy with their cause.
By looking he wanted to draw the name from the very thing.
When he was old, he tugged at his tobacco-stained beard:
"I prefer to lose thus than to win as they do."

Like Peter Breughel the father he fell suddenly
While attempting to look back between his spread-apart legs.

And still there stood the tree unattainable.
Veritable, true to the very core.

VIII

Between her and me there was a table, on the table a glass.
The chapped skin of her elbows touched the shining surface
In which the contour of shade under her armpit was reflected.
A drop of sweat thickened over her wavy lip.
And the space between her and me fractionized itself infinitely
Buzzing with pennate Eleatic arrows.
Not a year, not a hundred years of journey would exhaust it.
Had I overturned the table what would we have accomplished?
That act, a non-act, always no more than potential
Like the attempt to penetrate water, wood, minerals.
But she, too, looked at me as if I were a ring of Saturn
And knew I was aware that no one attains.
Thus were affirmed humanness, tenderness.

Translated from the Polish by the author

On the Other Side

> *Some hells present an appearance like the ruins of houses and cities*
> *after conflagrations, in which infernal spirits dwell and hide*
> *themselves. In the milder hells there is an appearance of rude huts,*
> *in some cases contiguous in the form of a city with lanes and streets.*
> —EMANUEL SWEDENBORG

Falling, I caught the curtain,
Its velvet was the last thing I could feel on earth
As I slid to the floor, howling: aah! aaah!

To the very end I could not believe that I too must . . .
Like everyone.

Then I trod in wheel-ruts
On an ill-paved road. Wooden shacks,
A lame tenement house in a field of weeds.
Potato patches fenced in with barbed wire.

They played as-if-cards, I smelled as-if-cabbage,
There was as-if-vodka, as-if-dirt, as-if-time.
I said: "See here . . . ," but they shrugged their shoulders,
Or averted their eyes. This land knew nothing of surprise.
Nor of flowers. Dry geraniums in tin cans,
A deception of greenery coated with sticky dust.
Nor of the future. Gramophones played,
Repeating endlessly things which had never been.
Conversations repeated things which had never been.
So that no one should guess where he was, or why.
I saw hungry dogs lengthening and shortening their muzzles,
And changing from mongrels, to greyhounds, then dachshunds,
As if to signify they were perhaps not quite dogs.
Huge flocks of crows, freezing in midair,
Exploded under the clouds . . .

Translated from the Polish by the author

Incantation

Human reason is beautiful and invincible.
No bars, no barbed wire, no pulping of books,
No sentence of banishment can prevail against it.
It establishes the universal ideas in language,
And guides our hand so we write Truth and Justice
With capital letters, lie and oppression with small.
It puts what should be above things as they are,
Is an enemy of despair and a friend of hope.
It does not know Jew from Greek or slave from master,
Giving us the estate of the world to manage.
It saves austere and transparent phrases
From the filthy discord of tortured words.
It says that everything is new under the sun,
Opens the congealed fist of the past.
Beautiful and very young are Philo-Sophia
And poetry; her ally in the service of the good.
As late as yesterday Nature celebrated their birth,

The news was brought to the mountains by a unicorn and an echo.
Their friendship will be glorious, their time has no limit. Their
enemies have delivered themselves to destruction.

Translated from the Polish by Robert Pinsky and the author

On Angels

All was taken away from you: white dresses,
wings, even existence.
Yet I believe you,
messengers.

There, where the world is turned inside out,
a heavy fabric embroidered with stars and beasts,
you stroll, inspecting the trustworthy seams.

Short is your stay here:
now and then at a matinal hour, if the sky is clear,
in a melody repeated by a bird,
or in the smell of apples at the close of day
when the light makes the orchards magic.

They say somebody has invented you
but to rue this does not sound convincing
for humans invented themselves as well.

The voice—no doubt it is a valid proof,
as it can belong only to radiant creatures,
weightless and winged (after all, why not?),
girdled with the lightning.

I have heard that voice many a time when asleep
and, what is strange, I understood more or less
an order or an appeal in an unearthly tongue:

day draws near
another one
do what you can.

Translated from the Polish by the author

Bypassing rue Descartes

Bypassing rue Descartes
I descended toward the Seine, shy, a traveler,
A young barbarian just come to the capital of the world.

We were many, from Jassy and Koloshvar, Wiino and Bucharest,
    Saigon and Marrakesh,
Ashamed to remember the customs of our homes,
About which nobody here should ever be told:
The clapping for servants, barefooted girls hurry in,
Dividing food with incantations,
Choral prayers recited by master and household together.

I had left the cloudy provinces behind,
I entered the universal, dazzled and desiring.

Soon enough, many from Jassy and Koloshvar, or Saigon or Marrakesh
Would be killed because they wanted to abolish the customs
    of their homes.

Soon enough, their peers were seizing power
In order to kill in the name of the universal, beautiful ideas.

Meanwhile the city behaved in accordance with its nature,
Rustling with throaty laughter in the dark,
Baking long breads and pouring wine into clay pitchers,
Buying fish, lemons, and garlic at street markets,
Indifferent as it was to honor and shame and greatness and glory,
Because that had been done already and had transformed itself
Into monuments representing nobody knows whom,
Into arias hardly audible and into turns of speech.

Again I lean on the rough granite of the embankment,
As if I had returned from travels through the underworlds
And suddenly saw in the light the reeling wheel of the seasons
Where empires have fallen and those once living are now dead.

There is no capital of the world, neither here nor anywhere else,
And the abolished customs are restored to their small fame
And now I know that the time of human generations is not like the
    time of the earth.

As to my heavy sins, I remember one most vividly:
How, one day, walking on a forest path along a stream,
I pushed a rock down onto a water snake coiled in the grass.

And what I have met with in life was the just punishment
Which reaches, sooner or later, the breaker of a taboo.

Translated from the Polish by Renata Gorczynski and
Robert Hass

ODYSSEAS ELYTIS
(GREECE, 1911–1996)

All Day Long We Walked in the Fields

All day long we walked in the fields
With our women, suns, and dogs
We played, sang, drank water
Fresh as it sprang from the ages.

In the afternoon we sat for a moment
And we looked deeply into each other's eyes
A butterfly flew from our hearts
It was whiter
Than the small branch at the tip of our dreams
We knew that it was never to disappear
That it did not remember at all what worms it bore.

At night we lit a fire
And round about it sang:

Fire, lovely fire, do not pity the logs
Fire, lovely fire, do not turn to ash
Fire, lovely fire, burn us, tell us of life.

We tell of life, we take it by the hands
We look into its eyes and it returns our look
And if this which makes us drunk is a magnet, we know it
And if this which gives us pain is bad, we have felt it
We tell of life, we go ahead
And say farewell to its birds, which are migrating.

We are of a good generation.

Translated from the Greek by Edmund Keeley and
Philip Sherrard

HO CH'I-FANG
(CHINA, 1912–1977)

Get Drunk

To Those Who Sing Ever So Gently

Get drunk, get drunk,
Those truly drunk are lucky
For paradise belongs to them.

If alcohol, books,
And lips that drip honey . . .
If none of these can cover up man's suffering,
If you proceed from being dead drunk to half sober
To fully awake finally,
Wouldn't you keep your hat cocked and

Your eyes half closed,
To act slightly intoxicated throughout your life?

The flies shivering in the cold wind
Flutter their wings before the paper windowpane,
Dreaming of dead bodies,
Of watermelon rinds in high summer,
And of a dreamless void.

In the epilogue of my ridicule
I hear my own shame:
"You too are only buzzing and buzzing
Like a fly."

If I were a fly,
I'd await the sound of a fly swatter
Smashing on my head.

Translated from the Chinese by Kai-yu Hsu

EDMOND JABÈS
(EGYPT/FRANCE, 1912–1991)

Dedication

To the remote sources of life and death revealed.
To the dust of the well.
To the rabbi-poets in whose mouths I put my words and whose
      names have, over the centuries, become mine.
To Sarah and Yukel.
To those, finally, whose roads of ink and blood go through
      words and men.
And, most of all, to you. To us. To you.

Translated from the French by Rosmarie Waldrop

MOUSHEGH ISHKHAN
(ARMENIA, 1913–1990)

The Armenian Language Is the Home of the Armenian

The Armenian language is the home
and haven where the wanderer can own
roof and wall and nourishment.
He can enter to find love and pride
locking the hyena and the storm outside.
For centuries its architects have toiled
to give its ceilings height.
How many peasants working
day and night have kept
its cupboards full, lamps lit, ovens hot.
Always rejuvenated, always old, it lasts
century to century on the path
where every Armenian can find it when he's lost
in the wilderness of his future or his past.

Translated from the Armenian by Diana Der-Hovanessian

AIMÉ CÉSAIRE
(MARTINIQUE, 1913–2008)

Ex-voto for a Shipwreck

Hélé hélélé the King is a great king
let his majesty deign to look up my anus to see
if it contains diamonds
let his majesty deign to explore my mouth to see
how many carats it contains
laugh tom-tom
laugh tom-tom
I carry the king's litter
I roll out the king's rug
I am the king's rug

I carry scrofula for the king
I am the king's parasol
laugh laugh tom-toms of the kraals
tom-toms of mines that laugh up their shafts
sacred tom-toms laughing about your rat and hyena teeth
right in the missionaries' faces
tom-toms of the forest
tom-toms of the desert
weep tom-tom
weep tom-tom
burned down to the impetuous silence of our shoeless tears
and roll
roll softly no longer than a speck of coal
the pure carbon duration of our endless major pangs
roll roll heavy speechless deliriums
russet lions without manes
tom-toms which protect my three souls my brain my heart my liver
hard tom-toms which very loudly uphold my star wind dwelling over
the blasted rock of my black head
and you brother tom-tom for whom sometimes all day long I keep a
    word now hot now cool in my mouth like the little known taste
    of vengeance
tom-toms of the Kalahari
tom-toms of Good Hope that cap the cape with your threats
O tom-tom of Zululand
Tom-tom of Shaka
tom, tom, tom
tom, tom, tom
King our mountains are mares in heat caught in the full convulsion of
    bad blood
King our plains are rivers vexed by the supplies of putrefactions
    drifting in from the sea and your caravels

Translated from the French by Clayton Eshleman and Annette J. Smith

Lagoonal Calendar

I inhabit a sacred wound
I inhabit imaginary ancestors
I inhabit an obscure will
I inhabit a long silence
I inhabit an irremediable thirst
I inhabit a one-thousand-year journey
I inhabit a three-hundred-year war
I inhabit an abandoned cult
between bulb and bulbil I inhabit an unexplored space
I inhabit not a vein of the basalt
but the rising tide of lava
which runs back up the gulch at full speed
to burn all the mosques
I accommodate myself as best I can to this avatar
to an absurdly botched version of paradise
    —it is much worse than a hell—
I inhabit from time to time one of my wounds
Each minute I change apartments
and any peace frightens me

    whirling fire
    ascidium like none other for the dust of strayed worlds
    having spat out my fresh-water entrails
    a volcano I remain with my loaves of words and my secret minerals

I inhabit thus a vast thought
but in most cases I prefer to confine myself
to the smallest of my ideas
or else I inhabit a magical formula
only its opening words
the rest being forgotten
I inhabit the ice jam
I inhabit the ice melting
I inhabit the face of a great disaster
I inhabit in most cases the driest udder
of the skinniest peak—the she-wolf of these clouds—

I inhabit the halo of the Cactaceae
I inhabit a herd of goats pulling
on the tit of the most desolate argan tree
To tell you the truth I no longer know my correct address
Bathyale or abyssal
I inhabit the octopuses' hole
I fight with the octopus over an octopus hole

   Brother lay off
a kelpy mess
twining dodder-like
      or unfurling porana-like
   it's all the same thing
      which the wave tosses
      to which the sun leeches
      which the wind whips
   sculpture in the round of my nothingness

The atmospheric or rather historic pressure
even if it makes certain of my words sumptuous
immeasurably increases my plight.

Translated from the French by Clayton Eshleman and
Annette J. Smith

All the Way from Akkad, from Elam, from Sumer

Awakener, uprooter
Suffered breath, hastener breath
Master of the three paths, you are facing a man
who has walked a lot.
All the way from Elam. From Akkad. From Sumer.
I have carried the commandant's body. I have carried the comman-
dant's railroad. I have carried the commandant's locomotive, the
commandant's cotton. On my wooly head which works so fine
without a little cushion I have carried God, the machine, the road—
the God of the commandant.
Master of the three paths I have carried under the sun, I have carried

in the fog I have carried over the ember shards of legionary ants
I have carried the parasol I have carried the explosives I have carried
the iron-collar.
All the way from Akkad. From Elam. From Sumer.
Master of the three paths, Master of the three channels, for once only
the first time since Akkad since Elam since Sumer may you grant
that—my muzzle apparently more tanned than the calluses on my
feet but in reality softer than the raven's scrupulous beak and as if
draped in bitter folds provided by my borrowed gray skin (a livery
that men force onto me every winter)
—I advance across the dead leaves with my little sorcerer steps

toward where the inexhaustible injunction of men thrown to the
knotted sneers of the hurricane threatens triumphantly.
All the way from Elam from Akkad from Sumer.

Translated from the French by Clayton Eshleman and
Annette J. Smith

ORHAN VELI KANIK

(TURKEY, 1914–1950)

Rumors

Who started the rumor
That I have a crush on Stiheyla?
I dare you to tell who saw me
Kissing Eleni
On the Winding Steps in broad daylight?
Do they say I grabbed Melahat and took her to Alemdar,
Is that what they're saying?
Well, I'll explain that later, but
Whose bottom do they claim I pinched on the streetcar?
And what's the one about the Galata brothels,
That I get loaded, the liquor goes to my head
And I rush down there?
Come off it, man.

Never mind all that,
I know what I'm doing.

And what's that story about my getting Mualla into a rowboat
And making her sing "Your grief is in my heart"?

Translated from the Turkish by Murat Nemet-Nejat

Poem with a Tail

We can't be seen together. Our paths are separate.
You belong to the butcher, I am an alley cat.
You eat from a nickeled plate.
I eat from the lion's mouth.
You dream of love. I dream of bones.

But your path isn't easy either, pal,
Not easy
To wag a tail every godforsaken day.

Translated from the Turkish by Murat Nemet-Nejat

Quantitative

I love beautiful women,
I also love working women;
But I love beautiful working women—
More.

Translated from the Turkish by Murat Nemet-Nejat

My Gold-Toothed Beauty

Come, my darling, come to me.
Let me buy you silk stockings.
Let me put you in taxis,
Let me take you to nightclubs.
Come,

Come, my gold-toothed beauty.
With your mascara, your perm, my whore,
Your cork-heeled shoes, your American style . . .
Here,
Come.

Translated from the Turkish by Murat Nemet-Nejat

JULIO CORTÁZAR
(ARGENTINA, 1914–1984)

Theme for a Tapestry

The general has only eighty men, and the enemy five thousand. In his tent the general curses and weeps. Then he writes an inspired proclamation and homing pigeons shower copies over the enemy camp. Two hundred foot desert to the general. There follows a skirmish which the general wins easily, and two regiments come over to his side. Three days later, the enemy has only eighty men and the general five thousand. Then the general writes another proclamation and seventy-nine men join up with him. Only one enemy is left, surrounded by the army of the general who waits in silence. The night passes and the enemy has not come over to his side. The general curses and weeps in his tent. At dawn the enemy slowly unsheathes his sword and advances on the general's tent. He goes in and looks at him. The army of the general disbands. The sun rises.

Translated from the Spanish by Paul Blackburn

Progress and Retrogression

They invented a kind of glass which let flies through. The fly would come, push a little with his head and pop, he was on the other side. Enormous happiness on the part of the fly.

All this was ruined by a Hungarian scientist when he discovered that the fly could enter but not get out, or vice versa, because he didn't know what gimmick was involved in the glass or the flexibility of its fibers, for it was very fibroid. They immediately invented a fly trap with a sugar cube inside, and many flies perished miserably. So ended any possible brotherhood with these animals, who are deserving of better luck.

Translated from the Spanish by Paul Blackburn

OCTAVIO PAZ
(MEXICO, 1914–1998)

The Key of Water

After Rishikesh
the Ganges is still green.
The glass horizon
breaks among the peaks.
We walk upon crystals.
Above and below
great gulfs of calm.
In the blue spaces
white rocks, black clouds.
You said:
      Le pays est plein de sources.
That night I washed my hands in your breasts.

Translated from the Spanish by Elizabeth Bishop

Sight, Touch

For Balthus

Light holds between its hands
the white hill and black oaks,
the path that goes on,
the tree that stays;

light is a stone that breathes
by the sleepwalking river,
light: a girl stretching,
a dark bundle dawning;

light shapes the breeze in the curtains,
makes a living body from each hour,
enters the room and slips out,
barefoot, on the edge of a knife;

light is born a woman in a mirror,
naked under diaphanous leaves,
chained by a look,
dissolved in a wink;

it touches the fruit and the unbodied,
it is a pitcher from which the eye drinks clarities,
a flame cut in blossom, a candle watching
where the blackwinged butterfly burns;

light opens the folds of the sheets
and the creases of puberty,
glows in the fireplace, its flames become shadows
that climb the walls, yearning ivy;

light does not absolve or condemn,
is neither just or unjust,
light with impalpable hands raises
the buildings of symmetry;

light escapes through a passage of mirrors
and returns to light:
is a hand that invents itself,
an eye that sees itself in its own inventions.

Light is time reflecting on time.

Translated from the Spanish by Mark Strand

Flame, Speech

I read in a poem:
to talk is divine.
But the gods don't speak:
they make and unmake worlds
while men do the talking.
They play frightening games
without words.

The spirit descends,
loosening tongues,
but doesn't speak words:
it speaks fire.
Lit by a god,
language becomes
a prophecy
of flames and a tower
of smoke and collapse
of syllables burned:
ash without meaning.

The word of man
is the daughter of death.
We talk because we are mortal:
words are not signs, they are years.
Saying what they say,
the words we are saying
say time: they name us.
We are time's names.

The dead are mute
but they also say
what we are saying.
Language is the house

of all, hanging over the abyss.
To talk is human.

Translated from the Spanish by Mark Strand

NICANOR PARRA
(CHILE, 1914–)

The Tablets

I dreamed I was in a desert and because I was sick of myself
I started beating a woman.
It was devilish cold, I had to do something,
Make a fire, take some exercise,
But I had a headache, I was tired,
All I wanted to do was sleep, die.
My suit was soggy with blood
And a few hairs were stuck among my fingers
—They belonged to my poor mother—
"Why do you abuse your mother," a stone asked me,
A dusty stone, "Why do you abuse her?"
I couldn't tell where these voices came from, they gave me the shivers,
I looked at my nails, I bit them,
I tried to think of something but without success,
All I saw around me was a desert
And the image of that idol
My god who was watching me do these things.
Then a few birds appeared
And at the same moment, in the dark, I discovered some slabs of rock.
With a supreme effort I managed to make out the tablets of the law:
"We are the tablets of the law," they said,
"Why do you abuse your mother?
See these birds that have come to perch on us,
They are here to record your crimes."
But I yawned, I was bored with these warnings.
"Get rid of those birds," I said aloud.
"No," one of the stones said,

"They stand for your different sins,
They're here to watch you."
So I turned back to my lady again
And started to let her have it harder than before.
I had to do something to keep awake.
I had no choice but to act
Or I would have fallen asleep among those rocks
And those birds.
So I took a box of matches out of one of my pockets
And decided to set fire to the bust of the god.
I was dreadfully cold, I had to get warm,
But that blaze only lasted a few seconds.
Out of my mind, I looked for the tablets again
But they had disappeared.
The rocks weren't there either.
My mother had abandoned me.
I beat my brow. But
There was nothing more I could do.

Translated from the Spanish by W. S. Merwin

A Man

A man's mother is very sick
He goes out to find a doctor
He's crying
In the street he sees his wife in the company of another man
They're holding hands
He follows a few steps behind them
From tree to tree
He's crying
Now he meets a friend from his youth
It's years since we've seen each other!
They go on to a bar
They talk, laugh
The man goes out to the patio for a piss
He sees a young girl
It's night

She's washing dishes
The man goes over to her
He takes her by the waist
They waltz
They go out into the street together
They laugh
There's an accident
The girl's lost consciousness
The man goes to telephone
He's crying
He comes to a house with lights on
He asks for a telephone
Somebody knows him
Hey stay and have something to eat
No
Where's the telephone
Have something to eat, hey eat something
Then go
He sits down to eat
He drinks like a condemned man
He laughs
They get him to recite something
He recites it
He ends up sleeping under a desk

Translated from the Spanish by W. S. Merwin

I Take Back Everything I've Said

Before I go
I'm supposed to get a last wish:
Generous reader
              burn this book
It's not at all what I wanted to say
Though it was written in blood
It's not what I wanted to say.

No lot could be sadder than mine
I was defeated by my own shadow:
My words took vengeance on me.

Forgive me, reader, good reader
If I cannot leave you
With a warm embrace, I leave you
With a forced and sad smile.

Maybe that's all I am
But listen to my last word:
I take back everything I've said.
With the greatest bitterness in the world
I take back everything I've said.

Translated from the Spanish by Miller Williams

FAIZ AHMED FAIZ
(PAKISTAN, 1914–1984)

You Tell Us What to Do

When we launched life
on the river of grief,
how vital were our arms, how ruby our blood.
With a few strokes, it seemed,
we would cross all pain,
we would soon disembark.
That didn't happen.
In the stillness of each wave we found invisible currents.
The boatmen, too, were unskilled,
their oars untested.
Investigate the matter as you will,
blame whomever, as much as you want,
but the river hasn't changed,
the raft is still the same.

Now *you* suggest what's to be done,
you tell us how to come ashore.

When we saw the wounds of our country
appear on our skins,
we believed each word of the healers.
Besides, we remembered so many cures,
it seemed at any moment
all troubles would end, each wound heal completely.
That didn't happen: our ailments
were so many, so deep within us
that all diagnoses proved false, each remedy useless.
Now do whatever, follow each clue,
accuse whomever, as much as you will,
our bodies are still the same,
our wounds still open.
Now tell us what we should do,
you tell us how to heal these wounds.

Translated from the Arabic by Agha Shahid Ali

Before You Came

Before you came,
things were as they should be:
the sky was the dead-end of sight,
the road was just a road, wine merely wine.

Now everything is like my heart,
a color at the edge of blood:
the grey of your absence, the color of poison, of thorns,
the gold when we meet, the season ablaze,
the yellow of autumn, the red of flowers, of flames,
and the black when you cover the earth
with the coal of dead fires.

And the sky, the road, the glass of wine?
The sky is a shirt wet with tears,

the road a vein about to break,
and the glass of wine a mirror in which
the sky, the road, the world keep changing.

Don't leave now that you're here—
Stay. So the world may become like itself again: so the sky
    may be the sky,
the road a road,
and the glass of wine not a mirror, just a glass of wine.

Translated from the Arabic by Naomi Lazard

KARL KROLOW
(GERMANY, 1915–1999)

Quite a Lot of Luck

It takes quite a lot of luck
For a body to start floating
On the air
With breast, shoulder and knee
And on this air
To meet another body
Travelling like itself.

The atmosphere turns them
Into two intimate torsos.
Unnoticed their delight
Describes gentle lines in the treetops.
For quite a while
They can still be heard whispering
And giving each other
That which is light in them.

ays begins
he earth.

been able to watch it.

Translated from the German by Michael Bullock

Unforeseen Events

Always something unexpected happens.
He who takes off one shirt
Has to take off three more
And a walk between two elms
Ends in the jungle.
He who looks at a woman
Is lost
For the moment comes
When she calls his glances
To account.
Even metaphysics
Begin by inconspicuously
Exciting hearts.

Astonishment paves the way
For the incomprehensible.
Unforeseen events
Redeem the minutes
Before death.
Even a hempen rope
Permits various decisions.

Translated from the German by Michael Bullock

SŎ CHŎNGJU
(KOREA, 1915–2000)

Self-portrait

Father was a serf, seldom came home at night.
At home my grandmother, old as

The shriveled root of leek,
And a blossoming date tree.
Big with child, Mother wanted just one apricot.

I was a mother's son with dirty fingernails
Under a lamp by the mud wall.
With bushy hair and staring eyes,
I am said to resemble Grandpa on Mother's side,
Who in 1894 went to sea and never returned.

For twenty-three years the wind has reared two-thirds of me,
And the world has become a more embarrassing place.
Some have read a convict in my eyes,
Others an idiot in my mouth.
Yet I will repent nothing.

At each dawn, brightly assailing,
The dews of poetry settled on my brow,
Mixed with drops of blood.
And I have come this far panting
Like a sick dog with his tongue hanging out
In the sun and in the shade.

Translated from the Korean by Peter H. Lee

Elephants of Thailand

The elephants of Thailand perform their bows extremely well.
To their mothers and fathers, of course;
and also to their offspring they bow
very well indeed.
            Familiar living creatures,
of course; and to living creatures
not so familiar, they perform their deep bows.
To anything that can be seen
as well as what might very well
never be seen they perform
their deep formal bows without fail.

They enjoy in the gap
between time and distance
their relatively uneventful independence.

Translated from the Korean by David R. McCann

CAMILO JOSÉ CELA
(SPAIN, 1916–2002)

from *Mrs. Caldwell Speaks to Her Son*

Chapter 112: The Clock Which Runs the City

The clock which runs the city, my son, has stopped, perhaps of old age, but the city has continued running with an imperceptible and perhaps healthful disorder.

The clock which runs the city from its high tower, my son, refused to go beyond seven thirty, the hour which lovers await to cover their faces with a disguise and lift a cold waxen hand to their hearts.

The clock which runs the city from the high tower which overlooks the rooftops, Eliacim, has died, as the birds, sailboats, clandestine sweethearts, lone wolves, the hermits of Onan, the glass in mirrors, die, with infinite discretion.

(Over the embalmed cadaver of our clock, Eliacim, of the clock which no longer runs the city, the dauntless sparrows, the daring witches of the city, refuse to fly. Perhaps it is a sad omen, my son, an omen even sadder than reality, the silent death of our clock.)

When I heard the news, my son, I thought I would become much sadder than, in fact, I later became.

I was fond of it, Eliacim, I should not tell you I wasn't, our old tree, the oldest tree in the city; but my heart, apparently, is hardening with the passage of time, becoming stiff with the swift course of pain.

I only gave the death of the oldest tree in the city, Eliacim, one day of tears, not counting mealtimes and the short time I did some shopping.

Its wood, which I bought from the city, will burn in my fireplace. What a pleasure, Eliacim, what a great pleasure!

Chapter 165: Street Musicians

With their accordion and violin, my son, the street musicians play in the doorways of taverns, in honor of the well-intentioned drinkers.

With their cornet and violin, my son, the street musicians play in the doorways of churches, in praise of the newlyweds who don't know how they will be able to live.

If it didn't cause gossiping, Eliacim, I would put all the street musicians I found playing polkas and marches in the doorways of taverns and churches in my house. Our house is large, my dear, as you know, and I think your mother and her street musicians would fit into it, her warm and aromatic street musicians, those who cover their heads with a cap with an oilcloth brim and those who have a lyre tattooed over their hearts. Street musicians, Eliacim, are usually heroes of the tiny tragedies which cast water over the life of men, perhaps so that the lowest spectators may be amused seeing how some men struggle against drowning.

But street musicians, Eliacim, who prefer to keep drowning little by little, like old whales, take no part in the fight they renounced in order to play music, from morning to night, while they wander slowly through the city, appearing at taverns and churches, in search of the kindly drinker and the poor groom who, almost by a miracle, can still give them enough for a meal.

On the cold days of winter, Eliacim, I think and think about the street musicians, the men who play sick violins, sick accordions, sick cornets and flutes, my son, and I feel a great remorse of conscience which I cannot avoid.

Yes, Eliacim; if it didn't cause gossip, I would fill our house with street musicians who, on April 17th, your birthday, would toast each other cheerfully and smilingly, and play, at the door of your empty room, the pieces which could please you most.

It would be a very happy day, Eliacim, an immensely happy day for everybody, but I don't have the courage, my son, I don't have, still! the necessary courage.

Translated from the Spanish by J. S. Bernstein

BERNARD DADIÉ
(CÔTE D'IVOIRE, 1916–)

I Thank You God

I thank you God for creating me Black,
For making of me
Porter of all sorrows,
Setting on my head
The World.
I wear the Centaur's hide
And I have carried the World since the first morning.

White is a colour for special occasions
Black the colour for every day
And I have carried the World since the first evening.

I am glad
Of the shape of my head
Made to carry the World,
Content

With the shape of my nose
That must snuff every wind of the World
Pleased
With the shape of my legs
Ready to run all the heats of the World.
I thank you God for creating me black
For making of me
Porter of all sorrows.

Thirty-six swords have pierced my heart.
Thirty-six fires have burnt my body.
And my blood on all calvaries has reddened the snow,
And my blood at every dawn has reddened all nature.

Still I am
Glad to carry the World,
Glad of my short arms
      of my long arms
           of the thickness of my lips.

I thank you God for creating me black.
White is a colour for special occasions
Black the colour for every day
And I have carried the World since the dawn of time. . . .
And My laugh over the World, through the night, creates the Day.

I thank you God for creating me black.

Translated from the French by John O. Reed and Clive Wake

GLORIA FUERTES
(SPAIN, 1917–1998)

Birds Nest

Birds nest in my arms,
on my shoulders, behind my knees,

between my breasts there are quail,
they must think I'm a tree.
The swans think I'm a fountain,
they all come down and drink when I talk.
When sheep pass, they pass over me,
and perched on my fingers, the sparrows eat,
the ants think I'm earth,
and the men think I'm nothing.

Translated from the Spanish by Philip Levine

Prayer

Our Father who is on earth,
whom I feel in the pine needle's prick,
in the blue shirt of the worker,
in the child bent over her embroidery,
winding the thread around a finger.
Our Father who is on earth,
in the furrow,
in the orchard,
in the mine,
in the harbor,
in the cinema,
in the wine,
in the doctor's office.
Our Father who is on earth,
where you reign over your glory and your hell,
and your limbo in the cafés
where the rich gather to drink.
Our Father who is in the public school,
and in the vegetable peddler
and in those that go hungry,
and in the poet, but never in the thief.
Our Father who is on earth,
an old man reading on a park bench in the Prado
or tossing bread to pigeons.

Our Father who is on earth,
in the cigarette, in the kiss,
in the ear of corn, in the chests
of all those who are decent.
Father who lives anywhere.
God who penetrates all emptiness,
you who end pain, who is on earth.
Our Father whom now we see,
and those who will see you soon here or in heaven.

Translated from the Spanish by Brian Barker

Now

Now I will tell you
how the worms
I kept in an empty soap carton
and fed white mulberry leaves,
changed themselves without my help,
curling into scoops of color,
and how later I watched them
transform into butterflies,
and all this just because it was May
and because insects possess a bit of magic.

Then I'll tell you
how Eloisa Muro,
fourth mistress of Cervantes,
was the author of *Don Quixote*.

For though I'm small, I know many things,
and my body is an endless eye
through which, unfortunately, I see everything.

Translated from the Spanish by Brian Barker

I Write Poetry, Gentlemen!

I write poetry, gentlemen, I write poetry,
but please don't call me poetess;
I swig my wine like the bricklayers do
and I have an assistant who talks to herself.
This world's a strange place;
things happen, gentlemen, that I don't disclose;
they build cases, for example, yet never build homes
for the poor who can't afford them.

And old maids are always having it out with their dogs,
married men with their mistresses,
yet no one says anything to the brutal tyrants.
And we read about the deaths and flip the pages,
and the people hate us and we say: that's life,
and they step on our necks and we don't get up.
All this happens, gentlemen, and I must say it.

Translated from the Spanish by Brian Barker

Autobiography

At the foot of the Cathedral of Burgos
my mother was born.
At the foot of the Cathedral of Madrid
my father was born.
At the foot of my mother I was born
one afternoon in the middle of Spain.
My father was a worker,
my mother was a seamstress.
I wanted to take off with the circus
but I'm only what I am.
When I was little
I went to a reformatory and a free school.
As a kid I was sickly
and summered in a sanatorium,
but now I get around.

I've had at least seven love affairs,
some bad daddies,
and a marvelous appetite.
Now I've got two minor convictions
and a kiss from time to time.

Translated from the Spanish by Philip Levine and Ada Long

ZELDA
(UKRAINE/ISRAEL, 1914–1984)

A Woman Who's Arrived at a Ripe Old Age

A woman who's arrived at a ripe old age
Has no memories of the madness of fire
Or of summer juices.
As her gossamer flesh melts into air
It shines in the dark like an ancient parable
Arousing disgust in earthy men
And in green leaves of a mulberry tree.

Translated from the Hebrew by Miriyam Glazer

JOHANNES BOBROWSKI
(GERMANY, 1917–1965)

Latvian Songs

My father the hawk.
Grandfather the wolf.
And my forefather the rapacious fish in the sea.

I, unbearded, a fool,
lurching against the fences,
my black hands strangling a lamb
in the early light. I,

who beat the animals
instead of the white
master, I follow the rattling caravans
on washed-out roads,

I pass through the glances
of the Gypsy women. Then
on the Baltic shore I meet Uexküll, the master.
He walks beneath the moon.

Behind him, the darkness speaks.

Translated from the German by Ruth Mead and Matthew Mead

PRIMO LEVI
(ITALY, 1919–1987)

August

Who stays in the city in August?
Only the poor and the mad,
Forgotten little old ladies,
Pensioners with their little dogs,
Thieves, some gentlemen and the cats.
Through the deserted streets
You hear a continual tapping of heels,
See women with plastic bags
In the streak of shade along the walls.
Under the fountain with its small tower
In the pool green with algae
There's a middle-aged naiad
About four inches long
With nothing on but a brassiere.
A few yards farther on,
Despite the well-known prohibition,
The begging pigeons
Surround you in a flock

And steal the bread out of your hand.
Rustling in the sky, in weary flight,
You hear the noontime demon.

Translated from the Italian by Ruth Feldman and Brian Swann

ANNA KAMIENSKA
(POLAND, 1920–1986)

Thanking

How to leave without thanking
animals and particularly the cat
for his being so separate
and for teaching us with his whole body the wisdom of concentration

Thank you walls
the great invisible photographs of my life thank you air
for the patient imprints of my loneliness

Thank you narrow table
untiring secretary
how many tears have I written into you
I've already changed into one of your lame legs

And you I thank for knowledge
breakable cup
it's you have always taught me departure
there are things more precious than ourselves

Just as before a wedding I'll have no time to thank you
all the corners and radiators
I thank every spoon
God bless you since who else is to bless you

And now all go away along with the crowd of holy statues
I'm fed up with you and fed up with thanking

The still night is looking at us with a chasm-like eye
what are we in that dark iris

Translated from the Polish by Tomasz P. Krzeszowski and
Desmond Graham

A Prayer That Will Be Answered

Lord let me suffer much
and then die

Let me walk through silence
and leave nothing behind not even fear

Make the world continue
let the ocean kiss the sand just as before

Let the grass stay green
so that the frogs can hide in it

so that someone can bury his face in it
and sob out his love

Make the day rise brightly
as if there were no more pain

And let my poem stand clear as a windowpane
bumped by a bumblebee's head

Translated from the Polish by Tomasz P. Krzeszowski and
Desmond Graham

PAUL CELAN

(GERMANY/ROMANIA, 1920–1970)

Memory of France

Together with me recall: the sky of Paris, that giant autumn crocus . . .
We went shopping for hearts at the flower girl's booth:
they were blue and they opened up in the water.
It began to rain in our room,
and our neighbour came in, Monsieur Le Songe, a lean little man.
We played cards, I lost the irises of my eyes;
you lent me your hair, I lost it, he struck us down.
He left by the door, the rain followed him out.
We were dead and were able to breathe.

Translated from the German by Michael Hamburger

Corona

Autumn eats its leaf out of my hand: we are friends.
From the nuts we shell time and we teach it to walk:
then time returns to the shell.

In the mirror it's Sunday,
in dream there is room for sleeping,
our mouths speak the truth.

My eye moves down to the sex of my loved one:
we look at each other,
we exchange dark words,
we love each other like poppy and recollection,
we sleep like wine in the conches,
like the sea in the moon's blood ray.

We stand by the window embracing, and people look up from the street:
it is time they knew!
It is time the stone made an effort to flower,

time unrest had a beating heart.
It is time it were time.

It is time

Translated from the German by Michael Hamburger

Deathfugue

Black milk of daybreak we drink it at evening
we drink it at midday and morning we drink it at night
we drink and we drink
we shovel a grave in the air there you won't lie too cramped
A man lives in the house he plays with his vipers he writes
he writes when it grows dark to Deutschland your golden hair Margareta
he writes it and steps out of doors and the stars are all sparkling, he
    whistles his hounds to come close
he whistles his Jews into rows has them shovel a grave in the ground
he commands us to play up for the dance.

Black milk of daybreak we drink you at night
we drink you at morning and midday we drink you at evening
we drink and we drink
A man lives in the house he plays with his vipers he writes
he writes when it grows dark to Deutschland your golden hair Margareta
Your ashen hair Shulamith we shovel a grave in the air there you won't
    lie too cramped

He shouts jab the earth deeper you lot there you others sing up and play
he grabs for the rod in his belt he swings it his eyes are so blue
jab your spades deeper you lot there you others play on for the dancing

Black milk of daybreak we drink you at night
we drink you at midday and morning we drink you at evening
we drink and we drink
a man lives in the house your goldenes Haar Margareta
your aschenes Haar Shulamith he plays his vipers

He shouts play death more sweetly this Death is a master from
    Deutschland
he shouts scrape your strings darker you'll rise then as smoke to the sky
you'll have a grave then in the clouds there you won't lie too cramped

Black milk of daybreak we drink you at night
we drink you at midday Death is a master aus Deutschland
we drink you at evening and morning we drink and we drink
this Death is ein Meister aus Deutschland his eye it is blue
he shoots you with shot made of lead shoots you level and true
a man lives in the house your goldenes Haar Margareta
he looses his hounds on us grants us a grave in the air
he plays with his vipers and daydreams der Tod ist ein Meister aus
    Deutschland

dein goldenes Haar Margareta
dein aschenes Haar Shulamith

Translated from the German by John Felstiner

Zurich, the Stork Inn

For Nelly Sachs

Of too much was our talk, of
too little. Of the You
and You-Again, of
how clarity troubles, of
Jewishness, of
your God.

Of
that.
On the day of an ascension, the
Minster stood over there, it sent
some gold across the water.

Of your God was our talk, I spoke
against him, I
let the heart that I had
hope:
for
his highest, death-rattled, his
quarrelling word—

Your eye looked on, looked away,
your mouth
spoke its way to the eye, and I heard:

We
don't know, you know,
we
don't know, do we?,
what
counts.

Translated from the German by Michael Hamburger

There was earth inside them

There was earth inside them, and
they dug.

They dug and they dug, so their day
went by for them, their night. And they did not praise God,
who, so they heard, wanted all this,
who, so they heard, knew all this.

They dug and heard nothing more;
they did not grow wise, invented no song,
thought up for themselves no language.
They dug.

There came a stillness, and there came a storm,
and all of the oceans came.

I dig, you dig, and the worm digs too,
and that singing out there says: They dig.

O one, o none, o no one, o you:
Where did the way lead when it led nowhere?
O you dig and I dig, and I dig towards you,
and on our finger the ring awakes.

Translated from the German by Michael Hamburger

I hear that the axe has flowered

I hear that the axe has flowered,
I hear that the place can't be named,

I hear that the bread which looks at him
heals the hanged man,
the bread baked for him by his wife,

I hear that they call life
our only refuge.

Translated from the German by Michael Hamburger

Psalm

No one moulds us again out of earth and clay,
no one conjures our dust.
No one.

Praised be your name, No one.
For your sake
we shall flower.
Towards
you.

A nothing
we were, are, shall

remain, flowering:
the nothing-, the
No one's rose.

With
our pistil soul-bright,
with our stamen heaven-ravaged,
our corolla red
with the crimson word which we sang
over, O over
the thorn.

Translated from the German by Michael Hamburger

Tenebrae

We are near, Lord,
near and at hand.

Handled already, Lord,
clawed and clawing as though
the body of each of us were
your body, Lord.

Pray, Lord,
pray to us,
we are near.

Askew we went there,
went there to bend
down to the trough, to the crater.

To be watered we went there, Lord.

It was blood, it was
what you shed, Lord.

It gleamed.

It cast your image into our eyes, Lord.
Our eyes and our mouths are so open and empty, Lord.
We have drunk, Lord.
The blood and the image that was in the blood, Lord.

Pray, Lord.
We are near.

Translated from the German by Michael Hamburger

JOÃO CABRAL DE MELO NETO
(BRAZIL, 1920–1999)

The Emptiness of Man

1

The emptiness of man is not like
any other: not like an empty coat
or empty sack (things which do not stand up
when empty, such as an empty man),
the emptiness of man is more like fullness
in swollen things which keep on swelling,
the way a sack must feel
that is being filled, or any sack at all.
The emptiness of man, this full emptiness,
is not like a sack of bricks' emptiness
or a sack of rivets', it does not have the pulse
that beats in a seed bag or bag of eggs.

2

The emptiness of man, though it resembles
fullness, and seems all of a piece, actually
is made of nothings, bits of emptiness,
like the sponge, empty when filled,

swollen like the sponge, with air, with empty air;
it has copied its very structure from the sponge,
it is made up in clusters, of bubbles, of non-grapes.
Man's empty fullness is like a sack
filled with sponges, is filled with emptiness;
man's emptiness, or swollen emptiness,
or the emptiness that swells by being empty.

Translated from the Portuguese by Galway Kinnell

TADEUSZ RÓŻEWICZ
(POLAND, 1921–)

Who Is a Poet

a poet is one who writes verses
and one who does not write verses

a poet is one who throws off fetters
and one who puts fetters on himself

a poet is one who believes
and one who cannot bring himself to believe

a poet is one who has told lies
and one who has been told lies

one who has been inclined to fall
and one who raises himself

a poet is one who tries to leave
and one who cannot leave

Translated from the Polish by Magnus Jan Krynski and
Robert A. Maguire

A Sketch for a Modern Love Poem

and yet whiteness
can be best described by greyness
a bird by a stone
sunflowers
in december

love poems of old
used to be descriptions of flesh
they described this and that
for instance eyelashes
and yet redness
should be described
by greyness the sun by rain
the poppies in november
the lips at night

the most palpable
description of bread
is that of hunger
there is in it
a humid porous core
a warm inside
sunflowers at night
the breasts the belly the thighs of Cybele

a transparent
source-like description
of water
is that of thirst
of ash
of desert
it provokes a mirage
clouds and trees enter
a mirror of water
lack hunger
absence

of flesh
is a description of love
in a modern love poem

Translated from the Polish by Czesław Miłosz

TYMOTEUSZ KARPOWICZ
(POLAND, 1921–2005)

A Lesson of Silence

Whenever a butterfly
happened to fold
too violently its wings—
there was a call: silence, please!

As soon as one feather
of a startled bird
jostled against a ray—
there was a call: silence, please!

In that way were taught
how to walk without noise
the elephant on his drum,
man on his earth.

The trees were rising
mute above the fields
as rises the hair
of the horror-stricken.

Translated from the Polish by Czesław Miłosz

Ecclesiastes

there is a time for opening the eyes and closing the bed
time for donning a shirt and shedding sleep

time for drowsy soap and half-awakened skin
time for the hair-brush and for sparks in the hair
time for trouser-legs time for shoe-laces time for buttons
for laddered stockings for the slipper's blindness
time for the fork and for the knife time for sausages and boiled eggs
time for the tram time for the conductress time for the policeman
time for good morning and time for goodbye
time for carrots peas and parsley
for tomato soup and shepherd's pie
time for trussing chicken and releasing forbidden speeds of thought
time for a cinema ticket or a ticket to nowhere
to a river perhaps perhaps to a cloud
there is finally a time of closed eyelids and the open bed
time for past present and future
praesens historicum and plusquamperfectum
time perfect and imperfect
time from wall to wall

Translated from the Polish by Adam Czerniawski

H. C. ARTMANN
(AUSTRIA, 1921–2000)

An Optician Has a Glass Heart

an optician has a glass heart with plexiglass hinges
he has a glass heart through which he wants no one to see
he has his heart in his brain, like others have hearts in their breasts
dark sparrows fly about the cosmopolitan shop of the optician
they are wearing red wigs and counterfeit billets-doux
they all have unlucky larvae tied before their beaks and come from a
    street of silk umbrellas
a danish wind whistles over skagerak and kattegat
a danish wind of milk and blood whistles over the umbrellas in all the streets
but now the dark sparrows whistle their message before the optician's
    heart of glass
the cosmopolitan optician's wife is still reclined on the sofa

her handsome lover is about to vanish on creamy white angel wings
in the garden behind the optician's home large poppies nod in the
    blue summer breeze
the vanishing lover nears the first bank of clouds
one can scarcely still see him with the naked eye
he has stitched his young days away behind his clean starched collar
his left wing beats the air more assuredly than his right
he has put several days behind him
one can barely discern him
he has vanished
the cosmopolitan optician whistles with the sparrows against the
    tedium of his work
his profits have always been small
patience has never brought him a cent
his heart of glass suffered an obvious crack that morning
patience has brought him no profit
even the stamped size of his shoes has grown noticeably smaller
his brain now registers nothing but the dark sparrows' false message
he accepts it as true
he lays his metals aside
he removes the magnifying glasses from the top shelf
he stamps with both feet on the various lenses
he hurls glasses for the farsighted into the jets of airplanes
he hurls glasses for the nearsighted into the oval eyes of electric
    locomotives
he nervously attempts to unscrew the complicated plexiglass hinges to
    his heart of glass
he mourns as well as he is able the obvious failure of this endeavour
that optician, whistle the sparrows, has a glass heart through which
    he wants no one to see
the optician establishes the anarchy of artificial eyes in his workroom
he dispatches miniature cannons to his worktable
he commands in a semi-loud voice with a glance at his pocket
    watch—fire!
he repeats to himself the sparrows' false message
he bolts up his heart against outside influences
he finally mounts his telescopic sight against the new machinery of
the huge evening sun

the sun for its part brings the more valuable screws and metal parts
    into safety
through the poppy gardens behind the optician's small home three
    peacocks swim in the whispering summer wind
the handsome lover of the optician's wife floats back again to the
    scene of his latest transgression
he has already emerged from the deepest cloud banks
the great poppy blossoms of the garden sway romantically in the blue
    summer wind
the cosmopolitan optician's wife is still reclined on the sofa

Translated from the German by Rosmarie Waldrop and
Harriett Watts

ERICH FRIED
(AUSTRIA, 1921–1988)

French Soldiers Mutiny—1917

For years the troops have gone
like lambs to the slaughter

but these are bleating
They are marching through the town

They are marching
and they are bleating like sheep

By bleating they cease to be
a herd of sheep

Author's note: Mutinying French soldiers actually did bleat as a protest.

Translated from the German by Stuart Hood

BLAGA DIMITROVA
(BULGARIA, 1922–)

Ars Poetica

Write each of your poems
as if it were your last.
In this century, saturated with strontium,
charged with terrorism,
flying with supersonic speed,
death comes with terrifying suddenness.
Send each of your words
like a last letter before execution,
a call carved on a prison wall.
You have no right to lie,
no right to play pretty little games.
You simply don't have the time
to correct your mistakes.
Write each of your poems,
tersely, mercilessly,
with blood—as if it were your last.

Translated from the Bulgarian by Ludmilla G. Popova-Wightman

VASKO POPA
(SERBIA, 1922–1991)

St. Sava's Journey

He journeys over the dark land

With his staff he cuts
The dark beyond him into four

He flings thick gloves
Changed into immense cats
At the grey army of mice

Amid the storm he releases his chains
And lashes the ancient oaken land
To the fixed stars

He lashes his wolves' paws
That no trace of the dark land
Should remain on them

He journeys without a path
And the path is born behind him

Translated from the Serbian by Anne Pennington

Prayer to the Wolf Shepherd

1

We pray to you wolf shepherd
Put us round your neck
So we needn't ride day and night
On ourselves

Feed us from your hand
So we needn't eat raw earth
And drink our own blood

Make a little room for us on your shoulders
So we needn't sleep far from ourselves
In the echoes of our howling

Find the newborn red stone
Fled from our breasts
So we needn't chase it to the world's end

We pray to you wolf shepherd

2

Beat us to death or accept us
As we are tattered maimed
And headless

We pray to you wolf shepherd

Clothe us in the hides
Stretched over the beaters' drums

Arm us with the paws
Made into handles
Of hunters' knives

Plant in our jaws the teeth
Strung in necklaces
Of bedworthy bitches

Translated from the Serbian by Anne Pennington

Wolf Ancestry

Under the lime trees in Sand
My great-grandfather Iliya Luka Morun
Found two wolflings

He put them between his donkey's ears
And brought them to the fold

He fed them on sheep's milk
And taught them to play
With the lambs of their own age

When they were strong he took them back
To the same place under the lime trees
Kissed them and signed them with the cross

Ever since childhood I've been waiting
For my years to equal
Great-grandfather's

To ask him
Which of those wolflings
Was me

Translated from the Serbian by Anne Pennington

Wolf Eyes

Before my christening they gave me
The name of one of the brothers
That the she-wolf suckled

All her life grandma will call me
In her flaxen Vlach tongue
Wolfling

Secretly she used to give me
Raw meat to eat
So I'd grow to be head-wolf

I believed
My eyes would begin to shine
In the dark

My eyes don't shine yet
Probably because the real dark
Hasn't yet begun to fall

Translated from the Serbian by Anne Pennington

Absolute Goal

Two Red Army men are carrying
Their dead comrade past our house

A little while ago my mother was feeding
All three with apple tart
And Vershats wine

My father advised the dead man
They should go over the roofs
And come out behind the nest of machine guns

The dead man laughed hugged my father
And together with the other two
Chose a shortcut

I watch the Red Army men

They put their comrade in a cart
With the crooked painted letters
T o   B e r l i n

Translated from the Serbian by Anne Pennington

The Tenants of the Little Box

Throw into the little box
A stone
You'll take out a bird

Throw in your shadow
You'll take out the shirt of happiness

Throw in your father's root
You'll take out the axle of the universe

The little box works for you

Throw into the little box
A mouse
You'll take out a quaking hill

Throw in your head
You'll take out two

The little box works for you

Translated from the Serbian by Charles Simic

The Craftsmen of the Little Box

Don't open the little box
Heaven's hat will fall out of her

Don't close her for any reason
She'll bite the trouser-leg of eternity

Don't drop her on the earth
The sun's eggs will break inside her

Don't throw her in the air
Earth's bones will break inside her

Don't hold her in your hands
The dough of the stars will go sour inside her

What are you doing for God's sake
Don't let her get out of your sight

Translated from the Serbian by Charles Simic

Last News About the Little Box

The little box which contains the world
Fell in love with herself
And conceived
Still another little box

The little box of the little box
Also fell in love with herself

And conceived
Still another little box

And so it went on forever

The world from the little box
Ought to be inside
The last offspring of the little box

But not one of the little boxes
Inside the little box in love with herself
Is the last one

Let's see you find the world now

Translated from the Serbian by Charles Simic

MIRON BIAŁOSZEWSKI
(POLAND, 1922–1983)

A Ballad of Going Down to the Store

First I went down to the street
by means of the stairs,
just imagine it,
by means of the stairs.

Then people known to people unknown
passed me by and I passed them by.
Regret
that you did not see
how people walk,
regret!

I entered a complete store:
lamps of glass were glowing.
I saw somebody—he sat down—

and what did I hear? what did I hear?
rustling of bags and human talk.

And indeed,
indeed,
I returned.

Translated from the Polish by Czesław Miłosz

PIER PAOLO PASOLINI
(ITALY, 1922–1975)

Prayer to My Mother

It's so hard to say in a son's words
what I'm so little like in my heart.

Only you in all the world know what my
heart always held, before any other love.

So, I must tell you something terrible to know:
From within your kindness my anguish grew.

You're irreplaceable. And because you are,
the life you gave me is condemned to loneliness.

And I don't want to be alone. I have an infinite
hunger for love, love of bodies without souls.

For the soul is inside you, it is you, but
you're my mother and your love's my slavery:

My childhood I lived a slave to this lofty
incurable sense of an immense obligation.

It was the only way to feel life,
the unique form, sole color; now, it's over.

We survive, in the confusion
of a life reborn outside reason.

I pray you, oh, I pray: Do not hope to die.
I'm here, alone, with you, in a future April . . .

Translated from the Italian by Norman MacAfee and
Luciano Martinengo

CHAIRIL ANWAR
(INDONESIA, 1922–1949)

Heaven

Like my mother, and my grandmother too,
plus seven generations before them,
I also seek admission to Heaven
which the Moslem party and the Mohammedan
Union say has rivers of milk
And thousands of houris all over.

But there's a contemplative voice inside me,
stubbornly mocking: Do you really think
the blue sea will go dry
—and what about the sly temptations
waiting in every port?
Anyway, who can say for sure
that there really are houris there
with voices as rich and husky as Nina's,
with eyes that flirt like Yati's?

Translated from the Indonesian by Burton Raffel

Tuti's Ice Cream

Between present and future happiness the abyss gapes,
My girl is licking happily at her ice cream;

This afternoon you're my love, I adorn you with cake and Coca-Cola.
Oh wife-in-training, we've stopped the clocks ticking.

You kissed skillfully, the scratches still hurt
—when we cycled I took you home—
Your blood was hot, oh you were a woman soon,
And the old man's dreams leaped at the moon.

Every day's whim invited you on, every day's whim was different.
Tomorrow we'll fight and turn our backs on each other:
Heaven is this minute's game.

I'm like you, everything ran by,
Me and Tuti and Hreyt and Amoy . . . dilapidated hearts.
Love's a danger that quickly fades.

Translated from the Indonesian by Burton Raffel

AUGUSTINHO NETO
(ANGOLA, 1922–1979)

Kinaxixi

I was glad to sit down
on a bench in Kinaxixi
at six o'clock of a hot evening
and just sit there . . .

Someone would come maybe to sit beside me

And I would see the black faces
of the people going uptown
in no hurry
expressing absence in the
jumbled Kimbundu they conversed in.

I would see the tired footsteps
of the servants whose fathers also were servants
looking for love here, glory there, wanting
something more than drunkenness in every
alcohol.

Neither happiness nor hate.

After the sun had set
lights would be turned on and I
would wander off
thinking that our life after all is simple
too simple
for anyone who is tired and still has to walk.

Translated from the Portuguese by W. S. Merwin

WISŁAWA SZYMBORSKA
(POLAND, 1923–)

I Am Too Near

I am too near to be dreamt of by him.
I do not fly over him, do not escape from him
under the roots of a tree. I am too near.
Not in my voice sings the fish in the net,
not from my finger rolls the ring.
I am too near. A big house is on fire
without me, calling for help. Too near
for a bell dangling from my hair to chime.
Too near to enter as a guest
before whom walls glide apart by themselves.
Never again will I die so lightly,
so much beyond my flesh, so inadvertently
as once in his dream. Too near.
I taste the sound, I see the glittering husk of this word
as I lie immobile in his embrace. He sleeps,

more accessible now to her, seen but once,
a cashier of a wandering circus with one lion,
than to me, who am at his side.
For her now in him a valley grows,
rusty-leaved, closed by a snowy mountain
in the dark blue air. I am too near
to fall to him from the sky. My scream
could wake him up. Poor thing
I am, limited to my shape,
I who was a birch, who was a lizard,
who would come out of my cocoons
shimmering the colours of my skins. Who possessed
the grace of disappearing from astonished eyes,
which is a wealth of wealths. I am near,
too near for him to dream of me.
I slide my arm from under the sleeper's head
and it is numb, full of swarming pins,
on the tip of each, waiting to be counted,
the fallen angels sit.

Translated from the Polish by Czesław Miłosz

Letters of the Dead

We read letters of the dead and are like helpless gods,
yet gods after all, for we know what happened after.
We know what money has never been returned.
How quickly widows married and whom they married.
The poor dead, the infatuated dead,
deceived, erring, clumsily circumspect.
We see grimaces and signs made behind their backs.
Our ears catch the rustling of last wills torn to pieces.
They sit before us, comic, as if on open sandwiches
or rush forward chasing their hats snatched by the wind.
Their bad taste, Napoleon, steam and electricity,
their lethal cures for curable illnesses,
their foolish apocalypse according to Saint John
and a false paradise according to Jean-Jacques . . .

We observe in silence their pawns on a chessboard,
except that their pawns were moved three squares forward.
Everything they had foreseen happened in a completely different way,
or slightly different, which amounts to completely different.
The most zealous among them look with hope into our eyes
for by their calculations they should see in them perfection.

Translated from the Polish by Czesław Miłosz

A Great Number

Four billion people on this earth,
while my imagination remains as it was.
It clumsily copes with great numbers.
Still it is sensitive to the particular.
It flutters in the dark like a flashlight,
and reveals the first random faces
while all the rest stay unheeded,
unthought of, unlamented.
Yet even Dante could not retain all that.
And what of us?
Even all the Muses could not help.

Non omnis moriar—a premature worry.
Yet do I live entire and does it suffice?
It never sufficed, and especially now.
I choose by discarding, for there is no other means
but what I discard is more numerous,
more dense, more insistent than it ever was.
A little poem, a sigh, cost indescribable losses.
A thunderous call is answered by my whisper.
I cannot express how much I pass over in silence.
A mouse at the foot of a mountain in labor.
Life lasts a few marks of a claw on the sand.
My dreams—even they are not, as they ought to be, populous.

There is more of loneliness in them than of crowds and noise.
Sometimes a person who died long ago drops in for a moment.

A door handle moves touched by a single hand.
An empty house is overgrown with annexes of an echo.
I run from the threshold down into the valley
that is silent, as if nobody's, anachronic.

How that open space is in me still—
I don't know.

Translated from the Polish by Czesław Miłosz

The Joy of Writing

Where is a written deer running through a written forest?
Whether to drink from written water
which will reflect its mouth like a carbon?
Why is it raising its head, does it hear something?
Propped on four legs borrowed from the truth
it pricks up its ears from under my fingers.
Silence—that word, too, is rustling on paper
and parts the branches caused by the word "forest."

Over a white page letters are ready to jump
and they may take a bad turn.
Sentences capable of bringing to bay,
and against which there is no help.
In a drop of ink there are quite a few
hunters squinting one eye,
ready to rush down a vertical pen,
to encircle the deer, to take aim.

They forget that this is not life here.
Other laws rule here, in black and white.
An instant will last as long as I desire.
It will allow a division into small eternities
each full of buckshot stopped in its flight.
If I command, nothing here will happen ever.
Not even a leaf will fall without my accord,
or a blade of grass bend under a dot of a hoof.

And so there is such a world
on which I impose an autonomous Fate?
A time which I bind with fetters of signs?
A life that at my command is perpetual?

The joy of writing.
A chance to make things stay.
A revenge of a mortal hand.

Translated from the Polish by Czesław Miłosz

In Praise of My Sister

My sister doesn't write poems,
and I don't think she'll suddenly start writing poems.
She is like her mother, who didn't write poems,
and like her father, who didn't write poems either.
Under my sister's roof I feel safe:
my sister's husband would rather die than write poems.
And—this begins to sound like a found poem—
none of my relations is engaged in writing poems.

There are no old poems in my sister's files
and there aren't any new ones in her handbag.
And when my sister invites me to lunch,
I know she has no plans to read me her poems.
Her soups are excellently improvised,
there is no coffee spilt on her manuscripts.

There are many families where no one writes poems,
but where they do—it's rarely just one person.
Sometimes poetry splashes down in cascades of generations,
creating terrible whirlpools in mutual feelings.

My sister cultivates a quite good spoken prose
and her writing's restricted to holiday postcards,
the text promising the same each year:
that when she returns

she'll tell us
all
all
all about it.

Translated from the Polish by Adam Czerniawski

Pietà

In the small town where the hero was born:
seeing the monument, praising it for its size,
shooing two hens off the steps of the abandoned museums,
finding out where the mother lives,
knocking and pushing the creaking door open.
She holds herself erect, hair combed straight, eyes clear.
Saying I've come from Poland.
Exchanging pleasantries. Asking questions loud and clear.
Yes, she loved him very much. Yes, he was always like that.
Yes, she was standing by the prison wall then.
Yes, she heard the salvo.
Regretting not bringing a tape recorder
and movie camera. Yes, she knows what those things are.
On the radio she had read his last letter.
On the television she had sung old lullabies.
Once she had even acted in a film, staring into
the klieg lights till the tears came. Yes, she is moved by the Memory.
Yes, she's a little tired. Yes, it will pass.
Getting up. Expressing thanks. Saying goodbye. Going out,
walking past the next batch of tourists.

Translated from the Polish by Magnus Jan Krynski and
Robert A. Maguire

Under a Certain Little Star

I apologize to coincidence for calling it necessity.
I apologize to necessity just in case I'm mistaken.
Let happiness be not angry that I take it as my own.

Let the dead not remember they scarcely smolder in my memory.
I apologize to time for the muchness of the world overlooked per second.
I apologize to old love for regarding the new as the first.
Forgive me, far-off wars, for bringing flowers home.
Forgive me, open wounds, for pricking my finger.
I apologize to those who cry out of the depths for the minuet-record.
I apologize to people at railway stations or sleeping at five in
    the morning.
Pardon me, hounded hope, for laughing now and again.
Pardon me, deserts, for not rushing up with a spoonful of water.
And you, O falcon, the same these many years, in that same cage,
forever staring motionless at that selfsame spot,
absolve me, even though you are but a stuffed bird.
I apologize to the cut-down tree for the table's four legs.
I apologize to big questions for small answers.
O Truth, do not pay me too much heed.
O Solemnity, be magnanimous unto me.
Endure, mystery of existence, that I pluck out the threads of your train.
Accuse me not, O soul, of possessing you but seldom.
I apologize to everything that I cannot be everywhere.
I apologize to everyone that I cannot be every man and woman.
I know that as long as I live nothing can justify me,
because I myself am an obstacle to myself.
Take it not amiss, O speech, that I borrow weighty words,
and later try hard to make them seem light.

Translated from the Polish by Magnus Jan Krynski and Robert A. Maguire

Homecoming

He was back. Said nothing.
But it was clear something had upset him.
He lay down in his suit.
Hid his head under the blanket.
Drew up his knees.
He's about forty, but not at this moment.
He exists—but only as much as in his mother's belly
behind seven skins, in protective darkness.

Tomorrow he is lecturing on homeostasis
in metagalactic space travel.
But now he's curled up and fallen asleep.

Translated from the Polish by Adam Czerniawski

The Terrorist, He Watches

The bomb will explode in the bar at twenty past one.
Now it's only sixteen minutes past.
Some will still have time to enter,
some to leave.

The terrorist's already on the other side.
That distance protects him from all harm
and well it's like the pictures:

A woman in a yellow jacket, she enters.
A man in dark glasses, he leaves.
Boys in jeans, they're talking.
Sixteen minutes past and four seconds.
The smaller one he's lucky, mounts his scooter,
but that taller chap he walks in.

Seventeen minutes and forty seconds.
A girl, she walks by, a green ribbon in her hair.
But that bus suddenly hides her.
Eighteen minutes past.
The girl's disappeared.
Was she stupid enough to go in, or wasn't she.
We shall see when they bring out the bodies.

Nineteen minutes past.
No one else appears to be going in.
On the other hand, a fat bald man leaves.
But seems to search his pockets and
at ten seconds to twenty past one
he returns to look for his wretched gloves.

It's twenty past one.
Time, how it drags.
Surely, it's now.
No, not quite.
Yes, now.
The bomb, it explodes.

Translated from the Polish by Adam Czerniawski

Children of the Epoch

We are the children of the epoch.
The epoch is political.

All my daily and nightly affairs,
all your daily and nightly affairs,
are political affairs.

Whether you want it or not,
your genes have a political past,
your skin a political tone,
your eyes a political color,
What you say resounds,
what you don't say is also
politically significant.

Even coming through the rye,
you walk with political steps
on political ground.

Apolitical poems are also political,
and in the sky there's a moon
that's no longer moonlike.

To be or not to be, that is a question.
Oh darling, what a question, give a suggestion.
A political question.

You don't have to be human
to acquire a political meaning.
It's enough to be petroleum,
cattle fodder, raw material.
Or just a conference table whose shape
was disputed for months.

In the meantime, people were killed.
Animals died,
houses burned,
fields grew wild,
as in distant
and less political epochs.

Translated from the Polish by Austin Flint

Hunger Camp at Jaslo

Write it. Write. In ordinary ink
on ordinary paper: they were given no food,
they all died of hunger. "All. How many?
It's a big meadow. How much grass
for each one?" Write: I don't know.
History counts its skeletons in round numbers.
A thousand and one remains a thousand,
as though the one had never existed:
an imaginary embryo, an empty cradle,
an ABC never read,
air that laughs, cries, grows,
emptiness running down steps toward the garden,
nobody's place in the line.

We stand in the meadow where it became flesh,
and the meadow is silent as a false witness.
Sunny. Green. Nearby, a forest
with wood for chewing and water under the bark—
every day a full ration of the view
until you go blind. Overhead, a bird—

the shadow of its life-giving wings
brushed their lips. Their jaws opened.
Teeth clacked against teeth.
At night, the sickle moon shone in the sky
and reaped wheat for their bread.
Hands came floating from blackened icons,
empty cups in their fingers.
On a spit of barbed wire,
a man was turning.
They sang with their mouths full of earth.
"A lovely song of how war strikes straight
at the heart." Write: how silent.
"Yes."

Translated from the Polish by Grazyna Drabik and Austin Flint

YVES BONNEFOY

(FRANCE, 1923–)

The Tree, the Lamp

The tree grows old in the tree, it is summer.
The bird leaps beyond birdsong and is gone.
The red of the dress illuminates and scatters
Away, in the sky, the lading of old sorrow.

O fragile country,
Like the flame of a lamp carried out of doors,
Sleep being close in the world's sap,
Simple the beating of the shared soul.

You too love the moment when the light of the lamps
Fades and dreams into daylight.
You know it's the darkness of your own heart healing,
The boat that reaches shore and falls.

Translated from the French by Richard Pevear

MIROSLAV HOLUB
(CZECHOSLOVAKIA, 1923–1998)

The Fly

She sat on the willow bark
watching
part of the battle of Crécy,
the shrieks,
the moans,
the wails,
the trampling and tumbling.

During the fourteenth charge
of the French cavalry
she mated
with a brown-eyed male fly
from Vadincourt.

She rubbed her legs together
sitting on a disemboweled horse
meditating
on the immortality of flies.

Relieved she alighted
on the blue tongue
of the Duke of Clervaux.

When silence settled
and the whisper of decay
softly circled the bodies

and just
a few arms and legs
twitched under the trees,

she began to lay her eggs
on the single eye

of Johann Uhr,
the Royal Armorer.

And so it came to pass—
she was eaten by a swift
fleeing
from the fires of Estrés

Translated from the Czech by Stuart Friebert and Dana Hábová

Man cursing the sea

Someone
just climbed to the top of the cliff
and started cursing the sea:

Stupid water, stupid pregnant water,
slimy copy of the sky,
hesitant hoverer between the sun and the moon,
pettifogging reckoner of shells,
fluid, loud-mouthed bull;
fertilizing the rocks with his blood,
suicidal sword
splintering itself on any promontory,
hydra, fragmenting the night,
breathing salty clouds of silence,
spreading jelly-like wings
in vain, in vain,
gorgon, devouring its own body,

water, you absurd flat skull of water—

Thus for a while he cursed the sea,
which licked his footprints in the sand
like a wounded dog.

And then he came down
and stroked
the small immense stormy mirror of the sea.

There you are, water, he said,
and went his way.

Translated from the Czech by Ian Milner and George Theiner

Zito the magician

To amuse His Royal Majesty he will change water into wine.
Frogs into footmen. Beetles into bailiffs. And make a Minister
out of a rat. He bows, and daisies grow from his finger-tips.
And a talking bird sits on his shoulder.

There.

Think up something else, demands His Royal Majesty.
Think up a black star. So he thinks up a black star.
Think up dry water. So he thinks up dry water.
Think up a river bound with straw-bands. So he does.

There.

Then along comes a student and asks: Think up sine alpha greater
     than one.
And Zito grows pale and sad. Terribly sorry. Sine is
Between plus one and minus one. Nothing you can do about that.
And he leaves the great royal empire, quietly weaves his way
Through the throng of courtiers, to his home
in a nutshell.

Translated from the Czech by George Theiner

Cinderella

Cinderella is sorting her peas:
bad ones those, good ones these,
yes and no, no and yes.
No cheating. No untruthfulness.

From somewhere the sound of dancing.
Somebody's horses are prancing.
Somebody's riding in state.

The slipper's no longer too small,
toes have been cut off for the ball.
This is the truth. Never doubt.

Cinderella is sorting her peas:
bad ones those, good ones these,
yes and no, no and yes.
No cheating. No untruthfulness.

Coaches drive to the palace door
and everybody bows before
the self-appointed bride.

No blood is flowing. Just red birds
from distant parts are clearly heard
as, plumage ruffled, they alight.

Cinderella is sorting her peas:
bad ones those, good ones these,
yes and no, no and yes.

No little nuts, no prince that charms
and we all long for mother's arms,
yet there is but one hope:

Cinderella is sorting her peas:
softly as one fits joints together

with finger gentle as a feather,
or as one kneads the dough for bread.

Translated from the Czech by George Theiner

GERRIT KOUWENAAR
(NETHERLANDS, 1923–)

Elba

for Constant

I wear a warning bloodcoat
and I stand on elba,
My name is napoleon, among others my name is napoleon
and I stand on elba.
I bear a hundred names
and I stand on elba.
I am the other side of a gentleman.
My dear generals, look at my beak
on elba.
Walk with me the parks of doubt and exile.
There are nights I sit up and beg like a beaked dog.
My rock is brown, as you can see.
My eye is the clockwork of your inventions:
atom bomb! Thank you, gentlemen!

But now that terror dwells in paris
on the cobblestones still tasting of my parades,
in the sidewalk cafés of colonel sartre,
out of the sea I profess the eiffel tower,
steel affiliation of fear
on elba.

You think I'm dead?
I stand here with saber, beak, bloodcoat.

My body is big and fat
and fat with the bones of hitler and bismarck and nietzsche and truman.
Chaplin is my lackey, but this I know:
he steals epaulettes for the fair
and tobacco for the slaves of soho,
he steals my history for marx—
generals, protest!

I stand like a cesspool on elba.
Oh generals, taste the lyricism of my rotting.
Repeat me and grow me.
I wait for you with spengler and gallows from the museum.
Deliver me, I cry, but do not hope.
The slaves no longer believe the beads, generals.
My name is among others napoleon of elba
and st. helena comes later.

Translated from the Dutch by Peter Nijmeijer

SADANAND REGE
(INDIA, 1923–1982)

Old Leaves from the Chinese Earth

*(I bought a Chinese book at a second-hand bookshop. I got a Japanese
chap to explain it to me. All that I could make out of it is what
follows—)*

I am Chiang Liang.
Once I was crossing the bridge,
There was an old man sitting there.
As soon as he saw me the old man removed
One of his shoes, and threw it, on purpose
Into the river
And said to me:
My good fellow, my shoe

Is fallen in the river
Please get it back to me.
I was furious. But I curbed my temper
And jumped into the river.
As soon as I came up with the shoe
He threw another into the river.
"Oh, there goes the other one too."
I dived into the river again
And returned with the other shoe
And the first one was thrown back into the river
I was frustrated; then he said:
Meet me here again after thirteen years.

After thirteen years . . .
There was not a soul on the bridge.
There was only the Sun blazing above it
The size of a tiger's jaw.
I waited for him a long time
Then came down and looked into the river
There was my own face behind the Sun
There was nobody on the bridge except the Sun,

But someone spoke out of my bones:
One shoe is life, the other is death . . .
I recognized the voice.

Translated from the Marathi by Dilip Chitre

ZAHRAD
(TURKEY, 1924–2007)

Cleaning Lentils

A lentil, a lentil, a lentil, a stone.
A green one, a black one, a green one, a stone.
A lentil, a lentil, a lentil, a word.
Suddenly a word, a lentil, a lentil, a word

next to another word. A word, a word, a word,
a speech. A word of nonsense.
Suddenly a song. A song, a song, suddenly
an old dream. A green, a green one, a black one
a stone. A lentil, a lentil, a lentil, a stone.

Translated from the Armenian by Diana Der-Hovanessian

ZBIGNIEW HERBERT
(POLAND, 1924–1998)

The Rain

When my older brother
came back from war
he had on his forehead a little silver star
and under the star
an abyss

a splinter of shrapnel
hit him at Verdun
or perhaps at Grünwald
(he'd forgotten the details)

he used to talk much
in many languages
but he liked most of all
the language of history

until losing breath
he commanded his dead pals to run
Roland Kowalski Hannibal

he shouted
that this was the last crusade
that Carthage soon would fall

and then sobbing confessed
that Napoleon did not like him

we looked at him
getting paler and paler
abandoned by his senses
he turned slowly into a monument

into musical shells of ears
entered a stone forest
and the skin of his face was secured
with the blind dry
buttons of eyes

nothing was left him
but touch

what stories
he told with his hands
in the right he had romances
in the left soldier's memories

they took my brother
and carried him out of town
he returns every fall
slim and very quiet
he does not want to come in
he knocks at the window for me

we walk together in the streets
and he recites to me
improbable tales
touching my face
with blind fingers of rain

Translated from the Polish by Czesław Miłosz and Peter Dale Scott

Report from Paradise

In paradise the work week is fixed at thirty hours
salaries are higher prices steadily go down
manual labour is not tiring (because of reduced gravity)
chopping wood is no harder than typing
the social system is stable and the rulers are wise
really in paradise one is better off than in whatever country

At first it was to have been different
luminous circles choirs and degrees of abstraction
but they were not able to separate exactly
the soul from the flesh and so it would come here
with a drop of fat a thread of muscle
it was necessary to face the consequences
to mix a grain of the absolute with a grain of clay
one more departure from doctrine the last departure
only John foresaw it: you will be resurrected in the flesh

not many behold God
he is only for those of 100 per cent pneuma
the rest listen to communiqués about miracles and floods
some day God will be seen by all
when it will happen nobody knows

As it is now every Saturday at noon
sirens sweetly bellow
and from the factories go the heavenly proletarians
awkwardly under their arms they carry their wings like violins

Translated from the Polish by Czesław Miłosz and Peter Dale Scott

Our Fear

Our fear
does not wear a night shirt
does not have owl's eyes

does not lift a casket lid
does not extinguish a candle

does not have a dead man's face either

our fear
is a scrap of paper
found in a pocket
"warn Wójcik
the place on Długa Street is hot"

our fear
does not rise on the wings of the tempest
does not sit on a church tower
it is down-to-earth

it has the shape
of a bundle made in haste
with warm clothing
provisions
and arms

our fear
does not have the face of a dead man
the dead are gentle to us
we carry them on our shoulders
sleep under the same blanket

close their eyes
adjust their lips
pick a dry spot
and bury them

not too deep
not too shallow

Translated from the Polish by Czesław Miłosz and Peter Dale Scott

Hen

The hen is the best example of what living constantly with humans leads to. She has completely lost the lightness and grace of a bird. Her tail sticks up over her protruding rump like a too large hat in bad taste. Her rare moments of ecstasy, when she stands on one leg and glues up her round eyes with filmy eyelids, are stunningly disgusting. And in addition, that parody of song, throat-slashed supplications over a thing unutterably comic: a round, white, maculated egg.

The hen brings to mind certain poets.

Translated from the Polish by Czesław Miłosz and Peter Dale Scott

Five Men

1

They take them out in the morning
to the stone courtyard
and put them against the wall

five men
two of them very young
the others middle-aged

nothing more
can be said about them

2

when the platoon
level their guns
everything suddenly appears
in the garish light
of obviousness

the yellow wall
the cold blue
the black wire on the wall
instead of a horizon

that is the moment
when the five senses rebel
they would gladly escape
like rats from a sinking ship

before the bullet reaches its destination
the eye will perceive the flight of the projectile
the ear record a steely rustle
the nostrils will be filled with biting smoke
a petal of blood will brush the palate
the touch will shrink and then slacken

now they lie on the ground
covered up to their eyes with shadow
the platoon walks away
their buttons straps
and steel helmets
are more alive
than those lying beside the wall

3

I did not learn this today
I knew it before yesterday

so why have I been writing
unimportant poems on flowers

what did the five talk of
the night before the execution

of prophetic dreams
of an escapade in a brothel

of automobile parts
of a sea voyage
of how when he had spades
he ought not to have opened
of how vodka is best
after wine you get a headache
of girls
of fruit
of life

thus one can use in poetry
names of Greek shepherds
one can attempt to catch the color of morning sky
write of love
and also
once again
in dead earnest
offer to the betrayed world
a rose

Translated from the Polish by Czesław Miłosz and Peter Dale Scott

My Father

My father liked Anatole France
and smoked Macedonian tobacco
with its blue clouds of fragrance
he savored a smile on narrow lips
and back in those far-away times
when he sat leaning over a book
I used to say: father is Sinbad
at times it's bitter for him with us

upon which he set off On a carpet
on the four winds Anxious we ran
after him in atlases but we lost him
In the end he'd come back take off
his odor put his slippers on again

the jangling of keys in his pockets
and days like drops like heavy drops
and time passes changing nothing

one holiday the net curtains down
he stepped through a windowpane
and didn't return I don't know if he
closed his eyes in grief or never
turned to look at us Once in a foreign
magazine I saw a photograph of him
he is now the governor of an island
where palm trees and liberalism grow

Translated from the Polish by Czesław Miłosz

What Mr. Cogito Thinks About Hell

The lowest circle of hell. Contrary to prevailing opinion it is inhabited neither by despots nor matricides, nor even by those who go after the bodies of others. It is the refuge of artists, full of mirrors, musical instruments, and pictures. At first glance this is the most luxurious infernal department, without tar, fire, or physical tortures.

Throughout the year competitions, festivals, and concerts are held here. There is no climax in the season. The climax is permanent and almost absolute. Every few months new trends come into being and nothing, it appears, is capable of stopping the triumphant march of the avant-garde.

Beelzebub loves art. He boasts that already his choruses, his poets, and his painters are nearly superior to those of heaven. He who has better art has better government—that's clear. Soon they will be able to measure their strength against one another at the Festival of the Two Worlds. And then we will see what remains of Dante, Fra Angelico, and Bach.

Beelzebub supports the arts. He provides his artists with calm, good board, and absolute isolation from hellish life.

Translated from the Polish by John Carpenter and Bogdana Carpenter

The Envoy of Mr. Cogito

Go where the others went before to the dark boundary
for the golden fleece of nothingness your last reward

go upright among those who are down on their knees
those with their backs turned those toppled in the dust

you have survived not so that you might live
you have little time you must give testimony

be courageous when reason fails you be courageous
in the final reckoning it is the only thing that counts

and your helpless Anger—may it be like the sea
whenever you hear the voice of the insulted and beaten

may you never be abandoned by your sister Scorn
for informers executioners cowards—they will win
go to your funeral with relief throw a lump of earth
a woodworm will write you a smooth-shaven life

and do not forgive in truth it is not in your power
to forgive in the name of those betrayed at dawn

beware however of overweening pride
examine your fool's face in the mirror
repeat: I was called—was there no one better than I

beware of dryness of heart love the morning spring
the bird with an unknown name the winter oak
the light on a wall the splendor of the sky
they do not need your warm breath
they are there to say: no one will console you

Keep watch—when a light on a hill gives a sign—rise and go
as long as the blood is still turning the dark star in your breast
repeat humanity's old incantations fairy tales and legends

for that is how you will attain the good you will not attain
repeat great words repeat them stubbornly
like those who crossed a desert and perished in the sand

for this they will reward you with what they have at hand
with the whip of laughter with murder on a garbage heap

go for only thus will you be admitted to the company of cold skulls
to the company of your forefathers: Gilgamesh Hector Roland
the defenders of the kingdom without bounds and the city of ashes

Be faithful Go

Translated from the Polish by John Carpenter and Bogdana Carpenter

NINA CASSIAN
(ROMANIA, 1924–)

Temptation

Call yourself alive? Look, I promise you
that for the first time you'll feel your pores opening
like fish mouths, and you'll actually be able to hear
your blood surging through all those lanes,
and you'll feel light gliding across the cornea
like the train of a dress. For the first time
you'll be aware of gravity
like a thorn in your heel,
and your shoulder blades will ache for want of wings.
Call yourself alive? I promise you
you'll be deafened by the sound of dust falling on furniture,
you'll feel your eyebrows turning to two gashes,
and every memory you have—will begin
at Genesis.

Translated from the Romanian by Brenda Walker and Andrea Deletant

CLARIBEL ALEGRÍA

(EL SALVADOR, 1924–)

From the Bridge

I have freed myself at last
it has been hard to break free:
near the end of the bridge
I pause
the water flows below
a turbulent water
sweeping fragments with it:
the voice of Carmen Lira
faces I loved
that disappeared.
From here
from the bridge
the perspective changes
I look backward
toward the beginning:
the hesitant silhouette
of a little girl
a doll
dangling from her hand
she lets it drop
and walks toward me
now she's an adolescent
gathers up her hair
and I recognize this gesture
stop girl
stop right there
if you come any closer
it will be difficult to talk
Don Chico died
after seven operations
they let him die
in a charity hospital
they closed Ricardo's school

and he died
during the earthquake
his heart failed.
Do you remember the massacre
that left Izalco without men?
You were seven.
How can I explain to you
nothing has changed
they keep on killing people daily?
It's better if you stop there
I remember you well at that age
you wrote honeyed poems
were horrified by violence
taught the neighborhood children
to read.
What would you say
if I told you that Pedro
your best student
rotted in jail
and that Sarita
the little blue-eyed girl
who made up stories
let herself be seduced
by the eldest son
of her employers
and afterwards sold herself
for twenty-five cents?
You've taken another step
you wear your hair short
have textbooks under your arm
poor deluded thing
you learned the consolations
of philosophy
before understanding
why you had to be consoled
your books spoke to you
of justice
and carefully omitted

the filth
that has always surrounded us
you went on with your verses
searched for order in chaos
and that was your goal
or perhaps your sentence.
You are coming closer now
your arms filled with children
it is easy to distract yourself
playing mother
and shrink the world
to a household.
Stop there
don't come any closer
you still won't recognize me
you still have to undergo
the deaths of Roque
of Rodolfo
all those innumerable deaths
that assail you
pursue you
define you
in order to dress in this plumage
(my plumage of mourning)
to peer out
through these pitiless
scrutinizing eyes
to have my claws
and this sharp beak.
I never found the order
I searched for
but always a sinister
and well-planned disorder
a prescribed disorder
that increases in the hands
of those who hold power
while the others

who clamor for
a more kindly world
a world with less hunger
and more hope
die tortured
in the prisons.
Don't come any closer
there's a stench of carrion
surrounding me.

Translated from the Spanish by D. J. Flakoll

YEHUDA AMICHAI
(ISRAEL, 1924–2000)

Yom Kippur

Yom Kippur without my father and mother
is no Yom Kippur.

All that's left of their blessing hands on my head
is the tremor, like the tremor of an engine
that kept going even after they died.

My mother died only five years ago,
her case is still pending
between the offices up there and the paperwork down here.

My father, who died long ago, has already risen
in some other place,
not in mine.

Yom Kippur without my father and mother
is no Yom Kippur. Therefore I eat
in order to remember
and drink so I won't forget,

And I sort out the vows
And classify the oaths by time and size.

During the day we used to shout, *Forgive us*,
and in the evening, *Open the gate to us*.
But I say, Forget us, forgo us, leave us alone
When your gate closes and day is gone.

The last sunlight broke
in the stained glass window of the synagogue.
The sunlight didn't break, we are broken.
the word "broken" is broken.

Translated from the Hebrew by Chana Bloch

I know a man

I know a man
who photographed the view he saw
from the window of the room where he made love
and not the face of the woman he loved there.

Translated from the Hebrew by Chana Bloch

Letter

To sit on the veranda of a hotel in Jerusalem
and to write: Sweetly pass the days
from desert to sea. And to write: Tears, here,
dry quickly. This little blot
is a tear that has melted ink. That's how
they wrote a hundred years ago. "I have
drawn a circle round it."

Time passes—like somebody who, on a telephone,
is laughing or weeping far away from me:
whatever I'm hearing I can't see.
And whatever I see I don't hear.

We were not careful when we said "next year"
or "a month ago." These words are like
glass splinters, which you can hurt yourself with,
or cut veins. Those who do things like that.

But you were beautiful, like the interpretation
of ancient books.
Surplus of women in your far country
brought you to me, but
other statistics have taken you
away from me.

To live is to build a ship and a harbor
at the same time. And to complete the harbor
long after the ship was drowned.

And to finish: I remember only
that there was mist. And whoever
remembers only mist—
what does he remember?

Translated from the Hebrew by Ted Hughes

A Man in His Life

A man doesn't have time in his life
to have time for everything.
He doesn't have seasons enough to have
a season for every purpose. Ecclesiastes
was wrong about that.

A man needs to love and to hate at the same moment,
to laugh and cry with the same eyes,
with the same hands to throw stones and to gather them,
to make love in war and war in love.
And to hate and forgive and remember and forget,
to arrange and confuse, to eat and to digest

what history
takes years and years to do.

A man doesn't have time.
When he loses he seeks, when he finds
he forgets, when he forgets he loves,
when he loves he begins to forget.

And his soul is seasoned, his soul
is very professional.
Only his body remains forever
an amateur. It tries and it misses,
gets muddled, doesn't learn a thing,
drunk and blind in its pleasures
and its pains.

He will die as figs die in autumn,
Shriveled and full of himself and sweet,
the leaves growing dry on the ground,
the bare branches pointing to the place
where there's time for everything.

Translated from the Hebrew by Chana Bloch

A Pity. We Were Such a Good Invention

They amputated
Your thighs off my hips.
As far as I'm concerned
They are all surgeons. All of them.

They dismantled us
Each from the other.
As far as I'm concerned
They are all engineers. All of them.

A pity. We were such a good
And loving invention.

An aeroplane made from a man and wife.
Wings and everything.
We hovered a little above the earth.

We even flew a little.

Translated from the Hebrew by Assia Gutmann

We Did It

We did it in front of the mirror
And in the light. We did it in the darkness,
In water, and in the high grass.

We did it with imagination and colors,
With confusion of reddish hair and brown
And with difficult gladdening
Exercises. We did it
Like wheels chariot-feats of prophets.
We did it six wings
And six legs

But the heavens
Were hard above us
Like the earth of the summer beneath.

Translated from the Hebrew by Assia Gutmann

Jerusalem Is Full of Used Jews

Jerusalem is full of used Jews, worn out by history,
Jews second-hand, slightly damaged, at bargain prices.
And the eye yearns toward Zion all the time. And all the eyes
of the living and the dead are cracked like eggs
on the rim of the bowl, to make the city
puff up rich and fat.

Jerusalem is full of tired Jews,
always goaded on again for holidays, for memorial days,
like circus bears dancing on aching legs.

What does Jerusalem need? It doesn't need a mayor,
it needs a ringmaster, whip in hand,
who can tame prophecies, train prophets to gallop
around and around in a circle, teach its stones to line up
in a bold, risky formation for the grand finale.

Later they'll jump back down again
to the sound of applause and wars.

And the eye yearns toward Zion and weeps.

Translated from the Hebrew by Chana Bloch

My Mother Once Told Me

Not to sleep with flowers in the room.
Since then I have not slept with flowers.
I sleep alone, without them.

There were many flowers.
But I've never had enough time.
And persons I love are already pushing themselves
Away from my life, like boats
Away from the shore.

My mother said
Not to sleep with flowers.
You won't sleep.
You won't sleep, mother of my childhood.

The bannister I clung to
When they dragged me off to school
Is long since burnt.

But my hands, clinging
Remain
Clinging.

Translated from the Hebrew by Assia Gutmann

A Dog After Love

After you left me
I let a dog smell at
My chest and my belly. It will fill its nose
And set out to find you.

I hope it will tear the
Testicles of your lover and bite off his penis
Or at least
Will bring me your stockings between his teeth.

Translated from the Hebrew by Assia Gutmann

Love Song

People use each other
as a healing for their pain. They put each other
on their existential wounds,
on the eye, on the cunt, on mouth and open hand.
They hold each other and won't let go.

Translated from the Hebrew by Assia Gutmann

When I Banged My Head on the Door

When I banged my head on the door, I screamed,
"My head, my head," and I screamed, "Door, door,"
and I didn't scream "Mama" and I didn't scream "God."
And I didn't prophesy a world at the End of Days
where there will be no more heads and doors.

When you stroked my head, I whispered,
"My head, my head," and I whispered, "Your hand, your hand,"
and I didn't whisper "Mama" or "God."
And I didn't have miraculous visions
of hands stroking heads in the heavens
as they split wide open.

Whatever I scream or say or whisper is only
to console myself: My head, my head.
Door, door. Your hand, your hand.

Translated from the Hebrew by Chana Bloch

A Letter of Recommendation

On summer nights I sleep naked
in Jerusalem. My bed
stands on the brink of a deep valley
without rolling down into it.

In the daytime I walk around with the Ten
Commandments on my lips
like an old tune someone hums to himself.

Oh touch me, touch me, good woman!
That's not a scar you feel under my shirt, that's
a letter of recommendation, folded up tight,
from my father:
"All the same, he's a good boy, and full of love."

I remember my father waking me for early prayers,
He would do it by gently stroking my forehead, not
by tearing away the blanket.

Since then I love him even more.
And as his reward, may he be wakened

gently and with love
on the Day of the Resurrection.

Translated from the Hebrew by Chana Bloch

The Diameter of the Bomb

The diameter of the bomb was thirty centimeters
and the diameter of its effective range about seven meters,
with four dead and eleven wounded.
And around these, in a larger circle
of pain and time, two hospitals are scattered
and one graveyard. But the young woman
who was buried in the city she came from,
at a distance of more than a hundred kilometers,
enlarges the circle considerably,
and the solitary man mourning her death
at the distant shores of a country far across the sea includes the entire
    world in the circle.
And I won't even mention the howl of orphans
that reaches up to the throne of God and
beyond, making
a circle with no end and no God.

Translated from the Hebrew by Chana Bloch

Gifts of Love

I gave them to you
for your earlobes, your fingers. I gilded
the time on your wrist,
I hung lots of glittery things on you
so you'd sway for me in the wind, so you'd chime softly over me
to soothe my sleep.

I comforted you with apples, as it says
in the Song of Songs,

I lined your bed with them,
so we could roll smoothly on red-apple bearings.

I covered your skin with a pink chiffon,
transparent as baby lizards—the ones with
black diamond eyes on summer nights.

You helped me live for a couple of months
without needing religion
or a point of view.

You gave me a letter opener made of silver.
Real letters aren't opened that way;
they're torn open,
torn, *torn*.

Translated from the Hebrew by Assia Gutmann

Tourist

She showed me her swaying hair
in the four winds of her coming.
I showed her some of my folding ways of life
and the trick, and the lock.
She asked after my street and my house
and I laughed loudly.
She showed me this long night
and the interior of her thirty years.
I showed her the place where I once laid tefillin.

I brought her chapters and verses
and sand from Eilat
and the handling of the Torah
and the manna of my death
and all the miracles that have not yet healed in me.

She showed me the stages of joy
and my childhood's double.

I revealed to her that King David is not buried in his tomb
and that I don't live in my life.

While I was reflecting and she was eating,
the city map lay open on the table—
her hand on Qatamon,
my hand on hers—
the cup covered the Old City,
ash dropped on the King David Hotel,
And an ancient weeping
allowed us to lie together.

Translated from the Hebrew by Assia Gutmann

PHILIPPE JACCOTTET

(SWITZERLAND, 1925–)

Distances

Swifts turn in the heights of the air;
higher still turn the invisible stars.
When day withdraws to the ends of the earth
their fires shine on a dark expanse of sand.

We live in a world of motion and distance.
The heart flies from tree to bird,
from bird to distant star,
from star to love; and love grows
in the quiet house, turning and working,
servant of thought, a lamp held in one hand.

Translated from the French by Derek Mahon

ÁNGEL GONZÁLEZ
(SPAIN, 1925–2008)

Diatribe Against the Dead

The dead are selfish:
they make us cry and don't care,
they stay quiet in the most inconvenient places,
they refuse to walk, we have to carry them
on our backs to the tomb
as if they were children. What a burden!
Unusually rigid, their faces
accuse us of something, or warn us;
they are the bad conscience, the bad example,
they are the worst things in our lives always, always.
The bad thing about the dead
is that there is no way you can kill them.
Their constant destructive labor
is for the reason incalculable.
Insensitive, distant, obstinate, cold,
with their insolence and their silence
they don't realize what they undo.

Translated from the Spanish by Steven Ford Brown and
Pedro Gutirrez Revuelta

Whatever You Want

When you have money, buy me a ring,
when you have nothing, give me a corner of your mouth,
when you don't know what to do, come with me
—but later don't say you didn't know what you were doing.

In the morning you gather bundles of firewood
and they turn into flowers in your arms.
I hold you up grasping the petals,
if you leave I'll take away your perfume.

But I've already told you:
if you decide to leave, here's the door:
its name is Angel and it leads to tears.

Translated from the Spanish by Steven Ford Brown and
Pedro Gutirrez Revuelta

EUGEN GOMRINGER
(BOLIVIA/SWITZERLAND/GERMANY, 1925–)

Streets and Flowers

streets
streets and flowers

flowers
flowers and women

streets
streets and women

streets and flowers and women and
an admirer

Translated from the German by Jerome Rothenberg

ROBERTO JUARROZ
(ARGENTINA, 1925–1995)

from *Ninth Vertical Poetry*

Snow has turned the world into a cemetery

Snow has turned the world into a cemetery.
But the world already was a cemetery
and the snow has only come to announce it.

The snow has only come to point,
with its slender jointless finger,
at the truly outrageous protagonist.

The snow is a fallen angel,
an angel who has lost patience.

Translated from the Spanish by Mary Crow

Life Draws a Tree

Life draws a tree
and death draws another one.
Life draws a nest
and death copies it.
Life draws a bird
to live in the nest
and right away death
draws another bird.

A hand that draws nothing
wanders among the drawings
and at times moves one of them.
For example:
a bird of life

occupies death's nest
on the tree that life drew.

Other times
the hand that draws nothing
blots out one drawing of the series.
For example:
the tree of death
holds the nest of death,
but there's no bird in it.

And other times
the hand that draws nothing
itself changes
into an extra image
in the shape of a bird,
in the shape of a tree,
in the shape of a nest.
And then, only then,
nothing's missing and nothing's left over.
For example:
two birds
occupy life's nest
in death's tree.

Or life's tree
holds two nests
with only one bird in them.

Or a single bird
lives in the one nest
on the tree of life
and the tree of death.

Translated from the Spanish by W. S. Merwin

from *Second Vertical Poetry*

Each one goes however he can

Each one goes however he can,
some with the breast ajar,
others with only one hand,
some with an identification in a pocket,
others with it in the soul,
some with the moon screwed into their blood,
and others without blood, or moon, or memories.

Each one goes, even though he can't,
some with love between their teeth,
others changing their skins,
some with life and death,
others with death and life,
some with their hand on their own shoulder,
others with it on somebody else's shoulder.

Each one goes because he's going,
some with someone up late between the eyebrows,
others whose paths never crossed anyone's,
some through the door that opens onto the road
or seems to,

others through the door that's drawn on the wall
or perhaps on the air,
some without having begun to live
and others without having begun to live.

But all of them go with their feet tied,
some by the path that they made,
others by the one they didn't make,
and all by the one that they will never make.

Translated from the Spanish by W. S. Merwin

ERNESTO CARDENAL

(NICARAGUA, 1925–)

"For Those Dead, Our Dead . . ."

When you get the nomination, the award, the
      promotion,
think about the ones who died.
When you are at the reception, on the delegation,
      on the commission,
think about the ones who died.
When you have won the vote, and the crowd
      congratulates you,
think about the ones who died.
When you're cheered as you go up to the speaker's
      platform with the leaders,
think about the ones who died.
When you're picked up at the airport in the big city,
      think about the ones who died.
When it's your turn to talk into the microphone,
      when the tv cameras focus on you,
think about the ones who died.
When you become the one who gives out the certificates,
      orders, permission,
think about the ones who died.
When the little old lady comes to you with her problem,
      her little piece of land,
think about the ones who died.
         See them without their shirts, being dragged,
      gushing blood, wearing hoods, blown to pieces,
submerged in tubs, getting electric shocks,
           their eyes gouged out,
      their throats cut, riddled with bullets,
dumped along the side of the road,
      in holes they dug themselves,
      in mass graves,
or just lying on the ground, enriching the soil of wild
      plants:

You represent them.
The ones who died
delegated you.

Translated from the Spanish by Jonathan Cohen

AHMAD SHAMLOU
(IRAN, 1925–2000)

Existence

If this is life—how low!
and I, how shamed, if I don't hang my lifetime's lamp
high on the dusty pine of this dead-end lane.

If this is life—how pure!
and I, how stained, if I don't plant my faith like a mountain,
eternal memorial, to grace this ephemeral earth.

Translated from the Persian by Zara Houshmand

INGEBORG BACHMANN
(AUSTRIA, 1926–1973)

Every Day

War is no longer declared
but continued. The unheard-of thing
is the everyday. The hero
keeps away from the fighters. The weak man
has moved up to the battle zones.
The uniform of the day is patience,
its decoration the humble star
of hope worn over the heart.

It is awarded
when nothing goes on,
when the barrage subsides,
when the enemy has grown invisible
and the shadow of everlasting arms
covers the sky.

It is awarded
for desertion of the flag,
for courage in the face of the friend,
for the betrayal of unworthy secrets
and for the nonobservance
of every order.

Translated from the German by Michael Hamburger

The Respite

A harder time is coming.
The end of the respite allowed us
appears on the skyline.
Soon you must tie your shoelace
and drive back the dogs to the marshland farms.
For the fishes' entrails
have grown cold in the wind.
Poorly the light of the lupins burns.
Your gaze gropes in the fog:
the end of the respite allowed us
appears on the skyline.

Over there your loved one sinks in the sand,
it rises towards her blown hair,
it cuts short her speaking,
it commands her to be silent,
it finds that she is mortal
and willing to part
after every embrace.

Do not look round.
Tie your shoelace.
Drive back the dogs.
Throw the fishes into the sea.
Put out the lupins!

A harder time is coming.

Translated from the German by Michael Hamburger

JAIME SABINES
(MEXICO, 1926–1999)

Pieces of Shadow

I don't know it for certain, but I imagine
that a man and a woman
fall in love one day,
little by little they come to be alone,
something in each heart tells them that they are alone,
alone on the earth they enter each other,
they go filling each other.

It all happens in silence. The way
light happens in the eye.
Love unites bodies.
They go on filling each other with silence.

One day they wake up, over their arms.
Then they think they know the whole thing,
They see themselves naked and they know the whole thing.

(I'm not sure about this. I imagine it.)

Translated from the Spanish by W. S. Merwin

JEAN-PIERRE ROSNAY
(FRANCE, 1926–)

Piazza San Marco

Imagine for yourself what was in my heart
I was in Venice for the very first time
Piazza San Marco
With a thousand lire in my pocket
About a thousand lire
The pigeons were drunk on music
You know Venice better than I do
You know the Italians
Their music their pigeons
I was totally adrift
At nine o'clock it suddenly occurred to me
That I hadn't eaten since the day before
The day before I had an orange for lunch
I stop a woman
She keeps on going
I'm lucky I bump into another
She laughs I laugh
But even before I have a line
ready in my mind
I remember I'm in Italy
And don't know the language
I catch a pigeon by the wing
It claps me on my hat and flies off
Imagine for yourself
What was in my heart
I was in Venice for the very first time
With a thousand lire in my pocket

Translated from the French by J. Kates

GÜNTER GRASS
(GERMANY, 1927–)

Happiness

An empty bus
hurtles through the starry night.
Perhaps the driver is singing
and is happy because he sings.

Translated from the German by Michael Hamburger

KIM NAM-JO
(KOREA, 1927–)

Foreign Flags

There I first glimpsed
such desolate loneliness.

Above the soaring towers of the old castle
at Heidelberg
a flag is waving
like a boat being rowed
like a windmill turning in the wind
waving on and on
until the threads grow thin
then casting away that body like a corpse
they raise a new flag

I wonder
what it's like to be up there all alone
in the sky with the drifting clouds,
what it's like
to be shaking all over, looking down
on the mutability of people and things?

There I first glimpsed
such adult prayer.

Translated from the Korean by Brother Anthony of Taizé

LUO FU
(CHINA, 1928–)

Song of Everlasting Regret

That rose, like all roses, only bloomed for one morning.
—H. BALZAC

1

From
The sound of water
Emperor Xuan of the Tang dynasty
Extracts the sorrow in a lock of black hair

2

In the genealogy of the Yang clan
She is
An expanse of white flesh
Lying right there on the first page
A rosebush in the mirror
In full flower, caressed by
What is called heaven-born beauty
A
Bubble
Waiting to be scooped up
From the Huaqing Pool

Heavenly music is everywhere
In Li Palace
The aroma of wine wafts in body odors

Lips, after being sucked hard
Can only moan
And the limbs outstretched on the ivory bed
Are mountains
And rivers too
A river sound asleep in another river
Underground rapids
Surge toward
The countryside
Until a white ballad
Breaks out of the soil

3

He raises his burned hand high
And cries out:
I make love
Because
I want to make love
Because
I am the emperor
Because we are used to encounters
Of flesh with blood

4

He begins to read newspapers, eat breakfast, watch her comb her hair,
    handle official papers in bed

                                        stamp a seal
                                        stamp a seal
                                        stamp a seal
                                        stamp a seal

From then on
The emperor no longer holds court in the morning

5

He is the emperor
But war
Is a puddle of
Sticky fluid
That cannot be wiped off
Under the brocade coverlets
Slaughter is far away
Distant beacon: fires snake upward, the sky is dumbfounded
By heartstopping hairstyles
Leather drums with flame-red tongues
Lick the earth

6

Rivers and streams
Burn between the thighs
War
May not be abandoned
Campaigns are affairs of state
My lady, women's blood can flow in only one direction
Now the armies refuse to budge
All right, all right, you are the willow catkins
Before the Mawei Slope
Let the wind in the square hold you aloft
A pile of expensive fertilizer
Is nourishing
Another rosebush
Or
Another incurable disease
In history

7

Regret probably begins in the middle of fire
He gazes out the window into the distance
His head

Sways with the flight of birds
His eyes change colors as the sun sets
The name that he cries out
Sinks into the echoes

All night long he paces around the room
In front of every window in Weiyang Palace
He stops
Cold pale fingers nip the candlewick
Amid muffled coughs
All the hibiscuses in the Forbidden City
Wilt overnight in
The autumn wind

He ties his beard into knot after knot, unties and ties it again, then
    walks with his hands behind his back, the sound of his footfalls
    footfalls footfalls a tuberose exploding behind the curtain, then he
    stretches out all ten fingers to grab a copy of the *Annotated Classic of*
    Waters, the water drip-dripping, he cannot understand at all why the
    river sobs instead of bellows when it flows through the palm of his hand
He throws on a gown and gets up
He sears his own skin
He is awakened by cold jade
       A thousand candles burn in a thousand rooms
       A bright moon shines on the sleepless
       A woman walks toward him along the wall
       Her face an illusion in the mist

8

Suddenly
He searches in a frenzy for that lock of black hair
And she hands over
A wisp of smoke
It is water and will rise to become a cloud
It is soil and will be trampled into parched moss
The face hiding among the leaves
Is more despairing than the sunset

A chrysanthemum at the corner of her mouth
A dark well in her eyes
A war raging in her body
A storm brewing
Within her palm
She no longer suffers from toothache
She will never again come down with
Tang dynasty measles
Her face dissolved in water is a relative white and an absolute black
She will no longer hold a saucer of salt and cry out with thirst
Her hands, which were used to being held
Now point
Tremblingly
To a cobbled road leading to Chang'an

9

Time: seventh day of the seventh month
Place: Palace of Longevity
A tall thin man in blue
A faceless woman
Flames still rising
In the white air
A pair of wings
Another pair
Fly into the moonlight outside the palace
Whispers
Receding farther and farther away
Glint bitterly

An echo or two reverberate through the storm

Translated from the Chinese by Michelle Yeh

HANS MAGNUS ENZENSBERGER

GERMANY (1929–)

last will and testament

get your flag out of my face, it tickles!
bury my cat inside, bury her over there,
where my chromatic garden used to be!

and get that tinny wreath off my chest, it's rattling too much;
toss it over to the statues on the garbage heap,
and give the ribbon to some biddies to doll themselves up.

say your prayers over the telephone, but first cut the wires,
or wrap them up in a handkerchief full of bread-crumbs
for the stupid fish in the puddles.

let the bishop stay at home and get plastered!
give him a barrel of rum,
he's going to be dry from the sermon.

and get off my back with your tombstones and stovepipe hats!
use the fancy marble to pave an alley where nobody lives,
an alley for pigeons.

my suitcase is full of scribbled pieces of paper for my little cousin,
who can fold them into airplanes, fancy ones for sailing off the bridge
so they drown in the river.

anything that's left (a pair of drawers a lighter a fancy birthstone
and an alarm clock) i want you to give to callisthenes the junk man
and toss in a fat tip.

as for the resurrection of the flesh however and life everlasting
i will, if it's all the same to you, take care of that on my own;
it's my affair, after all. live and be well!

there's a couple of butts left on the dresser.

Translated from the German by Jerome Rothenberg

ENRIQUE LIHN
(CHILE, 1929–1988)

Torture Chamber

Your alms are my salary
Your salary is the squaring of my circle, that I draw out
with my fingers to maintain their agility
Your calculator is my hand missing a finger with which
I keep myself from making calculation errors
Your alms are the capital I contribute when I go begging
Your appearance in Ahumada Mall is my debut
Your society is secret insofar as my tribe is concerned
Your personal security is my indecision
Your pocket handkerchief is my white flag
Your necktie is my Gordian knot
Your brand name suit is my backdrop
Your right shoe is my left shoe a dozen years later
The crease of your pants is the edge I couldn't cross
even though I disguised myself as you
after tearing your clothes off
Your ascension up the staircase at the Bank of Chile
is my dream of Jacob's ladder on which a blond angel
with painted wings descends
to pay, in hand to hand combat, all my debts
Your checkbook is my sack of papers when I get stoned
Your signature is my illiterate's game
Your $2 + 2 =$ four is my $2 - 2$
Your coming and going are my labyrinth in which

meditating I get lost pursued by a fly
Your office is the backstage where my name can be
condemned to death and transferred to another corpse
that will bear it in some friendly country
Your doctor's office is my torture chamber
Your torture chamber is the only hotel where I can be
received at any hour
without advance notice
Your order is my song
Your electric pen is what makes me a prolific author,
a goddam visionary, or the guy who remains silent—
depending on who I am at the moment
Your bad will is my blood
Your foot on my butt is my ascension to the heavens
that are what they are and not what God wants
Your tranquility is my being stabbed in the back
Your liberty is my everlasting flower
Your peace is mine forever and whenever I enjoy it eternally
and you for life
Your real life is the end of my imagination when I get stoned
Your house is my lost paradise which I'm going to feel I own
the next time I get stoned
Your wife is in that case my squashed kitten
Your toothpick is now my fork
Your fork is my spoon
Your knife is my temptation to slit your throat
when I suck on a joint
Your police dog is the guardian of my impropriety
Your German shepherd is my beheader at the door of your house
as if I weren't a cursed lost sheep
Your machine gun is the lover I fuck in my dreams
Your helmet is the mold in which they emptied
the head of my son when he was born
Your military march is my wedding processional
Your garbage dump is my pantheon
as long as the corpses aren't carried off.

Translated from the Spanish by Mary Crow

DAN PAGIS

(ROMANIA/ISRAEL, 1930–1986)

Autobiography

I died with the first blow and was buried
among the rocks of the field.
The raven taught my parents
what to do with me.

If my family is famous,
not a little of the credit goes to me.
My brother invented murder,
my parents invented grief,
I invented silence.

Afterward the well-known events took place.
Our inventions were perfected. One thing led to another,
orders were given. There were those who murdered in their own way,
grieved in their own way.

I won't mention names
out of consideration for the reader,
since at first the details horrify
though finally they're a bore:

you can die once, twice, even seven times,
but you can't die a thousand times.
I can.
My underground cells reach everywhere.

When Cain began to multiply on the face of the earth,
I began to multiply in the belly of the earth,
and my strength has long been greater than his.
His legions desert him and go over to me,
and even this is only half a revenge.

Translated from the Hebrew by Stephen Mitchell

Picture Postcard from Our Youth

On your piano a plaster Beethoven stands
and thinks: Thank goodness I've gone deaf.
Even the neighborhood sparrows are singing out of tune this morning.

Only the Kurdish peddler is being true to himself
as he limps along the street shouting *Old clothes!*
in his bargain-basement Hebrew.

It doesn't matter. From the tangle of voices, the one voice ascends.
A blue bell of air
arches above us.

Translated from the Hebrew by Stephen Mitchell

ADONIS
(SYRIA/LEBANON, 1930–)

A Mirror for the Twentieth Century

A coffin bearing the face of a boy
A book

Written on the belly of a crow
A wild beast hidden in a flower

A rock
Breathing with the lungs of a lunatic:

This is it
This is the Twentieth Century.

Translated from the Arabic by Abdullah al-Udhari

from The Desert: The Diary of Beirut Under Siege, 1982

I

3

I said: This street leads to our house. He said: No.
     You won't pass. And pointed his bullets at me.

Fine, in every street
     I have homes and friends.

5

The voice of the city is soft
The face of the city glows
Like a little boy telling his dreams to the night
And offering his chair to the morning.

6

They found people in sacks:
     One without a head
     One without a tongue or hands
     One strangled
     The rest without shape or names.
Have you gone mad? Please,
     Don't write about these things.

10

From the palm wine to the calmness of the desert . . . etc.
From the morning that smuggles its stomach and sleeps on the
     corpses of the refugees . . . etc.
From the streets, army vehicles, concentration of troops . . . etc.
From the shadows, men, women . . . etc.
From the bombs stuffed with the prayers of Muslims and infidels . . . etc.
From the flesh of iron that bleeds and sweats pus . . . etc.

From the fields that long for the wheat, the green and the workers . . . etc.
From the castles walling our bodies and bombarding us with
    darkness . . . etc.
From the myths of the dead which speak of life, express life . . . etc.
From the speech which is the slaughter, the slaughtered and the
    slaughterers . . . etc.
From the dark dark dark
I breathe, feel my body, search for you and him, myself and others,
And hang my death
Between my face and these bleeding words . . . etc.

12

The killing has changed the city's shape—This rock
        Is a boy's head
        This smoke people breathing.

16

Bourje Square—(inscriptions whispering their secrets
             to broken bridges . . .)
Bourje Square—(memory looking for itself
             in fire and dust . . .)
Bourje Square—(an open desert
             swept and dragged by the winds . . .)
Bourje Square—(witchcraft
             to see corpses moving/their limbs
             in a backstreet/their ghosts
             in a backstreet/you hear them sighing . . .)
Bourje Square—(west and east
             gallows standing,
             martyrs and guardians . . .)
Bourje Square—(a trail
               of caravans: myrrh
                      frankincense and musk
               and spices opening the festival . . .)
Bourje Square—(a trail
               of caravans: thunder

               and explosion and lightning
         and hurricanes opening the festival . . .)
Bourje Square—(I have called this era
                   by the name of this place)

II

1

My era tells me bluntly:
You do not belong.
I answer bluntly:
I do not belong,
I try to understand you.
Now I am a shadow
Lost in the desert
And shelter in the tent of a skull.

Translated from the Arabic by Abdullah al-Udhari

SHIN SHIFRA
(ISRAEL, 1931–)

Moonstruck

Uncle Yerocham was so worried
about Aunt Miriam he would
leave her alone so she'd know
what it feels like to sleep without him
he'd shut the door on her while she
fluttered like a dove in the large bed
covered the window
with a blanket locked the door
twice and again unlocked it
and all because at noon she dared
to mention, it doesn't matter
what, Mother guessed perhaps

he was simply jealous of her spirit
because that morning for no reason
her eyes shone with a nuptial light
and so he determined
to restrain her, she turns the house
into a grave, he yelled
at the top of his lungs, I was a child
on a family visit to the house
of Aunt Miriam and Uncle
Yerocham. Moonstruck, she walks
in her sleep, explained Uncle
Yerocham when they found
Aunt Miriam walking barefoot
at sunrise, only Mother guessed.

Translated from the Hebrew by Tsipi Keller

from A Woman Who Practices How to Live

2.

A woman who practices living may
go to the cinema on a first summer evening,
and doesn't, may go to a Danziger exhibit
at the Tel Aviv Museum, and doesn't, instead
she speaks on the phone with the gardener
in charge at the cemetery.

3.

To cover with aptenia her adjoining
lot, suggests the gardener, and she's evasive, he suggests
pine in her adjoining lot, and she's evasive, to uproot
a pine in her adjoining lot when the time comes,
doesn't feel right, she stammers, and the gardener in charge
    at the cemetery, mistaking her
motives, guarantees it's a good

omen for longevity, a plant, she requests, large, bougainvillea,
a temporary pot easily transported from place
to place, when the time comes, as I lived, she whispers
to herself, a woman who practices.

5.

A woman who practices living goes
to market to buy fish, the stench
of the sewage flowing in the gutter
rises up to her nose, chickens hang
from hooks, a man steering a cart
strikes her ankle, her eyes blurry from so many
pyramids of apples, pears, mangos,
at home she can't swallow the fish
the stench sticks in her throat.

Translated from the Hebrew by Tsipi Keller

TOMAS TRANSTRÖMER
(SWEDEN, 1931–)

Track

2 a.m.: moonlight. The train has stopped
out in a field. Far-off sparks of light from a town,
flickering coldly on the horizon.

As when a man goes so deep into his dream
he will never remember that he was there
when he returns again to his room.

Or when a person goes so deep into a sickness
that his days all become some flickering sparks, a swarm,
feeble and cold on the horizon.

The train is entirely motionless.
2 o'clock: strong moonlight, few stars.

Translated from the Swedish by Robert Bly

Grief Gondola, #2

I

Two old men, father-in-law and son-in-law, Liszt and Wagner,
    are staying on the Grande Canal
together with the restless woman who is married to King Midas
he who turns everything he touches into Wagner.
The green chill of the sea pushes up through the palace floors.
Wagner is a marked man, the well-known Caspar profile is more
    tired than before
        his face a white flag.
The gondola is heavily laden with their lives, two round trips and one
    one-way.

II

A window in the palace blows open, they grimace in the sudden draught.
Outside on the water, the garbage gondola appears, paddled by two
    one-oared bandits.
Liszt has composed a few chords so heavy they ought to be sent
to the mineralogical institute in Padua for analysis.
Meteorites!
Too heavy to rest, they are able only to sink and sink through the future
    all the way down
        to the year of the brownshirts.
The gondola is heavily laden with the huddled stones of the future.

III

Openings toward 1990.

March 25: Worry about Lithuania.
Dreamt I visited a large hospital.
No staff. Everyone was a patient.

In the same dream a newborn girl
who spoke in complete sentences.

IV

Compared to his son-in-law, who is a man of his time, Liszt is a
    moth-eaten grand seigneur.
It's a disguise.
The deep that tries out and discards various masks has chosen
    just this one for him—
the deep that wants to join the humans without showing its face.

V

Abbé Liszt is used to carrying his own suitcase through sleet and
    sunshine
and when the time comes to die there will be no one there
    to meet him at the station.
A tepid breeze of highly gifted cognac carries him off
    in the midst of an assignment.
He is never free of assignments.
Two thousand letters a year!
The schoolboy who writes the misspelled word one hundred times
    before he is allowed to go home.
The gondola is heavily laden with life, it is simple and black.

VI

Back to 1990.

Dreamt I drove a hundred miles in vain.
Then everything was magnified. Sparrows as large as hens
sang so that my ears popped.

Dreamt that I had drawn piano keys
on the kitchen table. I played on them, mutely.
The neighbors came in to listen.

VII

The clavier which has been silent through all of *Parsifal* (but it
    has listened)
      is at last allowed to say something.
Sighs . . . sospiri . . .
When Liszt plays tonight he holds down the sea-pedal
      so that the green force of the sea rises through the floor and
      flows together with all the stone of the building.
Good evening beautiful deep!
The gondola is heavily laden with life, it is simple and black.

VIII

Dreamt I was starting school but came late.
Everyone in the room wore white masks.
It was impossible to tell who was the teacher.

*Note: During late 1882 and early 1883 Liszt visited his daughter Cosima and her
husband, Richard Wagner. A few months later, Wagner died. Liszt's two pieces for
piano entitled "Trauer-Gondel" (Grief Gondola) were composed at that time.*

Translated from the Swedish by Malena Mörling

Vermeer

It's not a sheltered world. The noise begins over there, on the other
    side of the wall
where the alehouse is
with its laughter and quarrels, its rows of teeth, its tears, its chiming
    of clocks
and the psychotic brother-in-law, the murderer, in whose presence
    everyone feels fear.

The huge explosion and the emergency crew arriving late,
boats showing off on the canals, money slipping down into pockets—
     the wrong man's—
ultimatum piled on ultimatum,
wide-mouthed red flowers whose sweat reminds us of approaching war.

And then straight through the wall—from there—straight into the
     airy studio
and the seconds that have got permission to live for centuries.
Paintings that choose the name: *The Music Lesson*
or *A Woman in Blue Reading a Letter.*
She is here eight months pregnant, two hearts beating inside her.
The wall behind her holds a crinkly map of Terra Incognita.

Just breathe. An unidentifiable blue material has been tacked to the chairs.
Gold-headed tacks flew in with astronomical speed
and stopped right there
as if they had always been stillness and nothing else.

The ears experience a buzz, perhaps it's depth or perhaps height.
It's the pressure from the other side of the wall,
the pressure that makes each fact float
and makes the brushstroke firm.

Passing through walls hurts human beings, they get sick from it,
but we have no choice.
It's all one world. Now to the walls.
The walls are part of you.
One either knows that, or one doesn't; but it's the same for everyone
except for small children. There aren't any walls for them.

The airy sky has taken its place leaning against the wall.
It is like a prayer to what is empty.
And what is empty turns its face to us
and whispers:
"I am not empty, I am open."

Translated from the Swedish by Robert Bly

SHUNTARO TANIKAWA

(JAPAN, 1931–)

Growth

age three
there was no past for me

age five
my past went back to yesterday

age seven
my past went back to topknotted samurai

age eleven
my past went back to dinosaurs

age fourteen
my past agreed with the texts at school

age sixteen
I look at the infinity of my past with fear

age eighteen
I know not a thing about time

Translated from the Japanese by Harold Wright

"Porno-Bach"

Are those fingers, the ones playing Bach just now,
and these fingers really the same?
This thing of mine, getting long and getting short,
and not resembling a piano at all,
must be called a comical tool;
so how does this conventional thing
and the great Bach, by your soft fingers,

get joined together?
I, myself, have no idea!
Yet, that thing of yours and this of mine,
now the color of the naked heart,
feel so warm, so smooth
in endless surrender much like death,
and when in this transparent blood filled darkness
I unexpectedly seem to meet Bach face to face.

Translated from the Japanese by Harold Wright

Twenty Billion Light Years of Loneliness

Mankind on a little globe
Sleeps, awakes and works
Wishing at times to be friends with Mars.

Martians on a little globe
Are probably doing something; I don't know what
(Maybe sleep-sleeping, wear-wearing, or fret-fretting)
While wishing at times to be friends with Earth
This is a fact I'm sure of.

This thing called universal gravitation
Is the power of loneliness pulling together.

The universe is distorted
So all join in desire.

The universe goes on expanding
So all feel uneasy.

At the loneliness of twenty billion light years
Without thinking, I sneezed.

Translated from the Japanese by Harold Wright

Landscape with Yellow Birds

there are birds
so there is sky
there is sky
so there are balloons
there are balloons
so children are running
children are running
so there is laughter
there is laughter
so there is sadness
so there is prayer
and ground for kneeling
there is ground
so water is flowing
and there's today and tomorrow
there is a yellow bird
so with all colors forms and movements
there is the world

Translated from the Japanese by Harold Wright

KAZUKO SHIRAISHI
(JAPAN, 1931–)

The Donkey Speculates

Should she call   or not
Even though she wants to call   the donkey   wonders
As if she had become a nation
The line might be tapped
It's dangerous   to leak information   and
She thinks of the cute   mountain girl Heidi
Surrounded by sheep   mountain sheep   running through the
    green fields
Heidi   of the sweet   lips

Isn't she   too unsuspicious   too innocent   passionate   tossing
An ideal ball   to this side of the telephone
The donkey   like a housewife knitting   speculates
On this and that adding stitches   changing stitches

Translated from the Japanese by Samuel Grolmes and Yumiko Tsumura

TAHA MUHAMMAD ALI
(PALESTINIAN TERRITORIES, 1931–)

Abd el-Hadi Fights a Superpower

In his life
he neither wrote nor read.
In his life he
didn't cut down a single tree,
didn't slit the throat
of a single calf.
In his life he did not speak
of the New York Times
behind its back,
didn't raise
his voice to a soul
except in his saying:
"Come in, please,
by God, you can't refuse."

Nevertheless—
his case is hopeless,
his situation
desperate.
His God-given rights are a grain of salt
tossed into the sea.

Ladies and gentlemen of the jury:
about his enemies
my client knows not a thing.

And I can assure you,
were he to encounter
the entire crew
of the aircraft carrier Enterprise,
he'd serve them eggs
sunny side up,
and labneh
fresh from the bag.

Translated from the Arabic by Peter Cole, Yahya Hijazi, and
Gabriel Levin

BOGDAN CZAYKOWSKI
(POLAND, 1932–2007)

A Prayer

Throw me into a cloud o lord

but do not make me a drop of rain
I do not want to return to earth

throw me into a flower o lord

but do not make me a bee
I would die from an excess of industrious sweetness

throw me into a lake

but do not make me a fish o lord
I would not be able to become cold-blooded

throw me into a forest
like a pine cone on the grass
let no red-haired squirrels find me

throw me into a calm shape of a stone
but not on the pavement of a London street
o lord I worry and bite walls in this alien city

you who turn me over fire
pluck me from flames
and deposit me on a quiet white cloud

Translated from the Polish by Czesław Miłosz

REINER KUNZE
(GERMANY, 1933–)

The Bringers of Beethoven

For Ludvik Kundera

They set out to bring Beethoven
to everyone.
And as they had a record with them
they played for speedier understanding
Symphony no. 5, in C minor, opus 67

But the man M. said
it was too loud for him, he
was getting old

In the night the bringers of Beethoven put
up poles in streets and squares
hooked up cables, connected
loudspeakers, and with the dawn
for more thorough acquaintance came the strains of
Symphony no. 5, in C minor, opus 67,
came loud enough to be heard
in the mute fields.

But the man M. said he had a headache,
went home about noon, closed
doors and windows and praised
the thickness of the walls

Thus provoked, the bringers of Beethoven strung
wire on to the walls and hung
loudspeakers over the windows, and in
through the panes came
Symphony no. 5, in C minor, opus 67

But the man M. stepped out of the house and denounced
the bringers of Beethoven;
they all asked him what he had
against Beethoven

Thus attacked, the bringers of Beethoven knocked
on M.'s door and when they opened up they
forced a foot inside; praising the neatness of the place
they went in.
The conversation happened to turn
to Beethoven,
and to enliven the subject they happened
to have with them
Symphony no. 5, in C minor, opus 67

But the man M. hit the bringers of
Beethoven with an iron ladle.
He was arrested just in time.

M.'s act was called homicidal
by lawyers and judges of the bringers of Beethoven.
But they must not give up hoping.
He was sentenced
to Symphony no. 5, in C minor, opus 67,
by Ludwig van Beethoven

M. kicked and screamed,
until the loudspeakers stopped
beyond the mute fields

He was just too old, the bringers of Beethoven said.
But by M.'s coffin, they said,
are his children

And his children demanded
that over the coffin of
the man M. should be played
Symphony no. 5, in C minor, opus 67

Translated from the German by Gordon Brotherston and
Gisela Brotherston

ANDREI VOZNESENSKY

(RUSSIA, 1933–)

Darkmotherscream

Darkmotherscream is a Siberian dance,
cry from prison or a yell for help,
or, perhaps, God has another word for it—
ominous little grin—darkmotherscream.

Darkmotherscream is the ecstasy of the sexual gut;
We let the past sink into darkmotherscream also.
You, we—oooh with her eyes closed
woman moans in ecstasy—darkmother, darkmotherscream.

Darkmotherscream is the original mother of languages.
It is silly to trust mind, silly to argue against it.
Prognosticating by computers
We leave out darkmotherscream.

"How's it going?" Darkmotherscream.
"Motherscream! Motherscream!"
                    "OK, we'll do it, we'll do it."

The teachers can't handle darkmotherscream.
That is why Lermontov is untranslatable.
When the storm sang in Yelabuga,
What did it say to her? Darkmotherscream.

Meanwhile go on dancing, drunker and drunker.
"Shagadam magadam—darkmotherscream."
Don't forget—Rome fell
not having grasped the phrase: darkmotherscream.

Translated from the Russian by Robert Bly and Vera Dunham

KO UN
(KOREA, 1933–)

A cock crows at Donghyun's

A cock crows at Donghyun's
A cock crows at Yongsik's
A cock crows at Sunnam's
A cock crows at Gumchol's
Gumchol's grandpa has stopped breathing

Translated from the Korean by Brother Anthony of Taizé,
Gary Gach, and Young-moo Kim

What is this world?

What is this world?
Here's a butterfly fluttering by
and there's a spider's web

Translated from the Korean by Brother Anthony of Taizé,
Gary Gach, and Young-moo Kim

Dogs are barking in villages high and low

Dogs are barking in villages high and low
Will this evening's thief
Be called Kim or Park?

Translated from the Korean by Brother Anthony of Taizé,
Gary Gach, and Young-moo Kim

GENNADY AYGI
(RUSSIA, 1934–2006)

The People Are a Temple

And souls are candles, each lighting the other.

Translated from the Russian by Peter France

MUHAMMAD AL-MAGHUT
(SYRIA, 1934–2006)

The Postman's Fear

Prisoners everywhere
Send me all you have
Fears screams and boredom
Fishermen of all beaches

Send me all you have
Empty nets and seasickness

Peasants of every land
Send me all you have
Flowers rags
Mutilated breasts
Ripped-up bellies
And torn-out nails
To my address . . . any café
Any street in the world
I'm preparing a *huge file*
About human suffering
To present to God
Once it's signed by the lips of the hungry
And the eyelids of those still waiting
You wretched everywhere
What I fear most is
God could be *illiterate*

Translated from the Arabic by Abdullah al-Udhari

INGER CHRISTENSEN
(DENMARK, 1935–2008)

from *Alphabet*

1

apricot trees exist, apricot trees exist

2

bracken exists; and blackberries, blackberries;
bromine exists; and hydrogen, hydrogen

3

cicadas exist; chicory, chromium,
citrus trees; cicadas exist;
cicadas, cedars, cypresses, the cerebellum

4

doves exist, dreamers, and dolls;
killers exist, and doves, and doves;
haze, dioxin, and days; days
exist, days and death; and poems
exist; poems, days, death

5

early fall exists; aftertaste, afterthought;
seclusion and angels exist;
widows and elk exist; every
detail exists; memory, memory's light;
afterglow exists; oaks, elms,
junipers, sameness, loneliness exist;
eider ducks, spiders, and vinegar
exist, and the future, the future

6

fisherbird herons exist, with their grey-blue arching
backs, with their black-feathered crests and their
bright-feathered tails they exist; in colonies
they exist, in the so-called Old World;
fish, too, exist, and ospreys, ptarmigans,
falcons, sweetgrass, and the fleeces of sheep;
fig trees and the products of fission exist;
errors exist, instrumental, systemic,
random; remote control exists, and birds;
and fruit trees exist, fruit there in the orchard where
apricot trees exist, apricot trees exist

in countries whose warmth will call forth the exact
colour of apricots in the flesh

8

whisperings exist, whisperings exist
harvest, history, and Halley's

comet exist; hosts exist, hordes
high commanders, hollows, and within the hollows
half-shadows, within the half-shadows occasional

hares, occasional hanging leaves shading the hollow where
bracken exists, and blackberries, blackberries
occasional hares hidden under the leaves

and gardens exist, horticulture, the elder tree's
pale flowers, still as a seething hymn;
the half-moon exists, half-silk, and the whole
heliocentric haze that has dreamed
these devoted brains, their luck, and human skin

human skin and houses exist, with Hades
rehousing the horse and the dog and the shadows
of glory, hope; and the river of vengeance;
hail under stoneskies exists, the hydrangeas'
white, bright-shining, blue or greenish

fogs of deep, occasionally pink, a few
sterile patches exist, and beneath
the angled Armageddon of the arching heavens, poison,
the poison helicopter's humming harps above the henbane,
shepherd's purse, and flax, henbane, shepherd's purse
and flax; this last, hermetic writing,
written otherwise only by children; and wheat,
wheat in wheatfields exists, the head-spinning
horizontal knowledge of wheatfields, half-lives,
famine, and honey; and deepest in the heart,

otherwise as ever only deepest in the heart,
the roots of the hazel, the hazel that stands
on the hillslope of the heart, tough and hardy,
an accumulated weekday of Angelic orders;
high-speed, hyacinthic in its decay, life,
on earth as it is in heaven.

10

June nights exist, June nights exist,
the sky at long last as if lifted to heavenly
heights, simultaneously sinking, as tenderly as
when dreams can be seen before they are dreamed; a space
as if dizzied, as if filled with whiteness, an hourless

chiming of insects and dew, and no one in
this gossamer summer, no one comprehends that
early fall exists, aftertaste, afterthought;
just these reeling sets of restless ultrasounds
exist, the bat's ears of jade
turned toward the ticking haze;
never has the tilting of the planet been so pleasant,
never the zinc-white nights so white,

so defencelessly dissolved, gently ionized and
white, never the limit of invisibility so nearly
touched; June, June, your Jacob's ladders,
your sleeping creatures and their dreams exist,
a drift of galactic seed between
earth so earthly and sky so heavenly,
the vale of tears so still, so still, and tears
sinking, sinking like groundwater back
into earth; Earth; Earth in its trajectory
around the sun exists, Earth on its journey
along the Milky Way, Earth on its course with
its cargo of jasmine, jasper, iron,
iron curtains, omens, jubilation, Judas's kiss
kissed right and left, and virgin anger in

the streets, Jesus of salt; with the shadow of the
jacaranda over the river, with gyrfalcons, jet planes,
and January in the heart, with Jacopo della Quercia's
well Fonte Gala in Siena and with July
heavy as a bomb, with domestic brains
heart defects, quaking grass and strawberries
the ironwood's roots in the earthworm earth

Earth sung by Jayadeva in his mystical
poem from the 12th century, Earth with
the coastline of consciousness blue, with nests where
fisherbird herons exist, with their grey-blue arching
backs, or where bitterns exist, cryptic
and shy, or night herons, egrets,
with the wingbeat variations of hedge sparrows, cranes
and doves; Earth exists with Jullundur, Jabalpur and
the Jungfrau, with Jotunheim, the Jura,
with Jabrun, Jambo, Jogjakarta,
with duststorms, Dutchman's breeches
with water and land masses jolted by tremors
with Judenburg, Johannesburg, Jerusalem's Jerusalem

Translated from the Danish by Susanna Nied

ADÉLIA PRADO
(BRAZIL, 1935–)

Denouement

I have great admiration for ships
and for certain people's handwriting which I attempt to imitate.
Of my entire family, I'm the only one who has seen the ocean,
I describe it over and over; they say "hmm"
and continue circling the chicken coop with wire.
I tell about the spume, and the wearisome size of the waters;
they don't remember there's such a place as Kenya,
they'd never guess I'm thinking of Tanzania.

Eagerly they show me the lot: this is where the kitchen will be,
That's where we'll put in a garden.
So what do I do with the coast?
It was a pretty afternoon the day I planted myself in the window,
   between uncles,
and saw the man with his fly open,
the trellis angry with roses.
Hours and hours we talked unconsciously in Portuguese
as if it were the only language in the world.
Faith or no, I ask where are my people who are gone;
because I'm human, I zealously cover the pan of leftover sauce.
How could we know how to live a better life than this,
when even weeping it feels so good to be together?
Suffering belongs to no language.
I suffered and I suffer both in Minas Gerais and at the edge of the ocean.
I stand in awe of being alive. Oh, moon over the backlands,
oh, forests I don't need to see to get lost in,
oh, great cities and states of Brazil that I love as if I had invented them.
Being Brazilian places me in a way I find moving
And this, which without sinning I can call fate,
gives my desire a rest.
Taken all at once, it's far too intelligible; I can't take it.
Night! Make yourself useful and cover me with sleep.
Me and the thought of death just can't get used to each other.
I'll tremble with fear till the end.
And meanwhile everything is so small.
Compared to my heart's desire
the sea is a drop.

Translated from the Portuguese by Ellen Doré Watson

Serenade

Some night under a pale moon and geraniums
he would come with his incredible hands and mouth
to play the flute in the garden.
I am beginning to despair
and can see only two choices:

either go crazy or turn holy.
I, who reject and reprove
anything that's not natural as blood and veins,
discover that I cry daily,
my hair saddened, strand by strand,
my skin attacked by indecision.
When he comes, for it's clear that he's coming,
how will I go out onto the balcony without my youth?
He and the moon and the geraniums will be the same—
only women of all things grow old.
How will I open the window, unless I'm crazy?
How will I close it, unless I'm holy?

Translated from the Portuguese by Ellen Doré Watson

The Tenacious Devil Who Doesn't Exist

God's glory is greater
                  than this plane in the sky.
And his love,
           which is where my fear comes from,
that sea of delights
           where planes crash
           and ships founder,
I know oh so well,
and I also know what a disastrous thing it is
           to be the body of time,
                  to exist,
the intermittent terror.
Jonathan, if death is love
               then why
—if I'm so certain—am I still afraid?
How can a fish be happy when I'm not?
Strange, this business of being human.
I opened the door one evening,
and there was a toad
              with this throbbing gullet,
        a gentle toad.

And I thought: it's Jonathan in disguise
                    come to visit me.
Even so, I shooed him away with a broom
                    and went to watch television.
Under a starry sky,
        I was sleepless, astonished.
God's love is Beauty,
                    they're one in the same.
I want to be holy like Agnes
who flies on the wings of beetles
        singing to soothe me
                    with her little girl's voice:
"Cast off the chains
            around your neck,
            O captive daughter of Zion."
            Airplanes are scary
            because God is in them.
Embrace me, God, with Your
            flesh and blood arm.
        Sing with Your mouth
            to keep me innocent.

Translated from the Portuguese by Ellen Doré Watson

JORGE TEILLIER
(CHILE, 1935–1996)

End of the World

The day the world ends
will be clean and orderly
like the notebook
of the best student in the class.
The town drunk
will sleep in a ditch,
the express train will pass
without stopping at the station

and the regimental band
will endlessly practice
the march they have played in the square
                              for twenty years.

Only some children
will leave their kites tangled
in telephone lines
to run home crying
not knowing what to tell their mothers
and I will carve my initials
in the bark of a linden tree
knowing that it won't do any good.

The kids will play football
in the empty lot on the edge of town.
The holy sects will come out
                to sing on the street corners.
The crazy old woman will pass with her parasol.
And I will say to myself: "The world cannot end,
because here on the patio the pigeons and the sparrows
are still squabbling over the grain."

Translated from the Spanish by Miller Williams

SALAH NIAZI
(IRAQ, 1935–)

Third World

One per cent
Six per cent
Ten per cent
The government beams in pictures and papers,
And squats in printing presses
Capturing its days in stamps
Recording victories,
                Recording revenge.

Today's poet doesn't read figures,
His tomorrow is now.
                              If he's hungry he blocks the path of the rulers
If he's cold he steals the flag.

Translated from the Arabic by Abdullah al-Udhari

LARS GUSTAFSSON
(SWEDEN, 1936–)

Ballad of the Dogs

When Ibn Batutta, Arabian traveller,
physician, clear-eyed observer of the world,
born in Maghreb in the fourteenth century, came
to the city of Bulgar, he learnt about the Darkness.
This "Darkness" was a country, forty days' travel
further to the north. At the end of Ramadan,
when he broke his fast at sunset, he had barely time
to intone the night prayer before day
broke again. The birches glimmered whitely.
Ibn Batutta, Arabian traveller, journeyed
no further north than Bulgar. But the tales he heard
of the Darkness, and of the visits there, engrossed him.
This journey is made only by rich merchants,
who take hundreds of sledges with them, loaded
with food, drink and firewood, for the ground there
is covered with ice and no-one can keep his balance.
Except the dogs: their claws take firm hold
of the eternal ice. No trees, no stones,
no huts can serve the traveller as landmarks.
Only those long-lived dogs are guides into
the Country of the Darkness, those old dogs
who have made the journey many times before.
They can cost a thousand dinars, or even more,
since for their knowledge there is no substitute.
At meals they are always served before the men:

otherwise the leading dog grows angry
and escapes, leaving its master to his fate.
In the great Darkness. After they have travelled
for forty days the merchants make a halt,
place their wares on the ground and return to their camp.
Returning on the following day they find
heaps of sable, ermine, miniver,
set down a little apart from their own pile.
If the merchant is content with this exchange
he takes the skins. If not, he leaves them there.
Then the inhabitants of the Darkness raise
their bid with more furs, or else take back
everything they laid out before, rejecting
the foreigners' goods. Such is the way they trade.
Ibn Batutta returned to Maghreb, and there
at a great age he died. But these dogs,
mute but sagacious, lacking the power of speech
and yet with a blind certainty that guides them
across wind-polished ice into the Darkness,
will never leave us in peace.
We speak, and what we say knows more than we do.
We think, and what we thought runs on before us,
as if that thought knew something we didn't know.
Messages travel through history, a code
masquerading as ideas
but meant for someone other than ourselves.
The history of ideas is not a knowledge of the mind.
And the dogs go on, with sure and swishing steps,
deeper into the Darkness.

Translated from the Swedish by Philip Martin

MARIN SORESCU
(ROMANIA, 1936–1997)

Destiny

The hen I'd bought the night before,
Frozen,
Had come to life,
Had laid the biggest egg in the world
And had been awarded the Nobel Prize.

The phenomenal egg
Was passed from hand to hand,
In a few weeks it had gone round the world,
And round the sun
In 365 days.

The hen had received who knows how much strong currency
Valued in pails of grain
Which she never managed to eat

Because she was invited everywhere,
Gave lectures, granted interviews,
Was photographed.

Often the reporters insisted
That I should be there too
In the photograph
Beside her.

And so, after having served Art
All my life

Suddenly I'm famous
As a poultry-breeder.

Translated from the Romanian by Ted Hughes and Ioana Russell-Gebbett

With a Green Scarf

With a green scarf I blindfolded
the eyes of the trees
and asked them to catch me.

At once the trees caught me,
their leaves shaking with laughter.

I blindfolded the birds
with a scarf of clouds
and asked them to catch me.

The birds caught me
with a song.

Then with a smile I blindfolded
my sorrow
and the day after it caught me
with a love.

I blindfolded the sun
with my nights
and asked the sun to catch me.

I know where you are, the sun said,
just behind that time.
Don't bother to hide any longer.

Don't bother to hide any longer,
said all of them,
as well as all the feelings
I tried to blindfold.

Translated from the Romanian by Michael Hamburger

DAHLIA RAVIKOVITCH
(ISRAEL, 1936–2005)

Hovering at a Low Altitude

I am not here.
I am on those craggy eastern hills
streaked with ice
where grass doesn't grow
and a sweeping shadow overruns the slope.
A little shepherd girl
with a herd of goats,
black goats,
emerges suddenly
from an unseen tent.
She won't live out the day, that girl,
in the pasture.

I am not here.
Inside the gaping mouth of the mountain
a red globe flares
not yet a sun.
A lesion of frost, flushed and sickly,
revolves in that maw.

And the little one rose so early
to go to the pasture.
She doesn't walk with neck outstretched
and wanton glances.
She doesn't paint her eyes with kohl.
She doesn't ask, Whence cometh my help.

I am not here.
I've been in the mountains many days now.
The light will not scorch me. The frost cannot touch me.
Nothing can amaze me now.
I've seen worse things in my life.

I tuck my dress tight around my legs and hover
very close to the ground.
What ever was she thinking, that girl?
Wild to look at, unwashed.
For a moment she crouches down.
Her cheeks soft silk,
frostbite on the back of her hand.
She seems distracted, but no,
in fact she's alert.
She still has a few hours left.
But that's hardly the object of my meditations.
My thoughts, soft as down, cushion me comfortably.
I've found a very simple method,
not so much as a foot-breadth on land
and not flying, either—
hovering at a low altitude.

But as day tends toward noon,
many hours
after sunrise,
that man makes his way up the mountain.
He looks innocent enough.
The girl is right there, close by,
not another soul around.
And if she runs for cover, or cries out—
there's no place to hide in the mountains.

I am not here.
I'm above those savage mountain ranges
in the farthest reaches of the east.
No need to elaborate.
With a single hurling thrust one can hover
and whirl about with the speed of the wind.
Can make a getaway and persuade myself:
I haven't seen a thing.
And the little one, her eyes start from their sockets,
her palate is dry as a potsherd,

when a hard hand grasps her hair, gripping her
without a shred of pity.

Translated from the Hebrew by Chana Bloch and Chana Kronfeld

A Dress of Fire

for Yitzhak Livni

You know, she said, they made you a dress of fire.
Remember how Jason's wife burned in her dress?
It was Medea, she said, Medea did that to her.
You've got to be careful, she said,
they made you a dress that glows like an ember,
burns like coals.

Are you going to wear it, she said, don't wear it.
It's not the wind whistling, it's the poison seething.
You're not even a princess, what can you do to Medea?
Can't you tell one sound from another, she said,
it's not the wind whistling.

Remember, I told her, that time when I was six?
They shampooed my hair and I went out into the street.
The smell of shampoo trailed after me like a cloud.
Then I got sick from the wind and the rain.
I didn't know yet how to read Greek tragedies,
but that fragrance filled the air and I was very sick.
Now I can see it was an unnatural perfume.

What will become of you, she said, they made you a burning dress.
They made me a burning dress, I said. I know.
So why are you standing there, she said, you've got to be careful.
You know what a burning dress is, don't you?

I know, I said, but not about being careful.
The smell of that perfume gets me all confused.

I said to her: No one has to agree with me,
I don't put my trust in Greek tragedy.

But the dress, she said, the dress is on fire.
What are you saying, I shouted, what are you saying?
I'm not wearing a dress at all,
what's burning is me.

Translated from the Hebrew by Chana Bloch and Chana Kronfeld

VÉNUS KHOURY-GHATA
(LEBANON, 1937–)

from She Says

There were too many women for too few seasons
some of them turned themselves into willows to sweep the rivers
A dead-end village
the inhabitants' secrets were posted on swinging doors
the scent of wives handled in darkness impregnated the walls
No rain could erase it

The women existed through their fragrance
and the men had to search for them in the folds of sheets
in the stink of blood washed in copper pots

Monthly labor was the women's lot
they scrubbed at roofs soiled by the moon's excretions
and the menstrual blood of pubescent storks
till they wore the roof-tiles down

It appears that the rainbow was born there
of the rain which came before Noah
a dry rain which dripped pebbles and small stones

And then everything was white
the grass children's eyes the eyes of rabbits

Translated from the French by Marilyn Hacker

from Words

In those days   I know now   words declaimed the wind
besides pebbles there were moons but no lamps
the stars would emerge later from a brawl between two flintstones

I'll tell you everything there were five pebbles
one for each continent
vast enough   to contain a child of a different color

So there were   five children but no houses
windows but no walls
wind but no streets
the first man wore a stone around his neck

He made an arrangement with the first tree
an oak if I remember correctly
the one who got there first could drink up the ocean

Language at that time was a straight line reserved for birds
the letter "I" was the cleft of a female hummingbird
"h" a ladder with one rung necessary to replace a charred sun before
    nightfall
"o" a hole in the sole of the universe

Unlike the consonants with their rough garments
the vowels were naked
all the weaver's art consisted of humoring them
in the evening they counted each other to make sure no one was
    missing
in the rocky countries men slept without dreaming

Translated from the French by Marilyn Hacker

PENTTI SAARIKOSKI
(FINLAND, 1937–1983)

Potato Thief

The year was as long and dark as a bed,
I slept between two winds;
the bush was filling with black berries.

I went round two museums,
the first for turn-of-the-century middle-class interiors,
the second for state-purchased paintings
suitable for turn-of-the-century middle-class interiors.
The year was long and dark
the forest was pushing through the museums.

In summer the bush bloomed,
I very nearly bought a car
but then I stole a middle-class person's potatoes
and taught them how to behave themselves. Horrible summer!
Autumn gave us the moist glad eye from afar
and I was excluded from all restaurants.

I read some cardboard cut-out poets
with speech coming out of their mouths like writing;
the poets were sitting on wooden stools
in two forests and listening to the moon.

I slept without a pillow in a long and dark bed,
the police set off after me
and the potatoes thumbed their noses at the police.
The suns were small as black berries.
I hopped on a bike and fled from the world.
I pedaled up a hill and a girl was holding a basket,
a girl in a blue skirt, she sat on the bicycle rack.
At the top of the hill I took the girl's skirt off,
the girl opened her basket and tiny lions leapt straight out
and scrambled under the snow to hibernate.

The police were after me.
I leaped off the bicycle saddle through the moon into the sky.
I yelled "Last one through's a rotten egg."

Translated from the Finnish by Herbert Lomas

from Invitation to the Dance

XXII

Eating macaroni casserole
I'm reminded of the time in Belgrade
when I asked an East German official
can you really afford to lose talents
like Wolf Biermann and Rudolf Bahro
his reply was that in this phase
of historical development
the German Democratic Republic
did not need these men
the newspaper slid off my knees to the floor
I didn't say anything
what can you say to them
Guten Morgen and Gute Nacht

Translated from the Finnish by Anselm Hollo

OSCAR HAHN
(CHILE, 1938–)

Good Night, Dear

Good night, dear
may you dream about demons
and white cockroaches

and may you see eye-sockets
of death looking at you
from my eyes in flames

and let it not be a dream

Translated from the Spanish by James Hoggard

HAN YONGWUN
(KOREA, 1939–)

The Artist

I'm no artist but in bed
I can paint with my fingertip
your breast your mouth and cheeks,
and surely that crooked smile that floats around your eyebrows as you sleep.

When the neighbors are gone
and even the crickets quiet
I am still too shy to sing
the songs you taught me
to the sleeping cat.

I am not a poet but I can describe
your glance, your voice,
the way you walk in the garden
before coming to bed,
even each separate pebble
on the path that runs
the twenty steps from here to there.

Translated from the Korean by Bruce Taylor

AHARON SHABTAI

(ISRAEL, 1939–)

Rosh HaShanah

Even after the murder
of the child Muhammad on Rosh HaShanah,
the paper didn't go black.
In the same water in which the snipers
wash their uniforms,
I prepare my pasta,
and over it pour
olive oil in which I've browned
pine nuts,
which I cooked for two minutes with dried tomatoes,
crushed garlic, and a tablespoon of basil.
As I eat, the learned minister of foreign affairs
and public security
appears on the screen,
and when he's done
I write this poem.
For that's how it's always been—
the murderers murder,
the intellectuals make it palatable,
and the poet sings.

Translated from the Hebrew by Peter Cole

from *Metazivika*

16

My heart's so full of shit,
and that's the quality in me that sings:

Yesterday we fought with shouts
about money and you got hit—

your glasses flew off—
but the day before

I came to you with my tongue
from the ankle up to your ears

an hour and a half or more
(my cock, like the locomotive

in *La Bête Humaine* by Renoir
pulling the mouth and face around and around

—inside, forward and back—
the body rushing it blood

like fire within me and coal);
you screamed, and bit my lip,

like in Herodotus, where the story's told
of the female flying snake

which, as it comes to a climax,
pierces the throat of its mate.

Translated from the Hebrew by Peter Cole

28

When you were twenty, not wanting to miss even an hour
with your lover who was set to leave for Algiers

you faked a serious stomach ache and played the part so well
that you were taken from the studio to Hospital

Hôtel Dieu's emergency room, where, despite your denials,
an overly zealous doctor removed your appendix after he'd put you under.

Now you're asleep, and beside you I'm wide awake, still
thinking about that scar, that pale seal

branded across your belly for love of a distant and different man
who long ago drowned in the sea. Lord, how I envy him

who, packing a bag and adding some books and trousers,
suddenly gets a call and goes to answer.

Again and again I'm tempted to follow the way
he takes along that river, toward l'Île de la Cité:

with me he buys you flowers, climbs the stairs to the right ward
and the room that's draped in white, looks around, then moves toward

your bed, and there inside me you're waiting for him, breathless—
and he smothers your smiling mouth, like a pomegranate, in kisses . . .

Translated from the Hebrew by Peter Cole

JOSEPH BRODSKY
(RUSSIA, 1940–1996)

Elegy for John Donne

John Donne has sunk in sleep . . . All things beside
are sleeping too: walls, bed, and floor—all sleep.
The table, pictures, carpets, hooks and bolts,
clothes-closets, cupboards, candles, curtains—all
now sleep: the washbowl, bottle, tumbler, bread,
breadknife and china, crystal, pots and pans,
fresh linen, nightlamp, chests of drawers, a clock,
a mirror, stairway, doors. Night everywhere,
night in all things: in corners, in men's eyes,
in linen, in the papers on a desk,
in the wormed words of stale and sterile speech,
in logs and fire-tongs, in the blackened coals

of a dead fireplace—in each thing.
In undershirts, boots, stockings, shadows, shades,
behind the mirror, on the backs of chairs,
in bed and washbowl, on the crucifix,
in linen, in the broom beside the door,
in slippers. All these things have sunk in sleep.
Yes, all things sleep. The window. Snow beyond.
A roof-slope, whiter than a tablecloth,
the roof's high ridge. A neighborhood in snow,
carved to the quick by this sharp windowframe.
Arches and walls and windows—all asleep.
Wood paving-blocks, stone cobbles, gardens, grills.
No light will flare, no turning wheel will creak . . .
Chains, walled enclosures, ornaments, and curbs.
Doors with their rings, knobs, hooks are all asleep—
their locks and bars, their bolts and cunning keys.
One hears no whisper, rustle, thump, or thud.
Only the snow creaks. All men sleep. Dawn comes
not soon. All jails and locks have lapsed in sleep.
The iron weights in the fish-shop are asleep.
The carcasses of pigs sleep too. Backyards
and houses. Watch-dogs in their chains lie cold.
In cellars sleeping cats hold up their ears.
Mice sleep, and men. And London soundly sleeps.
A schooner nods at anchor. The salt sea
talks in its sleep with snows beneath her hull,
and melts into the distant sleeping sky.
John Donne has sunk in sleep, with him the sea.
Chalk cliffs now tower in sleep above the sand.
This Island sleeps, embraced by lonely dreams,
and every garden now is triple-barred.
The maples, pines, spruce, silver firs—all sleep.
On mountain slopes steep mountain-streams and paths
now sleep. Foxes and wolves. Bears in their dens.
The snowy drifts high at burrow-entrances.
All the birds sleep. Their songs are heard no more.
Nor is the crow's hoarse caw. 'Tis night. The owl's
dark, hollow laugh is silenced now.

The English countryside is still. Stars flame.
The mice are penitent. All creatures sleep.
The dead lie calmly in their graves and dream.
The living, in the oceans of their gowns,
sleep—each alone—within their beds. Or two
by two. Hills, woods, and rivers sleep. All birds
and beasts now sleep—nature alive and dead.
But still the snow spins white from the black sky.
There, high above men's heads, all are asleep.
The angels sleep. Saints—to their saintly shame—
have quite forgotten this our anxious world.
Dark Hell-fires sleep, and glorious Paradise.
No one goes forth from home at this bleak hour.
Even God has gone to sleep. Earth is estranged.
Eyes do not see, and ears perceive no sound.
The Devil sleeps. Harsh enmity has fallen
asleep with him on snowy English fields.
All horsemen sleep. And the Archangel, with
his trumpet. Horses, softly swaying, sleep.
And all the cherubim, in one great host
embracing, doze beneath St. Paul's high dome.
John Donne has sunk in sleep. His verses sleep.
His images, his rhymes, and his strong lines
fade out of view. Anxiety and sin,
alike grown slack, rest in his syllables.
And each verse whispers to its next of kin,
"Move on a bit." But each stands so remote
from Heaven's Gates, so poor, so pure and dense,
that all seem one. All are asleep. The vault
austere of iambs soars in sleep. Like guards,
the trochees stand and nod to left and right.
The vision of Lethean waters sleeps.
The poet's fame sleeps soundly at its side.
All trials, all sufferings, are sunk in sleep.
And vices sleep. Good lies in Evil's arms.
The prophets sleep. The bleaching snow seeks out,
through endless space, the last unwhitened spot.
All things have lapsed in sleep. The swarms of books,

the streams of words, cloaked in oblivion's ice,
sleep soundly. Every speech, each speech's truth,
is sleeping. Linked chains, sleeping, scarcely clank.
All soundly sleep: the saints, the Devil, God.
Their wicked servants. Children. Friends. The snow
alone sifts, rustling, on the darkened roads.
And there are no more sounds in the whole world.

But hark! Do you not hear in the chill night
a sound of sobs, the whispered voice of fear?
There someone stands, disclosed to winter's blast,
and weeps. There someone stands in the dense gloom.
His voice is thin. His voice is needle-thin,
yet without thread. And he in solitude
swims through the falling snow—cloaked in cold mist—
that stitches night to dawn. The lofty dawn.
"Whose sobs are those? My angel, is it thou?
Dost thou await my coming, there alone
beneath the snow? Dost walk—without my love—
in darkness home? Dost thou cry in the gloom?"
No answer.—"Is it you, oh cherubim,
whose muted tears put me in mind
of some sepulchral choir? Have you resolved
to quit my sleeping church? Is it not you?"
No answer.—"Is it thou, oh Paul? Thy voice
most certainly is coarsened by stern speech.
Hast thou not bowed thy grey head in the gloom
to weep?" But only silence makes reply.
"Has not that Hand protected my dull eyes,
that Hand which looms up here and in all times?
Is it not thou, Lord? No, my thought runs wild.
And yet how lofty is the voice that weeps."
No answer. Silence.—"Gabriel, hast thou
not blown thy trumpet to the roar of hounds?
But did I stand alone with open eyes
while horsemen saddled their swift steeds? Yet each
thing sleeps. Enveloped in huge gloom, the hounds
of Heaven race in packs. Oh Gabriel,

dost thou not sob, encompasséd about
by winter dark, alone, with thy great horn?"

"No, it is I, thy soul, John Donne, who speaks.
I grieve alone upon the heights of Heaven,
because my labors did bring forth to life
feelings and thoughts as heavy as stark chains.
Bearing this burden, thou couldst yet fly up
past those dark sins and passions, mounting higher.
Thou wast a bird, thy people didst thou see
in every place, as thou didst soar above
their sloping roofs. And thou didst glimpse the seas,
and distant lands, and Hell—first in thy dreams,
then waking. Thou didst see a jewelled Heaven
set in the wretched frame of men's low lusts.
Thou sawest Life: thine Island was its twin.
And thou didst face the ocean at its shores.
The howling dark stood close at every hand.
And thou didst soar past God, and then drop back,
for this harsh burden would not let thee rise
to that high vantage point from which this world
seems naught but ribboned rivers and tall towers—
that point from which, to him who downward stares,
this dread Last Judgment seems no longer dread.
The radiance of that Country does not fade.
From thence all here seems a faint, fevered dream.
From thence our Lord is but a light that gleams,
through fog, in window of the farthest house.
The fields lie fallow, furrowed by no plow.
The years lie fallow, and the centuries.
Forests alone stand, like a steady wall.
Enormous rains batter the dripping grass.
The first woodcutter—he whose withered steed,
in panic fear of thickets, blundered thence—
will mount a pine to catch a sudden glimpse
of fires in his own valley, far away.
All things are distant. What is near is dim.
The level glance slides from a roof remote.

All here is bright. No din of baying hound
or tolling bell disturbs the silent air.
And, sensing that all things are far away,
he'll wheel his horse back quickly toward the woods.
And instantly, reins, sledge, night, his poor steed,
himself—will melt into a Scriptural dream.

"But here I stand and weep. The road is gone.
I am condemned to live among these stones.
I cannot fly up in my body's flesh;
such flight at best will come to me through death
in the wet earth, when I've forgotten thee,
my world, forgotten thee once and for all.
I'll follow, in the torment of desire,
to stitch up this last parting with my flesh.
But hark! While here with weeping I disturb
thy rest, the busy snow whirls through the dark,
not melting, as it stitches up this hurt—
its needles flying back and forth, back, forth!
It is not I who sob. 'Tis thou, John Donne:
thou liest alone. Thy pans in cupboards sleep,
while snow builds drifts upon thy sleeping house—
while snow sifts down to earth from highest Heaven."

Like a wild bird, he sleeps in his cold nest,
his pure path and his thirst for purer life,
himself entrusting to that steady star
which now is closed in clouds. Like a wild bird,
his soul is pure, and his life's path on earth,
although it needs must wind through sin, is still
closer to nature than that tall crow's nest
which soars above the starlings' empty homes.
Like a wild bird, he too will wake at dawn;
but now he lies beneath a veil of white,
while snow and sleep stitch up the throbbing void
between his soul and his own dreaming flesh.
All things have sunk in sleep. But one last verse
awaits its end, baring its fangs to snarl

that earthly love is but a poet's duty,
while love celestial is an abbot's flesh.
Whatever millstone these swift waters turn
will grind the same coarse grain in this one world.
For though our life may be a thing to share,
who is there in this world to share our death?
Man's garment gapes with holes. It can be torn
by him who will, at this edge or at that.
It falls to shreds, and is made whole again.
Once more 'tis rent. And only the far sky,
in darkness, brings the healing needle home.
Sleep, John Donne, sleep. Sleep soundly, do not fret
thy soul. As for thy coat, 'tis torn; all limp
it hangs. But see, there from the clouds will shine
that star which made thy world endure till now.

Translated from the Russian by George L. Kline

A Prophecy

We'll go and live together by the shore;
huge dams will wall us from the continent.
A home-made lamp will hurl its warming glow
across the roundness of our centered space.
We shall wage war at cards, and cock an ear
to catch the crashing of the maddened surf.
We'll gently cough, or sigh a soundless sigh,
whenever the wind roars too raucously.

I shall be old, and you will still be young.
But, as the youngsters say, we'll count the time
that's left us till the new age breaks in days,
not years. In our reversed, small Netherland*

---

* The "Netherland" is "reversed" in the sense that it lies on the *sea* side of the
dam. The latter serves as a barrier not against the sea but against the mainland,
with its threat of atomic devastation.

we'll plant a kitchen-garden, you and I;
and we shall sizzle oysters by the door,
and drink the rays of the sun's octopus.

Let summer rains crash on our cucumbers;
we'll get as tanned as any Eskimo,
and you will run your fingers tenderly
along the virgin *V* where I'm unburned.*
I'll see my collarbone in the clear glass,
and glimpse a mirrored wave behind my back,
and my old Geiger counter, cased in tin,
that dangles from its faded, sweat-soaked strap.

When winter comes, unpitying, it will
twist off the thatch from our wood roof. And if
we make a child, we'll call the boy Andrei,
Anna the girl, so that our Russian speech,
imprinted on its wrinkled little face,
shall never be forgot. Our alphabet's
first sound is but the lengthening of a sigh
and thus may be affirmed for future time.

We shall wage war at cards until the tide's
retreating sinuosities draw us,
with all our trumps, down and away . . .
Our child will gaze in silence at a moth,
not fathoming its urgent moth-motives
for beating at our lamp. But then the time
will come when he must make his way back through
the dam that walls us from the continent.

Translated from the Russian by George L. Kline

---

* The V-shaped area on chest and collarbones shielded from the sun's rays by the
strap of the Geiger counter.

SAPARDI DJOKO DAMONNO
(INDONESIA, 1940–)

Who Are You

I am Adam
who ate the apple;
Adam suddenly aware of himself,
startled and ashamed,
I am Adam who realized
good and evil, passing
from one sin to another;
Adam continuously suspicious
of himself,
hiding his face.
I am Adam floundering
in the net of space and time,
with no help from reality:
paradise lost
because of my mistrust
of the Presence.
I am Adam
who heard God say

farewell, Adam.

Translated from the Indonesian by Burton Raffel

CAITLÍN MAUDE
(IRELAND, 1941–1982)

I Long for a Rhyme of Health

I long for a rhyme of health
a small fresh syllable
a poultice of words

to put the soul right
and make the body strong.

I long for a rhyme
to put the soul right.

Translated from the Gaelic by Pearse Hutchinson

TOMAŽ ŠALAMUN
(SLOVENIA, 1941–)

Pour un jeune Chalamoun qui se vend dans la rue

Powerful white teeth!
Membranes that enter the village of my eyes like
swords. I want your soul, to give it
to mine. I'm tired of
taking, I'd rather give myself.
Tu te rends compte? Am I to rent another
loft to dry our souls? This hotel
practice is costing me
enough already. I'm a professional and so are
you, only your trade is blank paper.
Every sheep, every cow is capital.
And I want my own sheep, my own
cows, not those stinking beasts
Alsatian peasants own. My animals are
history, because they give milk. But
you throw your paper away so that
store windows smell of your soul, which is
exuded from your books, as though they were some kind
of apple. Okay, give me your body for free, but this will
cost you. My job is not to
give my soul, just to take the money and not
give my soul.

Translated from the Slovenian by Michael Biggins

The Field of Ptuj

To my great-grandfather, General Franz Von Mally (1821–1893)

You were tired at the very beginning.
When like a trained monkey you posed
with your saber. At the ceremony
when you were made a baron. We forgive you
for looking ridiculous. You thought about duty
and the investment in future generations.
In Zadar you had grown bored. The troops
played cards, spread syphilis. Your wife
begged you to come back to Vienna.
Did you even notice when that Mr. Toplak
carried off your daughter? Your investment
had gone to Ptuj. When the messenger
brought the news that you disinherited her,
Baberle turned gray on the mountain road.
Dumbfounded she stared at her offspring.
She never understood the language of her children
raised by barbaric Slavic maids. It's written:
our mother lay down all white and kept
pressing the buzzer no one heard.
That's not the way you figured it, *mon général.*

Translated from the Slovenian by Christopher Merrill

MEIR WIESELTIER
(RUSSIA/ISRAEL, 1941–)

Abraham

The only thing in the world Abraham loved was God.
He didn't love the gods of others. Those people
slept with their wives every night and stuffed themselves with meat
    and wine.

Their gods were made of wood or clay and painted vermilion,
then sold like onions in the market to the highest bidder.
He figured out his own God, and made himself His chosen.

He loved that God above everything else in the world.
He wouldn't bow to the gods of others; he told them: if you go right
I'll go left, if you go left, I'll go right.
He told them: you can't accuse me of a get-rich scheme.
He refused to give or take anything
except with God. If only He'd asked
He'd have got it. Anything. Even Isaac the only son, the trusting heir
(but if there's a God, there's an angel).

Abraham didn't value a thing in the world but God.
Against Him, he never sinned, there was no difference between them.
Unlike Isaac who loved his uncouth son, unlike Jacob
who slaved for women, who limped from God's thrashing all night,
who saw angeled ladders only in dreams.
Not Abraham. He loved God and God loved him.
And together they counted the righteous of the cities before wiping
    them out.

Translated from the Hebrew by Shirley Kaufman

MAHMOUD DARWISH
(PALESTINIAN TERRITORIES, 1941–2008)

And We Love Life

And we love life if we find a way to it.
We dance in between martyrs and raise a minaret for violet or palm trees.

We love life if we find a way to it.

And we steal from the silkworm a thread to build a sky and fence in
    this departure.

We open the garden gate for the jasmine to go out as a beautiful day
    on the streets.

We love life if we find a way to it.

And we plant, where we settle, some fast growing plants, and harvest
    the dead.
We play the flute like the color of the faraway, sketch over the dirt
    corridor a neigh.
We write our names one stone at a time, O lightning make the night
    a bit clearer.

We love life if we find a way to it . . .

Translated from the Arabic by Fady Joudah

We Travel Like All People

We travel like all people, but we return to nothing . . . as if traveling
is the way of the clouds. We buried our loved ones in cloud shadows
and between tree roots then told our wives: Give birth to hundreds
of years so we can complete this departure
toward an hour of country and a meter of the impossible. We travel
in the carriages of the Psalms, sleep in the tents of prophets, come out
of gypsy words, measure space with a hoopoe's beak, or sing to distract the
    distance
from who we are, and wash the moonlight.
Your road is long so dream of seven women to carry this long road on your
    shoulders.
And shake the palm trees for the women so you may know their names
and the one who will birth Galilee's son.
We have a country of words. So speak, speak that I may lean
my path on a stone made of stone. We have a country of words.
Speak, speak that we may know an end to this travel!

Translated from the Arabic by Fady Joudah

On the Last Evening on This Earth

On the last evening on this earth, we sever our days
from our trees, and count the ribs we will carry along
and the ribs we will leave behind, right here . . . on the last evening
we bid nothing farewell, we don't find the time to end who we are . . .
everything remains the same, the place exchanges our dreams
and exchanges its visitors. Suddenly we are incapable of satire
since the place is ready to host the dust . . . Here on the last evening
we contemplate mountains surrounding clouds: a conquest and a
    counter-conquest
and an ancient time handing over our door keys to the new time
so enter, you conquerors, our homes and drink our wine
out of our simple *muwashah*. We are the night when midnight
    comes, no
horseman carries the dawn from the ways of the final Azaan . . .
our tea is hot and green so drink it, our pistachio fresh so eat it
and our beds are cedar green, so surrender to sleepiness
after this long siege, sleep on our dreams' feathers,
the sheets are ready, the perfume by the door is ready, and the mirrors
    are many
for you to enter them so we can leave them entire. In a little while we
    will search
for what was our history around your history in the distant lands
and ask ourselves in the end: Was the Andalus
right here or over there? On earth . . . or in the poem?

Translated from the Arabic by Fady Joudah

Remainder of a Life

If I were told:
By evening you will die,
so what will you do until then?
I would look at my wristwatch,
drink a glass of juice,
bite an apple,
contemplate at length an ant that has found its food,

then look at my wristwatch.
There'd be time left to shave my beard
and dive in a bath, obsess:
"There must be an adornment for writing,
so let it be a blue garment."
I'd sit until noon alive at my desk
but wouldn't see the trace of color in the words,
white, white, white . . .
I'd prepare my last lunch,
pour wine in two glasses: one for me
and one for the one who will come without appointment,
then I'd take a nap between two dreams.
But my snoring would wake me . . .
so I'd look at my wristwatch:
and there'd be time left for reading.
I'd read a chapter in Dante and half of a *mu'allaqah*
and see how my life goes from me
to the others, but I wouldn't ask who
would fill what's missing in it.
That's it, then?
That's it, that's it. Then what?
Then I'd comb my hair and throw away the poem . . .
this poem, in the trash,
and put on the latest fashion in Italian shirts,
parade myself in an entourage of Spanish violins,
and walk to the grave!

Translated from the Arabic by Fady Joudah

Viewpoint

The difference between narcissus
and sunflower
is a point of view: the first
stares at his image in water
and says there is no I but I
and the second looks
at the sun and says I am

what I worship.
And at night, difference shrinks
and interpretation widens.

Translated from the Arabic by Fady Joudah

LEI SHUYAN
(CHINA, 1942–)

Creation

With the scalpel of time
I cut mystic fissures in the brain.

All that has not yet happened
That has already happened
That will happen
Is rippling water within those fissures.

Where no beauty exists
I would create beauty.

I shall create a planet
And get it ready to collide with earth.

Translated from the Chinese by Fang Dai, Dennis Ding, and
Edward Morin

PATRICE KAYO
(CAMEROON, 1942–)

Song of the Initiate

All the wives of my father
      pulled my mother to bits

But their children cannot dance
It is I who have taken my father's stool
And my mother has become queen
All the wives of my father my wives
        and servants of my mother.

The mother of those who cannot dance
        has never borne children
Her children are nothing but epileptics
        The initiate alone with the chief.

If only I were a river!
I would roll down all silvery
And in the compound of the non-initiate
        I would become a swamp.

I am only a dealer in pigs
        and in chickens
But if you have any pearls or little bells
        I will buy them.
The only son alone
Is sure of his father's stool.
The panther's child does not fear the night
I can dance all the dances
And my mother eats nothing but the flesh of sparrowhawks.

Translated from the French by Gerald Moore

GYÖRGY PETRI
(HUNGARY, 1943–2000)

I Am Stuck, Lord, on Your Hook

I am stuck, Lord, on your hook.
I've been wriggling there, curled up,
for the past twenty-six years

alluringly, and yet
the line has never gone taut.
It's now clear
there are no fish in your river.
Lord, if you still have hopes,
choose some other worm. Being
among the elect
has been beautiful. All the same,
what I'd just like to do, right now,
is dry off and loll about in the sun.

Translated from the Hungarian by Clive Wilmer and George Gömöri

Night Song of the Personal Shadow

The rain is pissing down,
you scum.
And you, you are asleep
in your nice warm room—
that or stuffing the bird.
Me? Till six in the morning
I rot in the slackening rain.
I must wait for my relief, I've got to wait
till you crawl out of your hole,
get up from beside your old woman.
So the dope can be passed on
as to where you've flown.
You are flying, spreading your wings.
Don't you get into my hands—
I'll pluck you while you're in flight.
This sodding rain
is something I won't forget,
my raincoat swelling
double its normal weight
and the soles of my shoes.
While you
were arsing around
in the warm room.

The time will come
when I feed you to fish in the Danube.

Translated from the Hungarian by Clive Wilmer and George Gömöri

RYSZARD KRYNICKI
(AUSTRIA/POLAND, 1943–)

Save Me, Guide Me

Save me, shield me, faithful journey,
from my own lies and from our era.
Protect me, you, Angel and Guardian,
but you, White Cloud, guide me.

Keep me from thunder, hurricane,
immaculate truth, give me light.
Don't overlook me, little dove,
when you send us a sign from the heights.

Forgive me, twilight,
don't pierce me, spear of nightmares.
Don't bless me with madness,

wake me, morning star.

Translated from the Polish by Alissa Valles

FRANCESC PARCERISAS
(SPAIN, 1944–)

The Defeated

> *Those who invade the streets, in their sheepskin coats, their medals*
> *and their uniforms, are a different race.*
> —FELICIDAD BLANC, *ESPEJO DE SOMBRAS*

> *What is gained in losing*
> —ROBERT LOWELL

They are Franco's troops and they have won the battles.
For you there's nothing left but the grave or beyond,
the luckless marvel of waking up among the ashes.
You hear a shout: "It's them! They're coming!"
and feel like cowards, afraid, offended.
You were done down by an abject shadow of life.
And now, fifty years later—too young
to look for reparation—I can still see you,
silent with a trembling finger at your lips,
and I love you submitting to an order of great fear,
with the dignity of being in the right
or under nocturnal headlights of defeat.
Your silence has been a tangled wire,
showing us what is gained in losing.

Translated from the Catalan by Pearse Hutchinson

Act of Gratitude

Thank you, angel. Thank you, demons of the night.
Thank you, winter where the heart burns
arid tree-trunks of desire. Thank you,
bracing cold light, nocturnal water.
Thank you, midnight bile,
laurel of morning, hoopoe of dawn.
For what's odd, unexpected, wild,

for evil and pain, thank you.
For the sum of what we are
and are not,
for all we avoid
and all we crave.
Thanks for the lush words,
love and silver,
for yourself and myself.
Thank you for yes and for no.
For the ability to give thanks
and for rendering them unnecessary.
Thanks for fear,
for bread and oil,
for the night time.
Thank you for lovemaking
at the break of day, for the coin
discovered on the ground,
for your hand on my cheek,
the gush of the fountain.
Thank you for your eyes and lips,
for crying out my name with joy.
Many thanks, death, for your existence,
for making all these things
more vivid inside me—so very yours,
so beautiful, brimming, and complete.

Translated from the Catalan by Cyrus Cassells

ABBAS BEYDOUN
(LEBANON, 1945–)

White Lie

The truth is also blood.
And it might be a piece of tongue
or something severed from us.
We might find it in semen

or in dust if these two things
are not simply appearances
and if the blood does not suddenly
vanish or whiten as a lie.
Should we let the roses
or the strokes against the chest consume
those who lost their truth
as they fought their lies?
Is it the alarm clock's fault
or do we not permit
our clocks such precise appointments.
The sun is our tryst and
we do not know what it gathers now.
We are the meeting of strangers
and we do not ask why love drives free souls
and then abandons them, to scatter,
beneath the heavy rain.

Translated from the Arabic by Fady Joudah

HENRIK NORDBRANDT
(DENMARK, 1945–)

Our Love Is Like Byzantium

Our love is like Byzantium
must have been
on the last evening. There must have been
I imagine
a glow on the faces
of those who crowded the streets
or stood in small groups
on streetcorners and public squares
speaking together in low voices
that must have resembled
the glow your face has

when you brush your hair back
and look at me.

I imagine they haven't spoken
much, and about rather
ordinary things
that they have been trying to say
and have stopped
without having managed to express
what they wanted
and have been trying again
and given up again
and have been looking at each other
and lowered their eyes.

Very old icons, for instance,
have that kind of glow
the blaze of a burning city
or the glow which approaching death
leaves on photographs of people who died young
in the memory of those left behind.

When I turn towards you
in bed, I have a feeling
of stepping into a church
that was burned down long ago
and where only the darkness in the eyes of the icons
has remained
filled with the flames
which annihilated them.

Translated from the Danish by the author and Alexander Taylor

ADAM ZAGAJEWSKI

(POLAND, 1945–)

To Go to Lvov

To go to Lvov. Which station
for Lvov, if not in a dream, at dawn, when dew
gleams on a suitcase, when express
trains and bullet trains are being born. To leave
in haste for Lvov, night or day, in September
or in March. But only if Lvov exists,
if it is to be found within the frontiers and not just
in my new passport, if lances of trees
—of poplar and ash—still breathe aloud
like Indians, and if streams mumble
their dark Esperanto, and grass snakes like soft signs
in the Russian language disappear
into thickets. To pack and set off, to leave
without a trace, at noon, to vanish
like fainting maidens. And burdocks, green
armies of burdocks, and below, under the canvas
of a Venetian café, the snails converse
about eternity. But the cathedral rises,
you remember, so straight, as straight
as Sunday and white napkins and a bucket
full of raspberries standing on the floor, and
my desire which wasn't born yet,
only gardens and weeds and the amber
of Queen Anne cherries, and indecent Fredro.
There was always too much of Lvov, no one could
comprehend its boroughs, hear
the murmur of each stone scorched
by the sun, at night the Orthodox church's silence was unlike
that of the cathedral, the Jesuits
baptized plants, leaf by leaf, but they grew,
grew so mindlessly, and joy hovered
everywhere, in hallways and in coffee mills
revolving by themselves, in blue

teapots, in starch, which was the first
formalist, in drops of rain and in the thorns
of roses. Frozen forsythia yellowed by the window.
The bells pealed and the air vibrated, the cornets
of nuns sailed like schooners near
the theater, there was so much of the world that
it had to do encores over and over,
the audience was in frenzy and didn't want
to leave the house. My aunts couldn't have known
yet that I'd resurrect them,
and lived so trustfully, so singly;
servants, clean and ironed, ran for
fresh cream, inside the houses
a bit of anger and great expectation, Brzozowski
came as a visiting lecturer, one of my
uncles kept writing a poem entitled Why,
dedicated to the Almighty, and there was too much
of Lvov, it brimmed the container,
it burst glasses, overflowed
each pond, lake, smoked through every
chimney, turned into fire, storm,
laughed with lightning, grew meek,
returned home, read the New Testament,
slept on a sofa beside the Carpathian rug,
there was too much of Lvov, and now
there isn't any, it grew relentlessly
and the scissors cut it, chilly gardeners
as always in May, without mercy,
without love, ah, wait till warm June
comes with soft ferns, boundless
fields of summer, i.e., the reality.
But scissors cut it, along the line and through
the fiber, tailors, gardeners, censors
cut the body and the wreaths, pruning shears worked
diligently, as in a child's cutout
along the dotted line of a roe deer or a swan.
Scissors, penknives, and razor blades scratched,
cut, and shortened the voluptuous dresses

of prelates, of squares and houses, and trees
fell soundlessly, as in a jungle,
and the cathedral trembled, people bade goodbye
without handkerchiefs, no tears, such a dry
mouth, I won't see you anymore, so much death
awaits you, why must every city
become Jerusalem and every man a Jew,
and now in a hurry just
pack, always, each day,
and go breathless, go to Lvov, after all
it exists, quiet and pure as
a peach. It is everywhere.

Translated from the Polish by Renata Gorczynski

Late Beethoven

> *I haven't yet known a man who loved virtue as strongly as one
> loves beauty.*
>
> —CONFUCIUS

Nobody knows who she was, the Immortal
Beloved. Apart from that, everything is
clear. Feathery notes rest
peacefully on the threads of the staff
like martins just come
from the Atlantic. What would I have to be
in order to speak about him, he who's still
growing. Now we are walking alone
without ghosts or banners. Long live
chaos, say our solitary mouths.
We know that he dressed carelessly,
that he was given to fits of avarice, that he wasn't
always fair to his friends.
Friends are a hundred years
late with their impeccable smiles. Who
was the Immortal Beloved? Certainly,
he loved virtue more than beauty.

But a nameless god of beauty dwelled
in him and compelled his obedience.
He improvised for hours. A few minutes
of each improvisation were noted down.
These minutes belong neither to the nineteenth
nor to the twentieth century; as if hydrochloric
acid burned a window in velvet, thus
opening a passage to even
smoother velvet, thin as
a spiderweb. Now they name
ships and perfumes after him. They don't know who
the Immortal Beloved was, otherwise
new cities and pâtés would bear her
name. But it's useless. Only velvet
growing under velvet, like a leaf hidden
safely in another leaf. Light in darkness.
Unending adagios. That's how tired freedom
breathes. Biographers argue only
over details. Why he tormented
his nephew Karl so much. Why
he walked so fast. Why he didn't go
to London. Apart from that, everything is clear.
We don't know what music is. Who speaks
in it. To whom it is addressed. Why it is
so obstinately silent. Why it circles and returns
instead of giving a straight answer
as the Gospel demands. Prophecies
were not fulfilled. The Chinese didn't reach
the Rhine. Once more, it turned out that
the real world doesn't exist, to the immense
relief of antiquaries. The secret was hidden
somewhere else, not in soldiers'
knapsacks, but in a few notebooks.
Grillparzer, he, Chopin. Generals are
cast in lead and in tinsel to
give hell's flame a moment of respite
after kilowatts of straw. Unending adagios,

but first and foremost joy, wild
joy of shape, the laughing sister of death.

Translated from the Polish by Renata Gorczynski

Try to Praise the Mutilated World

Try to praise the mutilated world.
Remember June's long days,
and wild strawberries, drops of wine, the dew.
The nettles that methodically overgrow
the abandoned homesteads of exiles.
You must praise the mutilated world.
You watched the stylish yachts and ships;
one of them had a long trip ahead of it,
while salty oblivion awaited others.
You've seen the refugees heading nowhere,
you've heard the executioners sing joyfully.
You should praise the mutilated world.
Remember the moments when we were together
in a white room and the curtain fluttered.
Return in thought to the concert where music flared.
You gathered acorns in the park in autumn
and leaves eddied over the earth's scars.
Praise the mutilated world
and the grey feather a thrush lost,
and the gentle light that strays and vanishes
and returns.

Translated from the Polish by Clare Cavanagh

A Talk with Friedrich Nietzsche

Most highly respected Professor Nietzsche,
sometimes I seem to see you
on a sanatorium terrace at dawn
with fog descending and song bursting
the throats of the birds.

Not tall, head like a bullet,
you compose a new book
and a strange energy hovers around you.
Your thoughts parade
like enormous armies.

You know now that Anne Frank died,
and her classmates and friends, boys, girls,
and friends of her friends, and cousins
and friends of her cousins.

What are words, I want to ask you, what
is clarity and why do words keep burning
a century later, though the earth
weighs so much?

Clearly nothing links enlightenment
and the dark pain of cruelty.
At least two kingdoms exist,
if not more.

But if there's no God and no force
welds elements in repulsion,
then what are words really, and from whence
does their inner light come?

And from whence does joy come, and where
does nothingness go? Where is forgiveness?
Why do the incidental dreams vanish at dawn
and the great ones keep growing?

Translated from the Polish by Renata Gorczynski,
Benjamin Ivry, and C. K. Williams

Music Heard with You

Music I heard with you was more than music . . .

Music heard with you
will stay forever with us.

Grave Brahms and elegaic Schubert,
a few songs, Chopin's third sonata,

a couple of quartets with heart-
breaking chords (Beethoven, adagia),

the sadness of Shostakovich that
didn't want to die.

The great choruses of Bach's Passions,
as if someone had summoned us,

demanding joy,
pure and disinterested,

joy in which faith
is self-evident.

Some scraps of Lutoslawski
as fugitive as our thoughts.

A black woman singing blues
ran through us like shining steel,

even though it reached us on the street
of an ugly, dirty town.

Mahler's endless marches,
the trumpet's voice opening Symphony no. 5

and the first part of the Ninth
(you sometimes call him "malheur!").

Mozart's despair in the Requiem,
his buoyant piano concertos—

you hummed them better than I did,
but we both know that.

Music heard with you
will grow still with us.

Translated from the Polish by Clare Cavanagh

PATRIZIA CAVALLI
(ITALY, 1947–)

But first one must free oneself

But first one must free oneself
of the precise greed that produces us, that produces me sitting
in the corner of a bar
waiting with clerical passion
for the exact moment when
the little azure fires of the eyes opposite, of the eyes acclimatized to risk, the
trajectory precalculated, will demand a blush
from my face. And will obtain a blush.

Translated from the Italian by Robert McCracken and the author

Far from kingdoms

Far from kingdoms
how steady is the room!
Come, breathe close with me
so I may discover the sweetness
of many imperfections, some missing tooth,

some extra wrinkle, and your body
worn out slightly by carelessnesses

Translated from the Italian by Judith Baumel

AGI MISHOL
(HUNGARY, 1947–)

In the Supermarket

1.

Through the supermarket aisles I push a cart
as if I were the mother of two heads of cauliflower,
and navigate according to the verse-list
I improvised this morning over coffee.
Sale banners wave to shoppers
studying the labels on packaged foods
as Muzak entertains the frozen birds. And I too,
whose life is made of life, stride down the dog-food aisle
toward Mr. Flinker who confides in my ear that only the body
crumbles but the spirit remains young forever, believe me.
I believe, but now let me turn to Granny Smith and McIntosh.
Hurry hurry, folks, to the coriander,
hurry hurry, folks, I'm the supermarket bard,
I'll sing the rustle of cornflakes,
the curve of mutinous cucumbers,
until the cash register will hand me
the final printed version
of my poem.

2.

I stroll in the supermarket clad in the essence of my housewifery
when suddenly, near the pickles,
you kid me, "Agi-Bagi"

and then deviously
pinch my ass
near the delicatessen counter
while your wife vacillates
among the dairy products
hunts for you
for the final ruling:
Lowfat?
Nonfat?

3.

(In the lingerie department
I heard a woman say: Me,
I have nice legs
but my breasts are a flop.

With me, said another,
it's just the opposite.
My breasts are a knockout
but my legs are a flop.)

4.

I hugged you
and you hugged a watermelon
I loved you and you didn't
know what to do
with the watermelon
because your hands wanted
to hug me
but couldn't
let go of it
on the other hand
what
could you say, wait,

let me just put down
the watermelon?

Translated from the Hebrew by Tsipi Keller

A Little Prayer for Sunday

Give me a break
from flashing cops,
from HMOs and the temples
of social security,
from talking with my accountant,
and the Manpower jargon
of clerks
with helmet-like hair.

The partridge hunters
have been shooting here all morning,
and the dogcatcher
roams my countryside.
Newspapers—
filled with black-fisted fundamentalists,
high-strung poetry critics
and openmouthed bulldozers—
fall like leaves upon my house.

Why is it such a big deal to yield
to a woman like me
who lets other drivers
cut her off.

I who go to sleep with the hens
at the foot of the well-lit shopping malls—
Hear my prayer—

Please don't lay me down in the culture package.

I who am not exempt from anything—
Grant me
one day off
from the army.

Translated from the Hebrew by Lisa Katz

Woman Martyr

The evening goes blind, and you are only twenty.
—NATHAN ALTERMAN,
"LATE AFTERNOON IN THE MARKET"

You are only twenty
and your first pregnancy is a bomb.
Under your broad skirt you are pregnant with dynamite
and metal shavings. This is how you walk in the market,
ticking among the people, you, Andaleeb Takatka.

Someone loosened the screws in your head
and launched you toward the city;
even though you come from Bethlehem,
the Home of Bread, you chose a bakery.
And there you pulled the trigger out of yourself,
and together with the Sabbath loaves,
sesame and poppy seed,
you flung yourself into the sky.

Together with Rebecca Fink you flew up
with Yelena Konre'ev from the Caucasus
and Nissim Cohen from Afghanistan
and Suhila Houshy from Iran
and two Chinese you swept along
to death.

Since then, other matters
have obscured your story,

about which I speak all the time
without having anything to say.

Translated from the Hebrew by Lisa Katz

ELENA SHVARTS
(RUSSIA, 1948–)

Remembrance of Strange Hospitality

Once I had a taste
Of a girlfriend's milk,
My sister's milk—
Not to quench my thirst
But to satisfy my soul.
Into a cup she squeezed
Milk from her left breast
And in that simple vessel
It gently frothed, rejoiced.
There was something birdlike in its odor,
Whiffs of sheep and wolf, and something older
Than the Milky Way, it was
Somehow warm and dense.
A daughter in the wilderness
Once let her aged father drink
From her breasts and thus became
His mother. By this act of grace
Her whiteness drove away the dark,
A cradle substituted for a tomb
From the duct next to your heart
You offered me a drink—
I'm not a vampire, am I?—Horror.
It frothed and tinkled, warm
And sweet, soft, everlasting,
Crowding time back into a corner.

Translated from the Russian by Michael Molnar and Catriona Kelly

PABLO MEDINA

(CUBA, 1948–)

A Poem for the Epiphany

> *Ach, wie anders, wie schön*
> *Lebt der Himmel, lebt die Erde*
>
> —GOETHE

It snows because the door to heaven is open,
because God is tired of working
and the day needs to be left alone.
It snows because there is a widow hiding
under her mother's bed,
because the birds are resting their throats
and three wise men are offering gifts.
Because the clouds are singing
and trees have a right to exist,
because the horses of the past are returning.
They are grey and trot gently into the barn
never touching the ground.
It snows because the wind wants
to be water, because water
wants to be powder and powder wants
to seduce the eye. Because once in his life
the philosopher has to admit
to the poverty of thought.
Because the rich man cannot buy snow
and the poor man has to wear it on his eyebrows.
Because it makes the old dog think
his life has just begun. He runs
back and forth across the parking lot.
He rolls on the snow. He laps it up.
It snows because light and dark
are making love in a field where old age
has no meaning, where colors blur,

silence covers sound, sleep covers sorrow,
everything is death, everything is joy.

(for Ellen Jacko)

Translated from the Spanish by the author

PIOTR SOMMER
(POLAND, 1948–)

Transportist

Does such a word exist?
That's right.
Such an awfully busy
fellow, rushes here
and there, can't even
see, forgets
that he really is
between, that is, nowhere.

He transports words (from mouth to mouth),
gestures (from mother and friends
to child), and his own child
(from home out of the city),
by public transport, in fact,
out to unpolluted air.

But all those things
want to stop somewhere,
they can't always be
the object of transportation;
words stay behind the doors
of strangers' mouths, gestures
get written in the air
by strange hands, and the child
asked at school

for his father's occupation
answers shyly "transportist."

Translated from the Polish by Jarosław Anders and W. Martin

NOVICA TADIĆ

(SERBIA/YUGOSLAVIA, 1949–)

The Cats' Strike

The cat's cough wakes him at night.
He turns in bed, gets up.
Puts on his dressing-gown because it's cold.
Puts on his slippers because he's barefoot.
Slowly he approaches the window.
Drawing open the curtain, stares:
Below,
In the street,
As far as Republic Square
Thousands of phosphorescent flares
Thousands upon thousands of cats
Thousands upon thousands of raised tails.
Calmly
He closes the curtain.
And returns to his warm bed.
Yawning
He mutters:
        —*The cats' strike.*

Translated from the Serbian by Michael March and Dusan Puvacic

BEI DAO
(CHINA, 1949–)

Untitled

pedestrians lighting their own
lightbulb minds
the street heads for october's wild ideas

in tribute to a dog
shadow leans toward its experience

spring water's laid bare
the sleep underlying landscapes
we take turns hiding beneath
windows of endless light weeping

Li Po beats a drum and sings
calm and unhurried

Translated from the Chinese by David Hinton

Midnight Singer

a song
is a thief who's fled across rooftops
getting away with six colors
and leaving the red hour-hand
on 4 o'clock heaven
4 o'clock detonates
in the rooster's head
and it's 4 o'clock delirium

a song
is an ever hostile tree
across the border
it unleashes that promise
that wolf-pack feeding on tomorrow

a song
is a mirror that knows the body by heart
is the emperor of memory
is the waxen tongue
flame of talk
is the flower garden nurtured by myth
is a steam locomotive
bursting into the church

a song
is the death of a singer
his death-night
pressed into black records
singing over and over and over

Translated from the Chinese by David Hinton

DUODUO
(CHINA, 1951–)

Morning

in the morning or at any time, in the morning
you dream you wake up, you're afraid of waking up
so you say: you're afraid of the rope, afraid of the face
of a bird on a woman, so you dream of your father
speaking birdwords, drinking birdmilk
you dream your father is by himself
and by chance, not in the dream
had you, you dream the dream your father dreamed
you dream your father says: this is a dream a dead man dreamed.

you don't believe but you're inclined to believe
this is a dream, but a dream, your dream:
once, it was the handlebar on a bicycle
its shape squeezed into it by a hand
now, it droops from your father's belly

once it was a foetus refusing birth
now it is you crawling back to that handlebar
you've dreamed all the details in your dream
like the teeth your father left on the ground, flashing
and laughing at you, so you are not death
but a mere case of death: you've dreamed your dream's death.

Translated from the Chinese by Maghiel van Crevel

MARÍA NEGRONI
(ARGENTINA, 1951–)

The Baby

He who has nothing to hide,
has nothing to show

—MARGUERITE DE HAINAUT

My baby is playing in the bath, delighted. I begin
to wash his head and spend some time at this.
Then he begins. When I start to rinse his hair, I
can't find him. I turn around, and there he is
again. I don't understand what is happening, and
grow stern. I scold him. I don't like what he's
doing. The baby laughs, more and more amused,
glimmers for an instant, and vanishes again. My
impatience only makes things worse. He disap-
pears more and more quickly, doesn't even give
me time to protest. Through layers of uneasiness,
I glimpse his mischievous glance; my blindness is
his victory, my jealousy his passion. For a while, I
go on resisting: I don't know how to welcome
impotence. The baby just wants to play. The
game is dazzling and lasts a lifetime.

Translated from the Spanish by Anne Twitty

MIRIAM VAN HEE

(BELGIUM, 1952–)

Evening in Dún Laoghaire

1.

the lady from latvia recounted
how the people ended up where they did:
the finns steadily pushed the lapps
northwards

and the prussians were so belligerent,
do you hear, that they all
perished on their campaigns
of conquest

why are there so few
funny poems, sighed
the lady from latvia, she called the waiter
and asked him for more whisky, then
she looked outside and said
there was no one any more
who spoke prussian

2.

the sea and the air
had merged, only the lighthouses
still marked the horizon
they beckoned, not as a father or
a friend, they beckoned from
eternity, the freedom
of coming and going

finally only the palms
remained visible in the light

that came from the hotel rooms
and beyond that you could hear
the lashing of ropes against the masts

for everything there is a setting
for reunions, farewells
and for waiting

3.

the world is large, said
the lady from latvia,
europe, america, my father
died in siberia
we speak the oldest language
in europe, there aren't many of us
that's why we talk a lot,
we should wash out
our mouths with soap
my mother would say, where
is my mother now, why
can't I be silent, why
can't I cry?

life is long, said the lady
from latvia and you can't
trade it in

4.

from where I was seated I saw
an island where the sun
was shining now and then
as it did on me, downstairs
gulls were making their sounds
plaintive, busy and nervous:
they were at home

the island turned dark,
grey and then bright green again
as if it were blushing and I understood
that the sun was worshipped once
it was as if someone
was paying attention to you, even
when you were quite alone

Translated from the Flemish by Judith Wilkinson

Sycamores at Nîmes Station

their skin was beginning to wrinkle
they were growing old and would die
as we would but without fear
as if they were in on something
and we were not

already our parting was approaching
storm cloud, derailed trains
uncertainty there always was
certainty one might achieve
but how, how
to become like the trees

I felt that I would write
(because everything was always
as it could not remain)
of how we sat here
on a bench beneath sycamores
the sun shining, a dog barking
and chasing pigeons

Translated from the Flemish by Judith Wilkinson

NUALA NÍ DHOMHNAILL
(IRELAND, 1952–)

A Recovered Memory of Water

Sometimes when the mermaid's daughter
is in the bathroom
cleaning her teeth with a thick brush
and baking soda
she has the sense the room is filling
with water.

It starts at her feet and ankles
and slides further and further up
over her thighs and hips and waist.
In no time
It's up to her oxters.
She bends down into it to pick up
handtowels and washcloths and all such things
as are sodden with it.
They all look like seaweed—
like those long strands of kelp that used to be called
"mermaid-hair" or "foxtail."
Just as suddenly the water recedes
and in no time
the room's completely dry again.

A terrible sense of stress
is part and parcel of these emotions.
At the end of the day she has nothing else
to compare it to.
She doesn't have the vocabulary for any of it.
At her weekly therapy session
she has more than enough to be going on with
just to describe this strange phenomenon
and to express it properly
to the psychiatrist.

She doesn't have the terminology
or any of the points of reference
or any word at all that would give the slightest suggestion
as to what water might be.
"A transparent liquid," she says, doing as best she can.
"Right," says the therapist, "keep going."
He coaxes and cajoles her towards word-making.
She has another run at it.
"A thin flow," she calls it,
casting about gingerly in the midst of the words.
"A shiny film. Dripping stuff. Something wet."

Translated from the Irish by Paul Muldoon

As for the Quince

There came this bright young thing
with a Black & Decker
and cut down my quince-tree.
I stood with my mouth hanging open
while one by one
she trimmed off the branches.

When my husband got home that evening
and saw what had happened
he lost the rag,
as you might imagine.
"Why didn't you stop her?
What would she think
if I took the Black & Decker
round to her place
and cut down a quince-tree
belonging to her?
What would she make of that?"

Her ladyship came back next morning
while I was at breakfast.
She enquired about his reaction.

I told her straight
that he was wondering how she'd feel
if he took a Black & Decker
round to her house
and cut down a quince-tree of hers,
et cetera et cetera.

"O," says she, "that's very interesting."
There was a stress on the "very."
She lingered over the "ing."
She was remarkably calm and collected.

These are the times that are in it, so,
all a bit topsy-turvy.
The bottom falling out of my belly
as if I had got a kick up the arse
or a punch in the kidneys.
A fainting-fit coming over me
that took the legs from under me
and left me so zonked
I could barely lift a finger
till Wednesday.

As for the quince, it was safe and sound
and still somehow holding its ground.

Translated from the Irish by Paul Muldoon

MARÍA ELENA CRUZ VARELA

(CUBA, 1953–)

Kaleidoscope

All of us were there:
the one who fell marked by the water spurt
the one who ruined his countenance through ineptitude
the one who did not strike a flame

and violated the city in martial law.
The one who suffered the sin of clairvoyance
the one who fertilized with bizarre feces
the one who could not give more nails to the torture
the one who was not on time for the demolitions
the one who came early
the one who didn't come
and resolved by saying he wasn't informed.

All of us were there:
the innocent ones because they didn't know
and the guilty ones for legal ignorance
the more cultivated accomplices
the ones who fed themselves with prejudices
the more elaborated ones
the more cyclic ones
the singers with the lagger tone
the blind blind from not wanting to see
the ones subject to criticism
the critics subject to their dogmas
the denominators with their tabula rasa
the unbeaten facade
the marked backs

All of us were there
waiting for medals, and judgments.

Translated from the Spanish by Mairym Cruz-Bernal and
Deborah Digges

RICARDO CASTILLO

(MEXICO, 1954–)

Ode to the Urge

Urination is the major accomplishment of engineering
at least insofar as drainage is concerned.

Furthermore, to urinate is a pleasure.
What's there to say? One takes a leak
saluting love and friends,
one spills himself long into the throat of the world
to remind himself we're warm inside, and to stay tuned up.
All this is important
now that the world's emitting disaster signals,
intoxicated hiccups.
Because it's necessary, for pure love of life, to urinate
on the silver service,
on the seats of sports cars,
in swimming pools with underwater lights,
worth easily 15 or 16 times more than their owners.
To urinate until our throats ache,
right down to the last drops of blood.
To urinate on those who see life as a waltz,
to scream at them, Long live the Cumbia, señores,
Everybody up to shake his ass,
until we shake off this mystery we are
and the fucked-up love of suffering it.
And long live the Jarabe Zapateado, too,
because reality is in the back and to the right,
where you don't go wearing a tux.
(Nobody's yet gotten rid of TB by beating his chest.)
I'm pissing down from the manger of life,
I just want to be the greatest pisser in history,
Oh Mama, for the love of God, the greatest pisser in history.

Translated from the Spanish by Robert L. Jones

YU JIAN
(CHINA, 1954–)

Opus 39

During the years crowds jammed the streets
You lit off by yourself for Xinjiang

Maybe it's not so bad out there in the boonies
You really looked outlandish in a crowd
Try on those jeans now and see
How well they've lasted
Only three and a half years' wear and still like new
Remember the time
You and I got into that heavy rapping
That made everybody around clam up
You never went in for banging my ears
How well you know in your heart
That we struggle all our lives
Just to put on a front of being human
Always at a loss for what to do
When we're around good looking women
We're too dumb to even know how dumb we are
One of those women looked me up once
Said what a shame   with your swell voice
You could have made it as a baritone
Sometimes I think of you borrowing my money
I would stand at my gate
Trying to spot you among the scruffy men
I know you're going to come back here some day
Three short novels and a bottle of booze in your arms
Sitting in that rattan chair from Sichuan
Speaking for a couple of hours
As if the whole world were your audience
Now and again you'll glimpse yourself in the mirror
Heart brimming with sudden rushes of joy
Afterward you'll watch me a while in dead silence
Then go home with the empty bottle under your arm

Translated from the Chinese by Fang Dai, Dennis Ding, and
Edward Morin

IRINA RATUSHINSKAYA
(RUSSIA, 1954–)

I will live and survive and be asked:

I will live and survive and be asked:
How they slammed my head against a trestle,
How I had to freeze at nights,
How my hair started to turn gray . . .
But I'll smile. And I'll crack some joke
And brush away the encroaching shadow.
And I will render homage to the dry September '
That became my second birth.
And I'll be asked: "Doesn't it hurt you to remember?"
Not being deceived by my outward flippancy.
But the former names will detonate my memory—
Magnificent as an old cannon.
And I will tell of the best people in all the earth,
The most tender, but also the most invincible,
How they said farewell, how they went to be tortured,
How they waited for letters from their loved ones.
And I'll be asked: what helped us to live
When there were neither letters nor any news—only walls,
And the cold of the cell, and the blather of official lies,
And the sickening promises made in exchange for betrayal.
And I will tell of the first beauty
I saw in captivity.
A frost-covered window! No peepholes, nor walls,
Nor cell bars, nor the long-endured pain—
Only a blue radiance on a tiny pane of glass,
A lacy winding pattern—none more beautiful could be dreamt!
The more clearly you looked, the more powerfully blossomed
Those brigand forests, campfires and birds!
And how many times there was bitter cold weather
And how many windows sparkled after that one—
But never was it repeated,
That upheaval of rainbow ice!
And anyway, what good would it be to me now,

And what would be the pretext for that festival?
Such a gift can only be received once,
And once is probably enough.

Translated from the Russian by David McDuff

AMJAD NASSER
(JORDAN, 1955–)

Once Upon an Evening, in a Café

When your thoughts
don't take you too far
and you are silent
as you tremble
and gaze
at the trellis of your hands.

When the chariot of your imagination does not lead you into tunnels
lit up with apprehensions
and lightnings
as you remain silent
and tremble
gazing at the smoke twirling
around your wrist.

When the woman who lets
her scarf fall
through the evening's emptiness
greets you, and you don't
        acknowledge
her greeting, but rather
remain silent, and tremble
as you gaze
at the destinies that unfold, lurching
in your coffee cup.

When the new immigrants pass by
arm in arm with their local women
blabbering about time that flees
so soon, and you keep silent
as you tremble and gaze
at the table's
ambiguous wood.

When you don't sit with anyone
and remember war only
as a horseshoe, or a coat
riddled with bullets.

When, upon an evening, in a café
the faces pass by you
like copper clouds
as you listen
to cymbals that chime
in a faraway desert
or masts that break
in imaginary gulfs.

When the blind singer's
record spins, once upon an evening,
in a café, the customers sigh
and you walk toward the axe
where it leans against the tree.

Translated from the Arabic by S. V. Attalah

VERONICA VOLKOW
(MEXICO, 1955–)

The Washerwoman

She feels her hands, scabrous as fish,
blind fish striking against the rock,

incessantly against the rock for years and years;
she watches the night pierced with eyes,
humid, slippery glances,
the mute faces shifting, disappearing,
brilliant glances of girls,
the dazed look of exhausted mothers.
The day ends and people return to their houses
and water runs from the faucet monotonously as a song,
the water has lost the shape of pipes,
lost the memory of its mountain source
and has pounded out its course,
besieged by obstacles
like the feet, like the eyes, like the hands.
She looks at shadows people drag along,
shadows on the walls, corners, the streets,
fugitive ink that marks the beaten roads,
desperate roads, laborious,
looking for only, perhaps, a fidelity.

Translated from the Spanish by Forrest Gander

GU CHENG
(CHINA, 1956–1993)

Discovery

Of all the people who went into the snowy mountains,
Only Bulin discovered the path.
Though there's just a few metres of it,
Though Venus
Broke a tooth there,
None of this prevented
An Englishman from dying,
Lying in the middle of the road, smiling,
Orchids and tender leaves sprouting
From his ears,
And a rosy glow on his face.

What did that mean?
Bulin frowned
And at last he remembered:
When he was nine, he had come
To spend summer, and had planted a box of matches.
They sprouted, and bore
Berries the size of match heads.
The Englishman gobbled them up
Out of greed.

What a discovery! Unprecedented, perhaps—
     the berry a match bears is poisonous!
Bulin started the trip downhill
And reached the Lama temple made of manure.
He stood stock still, ready to be robbed of his secret
At knifepoint.
But it didn't work out that way. He could only
Sob his heart out
And lash thin copper cables around his stockings
To escape into the deep marshes.

There
Slippers clamoured in a frenzy
And turned into a cluster of frogs.

Translated from the Chinese by Eva Hung

from Forever Parted: Graveyard

3

I don't have an older brother
but I believe you
are my older brother.
In the sandpile,
in the cicada's shrill,
you made a clay tank
and gave it to me.

You made me a paper plane, too.
You taught me to write
characters, to string them artfully
together.
You were a giant
already in sixth grade.

I have an older sister
but I believe you are also
my older sister,
in the dazzle of morning light
skipping rope,
jumping so high,
turning from side to side
as part of the game
as if the brightly colored strands
could catapult you straight up to the sky,
but they were stretched too tight
and I ended up tangled
from standing too close.

And *him*!
Who is *he*?
who pulled the golden feathers from
the reed finch's wing,
spattering the whole earth
with tiny drops of blood,
or teased the borer beetle
with bounds and flame
and forced him to totter
across a window sill stage
for the crime of eating wood chips?
Who was that?
I don't know him,
a man, only.

Translated from the Chinese by J. P. Seaton and Mu Yi

ZHAI YONGMING
(CHINA, 1955–)

from Fourteen Plainsongs

for my mother

2

head bowed I hear: deep underground
bones talking with other bones
glittering eyes darting about
like the souls of the soil
in any kind of darkness
when listening to the daylight:
a rooster incessantly pecking at seeds as if it were all alone

Translated from the Chinese by Andrea Lingenfelter

MANSUR RAJIH
(YEMEN, 1958–)

The Fatherland

Do not despair, my friend:
The light that shines on our land
will remain chaste.
We still have time.

Maybe next year, the year after—
it will be enough.
We will see
the new face of Eban

smiling over our lives.
This land is good

and its history teaches us
we must not despair.

This land is happy.
Look, see the girls
painting their cheeks?
This land is continuously giving birth.

Yemen is a happy country,
the people die standing tall.

Translated from the Norwegian by Ren Powell

LUIS GARCÍA MONTERO
(SPAIN, 1958–)

Completely Friday

By the detergents and dish soap
by the orderly books and broom on the floor,
by the clean windows, by the table
without papers, notebooks or pens,
by the easy chairs without newspapers,
whoever approaches my house
will find a day
that is completely Friday.

That is how I find it
when I go out into the streets
and the cathedral has been
taken over by the world of the living
and in the supermarket
June becomes a bottle of gin,
sausages and dessert,
fan of light in the kiosk
of the flower shop,
city that undresses completely Friday.

As does my body
which recalls the memory of your body
and foretells your presence
in the restlessness of all it touches,
in the remote control for the music,
in the paper of the magazine,
in the ice melted away
just as the morning melts away
completely Friday.

When the front door opens
the icebox divines what my body knew
and suggests other titles for this poem:
completely you,
morning of the return, good love,
good company.

Translated from the Spanish by Katie King

ZHANG ER
(CHINA, 1960–)

from Cross River . Pick Lotus

9

How to describe sea
To someone who's never seen it?

He lives to ninety-nine, he wants it, to see it
To walk on its glass surface, to blow the seven trumpets.

At this joyous moment gigantic angel wings
Write prophecy all over the sky. How can I tell him

About sea storms, the choking waves
These things, right and wrong, that happen between us?

The prophecy he can't read is the world, tears
That become sea, sea that dries to salt.

On the brink of imagination, he's walking
Faster than us, a shadow white as our rumpled sheets.

Lick clean the moist forehead, the indescribable saltiness of the body
Building exercises that take the whole afternoon.

Resist the current, the waist laden with water sustains
A thousand years of sediment. The love that can't be contained.

He drifts downstream, pursues
Nothing. He enters the sea before us.

Translated from the Chinese by Rachel Levitsky

GUILLERMO SAAVEDRA
(ARGENTINA, 1960–)

On the Tomato

Brief Vaudevillian Hypotheses Apropos of This Androgynous Fruit

1

Behold the hero of the vegetable patch
a modest American marvel
with the face of a Chinese lantern.

2

Sheer light made of water:
a fleeting heart, pumping
muted cries of jubilation.

3

Her fancy dress, her festive
fantasy of red confirms a doubt:
she's a lady tossed in the salad by mistake.

16

A tomato rots: here lies
a misfortune greater
than the fall of an empire.

39

Voluptuous little flag:
he makes every dry spell
fresh.

41

To sink one's finger into
its soft flesh: a crime or copulation
as vague as your idea of bliss.

44

A tomato crosses the river
on a moonless night:
becomes a plum.

55

(Mark Twain)
A salad can be an anthem to joy
but the proof
is in the tomato.

60

To bite into a tomato thinking
of nothing: so the peak
of summer will burst in your mouth.

64

Columbus's was egg
and prophecy: America
is a tomato under sail.

66

A tomato was raised
by two elderly lemons:
now it's a sweet tangerine.

75

And yet, there is no more
voracious love than that of salt
searching for it on the plate.

97

The taste of tomato
remembered: the damp
face of a barefoot child.

Translated from the Spanish by Cindy Schuster

OKSANA ZABUZHKO

(UKRAINE, 1960–)

Letter from the Summer House

Dear _____,
The land's rusty again.
Acid rain: our blackened cucumber vines
Jut from the earth like scorched wire.
And I'm not sure about the orchard this year.
It needs a good cleaning up,
But I'm scared of those trees. When I walk
Among them, it feels like I'm going to step
On some carcass rotting in the tall grass,
Something crawling with worms, something smiling
Sickly in the hot sun.
And I get nervous over the sounds:
The day before yesterday, in the thicket, meowing,
The monotonous creaking of a tree,
The suppressed cackling of geese—all constantly
Straining for the same note. Do you remember
The dry elm, the one lightning turned
Into a giant charred bone last summer?
Sometimes I think it lords
Over the whole garden, infecting everything with rabid madness.
How do mad trees act?
Maybe they run amok like derailed streetcars. Anyway,
I keep an axe by the bed, just in case.
At least the butterflies are mating: we'll have
Caterpillars soon. Oh yes, the neighbour's daughter
Gave birth—a boy, a bit overdue. He had hair and teeth
Already, and could be a mutant,
Because yesterday, only nine days old, he shouted,
"Turn off the sky!", and hasn't said a word since.
Otherwise, he's a healthy baby.
So, there it is. If you can get away
For the weekend, bring me something to read,

Preferably in the language I don't know.
The ones I call mine are exhausted.

Kisses, love, O.

Translated from the Ukrainian by Douglas Smith

GHIRMAI YOHANNES
(ERITREA, 1961–)

Unjust Praise

In the beginning
The spirit moving
Upon the face of the waters
And in the breaking waves
Tasted salt

And I see fields of it
Drying on the shore.
We let in shallow lakes of sea
To evaporate,
And the salt

Accumulates along their edge
Thanks to the sunlight:
Crystal white,
Enough for everyone,
Harvested and sold

In every shop and on the roads:
Salt!—
In proper measure
Bringing out the taste,
The flavor and spirit

Of our food, hot or cold.
Why should pepper get
So much admiration
When salt does all the work?

Translated from the Tigrinya by Charles Cantalupo and Ghirmai Negash

MARCIN ŚWIETLICKI
(POLAND, 1961–)

M—Black Monday

The moment when all the town's streetlamps light up
simultaneously. The moment when you say
your incredible "no," and suddenly I don't know what
to do next: die? go away? not respond?
The moment in the sunshine when I watch you from the bus,
your face different from when you know I'm looking
—and now you can't see me, you're looking into nothing, into the glassy
sheen in front of me. Not me anymore, not with me,
not in this way, not here. Anything can
happen, since everything happens. Everything is defined
by three basic positions: man on top of woman,
woman on top of man, or the one right now
—woman and man divided by the light.

Translated from the Polish by Elżbieta Wójcik-Leese

Six Times Coltrane

To whom do I speak? Since I speak—and I do
speak in Polish———. Soon the sun will fall
beyond the edge. Soon, with a cold finger,
the run across the throat. Soon the run across
a cold city. To Nowhere. Settled in Nowhere
never will I be in Elsewhere. And to whom do I speak?
—in Polish, in the margins

of the light. An angel
unexpectedly speaks: "Now I want to strip for you, Mr."
(To whom does she speak?)

Translated from the Polish by Elżbieta Wójcik-Leese

XI CHUAN
(CHINA, 1963–)

After Wang Ximeng's Blue and Green Horizontal Landscape Scroll, *A Thousand Miles of Rivers and Mountains*

Green colors and blue colors flow together and form empty mountains. Some people are walking in them, but they're still empty mountains, as if the people walking there have no faces, but they are still people. No one should try to recognize themselves in these figures, or try to see the real mountains and waters of this world, nor should anyone think of trying to gain casual praise from Wang Ximeng. Wang Ximeng knows these small figures, and that not one is he himself. These are not his figures, and he cannot call out a single one by name. The figures acquire the mountains and waters, just as the mountains acquire the emerald and lapis, just as the waters acquire vastness and boats, just as Emperor Huizong got Wang Ximeng at eighteen years old, not knowing that Wang would die soon after he finished this thousand miles of rivers and mountains. The mountains and waters are nameless. Wang Ximeng realizes that people without names are just decorations in mountains and waters, just as flying birds know they are insignificant to men's games. And the birds meet in the sky. Meanwhile, people walking in the mountains have their own directions to travel and their own plans. These small figures, in white, walk, sit at leisure, go fishing, trade, surrounded by green colors and blue colors, just like, today, people, in black, go to banquets, concerts, and funerals, surrounded by golden colors and more golden colors. These small figures in white have never been born and so have never died; just like Wang Ximeng's landscape utopia, they are immune to pollution and invasion, and that is worth careful consideration. So people who are far away from social controls have no need to long for freedom, and people who haven't been destroyed by experience aren't concerned about forgetting. Wang Ximeng let the fishermen have infinite numbers of fishes to go fishing; he allowed limitless waters to run out from the mountains. According to him, happiness means the exact amount of blessing so that, immersed in the silence between mountains and waters, people can build bridges, waterwheels, roads, houses, and live quietly, just like the trees growing appropriately in the mountains, along the margins of water, or surrounding a village, and surrounding people. In the distance, the trees are like flowers. When they sway, it's the time when the clear wind is rising. When the clear wind is rising, it's time for people to sing. When people sing, it's time for an empty mountain to become an empty mountain.

Translated from the Chinese by Arthur Sze

DUNYA MIKHAIL
(IRAQ, 1965–)

The War Works Hard

How magnificent the war is!
How eager
and efficient!
Early in the morning,
it wakes up the sirens
and dispatches ambulances
to various places,
swings corpses through the air,
rolls stretchers to the wounded,
summons rain
from the eyes of mothers,
digs into the earth
dislodging many things
from under the ruins . . .
Some are lifeless and glistening,

others are pale and still throbbing . . .
It produces the most questions
in the minds of children,
entertains the gods
by shooting fireworks and
missiles
into the sky,
sows mines in the fields
and reaps punctures and blisters,
urges families to emigrate,
stands beside the clergymen
as they curse the devil
(poor devil, he remains
with one hand in the searing fire) . . .
The war continues working, day and night.
It inspires tyrants
to deliver long speeches,
awards medals to generals
and themes to poets.
It contributes to the industry
of artificial limbs,
provides food for flies,
adds pages to the history books,
achieves equality
between killer and killed,
teaches lovers to write letters,
accustoms young women to waiting,
fills the newspapers
with articles and pictures,
builds new houses
for the orphans,
invigorates the coffin makers,
gives grave diggers
a pat on the back
and paints a smile on the leader's face.
The war works with unparalleled diligence!

Yet no one gives it
a word of praise.

Translated from the Arabic by Elizabeth Winslow

ERNEST FARRÉS
(SPAIN, 1967–)

Summer Evening, 1947

Being a couple is twice the fun.
Being a couple is twice the cost.
Being a couple doubles your earning power
and your frustrated dreams.
Being a couple means a unity
stops you from being the indivisible
and unique thing you once were
for better or worse.
Being a couple is ruining your eyesight
together and shaking your booties in sync
and jogging side by side. Being a couple
brings the "added problem" of not being three or four.

Being a couple makes you talk it over. Being a couple,
I've sensed, languishes without conversation,
slipping eventually from the dynamic
to the stable EKG,
conversation that's very simple, so to speak,
conversation evocative of zen,
conversation with the social impact
of visceral gossip,
conversation rediscovered on the porch,
conversation that winds up interfering
with passionate moves.

Being a couple produces side effects:
it's the emotional contagion between people

who love one another, reconciling
their behavior, impulses,
mental states, what they didn't know
up to that point with the awareness
of having put an end to restraint.

Translated from the Catalan by Lawrence Venuti

Summer in the City, 1949

The man is looking for trouble,
thrills, sublime ecstasies, places
short on folklore, deals,
calculated approximations, objects
of desire that grab
your attention and keep
your cool, the latest rage
at your fingertips, binges,
infatuations, sexual icons,
irrefutable proofs, joyrides, advice
within parentheses, green lights, comfy shoes,
forms of expression that presuppose
supremacy, free tickets to the game,
ways of killing time that are reckless and frenzied,
the upper hand before bellyaching, answers
as plain as the nose on your face.
The woman, however, is looking for love.

Translated from the Catalan by Lawrence Venuti

TATJANA GROMAČA
(CROATIA, 1971–)

Lovers

A fat man and a fat woman kiss in the supermarket.
Their juicy, pinky tongues

lean awkwardly against each other
like two rolls on the bakery counter.
While they kiss, they can't cling to each other.
They come together at two points only:
the tip of their belly and the fiery flames of their tongue.
After lovemaking
they roll about in the sheets
like two happy hippos
in the zoo pool.

The fat man massages the fat woman's feet
a TV newsman's voice is in the background
and she feeds him tripe or honeycomb
from a pot that is on the floor.
Later on maybe she dresses him in her gowns
and puts a glaring lipstick on his lips.

They pay no attention to stains on the pillow
or breadcrumbs on the sheets,
to hairs, stretch marks, cellulite,
or varicose veins like railway tracks
on their short legs.
They are not frustrated with politics or the state of the country
or the bad living conditions,
these two passionate self-contained creatures
this perfect hermaphroditic cheese pie.

Translated from the Croatian by Mario Susko

LIDIJA DIMKOVSKA
(MACEDONIA, 1971–)

The Poem at the Beginning

Brodsky got scared, he got scared he might be hit
by a bomb, a watermelon or the evil eye of a Struga maiden,

and back then we still didn't have e-mail
for him to ask me in the Subject line: Is there a war going on in
    Macedonia?
so he didn't come. And those four days, they say,
the University of Michigan was being painted,
and at home the cleaning lady, Sevda from Bosnia,
had spilled some bleach in the living room and a terrible stench
spread all over the place.
Brodsky opened the windows and went out into the night
and had nowhere to go until the apartment was aired,
until the Department of Literature was painted.
For four days Brodsky wandered through Michigan, he went from
    church to church
(and when sad, they say, entered only the Orthodox)
and suddenly he came across the small Macedonian church
raised by old man Ilija in memory of his mother Petkana of Struga,
and just then it was Vespers, and two singers chanted in Macedonian:
Mother of God, rejoice, birthgiving Maria.
Brodsky listened and his hands got sweaty on his trousers
and every time they made the cross he choked
as if swimming in the waters of Genesis.
The Mother of God saw the collar on his shirt start crying,
then an old woman approached him with boiled wheat and told him:
Take some, son, this is in memory of my mother-in-law Petkana from
    Struga,
God bless her soul, she brought up my children.
Brodsky then searched his back pocket and took out the letter
about the Golden Wreath for Poetry '91. But the old woman
just kept on offering: Have some, son, have some of this wheat,
you're pale, take care you don't get sick, and as for wreaths—
God forbid, it's too early for you!
We the old must have our turn first!
Brodsky ate and cried, gulped and choked,
and on Monday, when the University opened again,
gave his literature students the following topic for their essays:
"What percentage of a man lives when he's alive
and what percentage dies when he dies?"

And for two hours he read and re-read
Marina Tsvetaeva's "Poem of the End."

Translated from the Macedonian by Ljubica Arsovska and Peggy Reid

POLINA BARSKOVA
(RUSSIA, 1977–)

Manuscript Found by Natasha Rostova During the Fire

I will try to live on earth without you.

I will try to live on earth without you.

I will become any object,
I don't care what—
I will be this speeding train.
This smoke
or a beautiful gay man laughing in the front seat.

A human body is defenseless
on earth.

It's a piece of fire-wood.
Ocean water hits it.
Lenin puts it on his official shoulder.

And therefore, in order not to suffer, a human spirit
lives
inside the wind and inside the wood and inside the shoulder of a
    great dictator.

But I will not be water. I will not be a fire.

I will be an eyelash.
A sponge washing your neck-hairs.
Or a verb, an adjective, I will become. Such a word

slightly lights your cheek.
What happened? Nothing.
Something visited? Nothing.

What was there you cannot whisper.
No smoke without fire, they whisper.
I will be a handful of smoke
over this lost city of Moscow.

I will console any man,
I will sleep with any man,
under the army's traveling horse carriages.

Translated from the Russian by Ilya Kaminsky

VALZHYNA MORT
(BELARUS, 1981–)

Belarusian

even our mothers have no idea how we got here
how we parted their legs and crawled out into the world
the way you crawl from the ruins after a bombing
we couldn't tell which of us was a girl or a boy
and we gorged on dirt thinking it was bread
and our future a gymnast on a thin
thread of the horizon was performing there
at the highest pitch
bitch
we grew up in a country where
first your door is stroked with chalk
and then at dark a chariot arrives
and no one sees you any more
but riding in those cars were neither
armed men nor
a wanderer with a scythe
this is how love loved to visit us

and snatch us veiled
completely free only in public toilets
where for a little change nobody cared what we were doing
we fought the summer heat the winter snow
and when we discovered we ourselves were the language
and our tongues were removed we started talking with our eyes
and when our eyes were poked out we talked with our hands
and when our hands were cut off we conversed with our toes
and when we were shot in the legs we nodded our head for yes
and shook our heads for no and when they ate our heads alive
we crawled back into the bellies of our sleeping mothers
as if into bomb shelters
to be born again
and there on the horizon our future's gymnast
was leaping through the fiery hoop
of the sun
screwed

Translated from the Belarusian by Franz Wright and
Elizabeth Oehlkers Wright

Men

Men arrive like a date on a calendar
they keep visiting once a month
men who've seen the bottom
of the deepest bottles
kings of both earth and heaven
and like the pearls from a torn necklace
trembling I scatter at their touch
their heartbeats open doors
vessels respond to their voice commands
and wind licks their faces like a crazy dog
and gallops after their train and roams
they undress me as if undressing themselves
and hold me in their arms like a saxophone
and oh this music these endless blues
like milk from breasts

those notes too high for human ears
those notes too low for gods
men who teach children to laugh
men who teach time how to run
men who love other men in club toilets
men who've kissed the hand of death herself
men who've never listened to my threats nightmares
which bound me to a chair
mama their lips fall on me
like burning planes
they are powerful patient
and when the world crashes
everyone runs for the shelters
they pause to pluck one of my lashes
mama not even mine
just anyone's mama
come back
rescue me find me
in this plane wreck

Translated from the Belarusian by Franz Wright and
Elizabeth Oehlkers Wright

YEN CHEN
(CHINA, TWENTIETH CENTURY)

The Plum Hint

Plums have bloomed, comrades.
Plum blossoms beckon you to come.
The productive team-captain plucks a branch,
and smiles as he walks into the village.

The snow on thousands of hills melted in one night.
A spout of water turns greener than before.
Listen! The cuckoo in the tree
also changes his new tune.

Outside the village, ponds are full,
ditches dug, and millets green.
Inside the village the cows are fat,
horses strong, and carts adorned.
Who is trying the new whip?
The snapping is so strong!

The windows are open in every house.
In every mansion the doors are wide.
Oh, spring has come!
without signs or signals in advance.

Plums have bloomed, comrades.
The plum gardens crimson like clouds.
O you thousands of full-blooming plums
are like the ten thousand hearts of our commune members.

Translated from the Chinese by Arthur Sze

JACOB NIBENEGENESABE
(CANADA, TWENTIETH CENTURY)

from The Wishing Bone Cycle

[2]

One time
all the noises met.
All the noises in the world
met in one place
and I was there
because they met in my house.
My wife said, "Who sent them?"
I said, "Fox or Rabbit,
yes one of those two.
They're both out for tricking me back today.
Both of them

are mad at me.
Rabbit is mad because I pulled
his brother's ear
and I held him up that way.
Then I ate him.
And Fox is mad because he wanted
to do those things first."
"Yes, then it had to be one of them,"
my wife said.
So, all the noises
were there.
These things happen.
Falling-tree noise was there.
Falling-rock noise was there.
Otter-mud-sliding noise was there.
All those noises, and more,
in my house.
"How long do you expect to stay?"
my wife asked them. "We need some sleep!"
They all answered at once!
That's why now my wife and I
sometimes can't hear well.
I should have wished them all away
first thing.

Translated from the Cree by Howard Norman

MALKA SHAKED
(ISRAEL, TWENTIETH CENTURY)

Shame

How ashamed I am.
My mother at my age
would stand on the balcony
and scream
the outrage of being a woman,

unravel her bitter reckoning to the winds
with maine shvartze yorn*
splitting the sky.
"Sha! She's crazy,
she's got no shame,"
my father would whisper to me
and hide my head in his arms
and I
to my shame
believed him.

Translated from the Hebrew by Shirley Kaufman

ANONYMOUS
(TWENTIETH CENTURY)

To the Earth (I)

The earth does not get fat
       It makes an end of those who wear the head plumes
The earth does not get fat
          It makes an end of those who act swiftly as heroes
Shall we die on earth?

Listen, O earth; we shall mourn because of you
Listen, shall we all die on the earth?

The earth does not get fat
       It makes an end of the chiefs
       Shall we all die on the earth?
The earth does not get fat
       It makes an end of the women-chiefs
       Shall we die on the earth?

----

*Yiddish: my black years

Listen, O earth; we shall mourn because of you
Listen, shall we all die on the earth?

The earth does not get fat
    It makes an end of the nobles
      Shall we die on the earth?
The earth does not get fat
    It makes an end of the royal women
      Shall we die on the earth?

Listen, O earth; we shall mourn because of you
Listen, shall we all die on the earth?

Translated from the Ngoni by Judith Gleason

ABOUT THE POETS

ADONIS was born in 1930 in Al Qassabin, Northern Syria, and divides his life between his home country, Lebanon, and France. In 1956, after a year-long imprisonment for political activities, Adonis fled Syria for Beirut, Lebanon. He joined a vibrant community of artists, writers, and exiles in Beirut, and cofounded and edited *Sh'ir*, and later *Muwaqaf,* both progressive journals of poetry and politics. Considered one of the Arab world's greatest living poets, Adonis is the author of numerous collections, including *Mihyar of Damascus* (2008) and *A Time Between Ashes and Roses* (2004).

ANNA AKHMATOVA was born in 1889 in Odessa on the Black Sea coast. In 1910 she married Nikolai Gumilev, who was a poet and leader of the Acmeist poetic movement. In 1921 he was shot as an alleged counter-revolutionary; Akhmatova published very little of her poetry from 1923 to 1940. In the thaw after Stalin's death her poetry began to be published again.

RAFAEL ALBERTI was a member of the Generation of '27, a group of Spanish poets known for revitalizing the art to a quality not seen since the sixteenth century. Alberti gradually turned away from the lyric traditions of his homeland, embracing communism and a more utilitarian style. After the Spanish Civil War, he fled the country and lived in exile, first in Argentina, then in Rome, before finally returning to Spain in 1977, after the death of Franco. He was the author of twenty-four volumes of poetry, several plays, and a five-volume autobiography.

CLARIBEL ALEGRÍA was born in Nicaragua in 1924 and moved to the United States in 1943. In 1985 Alegría returned to Nicaragua to aid in the country's reconstruction. Alegría's ideological and literary tendencies are a reflection of a literary current that gained momentum in Central America during the 1950s and 1960s known as *"la generación comprometida"* (the committed generation). Alegría has published numerous books of poetry, including *Casting Off* (2003); *Sorrow* (1999), which focuses on the death of her companion and translator, Darwin Flakoll; *Umbrales* (*Thresholds*, 1996); *Fuga de Canto Grande* (*Fugues*, 1992); and *La mujer del río/ Woman of the River* (1989), a bilingual edition. She is also a writer of novels and children's stories.

YEHUDA AMICHAI was born in Wurzburg, Germany, in 1924 and emigrated with his family to Palestine in 1936. He later became a naturalized Israeli citizen. Amichai published eleven volumes of poetry in Hebrew, two novels, and a book of short stories. His work has been translated into over thirty languages. His collections of poetry available in English include *Open Closed Open*; *The Selected Poetry of Yehuda Amichai: Newly Revised and Expanded Edition* (1996); *A Life of Poetry, 1948–1994* (1995); *Even a Fist Was Once an Open Palm with Fingers* (1989); and others.

JORGE CARRERA ANDRADE was born in Quito, Ecuador. His poetry is known for its lucid qualities and for its highly structured forms. However, his social concerns and the metaphors drawn from his own culture, particularly those of *"El hombre planetario"* ("The Planetary Man," 1959), lend a deep richness of imagery and feeling to his work.

CHAIRIL ANWAR was an Indonesian poet. Although he died young, Anwar transformed the Indonesian literary scene through the intense imagery of his poetry and through his rebellious stance toward religion and social convention. Today, he is considered one of the major poets from his region.

GUILLAUME APOLLINAIRE—Roman by birth, Polish by name (Wilhelm Albert Vladimir Apollinaris Kostrowitzky), Parisian by choice—died at thirty-eight in 1918. He was one of the leading figures in twentieth-century French poetry, a transitional figure whose work at once echoes the symbolists and anticipates the surrealists. His work in English includes *Alcools* and *Calligrammes: Poems of Peace and War (1913–1916)*.

H. C. ARTMANN was an Austrian poet. In 1947 his first publications were heard on radio and appeared in the newspaper *Neue Wege*. He was a founding member of the Anti PEN club in 1973.

ROSE AUSLANDER was a German writer. Her collections of poetry include *Der Regenbogen* (The Rainbow, 1939) and *Blinder Sommer* (Blind Summer, 1965).

GENNADY AYGI's work has been translated into some twenty languages. In the late 1950s, Boris Pasternak and Nâzim Hikmet urged Aygi to switch from writing in his mother tongue, Chuvash, to Russian. It was not until the 1960s that he was first published in Eastern Europe, and not until the late 1980s that his poems were allowed to be openly published in the Soviet Union and Chuvashia. Books of his available in the United States include *Selected Poems: 1954–1994*, *Salute to Singing*, and *Child-and-Rose*.

INGEBORG BACHMANN was an Austrian poet, dramatist, and novelist, a leading voice in postwar German literature. During her lifetime Bachmann was known first and foremost as a poet, but after she received the Büchner Prize, Germany's highest award for literature, in 1964, she turned her attention exclusively to fiction. In 1973 she fell asleep with a lighted cigarette and died three weeks later of burns suffered in the resulting fire.

POLINA BARSKOVA was born in Leningrad, studied at the University of California at Berkeley, and lives in the United States. She has published several volumes of poetry and is considered one of the most interesting Russian poets of her generation.

BEI DAO was born in Beijing. His pseudonym Bei Dao literally means "North Island," and was suggested by a friend as a reference to the poet's provenance from Northern China as well as his typical solitude. Bei Dao was one of the foremost poets of the Misty School, and his early poems were a source of inspiration during the April Fifth Democracy Movement of 1976, a peaceful demonstration in Tiananmen Square. He has been in exile from his native China since the Tiananmen Square massacre of 1989. His books of poetry include *Unlock*; *At the Sky's Edge: Poems 1991–1996*; *Landscape Over Zero*; *Forms of Distance*; *Old Snow*; and *The August Sleepwalker*.

GOTTFRIED BENN was raised in the small German village of Mansfeld, in an area which is now part of Poland. He wrote the collections *Morgue und andere Gedichte* (Morgue and Other Poems), *Söhne* (for Else Lasker-Schüler), *Fleisch* (Flesh), and *Statische Gedichte* (Static Poems).

ABBAS BEYDOUN was born in Sûr (Tyre), in Southern Lebanon, in 1945. He has been cultural editor of *As-Safir* newspaper in Beirut since 1997. He has published a novel and six collections of poetry.

MIRON BIAŁOSZEWSKI was born in Warsaw, Poland. His highly acclaimed *Memoir of the Warsaw Uprising* was published in 1970. Also a master of Polish experimental theater, he is the author of many poetry collections, including *Obroty rzeczy*, *Rachunek zachciankowy*, *Mylne wzruszenia*, *Było i było*, and *Poezje wybrane*.

ALEXANDER BLOK was born in St. Petersburg, Russia. He published his first collection, *Verses on a Beautiful Lady*, in 1905. Plays, essays, and poems appeared at regular intervals through to the outbreak of the Russian Revolution. In 1921 he was elected head of Petrograd's All-Russian Union of Poets. He died shortly thereafter.

JOHANNES BOBROWSKI was a German poet. Although he began publishing poetry during World War II, it was not until the publication of his 1961 collection, *Sarmatische Zeit*, that Bobrowski was recognized for his remarkable talent. His volumes in English include *Shadow Lands: Selected Poems*; *Selected Poems: Johannes Bobrowski and Horst Bienek* (1971); *From the Rivers: Selected Poems*; and *Under the Night's Edge*.

YVES BONNEFOY was born in Tours in 1923 and today is considered one of the strongest living poets of French language. *Du Mouvement et de* *l'immobilité de Douve* (On the Motion and Immobility of Douve, 1953) is perhaps Bonnefoy's best-known collection of poems.

JORGE LUIS BORGES was one of the great literary heroes of Argentina. His 1944 collection of short stories, *Ficciones,* is widely regarded as his masterwork. Although mostly known in this country as a fiction writer, Borges is also an accomplished poet whose work has influenced several generations of authors in the Spanish-speaking world.

BERTOLT BRECHT was one of Germany's best-known poets and also an acclaimed playwright. His social critiques, including *The Caucasian Chalk Circle, Mother Courage and Her Children,* and *The Threepenny Opera*, resonate with modern audiences and continue to be frequently performed.

ANDRÉ BRETON was a French writer, poet, and essayist who co-founded surrealism in Paris in 1919. His work and his experiments have influenced many generations of poets around the world. As a head (or "pope," as he was sometimes derisively called) of surrealists from the inception of the movement until his death, Breton authored surrealist manifestos in 1924 and 1930 and initiated several innovative methods of composition, among them automatic writing.

JOSEPH BRODSKY was born in 1940 in Leningrad, and began writing poetry when he was eighteen. Brodsky authored nine volumes of poetry, as well as several collections of essays, and received the Nobel Prize in Literature in 1987.

JOÃO CABRAL DE MELO NETO was a Brazilian poet. In 1942 he published his first collection, *Pedra do sono* (Stone of Sleep). Although his early work was marked by surrealist and cubist influences, his collection *O engenheiro* (The Engineer, 1945) revealed him as a leading voice of the Generation of '45, post–World War II poets notable for their austere style. Melo Neto gained widespread popularity with "*Morte e vida Severina*" (Death and Life of a Severino, 1955), a dramatic poem that made use of *literatura de cordel,* a popular narrative in verse. It was published in *Duas águas,* one of his more than thirty books of poetry.

DINO CAMPANA was born in Marradi, a mountain village in the Apennines. He is generally represented as the "wild man" of Italian poetry. His *Orphic Songs*, written in 1914, represent a "romanticized" and idealized vision that lashed out against the bourgeoisie and contemporary attitudes of the Italians.

ERNESTO CARDENAL is a major poet of the Spanish language well known in the United States as a spokesman for justice and self-determination in Latin America. Cardenal, who recognizes that poetry and art are closely tied to politics, used his poetry to protest the encroachments of outsiders in Nicaragua and supported the revolution that overthrew Somoza in 1979.

NINA CASSIAN, born in 1924 in Galati, Romania, has published over fifty books, including *Life Sentence: Selected Poems*, edited by William Jay Smith, plus works of fiction and books for children. Exiled from Romania in 1985, she is currently working on her memoirs and lives in New York City.

RICARDO CASTILLO's volumes of poetry include *El pobrecito señor X* and *La máquina del instante de formulación poética*. His poems have been included in several anthologies.

CONSTANTINE P. CAVAFY is regarded as the most important figure in twentieth-century Greek poetry. Cavafy remained virtually unrecognized in Greece until late in his career. He never offered a volume of his poems for sale during his lifetime, instead distributing privately printed pamphlets to friends and relatives. Close to one-third of his poems were never printed in any form while he lived. In book form, Cavafy's poems were first published without dates before World War II and reprinted in 1949. *Piimata* (The Poems of Constantine P. Cavafy) appeared posthumously in 1935 in Alexandria.

PATRIZIA CAVALLI was born in Todi and lives in Rome. Her books of poetry include *My Books Won't Change the World*, *The Sky*, *Poems*, and *Always Open Theater*. She is also noted for her translations from the French and English of various novels and plays, including works by Shakespeare and Molière.

CAMILO JOSÉ CELA was born in Iria Flavia, district of Padron. He was a Spanish writer known not only for his poetry, but for his prose and playwriting. His principal work of poetry is *Pisando la dudosa luz del día*. He won the Nobel Prize in Literature in 1989.

Paul Antschel, who wrote under the pseudonym **PAUL CELAN**, was born in Czernovitz, Bukovina, in Romania, on November 23, 1920. His parents were deported and eventually died in Nazi labor camps; Celan himself was confined for eighteen months in a Romanian labor camp before escaping to the Red Army. Celan's first book was published in 1947; it received very little critical attention. His second book, *Mohn und Gedächtnis* (Poppy and Memory), however, garnered tremendous acclaim and helped to establish his reputation. In 1960 he received the Georg Büchner Prize. During the 1960s he published more than six books of poetry. He committed suicide in 1970.

BLAISE CENDRARS was born in Switzerland of Swiss/Scottish descent. He was affiliated with the cubists and surrealists and was especially linked with Guillaume Apollinaire and Max Jacob. During the First World War he joined the French Foreign Legion, losing an arm in 1915. Afterward he turned his hand to writing partially autobiographical novels, which include *Gold*, *Dan Yack*, *Confessions of Dan Yack*, and *Moravagine*, and continued his obsessive wandering. Quiet during the 1930s, he began writing again in the Second World War while under surveillance as a potential subversive in Nazi-occupied France.

AIMÉ CÉSAIRE was born in Basse-Pointe, Martinique, and was a cofounder of the Negritude movement. His books of poetry in English include *Aimé Césaire: The Collected Poetry*; *Putting in Fetters*; *Lost Bodies*, with illustrations by Pablo Picasso; *Decapitated Sun*; *Miraculous Arms*; and *Notebook of a Return to the Homeland*.

RENÉ CHAR is one of the most influential modern French poets. Admired by Heidegger for the profundity of his poetic philosophy, he was also a hero of the French Resistance and in the 1960s a militant antinuclear protester. Associated with the surrealist movement for several years and a close friend of many painters, notably Braque, Giacometti, and

Picasso, he wrote poetry that miraculously, often challengingly, confronts the major twentieth-century moral, political, and artistic concerns.

INGER CHRISTENSEN was a prolific Danish poet, novelist, and essayist, whose major collections of poetry include *det* (1969) and *Alfabet* (1981). Christensen was considered the foremost experimentalist of her generation. In 1978 Christensen was appointed to the Danish Academy and in 1995 she became a member of Académie Européenne de Poésie.

JULIO CORTÁZAR was born in Brussels, grew up in Argentina, and lived for many years in Paris. His novels and stories include *Hopscotch*, *Blow-Up and Other Stories*, and *End of the Game*.

MARÍA ELENA CRUZ VARELA was the leader of the anti-Castro group Critirio Alternativo (Alternative Criteria) in Cuba. In 1991 the group published a manifesto demanding reforms, national debates, and free elections. Shortly afterward she was sentenced to two years in prison. After her release, she was kept under house arrest. In 1994, however, she was able to travel and left Cuba for the United States. She now lives with her daughter in exile in Puerto Rico.

BOGDAN CZAYKOWSKI was born in Poland in 1932 and was deported with his family to Russia in 1939. He grew up in England and earned a degree in Slavic literatures at the University of London. For many years he taught Polish literature at the University of British Columbia.

BERNARD DADIÉ is an Ivoirian poet, dramatist, novelist, and administrator. His first published work was a collection of poems, *Afrique debout* (Africa Upright). In the 1960s he published another collection of poems. Dadié's love of Africa's oral traditions caused him to collect and publish several more volumes of legends, fables, folktales, and proverbs.

SAPARDI DJOKO DAMONNO was born in Indonesia in 1940. He is a poet and professor at the University of Indonesia.

RUBÉN DARÍO was born in Metapa, Nicaragua, in a city that now bears the name Darío. He was one of the leaders and proponents of the *Modernismo* movement, which completely changed the landscape of Spanish-language poetry. A journalist and diplomat, he is now one of the more widely read of Spanish-language poets.

MAHMOUD DARWISH was a beloved and most popular poet in Palestine. Early in life, Darwish became politically active through his poetry and involvement in the Israeli Communist Party, Rakah. He spent a period as the editor of Rakah's newspaper, *Al-Ittihad* (Unity). Darwish's political advocacy brought him a great deal of negative Israeli attention, which included harassment and house arrest. Finally, in 1971, after years of hardship, Darwish left Israel and fled into exile in Beirut, Lebanon. By this time, he had established and upheld an outstanding reputation as one of the leading poets of the resistance. Among his accomplishments are the 1969 Lotus Prize and thirty compilations of poetry and prose. Darwish lived in Paris and was the editor of the Palestinian literary review *Al Karmel*. He died in 2008.

ROBERT DESNOS was born in Paris. He first published poems in the Dadaist magazine *Littérature* in 1919, and in 1922 he published his first book, *Rrose Selavy*. Between 1920 and 1930, Desnos published more than eight books of poetry, including *Language cuit* and *Deuil pour deuil*.

GERARDO DIEGO was an innovative Spanish poet. During the 1920s he wrote experimental poetry. His works include *Imagen* (1922), *Soria* (1923), and *Versos humanos* (Human Verses, 1925). *Angeles de Compostela* and *Alondra de verdad* (Lark of Truth) have been called his best works.

BLAGA DIMITROVA was born in Bulgaria in 1922 and was vice president of her country in the first democratic government after the fall of communism. Her books have been translated into more than twenty languages. She has won the Herder Prize, the Hristo G. Danov Prize, and the German Cogge Prize, and was awarded the French Medal of Merit for Freedom.

LIDIJA DIMKOVSKA grew up in Skopje, Macedonia, received a PhD in Romanian literature in Bucharest, and lives and works in Ljubljana, Slovenia. In addition to editing an anthology of young Macedonian poets, she has published four books of poetry and a novel in Macedonia. Her collection *Do Not Awaken Them with Hammers* was published by Ugly Duckling Presse.

CARLOS DRUMMOND DE ANDRADE was a Brazilian poet. The first of his numerous collections of poetry, *Alguma poesia* (Some Poetry, 1930), demonstrates both his affinity with the modernist movement and his own strong poetic personality. First translated into English by Elizabeth Bishop, his poems have influenced various leading American poets such as Donald Justice and Mark Strand.

DUODUO (real name Li Shizheng) was born in Beijing in 1951. He wrote his first poetry in 1972 and three years later also started to write prose. He was obliged to write clandestinely, publishing in samizdat publications. He left China for the first time the morning after the Tiananmen massacre that he had witnessed. *The Boy Who Catches Wasps: Selected Poetry of Duo Duo* was published in 2002.

GÜNTER EICH was a German lyricist, dramatist, and author. After being held as a prisoner of war, he was one of the founders in 1947 of Gruppe 47. Among his publications was *Abgelegene Gehöfte*. His work in English includes *Valuable Nail: Selected Poems*.

ODYSSEAS ELYTIS, a descendant of an old family of Lesbos, was born in Heraklion (Candia) on the island of Crete. Elytis's poetry has marked, through an active presence of over forty years, a broad spectrum. His poetry includes *To Axion Esti* (It Is Worthy). Elytis was awarded the Nobel Prize in Literature in 1979.

ISRAEL EMIOT wrote in Yiddish and survived both World War II and the Soviet camps. He is the author of several books of poetry, essays, and short fiction, and wrote for the *Jewish Daily Forward*. Besides his memoir, *The Birobidzhan Affair*, he wrote several volumes of verse in the United States. *Life in a Mirror*, an anthology of English translation of his poems and short stories, was published in 1976. He emigrated to the United States and died in Rochester, New York, in 1978.

HANS MAGNUS ENZENSBERGER is a German author, poet, translator, and editor. He sprang to fame as a member of the Gruppe 47, a radical opponent of both romantic socialism and blind industrialism. His early work was fiercely polemical, attacking technology's insidious power. His later work has returned to its more lyrical beginnings, to a concern with the individual rather than the poem.

FAIZ AHMED FAIZ began his career as the editor of the leftist English-language daily *Pakistan Times*, as well as the managing editor for the Urdu daily *Imroz*. Although his first volume of poetry, *Naqsh-e-Faryadi*, was published in Lucknow in 1941, he became widely known after the 1952 publication of *Dast-e Saba*, poems written during his imprisonment by the Pakistani government. After the miltary coup led by Zia-ul-Haq in 1979, Faiz lived in self-exile in Beirut writing for the Afro-Asia Writers Association journal, *Lotus*, until his return to Pakistan in 1982.

ERNEST FARRÉS is a journalist in Barcelona and the author of three volumes of poems in Catalan: *Clavar-ne una al mall i l'altra a l'enclusa* (1996), *Mosquits* (1998), and *Edward Hopper* (2006). He has also edited an anthology of young Catalan poets, *21 poetes del XXI* (2001).

JEAN FOLLAIN was a French author, poet, and corporate lawyer. His poetry includes *Usage du temps* (1943), *Exister* (1947), *Tout instant* (1957), *Appareil de la terre* (1964), and *Espaces d'instants* (1971). In 1970 he was awarded the Grand Prize of Poetry from L'Académie française for his life's work.

ERICH FRIED was an Austrian poet, broadcaster, translator, and essayist who settled in England. He was known for his political-minded poetry. He published several volumes of poetry as well as radio plays and a novel.

GLORIA FUERTES was born in 1918 in Madrid, Spain, where she lived most of her life. She worked at various office jobs and as a librarian to support her writing. Fuertes was part of the first generation of Spanish poets to come into prominence after the Civil War. She published fifteen books of poetry and thirty-four children's books before her death in 1998.

FEDERICO GARCÍA LORCA was one of the most important Spanish poets of the twentieth century. Also a dramatist and director, he was a member of the Generation of '27. His fame as a poet came in 1927 after the publication of *Gypsy Ballads* that year and *Poem of the Deep Song* in 1931. After his visit to the United States he wrote *Poet in New York*, which remains one of the finest examples of surrealist poetry in Spain.

LUIS GARCÍA MONTERO is one of the most popular poets writing in Spain today. He has received numerous awards for his work, including Spain's National Poetry Prize and the National Poetry Critics Prize.

García Montero is a professor of Spanish literature at the University of Granada.

YANKEV GLATSHTEYN (Jacob Glatstein) was one of the most important Jewish poets of the twentieth century and a founder of Yiddish modernism. In the 1920s, together with N. B. Minkov, Glatshteyn founded a new Yiddish literary school called *In zikh*, "in the self," or "introspective," which held that poetry should be beholden only to aesthetic criteria and not to political or social ends.

EUGEN GOMRINGER studied in Berne and was in contact with painters involved with concrete art. He was motivated by the visual arts movement to adopt the same philosophy in his poetry, and so *concrete poetry* was born in Europe. Since that time he has worked with many important artists, and has published numerous works.

ÁNGEL GONZÁLEZ was born in Oviedo and was a major Spanish poet of the twentieth century. His first book of poems, *Áspero mundo* (Harsh World), was an immediate critical success. His second book, *Grado elemental* (Elementary Grade), was published in Paris. He published eight more books of poetry.

GÜNTER GRASS was born in Danzig-Langfuhr of Polish-German parents. His first poetry was published in 1956 and his first play produced in 1957. His international breakthrough came with *The Tin Drum*. He was awarded the Nobel Prize in Literature in 1999.

TATJANA GROMAČA, a poet and fiction writer, works as a journalist for the *Feral Tribune*. Her first book of poems, *Something Wrong, Maybe?* was translated into German and Polish.

GU CHENG was one of the innovative writers of "misty poetry" (*menglung shi*) who emerged in the immediate post-Mao years. He began writing poetry as a child in Shandong province, where his parents had been exiled in 1969, during the Cultural Revolution. Gu Cheng went back to Beijing in 1974 and worked as a carpenter, an industrial painter, and a laborer, then worked as a newspaper and magazine editor. He began writing again and left China for Europe in 1987.

NICOLAS GUILLEN was a Cuban poet of social protest and a leader of the Afro-Cuban movement in the late 1920s and 1930s. His first volume of poetry was *Motivos de son* (Sound Themes, 1930), which was hailed as a masterpiece and widely imitated. Later volumes of poetry include *La paloma de vuelo popular: Elegías* (The Dove of Popular Flight: Elegies, 1958) and *Tengo* (I Have, 1964).

LARS GUSTAFSSON was born in Västerås, central Sweden, in 1936. His most recent publications have been the poetry collection *En tid i Xanadu* (2002) and the novel *Dekanen* (2003). In 2005–2006 he was Writer in Residence at Tübingen University, Germany.

OSCAR HAHN has published editions of his collected poems in his native Chile, as well as in Venezuela, Spain, Argentina, Greece, and other countries. He is currently a professor of Spanish at the University of Iowa.

MOISHE LEIB HALPERN was born in the Austro-Hungarian Empire and emigrated to the United States in 1898. He was part of the new American Yiddish movement called Di Yunge (The Young Ones).

HAN YONGWUN was a twentieth-century Korean Buddhist reformer and poet. He was one of the thirty-three members who signed the 1919 historical document as a representative of the people to declare Korea's independence from Japanese colonial control. His poems mainly concern his philosophical meditation on nature and the mystery of human experience.

ZBIGNIEW HERBERT was a spiritual leader of the anticommunist movement in Poland. His work has been translated into almost every European language, and he won numerous prizes, including the Jerusalem Prize and the T. S. Eliot Prize. His books include *Selected Poems*, *Report from the Besieged City and Other Poems*, *Mr Cogito*, *Still Life with a Bridle*, *King of the Ants*, and *Collected Poems*.

MIGUEL HERNÁNDEZ was a Spanish poet. His first book, *Perito en lunas* (Lunar Expert), was published in 1933. In 1936 he published *El rayo que no cesa* (Unceasing Lightning). Other works included *Viento del pueblo* (1937) and *El Hombre acecha* (1938). He also worked with Neruda on the publication of the influential journal *Caballo Verde para la Poesía*.

HIKMET, the first modern Turkish poet, was born in Sa-
he Ottoman Empire (now Thessaloniki, Greece). Many of his
have been translated into English, including *Things I Didn't Know I Loved*, *The Day Before Tomorrow*, *The Moscow Symphony*, and *Selected Poems*.

HO CH'I-FANG was a Chinese poet and fiction writer. His works in English include *Paths in Dreams: Selected Prose and Poetry of Ho Ch'i-fang*, translated and edited by Bonnie S. McDougall.

VLADIMIR HOLAN was a Czech poet. His collections include *Vanutí* (Breezing) and the political poems *Odpověď Francii* (The Reply to France), *Září 1938* (September 1938), and *Zpěv tříkrálový* (Twelfth Night Song).

MIROSLAV HOLUB was a poet and immunologist from Prague. His first poetry was published in 1947; by the mid-1950s he was associated with the young writers of the literary magazine *Květe*. His first verse collection was *Denní služba* (Day Duty), and his work was translated into many languages.

MOUSHEGH ISHKHAN was orphaned in the Armenian massacres at the age of two and was raised in Beirut. He graduated from the Jemaran. He had gone to Belgium to the University of Brussels in 1938, but World War II interrupted his studies and in 1940 he returned to Beirut. His first book of poems, *The Song the Houses Sing*, appeared in 1936.

EDMOND JABÈS was born in Cairo in 1912 and was a major voice in twentieth-century French poetry. Many of his books of prose and poetry have been translated into English, including *The Book of Dialogue* and *The Book of Margins*. His trilogy *Book of Questions* is considered one of the most important texts written in the French language after the Second World War.

PHILIPPE JACCOTTET was born in Switzerland in 1925. He is one of the most prominent figures of the immediate postwar generation of French poets. His work in English includes *Selected Poems* and *Under Clouded Skies with Beauregard*.

MAX JACOB was a French poet and artist whose circle of friends included Guillaume Apollinaire, Jean Cocteau, and Pablo Picasso. Born Jewish, he later converted to Catholicism. Jacob died of pneumonia in an internment camp.

JUAN RAMÓN JIMÉNEZ belonged to a group of writers in Spain who called themselves the *Modernistas*. Jiménez left Spain during the Spanish Civil War in 1936. He published *Españoles de tres mundos* (Spaniards of Three Worlds), *Voces de mi copla* (Voices of My Song), and *Animal de fondo* (Animal of Depth). Jiménez won the Nobel Prize in Literature in 1956.

ATTILA JÓZSEF was born in Budapest in 1906 and died, after apparently throwing himself under a train, in December 1937. He was considered one of the greatest Hungarian poets. His books in English include *A Transparent Lion* and *Winter Night: Selected Poems*.

ROBERTO JUARROZ was an Argentine poet famous for his *"Poesía vertical"* (Vertical Poetry). He published fourteen volumes of poetry in all, numbered successively 1 to 14, under the general title *Poesía vertical*, the first appearing in 1958 and the final one posthumously in 1997.

FRANZ KAFKA was born in Prague in 1883 and died of tuberculosis in a sanatorium near Vienna in 1924. After earning a law degree in 1906, he worked most of his adult life at the Workers Accident Insurance Company for the kingdom of Bohemia in Prague. Only a small portion of his writings were published during his lifetime; most of them, including the three unfinished novels *Amerika, The Trial*, and *The Castle*, were published posthumously.

ANNA KAMIENSKA, a major Polish writer widely acknowledged as a peer of Nobel Prize winners Wisława Szymborska and Czesław Miłosz, left a rich legacy that includes fifteen books of poetry; two volumes of notebooks; three volumes of commentaries on the Bible; and translations from several Slavic languages as well as from Hebrew, Latin, and French.

MITSUHARU KANEKO was one of the most prominent Japanese poets of the twentieth century. Drawing on his travels through Southeast Asia, he produced two great works: the book of poems *Same* (Sharks), published in

1937, and the prose account *Mareh Ran'in kikoh* (Malay and Dutch East Indies Travelogue) in 1940.

TYMOTEUSZ KARPOWICZ was born in Vilnius, Lithuania, in 1921. He published his first collection of poetry in 1958 and edited literary magazines such as the *Nowe Sygnaly* (New Signals), *Odra*, and *Poezja* (Poetry). He also wrote a number of radio plays and stage dramas. He later became professor of Polish at the University of Illinois at Chicago.

MARIE LUISE KASCHNITZ was a German poet. After World War II she emerged as an important lyric poet who combined modern and traditional verse forms with a highly original diction. Published poetry includes *Totentanz und Gedichte zur Zeit* (Dance of Death and Poems of the Times, 1947) and *Zukunftsmusik* (Music of the Future, 1950).

PATRICE KAYO was born in 1942 and is a poet, author, and scholar from Cameroon. He is the former director of *Le Cameroun littéraire* and author of numerous works in various genres—poems, fables, stories, essays—including *Tout le long des saisons* (1983), *Déchirements* (1983), *Les Sauterelles* (1986), and *Les fêtes tragiques* (2007).

DANIIL KHARMS was one of the founders of OBERIU, often described as Russia's last avant-garde group. His books in English translation include *Incidences*, translated by Neil Cornwell, and *The Man with the Black Coat*, translated by George Gibian. His work is also included in *OBERIU: An Anthology of Russian Absurdism*.

VELIMIR KHLEBNIKOV was a founding member of the Russian futurist movement and was generally regarded as a "poet's poet" whose work influenced many of his peers, including Mayakovsky, Pasternak, and Mandelstam. Notoriously difficult to translate into English, Khlebnikov is known for poems such as "Incantation by Laughter," "Bobeobi Sang the Lips," "The Grasshopper" (all 1908–1909), and "Snake Train" (1910).

VÉNUS KHOURY-GHATA is a Lebanese poet and novelist who lives in France. She has received the Prix Mallarmé, the Prix Apollinaire, and the Grand Prix de la Société des gens de lettres. Her collections include *Anthologie personelle*; *Elle dit*; *La Compassion des pierres*; and *Quelle est la nuit parmi les nuits*. Her volumes in English, translated by Marilyn Hacker, include *Here There Was Once a Country*; *She Says*; and *A House at the Edge of Tears*.

KIM NAM-JO was born in Taegu in 1927. She is one of Korea's leading poets. She has published numerous volumes of poetry and essays and has been awarded many major literary prizes. She served for a time as president of the Korean Poets' Association and has long been active in the Korean PEN Center.

KO UN is Korea's best-known living writer. After suffering during the Korean War, he became a Buddhist monk. He published his first poems in 1958, then returned to the world several years later. He became a leading spokesman in the struggle for freedom and democracy during the 1970s and 1980s, when he was often arrested and frequently imprisoned. He has published more than 120 volumes of poems, essays, and fiction. In recent years, selections from his work have been translated into at least fourteen languages.

EDVARD KOCBEK grew up in the section of present-day Slovenia that was then Austria-Hungary. His published poetry includes *Zemlja* (1934), *Groza* (1963), *Poročilo* (1969), and *Zbrane pesmi* (1977).

GERRIT KOUWENAAR was born in Amsterdam in 1923 and first published in clandestine publications during World War II. After the war he earned a living as a translator and journalist. His volumes *een geur van verbrande veren* (a smell of burnt feathers, 1991) and *de tijd staat open* (time is wide open, 1996) have won him universal critical acclaim.

KARL KROLOW was one of the more prominent German poets of the second half of the twentieth century. The sharply distinct phases of Krolow's work reflect the phases of German postwar poetry in general, giving his work a representative stature for the period; and his production as one of Germany's leading poetry critics is almost as impressive.

RYSZARD KRYNICKI was born in 1943 in Sankt Valentin, Austria, where his parents had been deported to a Nazi labor camp. In Poland in the 1960s he became a leading member of the "New Wave" group of poets, which included Adam Zagajewski and Stanisław Barańczak. He was co-editor of *Zapis*, the first independent literary magazine in Communist

Poland to be published outside the reach of official censorship. Krynicki is a distinguished translator of German-language poetry, in particular of Paul Celan and Nelly Sachs.

REINER KUNZE was born in 1933 and studied philosophy and journalism in Leipzig from 1951 to 1955. His poetry, prose, and essays (as well as translations) have won him numerous awards. In 1989 he gave the Lectures on Poetics at the University of Munich.

ELSE LASKER-SCHÜLER was one of the most outstanding German-language poets and writers of the twentieth century. Her first volume of poetry, *Styx*, appeared in 1902. A volume of poetry called the *Meine Wunder*, published in 1911, established Lasker-Schüler as the leading female representative of German expressionism. Several leading poets, including Yehuda Amichai, claimed to be influenced by her work.

LEI SHUYAN was born in Xi'an. He has published nine books of poetry and has won a number of awards. His work has been translated into several languages.

PRIMO LEVI was born in Turin in 1919. The son of educated middle-class Jewish parents, he graduated with a degree in chemistry and found a job as a research chemist in Milan. In December 1943 he was arrested as part of the antifascist resistance and deported to Auschwitz. After the war, Levi resumed his career as a chemist, retiring only in 1975. His account of his time in Auschwitz, *If This Is a Man*, was published in 1947, and he went on to write many other books, including *If Not Now, When?* and *The Periodic Table*, emerging not only as one of the most profound and haunting commentators on the Holocaust, but as a great writer on many twentieth-century themes.

ENRIQUE LIHN was born in Santiago in 1929. In addition to being a popular poet, he was also a novelist and playwright, and taught literature at the University of Chile. During the years when Chile was governed by a military junta, his work increasingly dealt with the social and human cost of the dictatorship. His final book, *Diario de muerte* (Diary of Dying), was written in the six weeks preceding his death.

JORGE DE LIMA is a Brazilian poet and novelist who became one of the representatives of regionalist poetry in Brazil in the 1920s. His best-known collections of poems include *A Túnica Inconsútil* (The Seamless Tunic), *Poemas Negros* (Black Poems), and *Invenção de Orfeu* (The Invention of Orpheus).

LUO FU is the pen name of Mo Luofu, who was born in Hengyang, Hunan province. He joined the military during the Sino-Japanese War (1937–1945) and moved to Taiwan in 1949. He held various posts until retiring from the navy in 1973. That year he also graduated with a BA in English from Tamkang University. He has been a full-time writer and translator since.

ANTONIO MACHADO was one of the great Spanish poets of the twentieth century and a leading member of the Spanish literary movement known as the Generation of '98. He defined poetry as "the essential word in time." Machado was born in Seville but spent most of his life in Castile. He visited Paris frequently and was well aware of the work of French poets of his time. During the Civil War, Machado fought on the Republican side, and at the end of the war fled to France, where he died in 1939.

MUHAMMAD AL-MAGHUT was a Syrian poet and playwright. He was considered to be one of the greatest and most original writers of modern Arabic. His first volume of poetry, *Huzn fi daw' al-Qamar* (Sorrow in Moonlight), appeared in 1959. Other volumes followed, including *Ghurfah bi-malayin al-Jidran* (A Room with Millions of Walls) in 1964.

OSIP MANDELSTAM was born and raised in St. Petersburg. Mandelstam first published his poems in *Apollyon* magazine, in 1910, then banded together with Anna Akhmatova and Nicholai Gumilev to form the Acmeist group, which advocated an aesthetic of exact description and chiseled form, as suggested by the title of Mandelstam's first book, *Stone* (1913). He published his second collection of poems, *Tristia*, in 1922, and an edition of collected poems in 1928. In 1934, after reading an epigram denouncing Stalin to friends, Mandelstam was arrested and sent into exile. He was arrested for "counterrevolutionary" activities in May 1938 and sentenced to five years in a labor camp; he died in the Gulag Archipelago, near Vladivostok, in 1938.

CAITLÍN MAUDE was an Irish poet, actress, and traditional singer. She was born in Casla, County Galway, and was an active member of the Dublin Irish-speaking community.

VLADIMIR MAYAKOVSKY was born in Georgia, moved to Russia when he was young, and joined the Bolsheviks. His propaganda work for the party eventually got him arrested; his time in prison was crucial to his artistic development. He went on to write *The Cloud in Trousers*, "I," "Back Home," and numerous other works. Although he is known as the best poet of the Soviet system, he is also a consummate love poet. He committed suicide in 1930.

PABLO MEDINA lived in Havana, Cuba, the first twelve years of his life, then moved with his family to New York City. He is the author of five collections of poetry, three novels, a memoir, and a book of translations, and his work has appeared in periodicals and anthologies in the United States and abroad. Medina has received several awards for his work, among them grants from the Lila Wallace Reader's Digest Fund, the National Endowment for the Arts, and the Rockefeller Foundation.

HENRI MICHAUX was a Belgian poet and artist who wrote in French. His body of work includes poetry, travelogues, and art criticism. Best known for his explorations of interior and exterior space, he traveled widely and thought of travel as a way to probe inner life, producing writings about imaginary countries and people.

DUNYA MIKHAIL published four collections of poetry in Arabic, including *The Psalms of Absence*, *Diary of a Wave Outside the Sea*, and *Almost Music*. In 2001 she was awarded the UN Human Rights Award for Freedom of Writing. Recently, her work *The War Works Hard* won PEN's Translation Award.

CZESŁAW MIŁOSZ was born in 1911 in Szetejnie, Lithuania. He survived World War II in Warsaw, publishing in the underground press, after which he was stationed in New York, Washington, and Paris as a cultural attaché from Poland. He defected to France in 1951, and in 1960 he accepted a position at the University of California at Berkeley. Although his writing was banned in Poland, he was nevertheless awarded the 1980 Nobel Prize in Literature. He died in 2004 in Kraków. He was called by Joseph Brodsky "one of the great poets of our time, perhaps the greatest."

AGI MISHOL was born in 1947 in Hungary and brought to Israel as a very young child. She is the author of twelve books of poetry and the winner of every major Israeli poetry prize, including the first Yehuda Amichai Prize in 2002. Her latest books, *New and Selected Works* and *Moment*, recently moved into their fifth and second printings, respectively. A teacher of poetry workshops and lecturer in literature, Mishol holds BA and MA degrees in Hebrew literature from Hebrew University in Jerusalem.

GABRIELA MISTRAL was the first Latin American woman to win the Nobel Prize in Literature. She was born in Chile and published her first collection of poems, *Desolación* (Despair), in 1922. *Ternura* (Tenderness), published in 1925, was a collection of poetry for children that celebrated the joys of birth and motherhood. Her later collections were *Questions* (1930) and *Tala* (1938). She won the Nobel Prize in 1945.

TATSUJI MIYOSHI was a Japanese poet, literary critic, and literary editor. His work often portrays loneliness and isolation as part of contemporary life, but is written in a complex, highly literary style reminiscent of classical Japanese poetry.

EUGENIO MONTALE is one of the few obvious "true masters" of the last fifty years of Italian literature. In 1925 he published his first collection of poems, *Ossi di seppia*, which quickly became one of the "classics" of contemporary Italian poetry. Other works include *Le occasioni* and *Finisterre*. He won the Nobel Prize in Literature in 1975.

VALZHYNA MORT was born in Minsk and currently lives in the United States. Her first collection, *I Am As Thin As Your Eyelashes*, was published in 2005. Her latest book, *Factory of Tears*, published by Copper Canyon Press, is the first translation of poetry from the Belarusian language to be published in the United States.

TAHA MUHAMMAD ALI was born in 1931 in a village in Galilee. He is a revered Palestinian poet whose collections in English include *Never Mind* and *So What*.

AMJAD NASSER was born in 1955 in al-Turra, Jordan. From 1976 he worked as a journalist in television and newspapers, then in the cultural section of *Al-Hadaf* journal in Beirut, and in Cyprus was arts editor of *Al-Ufq* magazine. Since 1987 he has been arts editor of *Al-Quds Al-Arabi* daily newspaper in London. He has published nine collections of poetry and two travel books. Three different volumes of selected poetry have been published, in Cairo in 1995 and in 1999 by the House of Poetry in Palestine.

MARÍA NEGRONI has published six collections of poems, two books of essays, a novel, and translations of, among others, Louise Labé, Valentine Penrose, Georges Bataille, H.D., and Charles Simic.

PABLO NERUDA led a life charged with poetic and political activity. In 1927 Neruda began his long career as a diplomat in the Latin American tradition of honoring poets with diplomatic assignments. He held various posts and wrote prolifically. Upon returning to Chile in 1943, he was elected to the Senate and joined the Communist Party. When the Chilean government moved to the right, they declared communism illegal and expelled Neruda from the Senate. He went into hiding. In 1952 the government withdrew the order to arrest leftist writers and political figures, and Neruda returned to Chile. He received numerous prestigious awards, including the International Peace Prize in 1950, the Lenin Peace Prize and the Stalin Peace Prize in 1953, and the Nobel Prize in Literature in 1971.

AUGUSTINHO NETO was the president of Angola as well as a poet. He first became known in 1948, when he published a volume of poems in Luanda and joined a national cultural movement. His work was published in a number of Portuguese and Angolan reviews and was included in Mário de Andrade's *Antologia da Poesia Negra de Expressão Portuguesa*.

VITESLAV NEZVAL was perhaps the most prolific writer in Prague during the 1920s and 1930s. An original member of the avant-garde group of artists *Devetsil* (Nine Forces), he was a founding figure of the Poetist movement. His best work is from the interwar period.

NUALA NÍ DHOMHNAILL was born in England and grew up in Ireland. Her books include *The Astrakhan Cloak, Pharaoh's Daughter, Selected Poems*, and *Spíonáin is Róiseanna*. She is one of the few female Irish poets who writes exclusively in Irish.

SALAH NIAZI was born in 1935 in Nasiriyah, Iraq, and has lived in Britain since 1963. He is a well-known poet and critic, and founding editor of the quarterly Arabic literary journal *Al Ightirab al Adabi*. He has published many collections of poetry and translated into Arabic Shakespeare's *Hamlet* and *Macbeth*, and James Joyce's *Ulysses*.

JACOB NIBENEGENESABE lived for ninety-four years on Lake Winnipeg, Canada. He was considered an excellent storyteller when it came to the traditional tales, but it is as an original poet that he made his greatest contributions to his people. In his series of poems using the magical "Wishing Bone" of a goose, Nibenegenesabe transformed himself into a "trickster," that is, someone capable of wishing things into existence, or wishing himself into various situations. Nibenegenesabe said of his special poetical powers that he was "curious to tell things past the old others" (meaning: things not discussed in older tales).

HENRIK NORDBRANDT holds a unique place in contemporary Danish literature, writing poetry that is imbued with the towns, landscapes, and climates of the Mediterranean region. Nordbrandt published his first collection, *Poems*, in 1966, when he was twenty-one. In 2000 he received the Nordic Council's prestigious literature prize for his twenty-first collection, *Dream Bridges*.

GIACOMO NOVENTA was a poet and essayist, born in Noventa di Piave, Veneto, Italy. A Catholic, he was involved in contemporary cultural debate and tried to fuse together Catholicism, socialism, and liberalism. His poems, *Versi e poesie* (1956, 1960), are written in his own style of cultured Venetian dialect that refers to German Romanticism. Among his books of essays are *Principio di una scienza nuova* (1937) and *I calzoni di Beethoven* (1965).

DAN PAGIS was born in Bukovina, Romania. During World War II, he was interned in a concentration camp for several years. He arrived in pre-state Israel in 1946 and became a teacher on a kibbutz. He received his PhD from the Hebrew University of Jerusalem, where he later became a professor of medieval Hebrew literature. A renowned poet, Dan Pagis published eight books of poetry, four studies of medieval poetry, and one book for children. He also published a critical edition of David Vogel's collected verse and collections of medieval poetry.

FRANCESC PARCERISAS is a poet, translator, and literary critic. He is the deputy director and head of the Department of Translation and

Interpretation at the Autonomous University of Barcelona. He has published several collections of poems and has received numerous prizes, including the 1966 Carles Riba Prize and the 1983 Critics' Prize for Catalan Poetry.

NICANOR PARRA, one of the most important Latin American poets of his time, is the originator of so-called antipoetry. *Poemas y antipoemas* (*Poems and Antipoems*, 1954), Parra's efforts to make poetry more accessible, gained him national and international fame. Parra also published *Versos de salón* (Verses of the Salon) and *Obra gruesa* (Big Work).

PIER PAOLO PASOLINI was an internationally acclaimed writer, poet, critic, actor, director, and filmmaker. Among his most noted films are his epic masterpiece *Accattone*, *The Gospel According to St. Matthew*, *Teorema*, and *Salò or the 120 Days of Sodom*. He was the author of several novels, most notably *The Ragazzi (Ragazzi di Vita)*, as well as books of short stories, essays, and collections of poetry.

BORIS PASTERNAK was born in Moscow. His volumes of poetry included *Sestra moya zhizn* (My Sister Life), *Temy i variatsii* (Themes and Variations), *Vysokaya bolezn* (Sublime Malady), and *Detstvo Lyuvers* (The Childhood of Luvers). Having survived in the age of Stalin's repressions, he published his novel, *Doctor Zhivago*, in 1957, and won the Nobel Prize in Literature in 1958.

CESARE PAVESE was born on his family's vacation farm in the country outside of Turin in northern Italy. Briefly exiled by the Fascist regime to Calabria in 1935, Pavese returned to Turin to work for the new publishing house of Giulio Einaudi, where he eventually became the editorial director. In 1936 he published a book of poems, *Lavorare stanca* (Hard Labor), and then turned to writing novels and short stories. His works in English include *Diaffections: Complete Poems 1930–1950*, *The Beach*, *The House on the Hill*, *Among Women Only*, *The Moon and the Bonfires*, and *The Devil in the Hills*, which is also published by NYRB Classics.

OCTAVIO PAZ was born and educated in Mexico City and lived for periods of time in Spain, France, and the United States. He entered the Mexican diplomatic service after World War II but resigned in 1968 to protest his government's repressive brutality against student demonstrations in Mexico City. His voluminous output of poems and essays made him a leading man of letters in Latin America, a fact recognized with his being awarded the Nobel Prize in Literature in 1990.

SANDRO PENNA was born in Perugia. His first collection of verse, *Poesie* (Poetry), was published in 1938 and later updated, first in 1957 and then in 1970, under the title *Tutte le poesie* (All the Poetry). He died in 1977.

FERNANDO PESSOA was born in Portugal. He was known for his creation of alter egos that he called heteronyms; at least seventy-two names besides Fernando Pessoa were "responsible" for the thousands of texts that he actually wrote and the many more that he only planned. He published his first book of English poems, *Antinous*, in 1918, followed by *Sonnets* (1918) and *English Poems* (1921), but released only a single book of Portuguese poems, *Mensagem,* in 1933.

GYÖRGY PETRI was a Hungarian satirist whose poetry set political and individual freedoms in relation to sex and death with a black humor that is almost medieval in feeling. His collections in English include *Eternal Monday: New & Selected Poems* and *Night Song of the Personal Shadow.*

FRANCIS PONGE was born in Montpellier, France, in 1899. His work became known in French literary circles in the early 1920s, primarily through publication in the *Nouvelle Revue Française.* In 1942 he published his great masterpiece, *Parti pris des choses.* Other works include *Soap, Things,* and *The Voice of Things.*

VASKO POPA was born in Serbia. During the war he fought with the communist partisans and was held in a Nazi concentration camp. For most of his life, he worked as an editor at several publishing houses. By his death he had published forty-three collections of poetry and was considered the leading poet of the language.

ADÉLIA PRADO is one of Brazil's foremost poets. *The Alphabet in the Park: Selected Poems of Adélia Prado*, translated by Ellen Doré Watson, was published by Wesleyan University Press in 1990.

JACQUES PRÉVERT was born in France and participated actively in the surrealist movement. His books include *Paroles* (Words, 1946), *Histoires* (Stories, 1963), *Spectacle* (1951), *La Pluie et le beau temps* (Rain and Good Weather, 1955), *Fatras* (1971), and *Choses et autres* (Things and Others, 1973).

SALVATORE QUASIMODO was born of Sicilian parents in Modica, near Syracuse. His publications include *La terra impareggiabile* (The Incomparable Earth), *Selected Poems*, *Giorno dopogiorno* (Day after Day), and *La vita non è sogno* (Life Is Not a Dream). Quasimodo was awarded the Nobel Prize in Literature in 1959.

RAYMOND QUENEAU was a French poet and novelist who aligned himself with Breton and the surrealists from 1924 to 1929. In 1960 he became the cofounder of Ouvroir de littérature potentielle (OuLiPo).

MIKLÓS RADNÓTI is one of the most frequently translated Hungarian poets of the twentieth century. Radnóti published his first collection of poems, *Pogány köszönto* (Pagan Salute), at the age of twenty-one. His other books include *Újmódi pásztorok éneke* (Song of Modern Shepherds, 1931). He was executed during World War II; his body was later found by his widow, a parcel of poems (including the one published here) still in his pocket.

MANSUR RAJIH was born in Yemen and was a prisoner of conscience from 1983 to 1998. Since then he has been living in exile in Norway. His poetry has been published in Norwegian and in the original Arabic in Yemen.

IRINA RATUSHINSKAYA was born in Odessa; she was imprisoned in Russia for her dissident activities and exiled from the country in 1986. She is the author of numerous collections of poetry and two memoirs.

DAHLIA RAVIKOVITCH was born in Ramat Gan, Israel, in 1936. Her language, rich inner life, and extreme sensitivity have won her an enthusiastic readership in Israel and abroad as one of the most brilliant and versatile Israeli poets. She has published ten books, mostly poetry.

SADANAND REGE began writing in the 1940s. He was a professor of English in Ramnarain Ruia College, Bombay. Among his collections of poems are *Aksharvel* and *Devapudhacha Diva*. He was the recipient of the Maharashtra State award and the Soviet Land Nehru award.

PIERRE REVERDY was a member of an avant-garde group that included such artists and writers as Guillaume Apollinaire, Max Jacob, Pablo Picasso, Juan Gris, and Georges Braque. With these and other artists, Reverdy helped develop cubism and surrealism. In 1917 he founded the monthly literary review *Nord-Sud*, which drew together the first cubists and surrealists. Although his work reflected both modes of thought, Reverdy sought more; he eventually became a Catholic and retired to a life of seclusion near the monastery of Solesmes.

RAINER MARIA RILKE was born in Prague. Rilke attended Charles University in Prague and several years later moved to Paris. In 1902 he became the friend, and for a time the secretary, of Rodin, and it was during his twelve-year Paris residence that Rilke enjoyed his greatest poetic activity. His first great work, *Das Stunden Buch* (*The Book of Hours*), appeared in 1906, followed in 1907 by *Neue Gedichte* (*New Poems*) and *Die Aufzeichnungen des Malte Laurids Brigge* (*The Notebooks of Malte Laurids Brigge*). When World War I broke out, Rilke was obliged to leave France, and during the war he lived in Munich. In 1919 he went to Switzerland, where he spent the last years of his life. It was here that he wrote his last two works, the *Duino Elegies* (1923) and the *Sonnets to Orpheus* (1923). With Neruda and Akhmatova, he is perhaps one of the most famous and influential poets of the twentieth century.

YANNIS RITSOS spent many years in sanatoriums, prisons, or in political exile while producing dozen of volumes of lyrics, dramas, and translations. During the Nazi occupation of Greece (1941–1944) and the subsequent Civil War (1946–1949), Ritsos fought with the communist guerrillas; after their defeat he was arrested and spent four years in prison camps. In 1967 Ritsos was arrested again by the Greek junta and exiled, and was prohibited from publishing until 1972. By the end of his life, and contrary to all odds, Ritsos had published over one hundred books, including numerous plays and essays.

JEAN-PIERRE ROSNAY was born in 1926 in France. Rosnay founded the quarterly *Vivre en poésie* in 1983 and the renowned Club des Poètes in Paris. Among his publications is *When a Poet Sees a Chestnut Tree*.

TADEUSZ RÓŻEWICZ, considered by many to be one of the most influential poets of postwar Poland, changed the sensibility of Polish poetry by stripping it of its rhetorical excesses and writing in a "prosaicized" voice of somber and powerful witness. He is also known as a playwright, essayist, and short story writer.

PENTTI SAARIKOSKI was a poet and a brilliant translator, the central figure in Finnish literature in the 1960s and 1970s. His translations include such classics as Homer's *Odyssey* and James Joyce's *Ulysses*. He published his first major work, *Mitä tapahtuu todella?* (What goes on really?), in 1962 and continued to publish into the 1970s. His works available in English include *The Dance Floor on the Mountain*, *Invitation to the Dance*, and *The Dark One's Dances*.

GUILLERMO SAAVEDRA was born in Buenos Aires in 1960. His books include the poetry collections *Caracol*, *Tentativas sobre Cage*, *El velador*, *La voz inútil*, and *Del tomate*. He is working on three other poetry books, *Pescado frito*, *Desocupado*, and *El corredor de fondo*. He lives in Buenos Aires, where he is the director of publications of the Complejo Teatral de Buenos Aires and director of the cultural journal *Las ranas*.

UMBERTO SABA was raised by his Jewish mother in the ghetto of Trieste, Italy. He is noted for his simple, lyrical autobiographical poems. He established his reputation as a poet with the publication of *Il canzoniere* (The Songbook, 1921). His collected poems of forty years were published in 1961 in a definitive edition bearing the same title.

JAIME SABINES was arguably Mexico's most popular contemporary poet. Known as "the sniper of literature," as he formed part of a group that transformed literature into reality, he published ten volumes of poetry, and his work has been translated into more than twelve languages. He was awarded Mexico's National Prize for Letters in 1983.

NELLY SACHS began her career as a poet after her emigration from Germany to Sweden in 1940. Her collections include *In den Wohnungen des Todes* (In the Houses of Death), *Sternverdunkelung* (Eclipse of Stars), *Und niemand weiss weiter* (And No One Knows Where to Go), and *Flucht und Verwandlung* (Flight and Metamorphosis). Sachs won the Nobel Prize in Literature in 1966.

TOMAŽ ŠALAMUN is the author of thirty-five books in Slovenian and has had books translated into most of the European languages. He lives in Ljubljana and occasionally teaches in the United States. His recent books in English include *The Book for My Brother*, *Row*, and *Woods and Chalices*.

GEORGE SEFERIS was born in 1900 in Smyrna, Greece. After law studies in Paris, he joined the Greek foreign service. After numerous government positions, Seferis eventually retired as ambassador to England. Influenced by the French symbolists, and later by T. S. Eliot and Ezra Pound, Seferis wrote most of his twelve books of poetry, essays, translations, diaries, and fiction while posted overseas. *Strophe* (1931) marked the advent of modernism in Greece. His work was translated by Henry Miller, Lawrence Durrell, and Rex Warner, among others. He was awarded the Nobel Prize in Literature in 1963, the first Greek to be so honored.

LÉOPOLD SÉDAR SENGHOR was president of Senegal and an internationally respected poet. Senghor's first collection of poetry, *Chants d'ombre* (Songs from the Shadows), was published in 1945, and his second, *Hosties noires* (Black Hosts), in 1948. That same year he also published *Anthologie de la nouvelle poésie nègre et malgache de langue française* (Anthology of New Black and Malagasy Poetry in the French Language).

AHARON SHABTAI was born in 1939 in Tel Aviv. Since the publication of his first book in 1966, Shabtai has published sixteen poetry books and has become one of the most acclaimed Israeli poets. Also an active translator of poetry from classical languages, he teaches Greek literature at Tel Aviv University.

MALKA SHAKED, a poet and literary critic, is retired from the Hebrew University of Jerusalem.

AHMAD SHAMLOU is recognized as one of Iran's greatest modern poets. In the 1950s he spent six months in hiding and another year in prison for his support of Mossadegh's nationalist movement. Eventually, in 1977, political oppression moved Shamlou to leave Iran, and he lived for two years in Princeton, New Jersey, and in England; he returned to Iran in 1979. In addition to twelve collections of his own poetry published between 1948 and 1978, he wrote several plays and a major analytical survey of

lore, *Ketab-i Kucheh* (Book of the Street), edited volumes of
nian poetry, and translated many French authors into Persian.

SHIFRA has published poetry, fiction, interviews with Israeli
writers, literary criticism, a children's book, and translations of Sumerian
and Akkadian literature. Shifra has been awarded the Ze'ev Prize, an An-
dersen Honor Citation, the Amichai Prize for Poetry, the President's Prize,
and the Brenner Prize for Poetry.

KAZUKO SHIRAISHI was born in Vancouver, Canada, in 1931 and
was taken to Japan by her family just prior to World War II. Her publica-
tions include many poetry books, such as *Seasons of Sacred Lust*, *Isso no ca-
noe, mirai e modoru* (A Canoe Returns to the Future), and *Sûnozoku* (Sand
Clan). Shiraishi lives in Tokyo.

ELENA SHVARTS is one of the best-known contemporary poets in
Russia. A familiar figure in the Leningrad underground culture of the 1970s
and 1980s, she is the author of numerous collections of poetry and also writes
prose.

LEONARDO SINISGALLI was born in Montemurro, in the prov-
ince of Potenza. He studied engineering and mathematics and worked as
an architect and graphic designer. His early collections focused on themes
from ancestral southern Italian myths. Later he adopted a more relaxed
style, analyzed the conflicts of existentialism and realism, and explored
scientific culture. His poetry in English includes *The Ellipse: Selected Poems*.

SŎ CHŎNGJU, known in Korea by the pen name Midang, was born in
the North Cholla province of Korea in 1915. His first poems were pub-
lished in the late 1930s; his first collection of poems dates from 1941. He
was for many years a professor at the Buddhist university, Dongguk Uni-
versity, in Seoul, where he is now professor emeritus.

EDITH SÖDERGRAN was born in St. Petersburg, Russia, and lived
in the Swedish-speaking part of southeast Finland. She was a pioneer of
free verse and was a distinct and powerful voice in Swedish poetry. A lead-
ing European modernist, she was highly regarded by her contemporaries
and influenced generations of Swedish poets. Edith Södergran died of tu-
berculosis at the age of thirty-one.

PIOTR SOMMER was born in Otwock, near Warsaw. He edits the Polish journal *World Literature*, has taught at several American universities, and has been a fellow of the International Writing Program at the University of Iowa and the National Humanities Center in North Carolina. His poetry collections include *What We're Remembered By*, *A Subsequent World*, *Lyrical Factor and Other Poems*, *New Relations of Words*, and *Continued*.

MARIN SORESCU was the most translated Romanian writer of the latter half of the twentieth century. More than a dozen books of his poetry and plays have appeared in English. He is the author of more than twenty collections of poetry, among them *Poems* (1965), *The Youth of Don Quixote* (1968), *Cough* (1970), *Fountains in the Sea* (1982), *Water of Life, Water of Death* (1987), *Poems Selected by Censorship* (1991), and *The Crossing* (1994). His valedictory volume, *The Bridge*, published posthumously in 1997, was composed during the final two months of his life, while he knew he was dying of liver cancer.

MARCIN ŚWIETLICKI was born in Lublin and studied at Jagiellonian University in Krakow. He has received the Trakl Prize and the Kościelski Foundation Prize, and has been nominated several times for the Nike Prize. His collections include *Cold Countries*, *Schism*, *Third Half*, *37 Poems on Vodka and Cigarettes*, and *Songs of a Profaner*.

ANNA SWIR (originally Świrszczyńska) was a Polish poet whose works deal with a variety of themes, including her experiences during World War II, motherhood, the female body, and sensuality. She was born in Warsaw and grew up as the poor daughter of an artist. She began publishing her poems in the 1930s. During the Nazi occupation of Poland she joined the Polish resistance movement in World War II and was a military nurse during the Warsaw Uprising. She also wrote for underground publications. In 1974 she published *Building the Barricade*, a volume of work that describes the pain and suffering she witnessed during that time.

WISŁAWA SZYMBORSKA was born in Kórnik in Western Poland. Szymborska made her debut in March 1945 with a poem, *"Szukam słowa"* ("I Am Looking for a Word"), in the daily *Dziennik Polski*. Szymborska has published sixteen collections of poetry. She won the Nobel Prize in Literature in 1996.

NOVICA TADIĆ was born in Montenegro and has lived in Belgrade for most of his life. He is one of the most celebrated Serbian poets today. His collections include *Night Mail*, translated by Charles Simic.

RABINDRANATH TAGORE was educated at home in India. Tagore had early success as a writer in his native Bengal. Among his fifty-odd volumes of poetry are *Manasi* (The Ideal One), *Sonar Tari* (The Golden Boat), *Gitanjali* (Song Offerings), *Gitimalya* (Wreath of Songs), and *Balaka* (The Flight of Cranes). He won the Nobel Prize in Literature in 1913.

SHUNTARO TANIKAWA was born in Tokyo in 1931. He published his first poems in the daily *Literary World* at eighteen, and in 1952 published his first book: *Twenty billion light years of solitude*. In poetry, moving away from the traditional haiku, he has experimented with free verse, looking for new metrics and rhythms.

JORGE TEILLIER, who has been called an important poet of his generation, was born in Lautaro, in the south of Chile, in 1935. Teillier studied history and geography at the University of Chile, and was later made editor of the university's *Bulletin*. He began writing poems when he was twelve, and his first book of poetry, *Para ángeles y gorriones* (For Angels and Sparrows), was published when he was twenty-one. He is the author of twelve collections of poems and many short stories and essays.

GEORG TRAKL was born in Salzburg, Austria. He published *Gedichte* (Poems) with the help of a patron, and later published *Sebastian im Traum* (Sebastian in the Dream), *Der Herbst des Einsamen* (The Autumn of the Lonely), and *Gesang des Abgeschiedenen* (Song of the Departed). His work has greatly influenced many generations of German poets, most notably, Paul Celan. After the translations of his poetry began to appear more widely in the United States in the 1960s and 1970s, he also influenced many American poets, such as James Wright.

TOMAS TRANSTRÖMER was born in Stockholm in 1931. His books of poetry in English include *The Great Enigma: New Collected Poems*, *The Half-Finished Heaven*, *New Collected Poems*, *For the Living and the Dead*, *Baltics*, *Paths*, *Windows and Stones*, and *Seventeen Poems*. He is one of the world's most regarded living poets. In 1997 the city of Västerås established the Tranströmer Prize.

MARINA TSVETAEVA was born in Moscow in 1892. After the revolution, while her husband, Sergei Efron, was fighting in the White Army, Tsvetaeva and her two small daughters were reduced to terrible poverty. Her younger daughter died of hunger. In 1921 Tsvetaeva emigrated, first to Berlin, then to Czechoslovakia, and then to Paris to join her husband. Her collection of poems *Mileposts I* was published in Moscow in 1922. In Prague Tsvetaeva wrote some of her finest poems, published in Paris in her collection *After Russia*. Other books she published during her emigré period include *Parting, Poems to Blok,* and *Psyche*. Two months after Tsvetaeva returned to Moscow, her daughter Ariadna was arrested; a month later her husband was arrested as well. When the Germans attacked Russia, Tsvetaeva was evacuated to Elabuga in Central Asia. She hanged herself on August 31, 1941.

TRISTAN TZARA was born in 1896 in Moineşti, Romania. He is mainly known as a cofounder—together with Marcel Iancu, Hugo Ball, Jean Arp, and Richard Huelsenbeck—and main theoretician of Dadaism, a movement that originated in Zürich, where Tzara had moved in 1915 during World War I. Tzara wrote the first Dada text in 1916 (*La Premiére Aventure cèleste de Monsieur Antipyrine*), followed by *Vingt-cinq poémes* in 1918, and the programmatic *Sept manisfestes Dada* in 1924. In 1936 he joined the Communist Party, having stopped writing Dada poetry around 1930. He died in 1963 in Paris.

GIUSEPPE UNGARETTI is an Italian poet who founded the Hermetic movement. His poetry developed in a coherent, original direction, evidenced in "Gay Shipwrecks." Other poems by Ungaretti are "The Promised Land," "An Old Man's Notebook," and "Death of the Seasons."

PAUL VALÉRY was born in the Mediterranean town of Sète, France. In 1917 Valéry published *La jeune parque* (The Young Fate*)*. A few years later he published *Album de vers anciens, 1890–1920* (Album of Old Verses). His second collection of poetry, *Charmes* (Charms), appeared in 1922.

CÉSAR VALLEJO was born in 1892 in the town of Santiago de Chuco, Peru, where he was brought up along with his eleven older brothers and sisters. Vallejo began writing poetry in 1913 and published his first collection, *Los heraldos negros*, in 1918. In 1922 he published *Trilce*. In 1923 he left his homeland for Paris. In 1931 he published his novel, *El Tugsteno*, and became a member of the Congress of Antifascist Writers in Madrid. Vallejo's next and final book, *Poemas humanos*, was not published until a year after his death in 1938.

MIRIAM VAN HEE is a Flemish poet. Her sixth collection of poems, *Achter de bergen* (Behind the Mountains, 1996), was awarded the Flemish Culture Prize for Poetry in 1998. That same year, her poems were collected in *Het verband tussen de dagen: Gedichten, 1978–1996* (The Link Between the Days: Poems, 1978–1996). Her latest collection, *De bramenpluk* (Blackberrying, 2002), includes poems about travel, landscapes, animals, art, and love. Van hee is also a Slavist and has translated works by authors such as Mandelstam and Akhmatova.

ORHAN VELI KANIK was a Turk who first wrote under the pen name Mehmed Ali Sel and published his early poems in the avant-garde literary review *Varl k* (Existence). In 1941 he published a volume of poetry, *Garip* (Strange). Other works included *Vazgecemediğim* (I Cannot Give Up, 1945) and *Karş* (Across, 1949).

VERONICA VOLKOW, a granddaughter of Trotsky, was born in Mexico in 1955. Her first collection of poems, *La Sicilia de cumas*, appeared in 1974. A half-dozen books of poetry followed. She is also the translator of American poets and the author of travel books on South America.

ANDREI VOZNESENSKY was born in Moscow in 1933 and published his first poems in 1958, giving numerous public readings of his works. One of the few Soviet poets allowed by the government to travel abroad after World War II, he was a popular reader of his own work in the United States and England.

ALEKSANDER WAT was born in Warsaw. He published a first book of poems, *Me from One Side and Me from the Other Side of My Pug Iron Stove*, in 1920 and, some years later, a collection of stories entitled *Lucifer Unemployed*. Wat was invited in 1964 to the University of California, Berkeley, where he wrote *My Century*, edited by Czesław Miłosz.

WEN I-TO was a pivotal figure in early twentieth-century Chinese poetry. He rejected classical Chinese, chose to write in the vernacular, and yet his work shows a confluence of the two. He came to the United States, where he studied at the Art Institute of Chicago and at Colorado College. When he returned to China, he became involved in the political turmoil of the time. On July 15, 1946, Wen gave an impassioned speech denouncing the Kuomintang government and was assassinated later that day.

MEIR WIESELTIER was born in Moscow in 1941, just before the Germans invaded Russia. He grew up in Netanya and, in 1955, moved to Tel Aviv, where he has lived ever since. His first poems were published when he was eighteen. His poetry includes *Burning Holy Books* and *Exit to the Sea*.

XI CHUAN (real name Liu Jun) is a poet, essayist, and translator, and has been recognized as one of the most dynamic poets living in China today. He has published four collections of poems, including *A Fictitious Family Tree* and *Roughly Speaking*, two books of essays, and one book of criticism, in addition to a play and numerous translations, including works of Ezra Pound, Jorge Luis Borges, and Czesław Miłosz. His own poetry and essays have been widely anthologized.

YEN CHEN published poetry in a Szechuan party newspaper in the late 1930s. No other information is available.

GHIRMAI YOHANNES, better known as San Diego, was born in Eritrea in 1961. An actor, poet, and writer, he has done television shows, children's programs, videos, advertising, stand-up comedy, and theater. *Unjust Praise* was first published in 1994.

YU JIAN was born in 1954 in the southwestern Chinese province of Yunnan. With the outbreak of the Cultural Revolution in 1966, his schooling was interrupted and he lived an "untied life," wandering the streets of Kunming with his friends while his parents were forced to leave home to undergo "re-education." In 1980, when university education once again became a possibility for young Chinese people, Yu Jian passed the entrance examinations for Yunnan University, becoming a student in the Department of Chinese Language and Literature. He became known as a student poet and was an energetic literary activist, helping to establish several literary clubs as well as edit various publications.

OKSANA ZABUZHKO was born in Kiev and is an associate scholar for the Institute of Philosophy of the Ukrainian Academy of Sciences. She is also Distinguished Professor of Creative Writing at Kiev Shevchanko University. She is the author of several collections of poetry and the autobiographical novel *Field Research in Ukrainian Sex*.

ADAM ZAGAJEWSKI lives in Poland and Chicago. He was born in Lwów in 1945 and first became well known as one of the leading poets of the Generation of '68, or the Polish New Wave (*Nowa fala*). Since 1988, he has served as a visiting associate professor of English in the Creative Writing Program at the University of Houston and currently teaches at the University of Chicago. He is currently coeditor of *Zeszyty literackie* (Literary Review), which is published in Paris.

ZAHRAD was a Western Armenian poet. He began writing under a pen name because he felt that his family would not be receptive to his work. Zahrad was characterized as "the huge oak tree of diasporan poetry, whose literary heritage had a deep and stable influence upon modern poetry of not only the diaspora, but also Armenia."

ZELDA (Shneurson Mishkowsky) was born into a famous Chassidic family in Ukraine. Known simply as Zelda, she began publishing poetry in 1968. She was awarded the Bialik Prize.

Author of six volumes of poetry, Chengdu-based **ZHAI YONGMING** is China's foremost feminist poet. Starting with her twenty-poem cycle *Woman* (1984), she has mounted a consistently forceful critique of traditional gender stereotypes in China's largely patriarchal society. Her powerful imagery and forthright voice have struck a chord with many readers, and Zhai has become an influential cultural figure. Her work has been translated into many languages, and she has read at many international poetry festivals.

ZHANG ER, born in Beijing, is the author of three collections of poetry in Chinese, most recently *Because of Mountain*. She has six chapbooks in English translation, among them *Carved Water* and *Sight Progress*. Her selected poems were published in two bilingual collections, *So Translating Rivers and Cities* and *Verses on Bird*. She coedited the bilingual volume *Another Kind of Nation: An Anthology of Contemporary Chinese Poetry*. She currently teaches at Evergreen State College in Washington.

ABOUT THE TRANSLATORS

AGHA SHAHID ALI was a poet from New Delhi. His volumes of poetry include *Call Me Ishmael Tonight: A Book of Ghazals*, *Rooms Are Never Finished*, *The Country Without a Post Office*, and *The Beloved Witness: Selected Poems*. He is also the author of *T. S. Eliot as Editor*, translator of *The Rebel's Silhouette: Selected Poems* by Faiz Ahmed Faiz, and editor of *Ravishing Disunities: Real Ghazals in English*. He died in 2001.

JAROSŁAW ANDERS was born in 1950 in Warsaw, Poland, and came to the United States in 1981. His translations include works by Hanna Krall and Zbigniew Herbert, and he has published many essays and reviews.

BROTHER ANTHONY OF TAIZÉ, along with Young-moo Kim and Gary G. Gach, translated Ko Un's *Ten Thousand Lives* (2004) and the forthcoming *Songs for Tomorrow*. He also translated *The Little Spring*, *The Novice at Songgwang Temple*, and *The Moon*.

DAVID ANTIN is a well-known American poet, critic, and performance artist. In the late 1960s, Antin began performing extemporaneously, improvising "talk poems" at readings and exhibitions. Since the late 1960s

Antin has lived in Southern California, where he taught for many years at the University of California, San Diego, in the experimental Visual Arts Department. He has been awarded Guggenheim Foundation and NEH fellowships and was also awarded the PEN Los Angeles Award for Poetry.

WILLIAM ARROWSMITH (1924–1992) was an American classicist. Arrowsmith translated Petronius's *Satyricon* (1959) and Aristophanes' plays *The Birds* (1961) and *The Clouds* (1962), as well as Euripides' *Alcestis, Cyclops, Heracles, Orestes, Hecuba*, and *The Bacchae*, among other works both classical and contemporary. He is also known for his writings on Italian film director Michelangelo Antonioni.

LJUBICA ARSOVSKA translated, with Peggy Reid, Lidija Dimkovska's *Do Not Awaken Them with Hammers*. She is editor in chief of the quarterly *Kulturen Zivot*, the leading cultural magazine in Macedonia, and translator of numerous books, plays, and poems.

S. V. ATTALAH has translated poetry by Walid al-Sheikh and Mahmoud Abu Hashhash, among others.

BRIAN BARKER studied at Virginia Commonwealth University, George Mason University, and the University of Houston, where he received an Academy of American Poets prize and several poetry fellowships. His collection *The Animal Gospels* won the Editors' Prize at Tupelo Press. He is an assistant professor at Murray State University.

JOHN BÁTKI translated Gyula Krúdy's *Sunflower*. His stories have appeared in *The New Yorker*. He has received the O. Henry Award for short fiction and has taught at Harvard University.

JUDITH BAUMEL is a poet, critic, and translator. She is an associate professor of English and director of the creative writing program at Adelphi University.

DAN BELLM has published three books of poetry, most recently *Practice*, winner of a 2009 California Book Award. His work has appeared in *The American Poetry Review, Poetry, Ploughshares, The Threepenny Review, Best American Spiritual Writing*, and *Word of Mouth: An Anthology of Gay American Poetry*. He is also a widely published translator of poetry and fiction from

Spanish and French, including *Sun on the Ceiling (Au soleil du plafond)* by Pierre Reverdy. He lives in San Francisco.

MICHAEL BENEDIKT's books of poetry include *The Badminton at Great Barrington: or, Gustave Mahler & the Chattanooga Choo-Choo*, *Night Cries*, *Mole Notes*, *Sky*, and *The Body*. He taught at Bennington, Sarah Lawrence, Vassar, and Hampshire colleges, and at Boston University. Michael Benedikt died in 2007.

MARY G. BERG is a professor of Spanish at Harvard University and the translator of many volumes, including *River of Sorrows* by Libertad Demitropulos.

STEPHEN BERG is the founder and coeditor of the *American Poetry Review*. He has published numerous books of poetry and translations and has received Guggenheim, NEA, Ford Foundation, Rockefeller, Dietrich, and Pew fellowships, as well as *Poetry* magazine's Frank O'Hara Memorial Prize.

ZACHARY SHOLEM BERGER has published poems, translations, and articles in English and Yiddish in a number of publications, including *Lyric*, *Forverts* (The Yiddish Forward), *Forward*, and *New York* magazine. Berger and his wife, Celeste Sollod, are the founders of Yiddish House, a publishing house specializing in Yiddish-language translations of classic children's books.

OLIVER BERNARD, born in 1925, has worked as an advisory teacher of drama, and was a director of the Speak a Poem Competition from its inception. He has lived in Norfolk (UK) for over thirty years.

J. S. BERNSTEIN translated works by Gabriel García Márquez and Camilo José Cela, among others.

ROSA BERUMEN is associate editor of *Poetry International*. She lives in San Diego.

JACK BEVAN is a poet and translator from the Italian.

MICHAEL BIGGINS is the head of the Slavic and East European Section and head of the International Studies Sections at the University of

Washington library. He is the coauthor of *Publishing in Yugoslavia's Successor States* and the translator of Tomaž Šalamun's *Ballad for Metka Krasovec* and Drago Jancar's *Mocking Desire* and *Northern Lights*.

ELIZABETH BISHOP is a major American poet and translator. She won numerous awards, including the Pulitzer Prize, the National Book Award, and the National Book Critics Circle Award, and was the first woman to receive the Neustadt International Prize for Literature. She spent many years in Brazil and translated into English a number of Latin American poets such as Octavio Paz, João Cabral de Melo Neto, and others. Her *Poems, Prose, and Letters* was published by the Library of America in 2008.

PAUL BLACKBURN was an American poet well known for his translations from Spanish of the medieval epic *Poema del Mio Cid*, of poetry by Federico García Lorca, Octavio Paz, and Pablo Picasso, and of the short stories of Julio Cortázar.

CHANA BLOCH is a poet, translator, and literary critic. Among her published works are three books of poems, five books of translation from Hebrew poetry, ancient and contemporary, and a critical study of George Herbert.

ROBERT BLY is the author of ten books of poetry and has edited and translated works of Swedish, German, Norwegian, and Persian poetry, including that of Neruda and Rilke. He received the National Book Award for poetry in 1968.

EAVAN BOLAND has published nine volumes of poetry, the most recent being *Domestic Violence* and *An Origin Like Water: Collected Poems 1967–87*, and a volume of prose, *Object Lessons: The Life of the Woman and the Poet in Our Time*.

GEOFFREY BOWNAS edited and translated, with Anthony Thwaite, *The Penguin Book of Japanese Verse*.

PETER BOYLE is an Australian poet living in Sydney. His first three collections of poetry, *Coming home from the world* (1994), *The Blue Cloud of Crying* (1997), and *What the painter saw in our faces* (2001), have received several awards. He has recently translated poetry by the Australian-based Chilean poet Juan Garrido-Salgado.

GEOFFREY BROCK is a poet and translator. His translations include Cesare Pavese's *Disaffections: Complete Poems 1930–1950*, Roberto Calasso's *K*, Umberto Eco's *Mysterious Flame of Queen Loana*, and Antonia Arslan's *Skylark Farm*. He teaches in the Arkansas Programs in Creative Writing and Translation.

GISELA BROTHERSTON, a native of Berlin, is a translator and landscape painter.

GORDON BROTHERSTON is the author of a dozen books and numerous translations and has lectured widely in Europe, North Africa, Australia, and North and Latin America. He is Honorary Professor, University of Manchester, and Professor Emeritus, University of Essex.

CLARENCE BROWN edited and did many of the translations for *The Portable Twentieth-Century Russian Reader*. He is the author of a prizewinning biography of Osip Mandelstam.

STEVEN FORD BROWN is a prolific editor and translator. His recent books include *Astonishing World: The Selected Poems of Ángel González, 1956–1986* (as editor and translator) and *Invited Guest: An Anthology of Twentieth-Century Southern Poetry* (as coeditor).

SUSAN M. BROWN translated *Poems of Fernando Pessoa* with Edwin Honig.

MICHAEL BULLOCK worked for many years as a freelance writer and translator. He produced essays, plays, works in translation, prose, and poetry. As well as being a prolific writer and translator, Bullock was the founder, and for five years editor, of the British poetry magazine *Expression*, as well as editor in chief of *Prism International*.

CHARLES CANTALUPO is a poet, scholar, critic, playwright, and teacher. He is recently the author of *Who Needs a Story? Contemporary Eritrean Poetry in Tigrinya, Tigre and Arabic* (2005). He has also published books on Thomas Hobbes and Ngugi wa Thiong'o, and he has written and directed the new documentary *Against All Odds: African Languages and Literatures into the 21st Century*. He is a professor of English, comparative literature, and African Studies at Penn State University.

BOGDANA CARPENTER is a professor of Slavic Languages and Literature at the University of Michigan. She has translated work by Zbigniew Herbert.

JOHN CARPENTER is a poet and literary critic. With Bogdana Carpenter he has translated seven volumes of poetry by Zbigniew Herbert.

CYRUS CASSELLS is the author of five books of poetry, for which he has received awards including a Lannan Fellowship, a Lambda Literary Award, two NEA fellowships, and a William Carlos Williams Award. He teaches in the MFA program of Texas State University at San Marcos.

CLARE CAVANAGH is an associate professor of Slavic and Gender Studies at Northwestern University and the Herman and Beulah Pearce Miller Research Professor in Literature. With Stanisław Barańczak, she translated Wisława Szymborska's *View with a Grain of Sand* and *Poems New and Collected*; she is also the translator of Adam Zagajewski's *Mysticism for Beginners, Another Beauty,* and *Without End: Selected Poems.*

DILIP CHITRE writes and translates Marathi and English. He has twice received the Sahitya Academy Award for his translations from Marathi. Chitre has published eighteen books, most recently the translation of a 3,200-line poem by Shri Jnandev, a thirteenth-century Marathi poet.

JONATHAN COHEN is a poet, translator, essayist, and scholar of inter-American literature. His translations include Ernesto Cardenal's *With Walker in Nicaragua and Other Early Poems, 1949–1954* and *From Nicaragua, with Love: Poems (1979–1986)* and works by Enrique Lihn, Pedro Mir, and Roque Dalton. His edited Cardenal collection *Pluriverse: New and Selected Poems* was published in 2009.

PETER COLE is the author of two collections of poetry, *Rift* and *Hymns & Qualms,* and has published nine books of translation from Hebrew and Arabic poetry and prose. Cole has received numerous awards for his poetry and translation, including the Modern Language Association's Scaglione Translation Prize for *Selected Poems of Shmuel HaNagid.*

PATRICK CREAGH is a prolific translator from the Italian.

MAGHIEL VAN CREVEL lectured at the University of Sydney and is currently a professor of Chinese language and literature at Leiden University. His publications include *Language Shattered: Contemporary Chinese Poetry and Duoduo* and *Chinese Poetry in Times of Mind, Mayhem, and Money.*

MARY CROW has published four collections of poetry and five collections of poetry in translation. Her most recent book of poems is *I Have Tasted the Apple*. Her poems and translations have appeared in hundreds of literary magazines.

MAIRYM CRUZ-BERNAL translated the work of María Elena Cruz Varela with Deborah Digges.

ADAM CZERNIAWSKI is a Polish poet, prose writer, and translator of Polish literature and philosophy into English. Born in 1934 in Warsaw, he left Poland in 1941. From 1941 to 1947 he lived in the Middle East. In 1947 Czerniawski arrived in England, where he studied literature and philosophy at the universities of London, Sussex, and Oxford. He currently lives in Wales.

ANDREA DELETANT translated the anthology *Silent Voices* with Brenda Walker.

DIANA DER-HOVANESSIAN is the author of over twenty books of poetry and translations. She works as a visiting poet and guest lecturer on American poetry, Armenian poetry in translation, and the literature of human rights at various universities in the United States and abroad.

DEBORAH DIGGES is the author of four books of poetry, including *Rough Music*.

W. S. DI PIERO is a poet, essayist, and translator. The most recent of his nine books of poems is *Chinese Apples: New and Selected Poems*. The latest of his four collections of essays is *City Dog*. His translations include Giacomo Leopardi's *Pensieri* (1984), *The Ellipse: Selected Poems of Leonardo Sinisgalli* (1983), and Euripides' *Ion* (1996).

DENNIS DING is chair of foreign languages at Guizhou University in China. His translations from English to Chinese include works by T. S.

Eliot, Ezra Pound, and Robert Frost. He is cotranslator of *The Red Azalea: Chinese Poetry Since the Cultural Revolution*.

MELVIN DIXON (1950–92) was a professor, writer, poet, and translator, and an important critical voice for African American scholarship.

GRAZYNA DRABIK is a translator of Polish poetry into English and Portuguese, with translations published in literary journals and anthologies in the United States and in Brazil. She is the coauthor of *The New New Yorkers: Portraits in Photos & Words*, an adjunct lecturer in the Department of English at City College–CUNY, and a contributing writer for the weekly cultural supplement of *Nowy Dziennik (The Polish Daily News)* in New York.

VERA DUNHAM translated from the Russian. With Richard Sheldon, she coauthored *In Stalin's Time: Middle Class Values in Soviet Fiction*.

JOSÉ A. ELGORRIAGA contributed translations to *The Other Shore: One Hundred Poems of Rafael Alberti*.

JONAS ELLERSTRÖM was born in Sweden in 1958. He is a writer, art critic, translator from the English and the French, and publisher. He has published two collections of his own poetry, a book on chess, and a book on Alice B. Toklas's cookbook. He has twice received the Karin and Karl Ragnar Gierow Prize from the Swedish Academy. He is currently working with Malena Mörling on an anthology, *Swedish Writers on Writing*, to be published by Trinity University Press in its series The Writer's World.

RICHARD ELLMAN was a prominent American/British literary critic and biographer of Irish writers such as James Joyce, Oscar Wilde, and William Butler Yeats.

CLAYTON ESHLEMAN has written or translated well over thirty books and has published hundreds of articles, essays, and poems throughout the world. He is the main American translator of César Vallejo (with José Rubia Barcia) and of Aimé Césaire (with Annette Smith). He received the National Book Award in 1979 for his cotranslation of César Vallejo's *Complete Posthumous Poetry*.

FANG DAI was born in Shanghai and has published several novels and stories in China, including *The Third Desire* and *The Curtain of Night*. He is cotranslator of *The Red Azalea: Chinese Poetry Since the Cultural Revolution*.

RAYMOND FEDERMAN (1928–2009) was born in France and emigrated to the United States in 1947. He published ten novels, five volumes of poems, four books of criticism on Samuel Beckett, three collections of essays, and numerous articles, essays, and translations. He was primarily a fiction writer.

RUTH FELDMAN has published five books of poetry and fifteen translations from the Italian. In 1999 Feldman and John P. Welle received the Raiziss/de Palchi Book Prize for their translation of Andrea Zanzotto's work *Peasant's Wake for Fellini's Casanova and Other Poems*.

JOHN FELSTINER has been a member of Stanford's English department since 1965. Teaching North American poetry in Chile in 1967–68 led to *Translating Neruda: The Way to Macchu Picchu*. He taught at the Hebrew University in Israel in 1974–75. His book *Paul Celan: Poet, Survivor, Jew*, and his *Selected Poems and Prose of Paul Celan* won various prizes. He coedited a Norton anthology of American Jewish literature and is a member of the American Academy of Arts and Sciences. His most recent book, *Can Poetry Save the Earth? A Field Guide to Nature Poems*, was published in 2009.

LAWRENCE FERLINGHETTI was born in New York and earned a doctoral degree in poetry at the Sorbonne in Paris. He was cofounder of both the magazine *City Lights* and the bookstore City Lights in San Francisco.

D. J. FLAKOLL was an American journalist and the husband of Claribel Alegría. Flakoll translated much of Alegría's work into English.

AUSTIN FLINT translated Wisława Szymborska's work from the Polish with Grazyna Drabik.

CAROLYN FORCHÉ is the author of four books of poetry: *Blue Hour*, *The Angel of History*, *The Country Between Us*, and *Gathering the Tribes*. She is also the editor of *Against Forgetting: Twentieth-Century Poetry of Witness*. Among her translations are Mahmoud Darwish's *Unfortunately, It Was*

Paradise: Selected Poems with Munir Akash, Claribel Alegria's *Flowers from the Volcano*, and Robert Desnos's *Selected Poetry*.

PETER FRANCE is Professor Emeritus of French at the University of Edinburgh, the author of *Politeness and Its Discontents*, and the editor of *The New Oxford Companion to Literature in French*.

STUART FRIEBERT has published seven volumes of translations, among them Karl Krolow's *What'll We Do with This Life?* and *On Account Of*.

RIKUTARO FUKUDA edited and translated, with Ichiro Kono, *An Anthology of Modern Japanese Poetry*.

GARY GACH is a poet, translator, and writer living in San Francisco. He is the author of *The Complete Idiot's Guide to Understanding Buddhism* and edited the Buddhist poetry anthology *What Book?* for Parallax Press.

FORREST GANDER's books include *Eye Against Eye*, *A Faithful Existence*, and the novel *As a Friend*. His translations include *No Shelter: Selected Poems of Pura Lopez Colome*; *Firefly Under the Tongue*, a collection of Coral Bracho's poems; and (with Kent Johnson) two books by Jaime Saenz, *The Night* and *Immanent Visitor*, which was a finalist for the 2003 PEN Award for Poetry in Translation.

REGINALD GIBBONS is a poet, fiction writer, translator, literary critic, artist, and professor of English, Classics, and Spanish and Portuguese at Northwestern University. In 2008 he published a new book of poems, *Creatures of a Day*, which was a finalist for the 2008 National Book Award for poetry. In 2008 he also published a volume of new translations of Sophocles, *Selected Poems: Odes and Fragments*.

GEORGE GIBIAN was a professor of Russian literature at Cornell from 1961 to his death in 1999. He wrote several books and edited a number of Russian classics for the W. W. Norton series, among them critical editions of *Crime and Punishment*, *War and Peace*, *Anna Karenina*, and *Dead Souls*. He was a major translator of Russian dramatists of the absurd and also of the works of Jaroslav Seifert.

J. L. GILI translated the work of Lorca with Stephen Spender.

MIRIYAM GLAZER is a professor of literature at the University of Judaism in Los Angeles, where she also studies for the Conservative rabbinate and teaches in the Ziegler School of Rabbinic Studies. She has edited several books, including *Dancing on the Edge of the World: Jewish Stories of Faith, Inspiration, and Love.*

JUDITH GLEASON holds a PhD from Columbia University and works as a psychotherapist in New York. Her books include *Leaf and Bone: African Praise-Poems.*

GEORGE GÖMÖRI was born in Hungary in 1934, fled because of his involvement in the Hungarian revolution of 1956, and came to rest in England, where he taught Polish and Hungarian at the University of Cambridge.

RENATA GORCZYNSKI is an essayist, a literary critic, and a teacher of journalism. She lives in Gdynia, Poland.

DESMOND GRAHAM was born in Surrey in 1940. His poems have appeared in *Ten North East Poets*, and he has published various pamphlets and four full collections. He has cotranslated from Polish the poems of Anna Kamienska: *Two Darknesses.*

GABRIEL GUDDING serves on the board of directors for the bilingual literary journal *Mandorla: Nueva Escritura de Las Américas.* His translations have appeared in *Poems for the Millennium*, vol. 3, *The Whole Island: Six Decades of Poetry from Cuba*, and *The Oxford Anthology of Latin American Poetry.*

PEDRO GUTIÉRREZ REVUELTA cotranslated *Astonishing World: The Selected Poems of Ángel González, 1956–1986.*

ASSIA GUTMANN was born in Berlin in 1927. She translated the work of Israeli poet Yehuda Amichai.

DANA HÁBOVÁ, one of the Czech Republic's top interpreters and translators, is particularly well known for her Czech subtitles for films.

MARILYN HACKER is the author of eleven books of poems, most recently *Essays on Departure: New and Selected Poems* and *Desesperanto.* Her translations include Vénus Khoury-Ghata's *Nettles* and *She Says*, and Guy

Goffette's *Charlestown Blues*. She edited the French and Francophone section of the Graywolf Press anthology *New European Poetries*. She was awarded the first Robert Fagles Translation Prize.

MICHAEL HAMBURGER was a noted British translator, poet, critic, memoirist, and academic. He was known in particular for his translations of Friedrich Hölderlin, Paul Celan, Gottfried Benn, and W. G. Sebald from the German and for his work in literary criticism.

C. G. HANZLICEK is the author of seven books of poetry. He has translated Native American songs, *A Bird's Companion*, and poems from the Czech, *Mirroring: Selected Poems of Vladimir Holan*.

ROBERT HASS was born in San Francisco and lives in Berkeley, California, where he teaches at the University of California. He served as Poet Laureate of the United States from 1995 to 1997. A MacArthur fellow and a two-time winner of the National Book Critics Circle Award, he has published poems, literary essays, and translations.

H. R. HAYS received degrees from Cornell University and Columbia University and had a long and varied career as a poet, novelist, critic, playwright, translator, social anthropologist, and educator.

MAX HAYWARD (1924–1979) was a British lecturer and a scholar and translator of Russian literature. Hayward became a well-known authority on Russian literature. He was best known as a translator (often jointly with colleagues) of the works of Vladimir Mayakovsky, Isaac Babel, Nadezhda Mandelstam, Anna Akhmatova, and many others.

JUDITH HEMSCHEMEYER translated *The Complete Poems of Anna Akhmatova*.

YAHYA HIJAZI translates the work of Taha Muhammad Ali with Peter Cole and Gabriel Levin.

DAVID HINTON has translated many volumes of classical Chinese poetry. He is the first translator in over a century to translate the four seminal masterworks of Chinese philosophy: *Tao Te Ching*, *Chuang Tzu*, *Analects*, and *Mencius*.

MICHAEL HOFMANN was born in Freiburg, Germany, and lives in London. He has translated more than thirty books from the German and has won the Helen and Kurt Wolff Translator's Prize and the Schlegel-Tieck Prize. In 2005 he edited *The Faber Book of Twentieth-Century German Poetry*.

JAMES HOGGARD is the author of sixteen books, including six collections of translations, three of them collections of poems by Oscar Hahn.

PETER HOIDA is a poet, translator, and abstract painter. His publications include *The Selected Poems of Blaise Cendrars*.

JOHN HOLLANDER is the author of more than a dozen volumes of poetry and seven books of criticism, and the editor and coeditor of many anthologies.

ANSELM HOLLO is a poet and literary translator and a professor in the Jack Kerouac School of Disembodied Poetics at Naropa University in Boulder, Colorado.

EDWIN HONIG translated a number of works by Fernando Pessoa.

STUART HOOD translated work by Ernst Jünger, Erich Fried, Dario Fo, and Pier Paolo Pasolini. His novels include *A Storm from Paradise* and *The Upper Hand*.

ZARA HOUSHMAND is an Iranian-American writer and theater artist. She coauthored *A Mirror Garden* (2007) with Monir Shahroudy Farmanfarmaian and has published poetry in the anthologies *Let Me Tell You Where I've Been* (2006) and *A World Between* (1999), and in numerous journals. Her translations from the Persian received the first commissioning grant from the National Theatre Translation Fund, and have been published in journals and anthologies including *Literature from the Axis of Evil*, (2006) *Words Without Borders*, (2007) and *Strange Times, My Dear: The PEN Anthology of Contemporary Iranian Literature* (2006).

TED HUGHES's lengthy career included over a dozen books of poetry, translations, nonfiction, and children's books. His books of poems include *Wolfwatching* (1990), *Flowers and Insects* (1986), *Selected Poems 1957–1981* (1982), *Moortown* (1980), *Cave Birds* (1979), *Crow* (1971), and *Lupercal* (1960).

...won many of Europe's highest literary honors, and was appointed ...ureate of England in 1984, a post he held until his death in 1998.

EVA HUNG is the author of *Translations and Cultural Change* (2005).

PEARSE HUTCHINSON was born in Glasgow in 1927 of Irish parents. His books include *Watching the Morning Grow*, *The Frost Is All Over*, *Selected Poems*, *Climbing the Light*, *The Soul That Kissed the Body*, *Barnsley Main Seam*, *Collected Poems*, and *Done Into English*.

JAMES E. IRBY translated many works by Jorge Luis Borges.

BENJAMIN IVRY is the author of biographies of Ravel, Poulenc, and Rimbaud, and translator from the French of authors such as Gide, Verne, and Balthus.

ROBERT L. JONES has translated the work of Ricardo Castillo and other Spanish-language poets.

FADY JOUDAH is a physician specializing in internal medicine, and has been a field member of Doctors Without Borders since 2001. His poetry has appeared in the *Kenyon Review*, *Prairie Schooner*, *Bellingham Review*, and *Crab Orchard*, among others. He translated Mahmoud Darwish's *The Butterfly's Burden*.

KAI-YU HSU (1922–1982) was a poet, artist, and scholar. He translated work by Wen I-to and wrote the definitive biography of the poet.

J. KATES is an author and translator. He has translated work by Moisei Fishbein, Mikhail Rodionov, and Alexander Stessin, among others.

LISA KATZ, born in New York, is a poet and translator living in Israel since 1983. *Reconstruction*, a volume of her poetry translated into Hebrew, was published in 2008 by Am Oved Press. A bilingual edition of her translations of Admiel Kosman is forthcoming from Zephyr Press.

SHIRLEY KAUFMAN is an American poet and translator who has lived in Jerusalem for thirty years. She is the author of seven books of poetry and several translations from the Hebrew.

EDMUND KEELEY is the author of seven novels, nine volumes of nonfiction, and fourteen volumes of poetry in translation. He taught English, creative writing, and Hellenic studies at Princeton for forty years and retired in 1994 as Charles Barnwell Straut Professor of English. His awards include the Rome Prize for fiction and the Award in Literature from the American Academy of Arts and Letters, the Landon Prize for Translation from the Academy of American Poets, the PEN/Ralph Manheim Medal for Translation, and the Criticos Prize for nonfiction. His latest books are *Inventing Paradise: The Greek Journey, 1937–47* (1999), *On Translation: Reflections and Conversations* (2000), and a novel, *Some Wine for Remembrance* (2001).

TSIPI KELLER was born in Prague, was raised in Israel, and has been living in the United States since 1974. Her short fiction and poetry translations have appeared in various journals and anthologies. She is the recipient of several literary awards, including a National Endowment for the Arts Translation Fellowship.

CATRIONA KELLY is a professor of Russian at the University of Oxford. She works on Russian literature and on Russian cultural history, particularly Russian modernism, gender history, the history of childhood, and national identity.

ROBERT KELLY is a prolific poet, fiction writer, essayist, and translator. He teaches at Bard College.

JANE KENYON's volumes of poetry include *From Room to Room*, *The Boat of Quiet Hours*, *Let Evening Come*, *Constance*, *Otherwise: New & Selected Poems*, and *Collected Poems*. She died in 1995.

KIM YOUNG-MOO was a professor of English literature at Seoul National University and published three volumes of his poetry. With Brother Anthony of Taizé, he translated and published poems by a number of Korean writers, including Ko Un.

KATIE KING is a writer, lecturer, and media consultant in London. She has lived and worked in Spain, Mexico, Central America, and Brazil. She studied at the University of Seville, the University of Washington in Seattle, and Columbia University in New York and holds degrees in Spanish literature and journalism.

KINNELL is the author of ten books of poetry. He has also translations of works by Yves Bonnefoy, Yvanne Goll, François and Rainer Maria Rilke. His *Selected Poems* (1980) was awarded both the Pulitzer Prize and the National Book Award. He served as chancellor of the American Academy of American Poets from 2001 to 2007.

GEORGE L. KLINE translated Joseph Brodsky's *Selected Poems*.

ICHIRO KÔNO edited and translated, with Rikutaro Fukuda, *An Anthology of Modern Japanese Poetry*.

CHANA KRONFELD is a professor of Hebrew and comparative literature at the University of California at Berkeley. With Chana Bloch she received the PEN Translation Award for their translation of Yehuda Amichai's *Open Closed Open* and an NEA Fellowship for *The Poetry of Dahlia Ravikovitch*.

MAGNUS JAN KRYNSKI was a professor emeritus of Slavic languages and literature at Duke University, Durham, North Carolina. He was a specialist in twentieth-century Polish literature and translated three volumes of poetry into English.

TOMASZ P. KRZESZOWSKI edited and translated, with Desmond Graham, Anna Kamienska's *Two Darknesses*.

WILLIAM T. KULIK translated works by Robert Desnos and Max Jacob, among others.

STANLEY KUNITZ was poet laureate of the United States from 2000 to 2001. His many honors included the Pulitzer Prize and the National Book Award.

NAOMI LAZARD is a writer and translator whose work appears in *A Book of Luminous Things*, *Lives Through Literature*, *The True Subject*, and *Ordinances* (1984).

PETER H. LEE is a professor of Korean and comparative literature at the University of California, Los Angeles. He was on the editorial board for the *Dictionary of Literary Themes and Motifs*.

MUNA LEE DE MUÑOZ MARÍN was a famous poet, historian, translator, activist, essayist, and (as Newton Gayle) a fiction writer. In 1918, Muna Lee moved to New York City and began working as a "confidential translator" for the U.S. Secret Service, a job for which she had qualified by teaching herself Spanish in two weeks. For the rest of the First World War, she translated and censored mail written in Spanish, Portuguese, and French and developed an interest in the new Pan-American movement.

URSULA K. LE GUIN writes both poetry and prose, and in various modes including realistic fiction, science fiction, fantasy, young children's books, books for young adults, screenplays, essays, verbal texts for musicians, and voicetexts. She has published seven books of poetry, twenty-two novels, over a hundred short stories (collected in eleven volumes), four collections of essays, twelve books for children, and four volumes of translation.

J. B. LEISHMAN translated the works of Rainer Maria Rilke and also wrote studies of John Donne and Shakespeare.

GABRIEL LEVIN is a poet and translator living in Jerusalem.

PHILIP LEVINE is the author of sixteen books of poetry, most recently *Breath*. Levine has also published a collection of essays, *The Bread of Time: Toward an Autobiography*, edited *The Essential Keats*, and coedited and translated two books: *Off the Map: Selected Poems of Gloria Fuertes* (with Ada Long) and *Tarumba: The Selected Poems of Jaime Sabines* (with Ernesto Trejo).

RACHEL LEVITSKY's first full-length volume, *Under the Sun,* was published in 2003. She is the author of five poetry chapbooks. A past fellow of the MacDowell Colony and Lower Manhattan Cultural Council, she teaches at Pratt Institute.

ANDREA LINGENFELTER is a poet and translator of contemporary Chinese poetry, fiction, and (on occasion) film subtitles. Her translations of contemporary Chinese poetry have appeared in a number of literary journals and anthologies. She is also the translator of the novels *Candy* by Mian Mian and *Farewell My Concubine* by Lilian Lee. In 2008 she received a

PEN Translation Fund Grant to translate Annie Baobei's 2006 novel, *Padma*. Her translations of Zhai Yongming's poetry are forthcoming from Zephyr Press.

HERBERT LOMAS edited and translated *Contemporary Finnish Poetry*. He is a member of the Finnish Academy and was made Knight First Class, Order of the White Rose of Finland, for his services to Finnish literature.

ADA LONG, a PhD and founding director of the University of Alabama at Birmingham's nationally recognized honors program, is a professor in the Department of English.

ROBERT LOWELL was born in Boston into an old and prominent family that included the poets Amy Lowell and James Russell Lowell. His *Lord Weary's Castle* won the Pulitzer Prize in 1947 and was followed by many books, including *Life Studies* and *For the Union Dead*. His acclaimed volume *Imitations*, a collection of loose translations of poems by classical and modern European poets, including Rilke, Montale, Akhmatova, and Pasternak, was awarded the 1962 Bollingen Poetry Translation Prize.

NORMAN MACAFEE is a writer, translator, visual artist, and editor. His books of poetry include *One Class: Selected Poems, 1965–2005*, *A New Requiem*, and *The Coming of Fascism to America*. MacAfee has translated (with Luciano Martinengo) the only edition of the major poems of the Italian filmmaker and poet Pier Paolo Pasolini.

ROBERT A. MAGUIRE was a professor of Slavic literature at Columbia. He translated words by Gogol, Bely, and others.

DEREK MAHON was born in Belfast, Northern Ireland, in 1941. He was educated at Trinity College in Dublin. He translated *Racine's Phaedra*; *Selected Poems* by Philippe Jaccottet, which won the Scott-Manriet Translation Prize; and *The Chimeras* by Nerval.

DENNIS MALONEY is the founding editor and publisher of White Pine Press.

MICHAEL MARCH was born in 1946 in New York. He is the author of *Goya*, *Disappearance*, and *When She Danced*, and the cotranslator of Zbigniew Herbert's *Barbarian in the Garden*.

S. J. MARKS translated Miklós Radnóti's *Clouded Sky* with Steven Polgar and Stephen Berg.

PHILIP MARTIN was an Australian academic, poet, translator, critic, and broadcaster. Born in Melbourne, Martin taught English at Monash University, and his poems have been published, anthologized, and broadcast both in Australia and overseas.

W. MARTIN is a doctoral candidate in comparative literature at the University of Chicago. As an editor and translator, he has been instrumental in introducing many younger Polish poets and prose writers to English-speaking readers.

LUCIANO MARTINENGO translated Pier Paolo Pasolini's *Poems* with Norman MacAfee.

DAVID R. McCANN is Korea Foundation Professor of Korean Literature in the Department of East Asian Languages and Civilizations as well as director of the Korea Institute at Harvard University. His many books include *Traveler Maps: Poems by Ko Un*, *The Columbia Anthology of Modern Korean Poetry*, *Early Korean Literature: Selections and Introductions*, *War and Democracy: A Comparative Study of the Korean War and the Peloponnesian War*, and *The Classical Moment: Views from Seven Literatures*.

ROBERT McCRACKEN translated work by Patrizia Cavalli with the author.

DAVID McDUFF translates from Swedish, Icelandic, Russian, and Finnish. His translations of four novels by Dostoevsky are available in Penguin Classics.

HEATHER McHUGH was raised in Virginia and educated at Harvard University. Her books of poetry include *Eyeshot*, which was shortlisted for the Pulitzer Prize; *The Father of Predicaments*; *Hinge & Sign: Poems 1968–1993*, a finalist for the National Book Award and named a "Notable Book of the Year" by the *New York Times Book Review*; *Shades*; *To the Quick*; *A World of Difference*; and *Dangers*.

RICHARD McKANE is a prolific translator of Russian poetry, including Anna Akhmatova's *Selected Poems* and, with Elizabeth McKane, Osip Mandelstam's *Moscow Notebooks* and *Voronezh Notebooks*.

JAMIE McKENDRICK is a poet and translator. He edited *The Faber Book of Twentieth-Century Italian Poems*.

MATTHEW MEAD and **RUTH MEAD** translated Johannes Bobrowski's *Shadow Lands: Selected Poems*.

CHRISTOPHER MERRILL has published four collections of poetry, including *Watch Fire*, for which he received the Peter I. B. Lavan Younger Poets Award from the Academy of American Poets. He directs the International Writing Program at the University of Iowa.

W. S. MERWIN was born in 1927. His many awards include the 2005 National Book Award in Poetry, the Pulitzer Prize in poetry, the Tanning Prize, the Bollingen Award, the Ruth Lily Poetry Prize, and the 2006 Bobbitt Poetry Prize, as well as fellowships from the Rockefeller and the Guggenheim Foundations and the National Endowment for the Arts. He is the author of dozens of books of poetry and prose.

ROBERT MEZEY was educated at Kenyon, Iowa, and Stanford, and has taught at Western Reserve, Fresno State, the University of Utah, Franklin and Marshall, and elsewhere. His poems, prose, and translations have been appearing since 1953 in many journals, including the *New York Review of Books*, *Hudson Review*, the *New Republic*, *The New Yorker*, *Harper's*, and others.

IAN MILNER was a New Zealand–born critic, translator, and academic. He was formerly a professor of English at Charles University, Prague.

CZESŁAW MIŁOSZ was born in 1911 in Szetejnie, Lithuania. He survived World War II in Warsaw, publishing in the underground press, after which he was stationed in New York, Washington, and Paris as a cultural attaché from Poland. He defected to France in 1951, and in 1960 he accepted a position at the University of California at Berkeley. Although his writing was banned in Poland, he was nevertheless awarded the 1980 Nobel Prize in Literature. He died in 2004 in Kraków. He was called by Joseph Brodsky "one of the great poets of our time, perhaps the greatest."

STEPHEN MITCHELL's numerous translations include *The Book of Job, A Book of Psalms*, and *Genesis*.

MICHAEL MOLNAR translated *Paradise: Selected Poems of Elena Shvarts*.

GERALD MOORE coedited, with Ulli Beier, *The Penguin Book of Modern African Poetry*.

EDWARD MORIN is the author of several poetry collections, including *The Dust of Our City* and *Labor Day at Walden Pond*. With Fang Dai and Dennis Ding, he translated *The Red Azalea: Chinese Poetry Since the Cultural Revolution*.

MALENA MÖRLING is a poet and translator. Her poems have been published in *Ploughshares* and *New England Review*, and her translations into Swedish of Philip Levine's poems have been published in the Swedish journal *Artes*.

MU YI translated, with J. P. Seaton, the poetry of Gu Cheng for *Out of the Howling Storm: The New Chinese Poetry*, edited by Tony Barnstone.

WILLA MUIR and **EDWIN MUIR** translated Kafka's *Amerika, The Castle,* and *The Trial,* among other works.

PAUL MULDOON is the author of *Horse Latitudes, Moy Sand and Gravel,* and *Poems 1968–1998*, among others.

LEONARD NATHAN was a poet and critic, a master of the short lyric who helped found the Department of Rhetoric at the University of California at Berkeley. He is the author of seventeen books of poetry.

GHIRMAI NEGASH is an assistant professor of English and African literature at Ohio University and associate director of the Center for African Studies. He was the founder and formerly chair of the Department of

Eritrean Languages and Literature at the University of Asmara, Eritrea. His publications include *Who Needs a Story?* coedited and translated with Charles Cantalupo.

MURAT NEMET-NEJAT is a poet, translator, and essayist. He edited *Eda: An Anthology of Contemporary Turkish Poetry*. His books of translations also include Ece Ayhan's *Blind Cat Black and Orthodoxies* and Orhan Veli Kanlk's *I, Orhan Veli*.

SUSANNA NIED is known for her translations and her writing on nature and the environment, women, science, and philosophy. Her publications include the translation of Inger Christensen's *Alphabet*.

PETER NIJMEIJER is a poet, translator, and reviewer. He has translated poems by Paul Celan, Hans Magnus Enzensberger, Tadeusz Rózewicz, Francis Ponge, Charles Tomlinson, and Seamus Heaney.

JOHN NIST edited and translated the anthology *Modern Brazilian Poetry*.

HENRIK NORDBRANDT published his first collection, *Poems*, in 1966. In 2000 he received the Nordic Council's prestigious literature prize for his twenty-first collection, *Dream Bridges*.

HOWARD NORMAN edited and translated the anthology *The Wishing Bone Cycle: Narrative Poems of the Cree Indians*.

MARTIN PAUL translated, with José A. Elgorriaga, poetry by Rafael Alberti in *The Other Shore: 100 Poems by Rafael Alberti*.

ANNE PENNINGTON worked very closely with Vasko Popa in translating his poetry until her death in 1981. She taught at Lady Margaret Hall, Oxford, where she was a professor of Comparative Slavonic Philology.

DENIZ PERIN is a Turkish-American writer and translator living in San Diego, California. She is working on a collection of poems about Turkey and has recently completed the translation of Ece Temelkuran's *Book of the Edge*.

RICHARD PEVEAR works mainly as a literary translator, translating from French, Italian, Spanish, and (in collaboration with Larissa Volokhonsky) from Russian. He has published some twenty-six books, including works by Alain, Yves Bonnefoy, and Alberto Savinio, and a series of Russian classics. He has also published two collections of poetry.

ROBERT PINSKY is the author of several collections of poetry, most recently *Gulf Music: Poems* and *Jersey Rain*. He has published two acclaimed works of translation: *The Inferno of Dante*, which was a Book-of-the-Month-Club Editor's Choice and received both the *Los Angeles Times* Book Prize and the Harold Morton Landon Translation Award, and *The Separate Notebooks* by Czesław Miłosz.

STEVEN POLGAR translated Miklós Radnóti's *Clouded Sky* with S. J. Marks and Stephen Berg.

LUDMILLA G. POPOVA-WIGHTMAN was born in Bulgaria and lives in Princeton. She is a member of the Princeton Research Forum and has published translations from the Bulgarian in *Partisan Review*, the *Literary Review*, the *New York Review of Books*, *Poetry East*, and in print anthologies.

REN POWELL is an American writer living in Norway. She has published two books of poetry and ten books of translations.

DUSAN PUVACIC taught in the Department of Central and South-Eastern European Studies, Lonsdale College, the University of Lancaster, and was coeditor of *Kritika*.

WILLIAM RADICE has pursued a double career as a poet and as a scholar and translator of Bengali, and has written or edited nearly thirty books. He also translates from the German.

BURTON RAFFEL is a translator, poet, and teacher. His books include fiction and poetry, translations, literary and historical criticism, teaching texts and anthologies, and annotated editions of Shakespeare and Milton.

GEORGE REAVEY (1907–1976) was a Russian-born Irish surrealist poet, publisher, translator, and art collector. Reavey's translations and critical prose helped introduce twentieth-century Russian poetry to an English-speaking audience.

JOHN O. REED edited and translated, with Clive Wake, *A Book of African Verse*; *A New Book of African Verse*; *French African Verse*; and Léopold Sédar Senghor's *Prose and Poetry* and *Selected Poems*.

ALASTAIR REID is a poet, a prose writer, a translator, and a traveler. He has published over forty books, and his writings have been widely translated.

PEGGY REID translated the work of Lidija Dimkovska with Ljubica Arsovska.

MICHAEL ROLOFF's translations from the German include works by Hermann Hesse and Peter Handke.

BRINA MENACHOVSKY ROSE translated Israel Emiot's *Siberia* with Leah Zazulyer.

JEROME ROTHENBERG, born in 1931, is an internationally known American poet, translator, and anthologist noted for his work in ethno-poetics and poetry performance. His published works include four books of poetry in translation—from Schwitters, Lorca, Picasso, and Nezval—and a book of selected translations, *Writing Through*.

JOSÉ RUBIA BARCIA (1914–1997) was a distinguished professor of twentieth-century Spanish literature who also served as the chair of UCLA's Department of Spanish and Portuguese. His translations of César Vallejo's poetry, done in collaboration with Clayton Eshleman, received the National Book Award in 1979.

IOANA RUSSELL-GEBBETT translated poems by Marin Sorescu with Ted Hughes and D. J. Enright.

I. L. SALOMON translated works by Carlo Betocci, Dino Campana, and others.

STEPHEN SARTARELLI is a poet and translator. He received the 2001 Raiziss/de Palchi Translation Award from the Academy of American Poets for *Songbook: The Selected Poems of Umberto Saba*.

TEO SAVORY translated collections by Jacques Prévert, Günter Eich, Francis Jammes, and Raymond Queneau.

MINAS SAVVAS's poetry, translations, and criticism have appeared in numerous publications, including the *New York Review of Books, World Literature Today,* and *Poetry International.* He is one of the first, and most prolific, translators of Yannis Ritsos, and published *Peculiar Gestures* and *Subterranean Horses.* For many years he has taught at San Diego State University.

YUKI SAWA edited and translated, with Edith Marcombe Shiffert, *An Anthology of Modern Japanese Poetry.*

MICHAEL SCAMMELL was born in England in 1935. He has translated the work of Fyodor Dostoyevsky, Leo Tolstoy, Vladimir Nabokov, and Alexander Solzhenitsyn, among many others.

PAUL SCHMIDT was a translator, poet, actor, librettist, playwright, and essayist. He published four volumes of his translations of Velimir Khlebnikov.

CINDY SCHUSTER is a poet and translator. She is cotranslator of the anthology *Cubana: Contemporary Fiction by Cuban Women* (1998). Her translations of fiction and poetry have appeared in various anthologies and journals, including *Words Without Borders: The World Through the Eyes of Writers, New Short Fiction from Cuba, Poetry International, The American Voice, Exquisite Corpse,* and *Compost.*

PETER DALE SCOTT, a former Canadian diplomat and English professor at the University of California at Berkeley, is a poet, writer, and researcher. His chief poetry books are the three volumes of his trilogy *Seculum: Coming to Jakarta: A Poem About Terror; Listening to the Candle: A Poem on Impulse;* and *Minding the Darkness: A Poem for the Year 2000.*

J. P. SEATON translates Chinese poetry.

HARVEY SHAPIRO is the author of many books, including *How Charlie Shavers Died and Other Poems* (2001) and *National Cold Storage Company*

(1988). He has taught at Cornell University, Bard College, Columbia University, and Yale University, and has served as editor of the *New York Times Book Review* and senior editor of the *New York Times Magazine*.

ROGER SHATTUCK was a major literary scholar and the author of sixteen books.

PHILIP SHERRARD was a poet, translator, theologian, and scholar. His translations included works by Cavafy, Seferis, Elytis, and Gatsos.

EDITH MARCOMBE SHIFFERT was a founder and Far Eastern editor of *Poetry Northwest*. With Yuki Sawa, she edited and translated *An Anthology of Modern Japanese Poetry*.

CHARLES SIMIC was born in 1938 in Belgrade. His first full-length collection of poems, *What the Grass Says*, was published in 1967. Since then he has published more than sixty books in the United States and abroad, twenty titles of his own poetry among them. Simic has also published numerous translations of French, Serbian, Croatian, Macedonian, and Slovenian poetry.

DANIEL SIMKO translated *Autumn Sonata: The Poems of Georg Trakl*.

G. SINGH translated works by Italian poets including Eugenio Montale, Alfonso Gatto, and Giovanni Rabini.

ANNETTE J. SMITH edited and translated, with Clayton Eshleman, Aimé Césaire's *Collected Poems*.

DOUGLAS SMITH is an awarding-winning historian and translator and a Resident Scholar at the University of Washington's Henry M. Jackson School of International Studies.

SIR STEPHEN HAROLD SPENDER was born in 1909 in London. He attended Oxford University and fought in the Spanish Civil War. Spender's books of poetry include *Twenty Poems* (1930), *Vienna* (1934), *The Still Centre* (1939), *Poems of Dedication* (1946), and *The Generous Days* (1971). Spender was a professor of English at University College, London, from 1970 to 1977, and gave frequent lecture tours in the United States.

MARK STRAND is the author of numerous collections of poetry, including *Man and Camel* (2006) and *Blizzard of One* (1998), which won the Pulitzer Prize. He has also published two books of prose and several volumes of translation (of works by Rafael Alberti and Carlos Drummond de Andrade, among others).

MARIO SUSKO was born in Croatia in 1941. He received his MA and PhD from SUNY at Stony Brook in the 1970s, and has lived in the United States on and off for the past thirty-two years. A prolific poet, translator, and university professor, he is the author of twenty-two poetry collections and numerous translations from modern American literature. A witness to and survivor of the war in Bosnia, he returned to the United States at the end of 1993.

BRIAN SWANN has published a number of collections of poetry and fiction, including *Wearing the Morning Star: Native American Song-Poems* and *Coming to Light: Contemporary Translations of the Native Literatures of North America*. He teaches at the Cooper Union in New York City.

ARTHUR SZE is the author of eight books of poetry, including *The Ginkgo Light, Quipu, The Redshifting Web: Poems 1970–1998*, and *Archipelago* (1995). He is also a celebrated translator, and released *The Silk Dragon: Translations from the Chinese* in 2001.

VENO TAUFER is a Slovenian poet, playwright, essayist, and translator. In 1989 he was cofounder of the first Slovenian democratic party and coauthor of the 1989 May Declaration, the basic document of the pluralistic democracy and independence of Slovenia. From 2000 to 2006 he was chair of the Writers for Peace Committee of International PEN.

ALEXANDER TAYLOR was the founder and codirector of Curbstone Press and a leading light in the world of independent publishing. He was a teacher of English for over thirty years and a translator of Danish literature. His own poetry has been published in English, Danish, Bulgarian, and Serbo-Croatian.

BRUCE TAYLOR is a professor emeritus at the University of Wisconsin at Eau Claire. He is the author of seven collections of poetry and the editor of eight anthologies.

EINER was a major translator from Czech and editor of the *rship* issued by Writers & Scholars International.

THWAITE was born in Chester, England, in 1930. He spent ldhood in Yorkshire but was evacuated to the United States during the Second World War. An acclaimed writer and poet, he has worked as a broadcaster, critic, reviewer, and academic.

YUMIKO TSUMURA was born and educated in Japan. She received an MFA in poetry and translation from the Writers' Workshop at the University of Iowa. Her poetry has appeared in many literary journals. Her translations of modern Japanese poetry and fiction in collaboration with her husband, Samuel Grolmes, have appeared in *New Direction Annuals, Literature East West, Mundus Artium*, and other journals.

ANNE TWITTY is a winner of a PEN Award for Poetry in Translation. Her translations include *Say Nothing: Poems of Jalal al-Din Rumi*.

ABDULLAH AL-UDHARI was born in Taiz, Yemen, in 1941, and has lived in London since 1962. In 1974 he founded and edited *TR*, an Anglo-Arab literary and arts magazine. He is a literary historian, poet, and storyteller, and the author of *Voice Without Passport, The Arab Creation Myth, Victims of a Map*, and *Modern Poetry of the Arab World*.

JEAN VALENTINE won the Yale Younger Poets Award for her first book, *Dream Barker*, in 1965. Her tenth and most recent book of poetry is *Little Boat*. Her previous collection, *Door in the Mountain: New and Collected Poems 1965–2003*, was the winner of the 2004 National Book Award for poetry.

ALISSA VALLES was born in Amsterdam to an American father and a Dutch mother, grew up in the United States and the Netherlands, and studied Slavic languages in London, Russia, and Poland. She is the editor and translator of Zbigniew Herbert's *Collected Poems* and a contributing editor to the Graywolf anthology *New European Poets*. Her translations have appeared in the *New York Review of Books, The New Yorker, Ploughshares*, and elsewhere. Her own poetry is collected in *Orphan Fire*.

LAWRENCE VENUTI is a translator as well as a translation theorist and historian. He translates from Italian, French, and Catalan into English.

Recent translations include Antonia Pozzi's *Breath: Poems and Letters* (2002), the anthology *Italy: A Traveler's Literary Companion* (2003), and Massimo Carlotto's crime novel *Death's Dark Abyss* (2006). He is the author of *The Translator's Invisibility* (2nd ed., 2008) and *The Scandals of Translation* (1998) and the editor of *The Translation Studies Reader* (2nd ed., 2004). He is a professor of English at Temple University.

CLIVE WAKE edited and translated, with John O. Reed, *A Book of African Verse*; *A New Book of African Verse*; *French African Verse*; and *The Selected Poems of Léopold Sédar Senghor*.

ROSMARIE WALDROP began publishing her poetry in English in the late 1960s and since 1968 has been coeditor and publisher of Burning Deck Press with her husband, the poet and translator Keith Waldrop. She is the author of more than three dozen books of poetry, fiction, and criticism, and the translator of more than twenty books.

BRENDA WALKER is an associate professor of English and cultural studies at the University of Western Australia. She has been a visiting fellow at Stanford University.

ELLEN DORÉ WATSON is the author of four books of poetry, most recently *This Sharpening*, and the translator of many books from Brazilian Portuguese. She directs the Poetry Center at Smith College.

HARRIETT WATTS is a research associate at the Center for European Studies at Harvard University.

RUTH WHITMAN was a poet and longtime Radcliffe Seminars instructor. She published seven books of poems, including *Tamsen Donner: A Woman's Journey*. From 1980 to 1995 she was the poetry editor of the *Radcliffe Quarterly*. Her other books of poems include *Laughing Gas*, *Permanent Address*, and *Marriage Wig and Other Poems*.

JUDITH WILKINSON is a British poet and translator. She has published poetry, translations, and articles in various journals, including *Envoi*, *English Studies*, *PN Review*, *Chapman*, *The Manhattan Review*, and *Poetry London*. Her translation of Miriam Van hee's *Instead of Silence* was published in 2007.

JOHN WILLETT (1917–2002) was a translator and a scholar famous for translating the work of Bertolt Brecht into English. His translations include *Life of Galileo*, *The Good Person of Setzuan*, *The Resistible Rise of Arturo Ui*, and *Mother Courage and Her Children*.

C. K. WILLIAMS was born in 1936 in Newark, New Jersey. He is the author of numerous books of poetry, including *The Singing*. Williams has also published five works of translation: *Selected Poems of Francis Ponge*; *Canvas*, by Adam Zagajewski (with Renata Gorczynski and Benjamin Ivry); *The Bacchae of Euripides*; *The Lark. The Thrush. The Starling.* (Poems from Issa); and *Women of Trachis*, by Sophocles (with Gregory Dickerson).

MILLER WILLIAMS is one of the foremost American poets of the post–World War II era. For thirty-three years, he was a professor of English, foreign languages, and comparative literature at the University of Arkansas at Fayetteville and was a key figure in the university's nationally known programs in creative writing and translation. He is the author, editor, or translator of thirty-one volumes of poetry, literary criticism, and fiction.

CLIVE WILMER is a fellow of Sidney Sussex College, Cambridge. His most recent collection of poems is *The Mystery of Things*.

ELIZABETH WINSLOW is a fiction writer and a graduate of the Iowa Writers' Workshop. Her translation of Dunya Mikhail's *The War Works Hard* won the PEN prize for translation in 2004 and was published by New Directions in 2005.

ELŻBIETA WÓJCIK-LEESE has published translations of Polish poetry in *Poetry Review*, *Poetry London*, *Poetry Wales*, *Modern Poetry in Translation*, *Poetry Ireland*, and elsewhere. She coedits *Przekładaniec: A Journal of Literary Translation*.

ELIZABETH OEHLKERS WRIGHT's translations of contemporary German poets have appeared in such journals as *Agni* and *Seneca Review*. She cotranslated Valzhyna Mort's poetry with her husband, Franz Wright, and has received NEA and ALTA fellowships.

FRANZ WRIGHT received the Pulitzer Prize in poetry for *Walking to Martha's Vineyard*. He is the author of numerous books of poetry, including

Ill Lit: Selected and New Poems, and critically acclaimed translations of Rainer Maria Rilke and Valzhyna Mort. Wright teaches at Brandeis University.

HAROLD WRIGHT is an emeritus professor of Japanese at Antioch College. His translations from the Japanese include Shuntaro Tanikawa's *Map of Days* and *Selected Poems*.

MICHELLE YEH is a professor of East Asian Languages and Cultures at the University of California, Davis.

DAVID YOUNG translated *Five Tang Poets* and, with Jiann I. Lin, *The Clouds Float North*, a collection of poems by Yu Xuan-ji.

LEAH ZAZULYER is a poet, translator, prose writer, former school psychologist, special education teacher, and mediator. Her publications and prizes include two chapbooks of her own poetry, and *Siberia*, poems by Israel Emiot. She is working on a selected/collected volume of all Emiot's poetry.

PERMISSIONS

Every effort has been made to trace the ownership of copyrighted material and to make full acknowledgment of its use. The editors regret any errors or omissions, which will be corrected in subsequent editions upon notification in writing to the publisher.

Adonis, from "A Mirror for the Twentieth Century". and from "The Desert: The Diary of Beirut Under Siege, 1982," translated by Abdullah al-Udhari. Reprinted by permission of the author.

Anna Akhmatova, "Requiem" from *Poems of Akhmatova*, selected, translated, and introduced by Stanley Kunitz and Max Hayward. Originally published by Little, Brown and used courtesy of Darhansoff, Verrill, Feldman Literary Agents. "A Land Not Mine" translated by Jane Kenyon. From *The Collected Poems of Jane Kenyon*. Reprinted by permission of Graywolf Press. "Our Own Land." From *Selected Poems*. © Richard McKane, translation. Reprinted by permission of Bloodaxe Books. "Northern Elegies, Fourth" from *Complete Poems of Anna Akhmatova*, translated by Judith Hemschemeyer, edited and introduced by Roberta Reeder. Copyright © 1989, 1992, 1997 by Judith

Hemschemeyer. Reprinted with the permission of Zephyr Press, www .zephyrpress.org.

Rafael Alberti, "Song 35," from *Ballads and Songs of the Paranas*. Translated by José A. Elgorriaga and Martin Paul. Reprinted by permission of the Carmen Balcells Agency.

Claribel Alegría, "From the Bridge," translated by D. J. Flakoll, from *Woman of the River: Bilingual Edition*. © 1989 Claribel Alegría and D. J. Flakoll. Reprinted by permission of the University of Pittsburgh Press.

Yehuda Amichai, "Yom Kippur," "I Know a Man," "A Man in His Life," "Jerusalem Is Full of Used Jews," "When I Banged My Head on the Door," "A Letter of Recommendation," and "The Diameter of the Bomb," translated by Chana Bloch, from *Selected Poetry of Yehuda Amichai*, edited and translated by Chana Bloch and Stephen Mitchell. By permission of the University of California Press. "A Pity. We Were Such a Good Invention," "We Did It," "My Mother Once Told Me," "A Dog After Love," "Love Song," and "Gifts of Love," translated by Assia Gutmann, from *Love Poems*: © 1981 by Yehuda Amichai. Reprinted by permission of HarperCollins Publishers and Hanah Amichai. "Letter," translated by Ted Hughes, from *Amen*. © 1977 by Yehuda Amichai. Reprinted by permission of HarperCollins Publishers and Hanah Amichai.

Jorge Carrera Andrade, "The Guest." Translated by Muna Lee de Muñoz Marín. From *Anthology of Contemporary Latin-American Poetry*. © 1947 New Directions Publishing Corp. Reprinted by permission of New Directions Publishing Corp.

Anonymous, "To the Earth (I)," translated by Judith Gleason. Reprinted by permission of the translator.

Chairil Anwar, "Heaven" and "Tuti's Ice Cream" from *The Voice of the Night: The Complete Prose & Poetry of Chairil Anwar*, translated by Burton Raffel. Reprinted by permission of Ohio University Press/Swallow Press, Athens, Ohio (www.ohioswallow.com).

Guillaume Apollinaire, "The Little Car" from *Guillaume Apollinaire: Selected Poems*. Translated by Oliver Bernard. Published by Anvil Press Poetry in 1986. By permission of Anvil Press Poetry. "Hotel" and "Zone," translated by Roger Shattuck, from *Selected Writings*. © 1971 by Roger Shattuck. Reprinted by permission of New Directions Publishing Corp.

H. C. Artmann, "An Optician Has a Glass Heart," translated by Rosmarie Waldrop and Harriet Watts, from *Six Major Austrian Poets*. Reprinted by permission of the translator.

Rose Auslander, "Motherland." Translated by Eavan Boland. From *After Every War*. © 2004 by Eavan Boland. Published by Princeton University Press. Reprinted by permission of Princeton University Press.

Gennady Aygi, "The People Are a Temple," translated by Peter France, from *Child and Rose*. © 1982, 1984, 1989, 1991, 1992, 1993, 1995, 2002 by Gennady Aygi. Translation © 1989, 1997, 2003 by Peter France. Compilation © 2003 by New Directions. Reprinted by permission of New Directions Publishing Corp.

Ingeborg Bachmann, "Every Day" and "The Respite," translated by Michael Hamburger, from *The Faber Book of Modern European Poetry*. Reprinted by permission of the estate of Michael Hamburger.

Polina Barskova, "Manuscript Found by Natasha Rostova During the Fire," translated by Ilya Kaminsky. By permission of the author and translator.

Bei Dao, "Midnight Singer" and "Untitled," translated by David Hinton, from *At the Sky's Edge: Poems 1991–1996*. © 1995 by David Hinton. Reprinted by permission of New Directions Publishing Corp. From *Bei Dao: Forms of Distance*, published by Anvil Press Poetry, 1994. Reprinted by permission of Anvil Press Poetry.

Gottfried Benn, "This Is Bad," translated by Harvey Shapiro. Reprinted by permission of the translator. "Chopin," translated by Michael Hofmann, from *Twentieth-Century German Poetry: An Anthology*, edited by Michael Hofmann. © 2005 by Michael Hofmann. Reprinted by permission of Farrar, Straus and Giroux, LLC.

Abbas Beydoun, "White Lie," translated by Fady Joudah. Reprinted by permission of the translator.

Miron Białoszewski, "A Ballad of Going Down to the Store," translated by Czesław Miłosz, from *Postwar Polish Poetry, Third Edition.* © 1965, 1983 by Czsesław Miłosz. Reprinted by permission of The Wylie Agency, Inc.

Alexander Blok, "[Night. Street. Lamp. Drugstore.]," translated by Ilya Kaminsky. © 2009 by Ilya Kaminsky. By permission of the translator.

Johannes Bobrowski, "Latvian Songs," translated by Ruth and Matthew Mead, from *Shadowlands: Selected Poems.* © 1984 by Ruth and Matthew Mead. Reprinted by permission of New Directions Publishing Corp. and Anvil Press Poetry.

Yves Bonnefoy, "The Tree, the Lamp," translated by Richard Pevear, from *Poems 1955–75.* Translation © 1985 by Random House, Inc. Reprinted by permission of Random House.

Jorge Luis Borges, "Borges and I" and "Everything and Nothing," translated by James E. Irby, from *Labyrinths.* © 1962, 1964 by New Directions Publishing Corp. Reprinted by permission of New Directions Publishing Corp. and Gerald Pollinger Ltd.

Bertolt Brecht, "I, the Survivor" and "Motto," translated by John Willett, in *Bertolt Brecht: Poems 1913–1956*, published by Methuen in 1976. Reprinted by permission of Methuen.

André Breton, "Free Union," translated by David Antin. Reprinted by permission of the translator.

Joseph Brodsky, "Elegy for John Donne" and "A Prophecy," translated by George L. Kline, from *Joseph Brodsky: Selected Poems*, published by

Harper & Row 1973. © 1973 by George L. Kline. Reprinted by permission of Farrar, Straus and Giroux, LLC.

João Cabral de Melo Neto, "The Emptiness of Man," translated by Galway Kinnell, in *João Cabral de Melo Neto: Selected Poetry*. © 1994 by Djelal Kadir and reprinted by permission of Wesleyan University Press, www.wesleyan.edu/wespress.

Dino Campana, "Journey to Montevideo," translated by I. L. Salomon, from *Orphic Songs*. Translation © 1968 by I. L. Salomon. Reprinted by permission of City Lights Books.

Ernesto Cardenal, "For Those Dead, Our Dead . . . ," translated by Jonathan Cohen. Reprinted by permission of Jonathan Cohen.

Nina Cassian, "Temptation," translated by Brenda Walker and Andrea Deletant from *Life Sentence, Selected Poems* by Nina Cassian, edited by William Jay Smith. © 1990 by Nina Cassian. Published by Anvil Press Poetry in 1990. New edition 1998. Reprinted by permission of Anvil Press Poetry and W. W. Norton and Co., Inc.

Ricardo Castillo, "Ode to the Urge," translated by Robert L. Jones, from *Light from a Nearby Window: Contemporary Mexican Poetry*. Translation © 1993 by Robert L. Jones. Reprinted by permission of City Lights Books.

Constantine P. Cavafy, "The City," "Ithaka," and "Body, Remember," from Edmund Keeley, *George Seferis*. © 1967 Princeton University Press, 1995 renewed PUP/1995 revised edition. Reprinted by permission of Princeton University Press. "Waiting for the Barbarians," from *Selected Poems*. © 1972 Edmund Keeley and Philip Sherrard, translation. Reprinted by permission of Princeton University Press.

Patrizia Cavalli, "But first one must free oneself" and "Far from Kingdoms," translated by Patrizia Cavalli and Robert McCracken, from *My Poems Will Not Change the World*. Reprinted by permission of Exile Editions.

Camilo José Cela, "The Clock Which Runs the City" and "Street Musicians," translated by J. S. Bernstein, from *Mrs. Caldwell Speaks to Her Son*, published by Cornell University Press. Reprinted by permission of the Carmen Balcells Agency.

Paul Celan, "Deathfugue," from *Selected Poems and Prose of Paul Celan*, translated by John Felstiner. © 2001 by John Felstiner. Used by permission of W. W. Norton & Company, Inc. Paul Celan, *Mohn und Gedächtnis*. Gedichte © 1952 Deutsche Verlags-Anstalt, Munich, a member of Verlagsgruppe Random House GmbH. "Zurich, the Stork Inn," "There was earth inside them," "I hear that the axe has flowered," "Memory of France," "Psalm," "Corona," and "Tenebrae," translated by Michael Hamburger, from *The Poems of Paul Celan*, published by Persea Books. Reprinted by permission of Persea Books.

Blaise Cendrars, "White Suit," translated by Pete Hoida. Reprinted by permission of the translator.

Aimé Césaire, "Ex-voto for a Shipwreck," "Lagoonal Calendar," and "All the Way from Akkad, from Elam, from Sumer," translated by Clayton Eshleman and Annette J. Smith. From *Aimé Césaire: The Collected Poetry*. © University of California Press. Reprinted by permission of University of California Press.

René Char, "The Gods Are Back," translated by Peter Boyle. Reprinted by permission of the translator.

Inger Christensen, from "Alphabet," translated by Susanna Nied, from *Alphabet*. © 1981, 2000 by Inger Christensen, translation © 2000 by Susanna Nied. Reprinted by permission of New Directions Publishing Corp.

Julio Cortázar, "Theme for a Tapestry" and "Progress and Retrogression," translated by Paul Blackburn, from *Cronopios and Famas*. © 1962 by Julio Cortázar and the heirs of Julio Cortázar. Translation © 1969 by Random House, Inc. Reprinted by permission of New Directions Publishing Corp. and the Carmen Balcells Agency.

María Elena Cruz Varela, "Kaleidoscope," translated by Mairym Cruz-Bernal and Deborah Digges, from *Ballad of the Blood: The Collected Poems of Maria Elena Cruz Varela*. Reprinted by permission of HarperCollins Publishers.

Bogdan Czaykowski, "A Prayer," translated by Czesław Miłosz, from *Postwar Polish Poetry, Third Edition*. © 1965, 1983 Czesław Miłosz. Reprinted by permission of The Wylie Agency, Inc.

Bernard Dadié, "I Thank You God," translated by John O. Reed and Clive Wake, from *French African Verse*, Heinemann Educational Books, Ltd. Reprinted by permission of Random House UK.

Sapardi Djoko Damonno, "Who Are You," translated by Burton Raffel, from *Poetry in Our World*, edited by Jeffrey Pine. Reprinted by permission of HarperCollins.

Rubén Darío, "The Wandering Song," translated by Gabriel Gudding. © 2008 by Gabriel Gudding. Published in *Words Without Borders*, May 2008. Reprinted by permission of *Words Without Borders*.

Mahmoud Darwish, "We Travel Like All People," "And We Love Life," "On the Last Evening on This Earth," "Remainder of a Life," and "Viewpoint," translated by Fady Joudah. © Mahmoud Darwish. Translations © 2009 by Fady Joudah. By permission of the estate of Mahmoud Darwish and the translators.

Robert Desnos, "I've Dreamed of You So Much," translated by Carolyn Forché and William T. Kulik, from *Selected Poems of Robert Desnos*. © 1991 Ecco Press. Reprinted by permission of the translators.

Gerardo Diego, "Julio Campal," translated by Robert Mezey, from *Roots & Wings: Poetry from Spain 1900–1975*. © 1976, 2005 Hardie St. Martin. Reprinted by permission of White Pine Press.

Blaga Dimitrova, "Ars Poetica," translated by Ludmilla Popova-Wightman. Reprinted by permission of the translator.

Lidija Dimkovska, "The Poem at the Beginning," translated by Ljubica Arsovska and Peggy Reid, from *Do Not Awaken Them with Hammers.* © 2006 by Ugly Duckling Presse. Reprinted by permission of Ugly Duckling Presse.

Carlos Drummond de Andrade, "Seven-Sided Poem," "Don't Kill Yourself," "Infancy," "Family Portrait," and "In the Middle of the Road There Was a Stone," translated by Elizabeth Bishop. Reprinted by permission of Farrar, Straus and Giroux, LLC. "Your Shoulders Hold Up the World," translated by Mark Strand, in *Another Republic: 17 European and South American Writers,* edited by Charles Simic and Mark Strand. © 1976 by Charles Simic and Mark Strand. Reprinted by permission of HarperCollins Publishers.

Duoduo, "Morning," translated by Maghiel van Crevel. Reprinted by permission of the translator.

Günter Eich, "Inventory," translated by David Young, from *Valuable Nail.* English translation © 1981. Reprinted by permission of Oberlin College Press, www.oberlin.edu/ocpress/.

Odysseas Elytis, "All Day Long We Walked in the Fields." From Edmund Keeley, *Voices of Modern Greece.* © 1981 Princeton University Press. Reprinted by permission of Princeton University Press.

Israel Emiot, "A Prayer in Nineteen Forty-Three," translated by Leah Zazulyer and Brina Menachovsky Rose. Reprinted by permission of the translators.

Hans Magnus Enzensberger, "last will and testament," translated by Jerome Rothenberg. Reprinted by permission of the translator.

Faiz Ahmed Faiz, "Before You Came," translated by Naomi Lazard, from *The True Subject.* © 1987 Princeton University Press. Reprinted by permission of Princeton University Press. "You Tell Us What to Do," translated by Agha Shahid Ali, from *The Rebel's Silhouette: Selected Poems.* © 1991 by Agha Shahid Ali and published by the University of Massachusetts Press. Reprinted by permission of the University of Massachusetts Press.

Ernest Farrés, "Summer Evening, 1947," and "Summer in the City, 1949," translated by Lawrence Venuti. © 2007 by Lawrence Venuti. Published in *Words Without Borders*, October 2007. Reprinted by permission of *Words Without Borders*.

Jean Follain, "Face the Animal," translated by Heather McHugh, from *D'Après Tout*. © 1981 Princeton University Press. Reprinted by permission of Princeton University Press. "Music of Spheres" and "A Mirror," translated by Czesław Miłosz and Robert Hass. Reprinted by permission of Gallimard.

Erich Fried, "French Soldiers Mutiny—1917," translated by Stuart Hood, © John Calder Publishers Ltd and the Estate of Erich Fried, 1987; translation © Stuart Hood, 1987. Reprinted by permission of Calder Publications (UK) Ltd.

Gloria Fuertes, "Autobiography", translated by Philip Levine, from *Off the Map*, translated and edited by Philip Levine and Ada Long (Wesleyan University Press, 1984). © 1984 by Philip Levine and Ada Long and reprinted by permission of Wesleyan University Press. "Birds Nest," translated by Philip Levine. Reprinted by permission of the translator. "Prayer," "Now," and "I Write Poetry, Gentlemen!" translated by Brian Barker, published in *Words Without Borders*, September 2005. Reprinted by permission of *Words Without Borders*.

Reginald Gibbons, "Lemon Trees," after Eugenio Montale. Reprinted by permission of the author.

Federico García Lorca, "Sanchez Mejias/Lament for Ignacio Sanchez Mejias," translated by Stephen Spender and J. L. Gili, "Despidida/Farewell," "El nino mudo/The Little Mute Boy," translated by W. S. Merwin, "Rundown Church," "City That Does Not Sleep," "Little Infinite Poem," and "Song of the Cuban Blacks," translated by Robert Bly. © Herederos de Federico García Lorca. Translations © Herederos de Federico García Lorca and Stephen Splender, J. L.Gili, W. S. Merwin, Robert Bly. For information regarding rights and permissions, please contact lorca@artslaw.co.uk or William Peter Kosmas, Esq., 8 Franklin Square, London W14 9UU.

Luis García Montero, "Completely Friday," translated by Katie King. Published in *Words Without Borders*, July 2005. © 2005 by Katie King. Reprinted by permission of *Words Without Borders*.

Yankev Glatshteyn, "Mozart," translated by Ruth Whitman, from *Anthology of Modern Yiddish Poetry*. "A Song," translated by Zachary Sholem Berger, published in *Words Without Borders*, August 2004. Reprinted by permission of *Words Without Borders*.

Eugen Gomringer, "Streets and Flowers," translated by Jerome Rothenberg. Reprinted by permission of the translator.

Ángel González, "Diatribe Against the Dead" and "Whatever You Want," in *Astonishing World: The Selected Poems of Ángel González 1956–1986*, translated by Steven Ford Brown and Pedro Gutiérrez Revuelta (Minneapolis: Milkweed Editions, 1993). Spanish language © 1986 by Ángel González. English translation © 1993 by Steven Ford Brown and Pedro Gutiérrez Revuelta. Reprinted by permission of Milkweed Editions.

Günter Grass, "Happiness," translated by Michael Hamburger. From *Selected Poems* by Günter Grass. © 1966 Martin, Secker & Warburg, Limited. Reprinted by permission of Houghton Mifflin Harcourt Publishing Company.

Tatjana Gromača, "Lovers," translated by Mario Susko. Reprinted by permission of the translator.

Gu Cheng, "Discovery," translated by Eva Hung, and from "Forever Parted: Graveyard: 3. I don't have an older brother but I believe you . . . ," translated by J. P. Seaton and Mu Yi, in *Out of the Howling Storm*. © 1993 Wesleyan University and reprinted by permission of Wesleyan University Press, www.wesleyan.edu/wespress.

Nicolas Guillen, "Sensemayá (Chant for Killing a Snake)," translated by H. R. Hays. © H. R. Hays. Reprinted by permission of Ann Elmo Agency, Inc.

Lars Gustafsson, "Ballad of the Dogs," translated by Philip Martin, from *Stillness of the World before Bach*. © 1980 by Lars Gustafsson, translation © 1982 by Philip Martin. Reprinted by permission of New Directions Publishing Corp.

Oscar Hahn, "Good Night, Dear," translated by James Hoggard. Reprinted by permission of the author and the translator.

Moishe Leib Halpern, "Man, That Ape," translated by John Hollander, from *An Anthology of Modern Yiddish Poetry*, selected and translated by Irving Howe and Eliezer Greenberg (Holt, Rinehart and Winston, 1969). Reprinted by permission of the translator.

Han Yongwun, "The Artist," translated by Bruce Taylor. Reprinted by permission of the translator.

Zbigniew Herbert, "The Rain," "Report from Paradise," "Our Fear," "Hen," and "Five Men," translated by Czesław Miłosz and Peter Dale Scott, and "My Father," translated by Czesław Miłosz, from *The Collected Poems: 1956–1998* by Zbigniew Herbert. Translated and edited by Alissa Valles with additional translations by Czesław Miłosz and Peter Dale Scott. © 2007 the Estate of Zbigniew Herbert. Reprinted by permission of HarperCollins Publishers. "What Mr. Cogito Thinks About Hell" and "The Envoy of Mr. Cogito," translated by John Carpenter and Bogdana Carpenter, from *Mr. Cogito*. Translation © 1993 by John Carpenter and Bogdana Carpenter. © 1974 by Zbigniew Herbert. Reprinted by permission of HarperCollins and the Andrew Wylie Agency.

Miguel Hernández, "Lullabies of the Onion," translated by Philip Levine. Reprinted by permission of the translator.

Nâzim Hikmet, "Things I Didn't Know I Loved," "Since I Was Thrown Inside," "Angina Pectoris," and "On Living." © Nâzim Hikmet. By permission of the estate of Nâzim Hikmet. Translations © 2009 by Deniz Perin. By permission of the translator.

Ho Ch'i-fang, "Get Drunk," translated by Kai-yu Hsu, from *Twentieth-Century Chinese Poetry*. © 1963 by Kai-yu Hsu.

Vladimir Holan, "May, 1945," "June, July, and August, 1945," and "Resurrection," translated by C. G. Hanzlicek and Dana Hábová. From *Mirroring: Selected Poems of Vladimir Holan*. © 1985 C. G. Hanzlicek. Reprinted by permission of Wesleyan University Press, www.wesleyan.edu/wespress.

Miroslav Holub, "Cinderella," "Man cursing the sea" and "Zito the magician." From *Poems Before & After*, translated by George Theiner, Ewald Osers, et al. (Bloodaxe Books, 2006). Reprinted by permission of Bloodaxe Books. "The Fly," translated by Stuart Friebert and Dana Hábová, from *Intensive Care: Selected and New Poems*. © 1996 Oberlin College Press. Reprinted by permission of Oberlin College Press.

Moushegh Ishkhan, "The Armenian Language Is the Home of the Armenian," translated by Diana Der-Hovanessian. Reprinted by permission of the translator.

Edmond Jabès, "Dedication," translated by Rosmarie Waldrop, in *The Book of Questions*. © 1984 by Rosmarie Waldrop and reprinted by permission of Wesleyan University Press, www.wesleyan.edu/wespress.

Max Jacob, "Mystery of the Sky," translated by William T. Kulik, from *Dreaming the Miracle: Three French Prose Poets: Max Jacob, Jean Follain, Francis Ponge*. Translation © 2003 William T. Kulik. Reprinted by permission of White Pine Press, Buffalo, New York.

Juan Ramón Jiménez, "Oceans," translated by Robert Bly. Reprinted by permission of the translator.

Attila József, "The Seventh," translated by John Bátki. Reprinted by permission of the translator.

Roberto Juarroz, from *Ninth Vertical Poetry*: "Snow has turned the world into a cemetery," translated by Mary Crow. © Mary Crow.

Reprinted by permission of the translator. From *Second Vertical Poetry*: "Life Draws a Tree" and "Each one goes however he can," translated by W. S. Merwin. © W. S. Merwin, reprinted by permission of The Wylie Agency LLC.

Franz Kafka, "On Parables," translated by Willa Muir and Edwin Muir. Reprinted by permission of Random House.

Anna Kamienska, "Thanking" and "A Prayer That Will Be Answered," translated by Tomasz P. Krzeszowski and Desmond Graham, from *Two Darknesses*. Reprinted by permission of Flambard Press.

Mitsuharu Kaneko, "Opposition," translated by Geoffrey Bownas and Anthony Thwaite, from *The Penguin Book of Japanese Verse*. © 1964 Geoffrey Bownas and Anthony Thwaite. Reprinted by permission of the translators.

Tymoteusz Karpowicz, "A Lesson of Silence," translated by Czesław Miłosz, from *Postwar Polish Poetry, Third Edition*. © 1965, 1983 Czesław Miłosz. Reprinted by permission of The Wylie Agency, Inc. "Ecclesiastes," translated by Adam Czerniawski. Reprinted by permission of the translator.

Marie Luise Kaschnitz, "Hiroshima," translated by Eavan Boland, from *After Every War*. © 2004 Eavan Boland. Reprinted by permission of Princeton University Press.

Patrice Kayo, "Song of the Initiate," translated by Gerald Moore, from *Modern African Poetry*.

Daniil Kharms, "The Beginning of a Beautiful Day (A Symphony)," translated by George Gibian, from *The Man in the Black Coat: Russia's Lost Literature of the Absurd*.

Velimir Khlebnikov, "Incantation by Laughter," from *The King of Time* by Velimir Khlebnikov, translated by Paul Schmidt, edited by Charlotte Douglas. © 1985 by the Dia Art Foundation. Reprinted by permission of Harvard University Press.

Vénus Khoury-Ghata, "She Says" and "Words," translated by Marilyn Hacker, from *She Says*. © Vénus Khoury-Ghata. Translation © 2003 by Marilyn Hacker. Reprinted by permission of Graywolf Press.

Kim Nam-Jo, "Foreign Flags," translated by Brother Anthony of Taizé. Reprinted by permission of the translator.

Ko Un, "A cock crows at Donghyun's," "What is this world?" and "Dogs are barking in villages high and low" from *Flowers of a Moment*, translated by Brother Anthony of Taizé, Young-moo Kim, and Gary Gach. Translation © 2006 by Brother Anthony of Taizé, Young-moo Kim, and Gary Gach. Reprinted by permission of BOA Editions, Ltd., www.boaeditinos.org.

Edvard Kocbek, "Longing for Jail," translated by Michael Scammell and Veno Taufer. From *Nothing Is Lost*. © 1990 by Matjaz Kocbek and Jurij Kocbek. Translation © 2004 Michael Scammell and Veno Taufer. Reprinted by permission of Princeton University Press.

Gerrit Kouwenaar, "Elba," translated by Peter Nijmeijer, from *Dutch Interior*, edited by James Holmes and William Jay Smith. © 1994 Columbia University Press. Reprinted by permission of the publisher.

Karl Krolow, "Quite a Lot of Luck" and "Unforeseen Events," translated by Michael Bullock, from *Foreign Bodies*. © 1969 Michael Bullock. Reprinted by permission of Suhrkampf Verlag GmbH & Co.

Ryszard Krynicki, "Save Me, Guide Me," translated by Alissa Valles. © 2005 by Alissa Valles. Published in *Words Without Borders*, September 2005. Reprinted by permission of *Words Without Borders*.

Reiner Kunze, "The Bringers of Beethoven," translated by Gordon Brotherston and Gisela Brotherston. Reprinted by permission of the translators.

Else Lasker-Schüler, "In the Evening." From *After Every War*. © 2004 Eavan Boland. Reprinted by permission of Princeton University Press.

Lei Shuyan, "Creation," translated by Fang Dai, Dennis Ding, and Edward Morin, from *The Red Azalea: Chinese Poetry Since the Cultural Revolution*. © 1990 University of Hawaii Press. Reprinted by permission of University of Hawaii Press.

Primo Levi, "August," translated by Ruth Feldman and Brian Swann, from *Collected Poems* by Primo Levi. English translation © 1988 by Ruth Feldman and Brian Swann. Reprinted by permission of Faber and Faber, Inc., an affiliate of Farrar, Straus and Giroux, LLC.

Enrique Lihn, "Torture Chamber," translated by Mary Crow. © 1991 Mary Crow. Reprinted by permission of the translator.

Jorge de Lima, "Distribution of Poetry," translated by John Nist, from *Modern Brazilian Poetry*. © 1962 by John Nist.

Robert Lowell, "Wild Vines," "Sparrow Hills," and "To Anna Akhmatova," all after Pasternak, from *Imitations*. © 1959 by Robert Lowell. Reprinted by permission of Farrar, Straus and Giroux, LLC.

Luo Fu, "Song of Everlasting Regret," translated by Michelle Yeh, from *Anthology of Modern Chinese Poetry*. © 1994 Yale University Press. Reprinted by permission of Yale University Press.

Antonio Machado, "I Never Sought the Glory," translated by Katie King. © 2009 by Katie King. Reprinted by permission of the translator. "Last Night, as I Was Sleeping," translated by Robert Bly. From *Times Alone: Selected Poems of Antonio Machado*. © 1983 Antonio Machado and reprinted by permission of Wesleyan University Press, www.wesleyan.edu/wespress/. "The best of the good people," "Don't be surprised, dear friends," "The cricket in his cage," and "Pay attention," translated by Mary G. Berg and Dennis Maloney, from *There Is No Road*. © 2003 Mary G. Berg and Dennis Maloney, translation. Reprinted by permission of White Pine Press, www.whitepine.org. "Eyes," translated by Rosa Berumen. Copyright © 2009 Rosa Berumen. By permission of the translator.

Muhammad al-Maghut, "The Postman's Fear," translated by Abdullah al-Udhari, from *Modern Poetry of the Arab World*.

Derek Mahon, "Distances" (after Philippe Jaccottet). From *Words in the Air* (1998). By kind permission of the author and The Gallery Press, Loughcrew, Oldcastle, County Meath, Ireland.

Osip Mandelstam, "O Lord, help me to live through this night," "#116 Take from my palms, to soothe your heart," "#221 Leningrad," "#393 Pear blossom and cherry blossom aim at me," "#395 Through Kiev, through the streets of the monster," "#296 Your thin shoulders are for turning red under whips," and "The Stalin Epigram," translated by Clarence Brown and W. S. Merwin, from *Osip Mandelstam: Selected Poems*. © 1973 by Clarence Brown and W. S. Merwin. Reprinted by permission of Simon & Schuster.

Caitlín Maude, "I Long for a Rhyme of Health," translated by Pearse Hutchinson, from *Done into English*. © 2003 by Pearse Hutchinson. Reprinted by kind permission of the author and The Gallery Press, Loughcrew, Oldcastle, County Meath, Ireland.

Vladimir Mayakovsky, "Past One O'Clock" and from "The Cloud in Trousers," translated by Max Hayward and George Reavey, from *The Bedbug and Selected Poetry*. © 1960 by Harper & Row. Reprinted by permission of HarperCollins Publishers and Weidenfeld & Nicolson Ltd.

Pablo Medina, "A Poem for the Epiphany," translated by Pablo Medina, from *Burnt Sugar: Contemporary Cuban Poetry*, edited by Lori Marie Carlson and Oscar Hijuelos. Reprinted by permission of Lori Marie Carlson.

Henri Michaux, from "I Am Writing to You from a Far-off Country," translated by Richard Ellmann, from *Selected Writings*. © 1968 New Directions Publishing Corp. Reprinted by permission of New Directions Publishing Corp.

Dunya Mikhail, "The War Works Hard," translated by Elizabeth Winslow, from *The War Works Hard*. © 1993, 1997, 2000, 2005 Dunya Mikhail. Reprinted by permission of New Directions Publishing Corp.

Czesław Miłosz, "Dedication," "A Gift," "Winter," "And the City Stood in Its Brightness," "Throughout Our Lands: 1, 3, 11, 14," "A Felicitous Life," "Mittelbergheim," "A Poor Christian Looks at the Ghetto," "Café," from "Bobo's Metamorphosis," "On the Other Side," "Incantation," "On Angels," "Bypassing rue Descartes," and "A Song on the End of the World," from *New and Collected Poems: 1931–2001*. © 1988, 1991, 1995, 2001 by Czesław Miłosz Royalties, Inc., and The Wylie Agency, Inc. Reprinted by permission of HarperCollins Publishers.

Agi Mishol, "A Little Prayer for Sunday" and "Woman Martyr," translated by Lisa Katz, from *Look There: New and Selected Poems*. © 2006 by Agi Mishol. English-language translation © 2006 by Lisa Katz. Reprinted by permission of Graywolf Press, Saint Paul, Minnesota. "In the Supermarket," translated by Tsipi Keller. Reprinted by permission of the translator.

Gabriela Mistral, "The Footprint," translated by Ursula K. Le Guin, from *Selected Poems of Gabriela Mistral*. © 2003 University of New Mexico Press. Reprinted by permission of University of New Mexico Press.

Tatsuji Miyoshi, "The Ground," translated by Ichiro Kôno and Rikutaro Fukuda, from *An Anthology of Modern Japanese Poetry*, published by Kenkyusha, 1957. © 1957 by Ichiro Kôno and Rikutaro Fukuda. "Great Aso," translated by Edith Marcombe Shiffert and Yuki Sawa, from *An Anthology of Modern Japanese Poetry*. © 1972 by the Charles E. Tuttle Co.

Eugenio Montale, "Xenia I," "To Conclude," and "In the Smoke," translated by G. Singh, from *New Poems*, ©1990, 1972 by Eugenio Montale and G. Singh. Reprinted by permission of New Directions Publishing Corp.

Valzhyna Mort, "Belarusian" and "Men," translated by Franz Wright and Elizabeth Oehlkers Wright. Published in *Words Without Borders*, September 2005. © 2005 by Franz Wright. Reprinted by permission of *Words Without Borders*.

Taha Muhammad Ali, "Abd el-Hadi Fights a Superpower," from *So What: New & Selected Poems 1971–2005*, translated by Peter Cole,

Yahya Hijazi, and Gabriel Levin. © 2006 by Taha Muhammad Ali. Translation © 2000, 2006 by Peter Cole, Yahya Hijazi, and Gabriel Levin. Reprinted by permission of Copper Canyon Press, www .coppercanyonpress.org.

Amjad Nasser, "Once Upon an Evening in a Café." Translated by S. V. Attalah. By permission of the author.

María Negroni, "The Baby," translated by Anne Twitty, from *Night Journey*. © 2002 María Negroni; translation and introduction © 2002 Princeton University Press. Reprinted by permission of Princeton University Press.

Pablo Neruda, "Nothing More" and "Too Many Names," translated by Alastair Reid, from *Extravagaria*. Translation © 1974 by Alastair Reid. Reprinted by permission of Farrar, Straus and Giroux, LLC. "Body of a Woman," "I Remember You as You Were," "Walking Around," and "Tonight I Can Write," translated by W. S. Merwin, from *Twenty Love Poems and a Song of Despair*. Translations © W. S. Merwin. Reprinted by permission of The Wylie Agency LLC. "Nothing but Death" and "Ode to My Socks," translated by Robert Bly, from *Neruda & Vallejo: Selected Poems*. © 1993 by Robert Bly. Reprinted by permission of the translator. "Keeping Still," translated by Dan Bellm. By permission of the Carmen Balcells Agency and the translator.

Augustinho Neto, "Kinaxixi," translated by W. S. Merwin. © W. S. Merwin. Reprinted by permission of The Wylie Agency LLC.

Viteslav Nezval, "Woman in Plural," translated by Jerome Rothenberg, from *Antilyrik and Other Poems*. © 2001. Reprinted by permission of Green Integer Books, www.greeninteger.com.

Nuala Ní Dhomhnaill, "A Recovered Memory of Water," translated by Paul Muldoon, from *The Fifty Minute Mermaid*. "As for the Quince," translated by Paul Muldoon, from *Pharaoh's Daughter*. Reprinted by kind permission of the author and The Gallery Press, Loughcrew, Oldcastle, County Meath, Ireland.

Salah Niazi, "Third World," translated by Abdullah al-Udhari, from *Modern Poetry of the Arab World*.

Jacob Nibenegenesabe, from "The Wishing Bone Cycle, #2," translated by Howard Norman, from *The Wishing Bone Cycle*. © by Howard Norman.

Henrik Nordbrandt, "Our Love Is Like Byzantium," translated by Alexander Taylor and the author, from *Selected Poems*. Translation © 1978 by Alexander Taylor and Henrik Nordbrandt. Reprinted by permission of Curbstone Press.

Giacomo Noventa, "What's Beyond," translated by Pearse Hutchinson, from *Done into English*. © 2003 by Pearse Hutchinson. Reprinted by kind permission of the author and The Gallery Press, Loughcrew, Oldcastle, County Meath, Ireland.

Dan Pagis, "Picture Postcard from Our Youth" and "Autobiography," translated by Stephen Mitchell, from *The Selected Poetry of Dan Pagis*. © 1996 Dan Pagis. Reprinted by permission of The University of California Press.

Francesc Parcerisas, "The Defeated," translated by Pearse Hutchinson, from *Done into English*. © 2003 by Pearse Hutchinson. Reprinted by kind permission of the author and The Gallery Press, Loughcrew, Oldcastle, County Meath, Ireland. "Act of Gratitude," translated by Cyrus Cassells. Reprinted by permission of the translator.

Nicanor Parra, "The Tablets," "A Man," translated by W. S. Merwin, from *Antipoems: New and Selected*. © 1985 Nicanor Parra. Reprinted by permission of New Directions Publishing Corp. "I Take Back Everything I've Said," translated by Miller Williams, from *Poems and Antipoems*. © 1972 by Nicanor Parra and Miller Williams. Reprinted by permission of New Directions Publishing Corp.

Pier Paolo Pasolini, "Prayer to My Mother," translated by Norman MacAfee and Luciano Martinengo, from *Poems*. Translation © 1982 by Norman MacAfee. Reprinted by permission of Farrar, Straus and Giroux, LLC.

Boris Pasternak, "A Wedding," translated by Robert Hass and Stephen Mitchell, from *Into the Garden: A Wedding Anthology*. © 1993 by Robert Hass and Stephen Mitchell. Reprinted by permission of Harper Collins Publishers.

Cesare Pavese, "Death will come and will have your eyes," translated by Geoffrey Brock, from *Disaffections: Complete Poems 1930–1950*. © 1998 by Giulio Einaudi editore s.p.a., Torino. Translation © 2002 by Geoffrey Brock. Reprinted by permission of Copper Canyon Press, www.coppercanyonpress.org. "Words from Confinement," translated by William Arrowsmith, from *Hard Labor*. Reprinted by permission of HarperCollins.

Octavio Paz, "Flame, Speech," translated by Mark Strand, from *A Draft of Shadows*. © 1987 Mark Strand. Reprinted by permission of New Directions Publishing Corp. "Sight, Touch," translated by Eliot Weinberger, from *Collected Poems 1957–1987*, © 1987 by Octavio Paz and Eliot Weinberger. Reprinted by permission of New Directions Publishing Corp. "The Key of Water" by Octavio Paz, translated by Elizabeth Bishop, from *The Complete Poems 1927–1979* by Elizabeth Bishop. © 1979, 1983 by Alice Helen Methfessel. Reprinted by permission of Farrar, Straus and Giroux, LLC.

Sandro Penna, "Maybe I'm getting old, staying seated," "A glass of milk and a piazza," "Look at the workers on the green field," "The accused has only words," translated by W. S. Di Piero, from *This Strange Joy: Selected Poems of Sandro Penna* (Ohio State Unversity Press, 1982). © 1982 by W. S. Di Piero. Reprinted by permission of the translator.

Fernando Pessoa, "If they want me to be a mystic, fine. I'm a mystic." translated by Edwin Honig, from *Poems of Fernando Pessoa*. © 1986 by Edwin Honig and Susan M. Brown. Reprinted by permission of City Lights Books.

György Petri, "I Am Stuck, Lord, on Your Hook" and "Night Song of the Personal Shadow," translated by Clive Wilmer and George

Gömöri, from *Night Song of the Personal Shadow*. Published by Bloodaxe Books in 1991. Reprinted by permission of the translators.

Francis Ponge, "The Pleasures of the Door," translated by Raymond Federman. © 1942 Editions Gallimard. Reprinted by permission of the translator and Editions Gallimard.

Vasko Popa, "St. Sava's Journey," translated by Anne Pennington, from *Vasko Popa: Collected Poems*, revised and expanded by Francis R. Jones. © 1977. Published by Anvil Press Poetry in 1997. Reprinted by permission of the publisher. "Prayer to the Wolf Shepherd," "Wolf Ancestry," "Wolf Eyes," and "Absolute Goal," from *Vasko Popa: Collected Poems 1943–1976*. © Vasko Popa 1952, 1956, 1965, 1968, 1972, 1975. Translations © Anne Pennington 1969, 1973, 1977. Reprinted by permission of Persea Books and Carcanet Press. "The Tenants of the Little Box," "The Craftsmen of the Little Box," and "Last News About the Little Box," translated by Charles Simic, from *Another Republic: 17 European and South American Writers*. © 1976 Charles Simic and Mark Strand. Reprinted by permission of HarperCollins Publishers.

Adélia Prado, "Denouement" and "Serenade," translated by Ellen Doré Watson, from *The Alphabet in the Park*. © 1990 by Ellen Doré Watson and reprinted by permission of Wesleyan University Press, www.wesleyan.edu/wespress/. "The Tenacious Devil Who Doesn't Exist," translated by Ellen Doré Watson. © 2009 by Ellen Doré Watson. Published by permission of the author and the translator.

Jacques Prévert, "Barbara," translated by Lawrence Ferlinghetti, from *Paroles*. © 1958 Lawrence Ferlinghetti. Reprinted by permission of City Lights Books.

Salvatore Quasimodo, "And Suddenly It's Evening" and "Only If Love Should Pierce You," translated by Jack Bevan, from *Salvatore Quasimodo: Complete Poems*. Published by Anvil Press Poetry in 1983. Reprinted by permission of the publisher.

Raymond Queneau, "The Human Species," translated by Teo Savory, from *Raymond Queneau: Poems*. Published by Unicorn Press, 1971.

From *L'Instant fatal*. © 1948 Editions Gallimard. Reprinted by permission of Editions Gallimard. "If You Imagine," translated by Michael Benedikt. Published in *Modern Poetry in Translation*, summer 1966. From *Si tu t'imagines*. © 1948 Editions Gallimard. Reprinted by permission of Editions Gallimard.

Miklós Radnóti, "Postcard," translated by Steven Polgar, Stephen Berg, and S. J. Marks, from *Clouded Sky*. © 1972 Sheep Meadow Press. Reprinted by permission of the translators.

Mansur Rajih, "The Fatherland," translated by Ren Powell. Published in *Words Without Borders*, September 2005. Reprinted by permission of *Words Without Borders*.

Irina Ratushinskaya, "I will live and survive and be asked:" translated by David McDuff. Reprinted by permission of the translator.

Dahlia Ravikovitch, "A Dress of Fire" and "Hovering at a Low Altitude," translated by Chana Bloch and Chana Kronfeld. From *Hovering at a Low Altitude* (W. W. Norton, 2009). © Chana Bloch and Chana Kronfeld. Reprinted by permission of the translators.

Sadanand Rege, "Old Leaves from the Chinese Earth," translated by Dilip Chitre, from *An Anthology of Marathi Poetry (1945–65)*, edited by Dilip Chitre (Nirmala Sadanand Publishers, 1967). © International Association for Cultural Freedom. Reprinted by permission of the translator.

Pierre Reverdy, "The Book," "Fruit Bowl," and "Bottle," translated by Dan Bellm. By permission of Flammarion and the translator.

Rainer Maria Rilke, "The Eighth Duino Elegy," translated by Robert Kelly. Reprinted by permission of the translator. "Orpheus. Eurydice. Hermes," translated by J. B. Leishman. Reprinted by permission of Suhrkampf Verlag GmbH & Co. "Sometimes a Man Stands Up During Supper," translated by Robert Bly. Reprinted by permission of the translator. "Autumn Day," translated by John Felstiner. Reprinted by permission of the translator.

Yannis Ritsos, "The Meaning of Simplicity," translated by Edmund Keeley, from *Repetitions, Testimonies, Parentheses*. © 1991 Princeton University Press. Reprinted by permission of Princeton University Press. "Wonder," "Beauty," and "Audible and Inaudible," translated by Minas Savvas. Reprinted by permission of the translator.

Jean-Pierre Rosnay, "Piazza San Marco," translated by J. Kates. © J. Kates. Reprinted by permission of the translator.

Tadeusz Różewicz, "A Sketch for a Modern Love Poem," from *Postwar Polish Poetry, Third Edition*. © 1965, 1983 Czesław Miłosz. Reprinted by permission of The Wylie Agency, Inc. "Who Is a Poet," translated by Magnus Jan Krynski and Robert Maguire, from *The Survivor and Other Poems*. © Princeton University Press. Reprinted by permission of Princeton University Press.

Pentti Saarikoski, "Potato Thief," translated by Herbert Lomas. Reprinted by permission of the translator. From "Invitation to the Dance, #XXII," translated by Anselm Hollo. Reprinted by permission of the translator.

Guillermo Saavedra, from "On the Tomato," translated by Cindy Schuster. © 2007 by Cindy Schuster. Published in *Words Without Borders*, May 2007. Reprinted by permission of *Words Without Borders*.

Umberto Saba, "The Goat," translated by Stephen Sartarelli, from *Songbook: Selected Poems from the* Canzoniere *of Umberto Saba*. Translation © 1998 by Stephen Sartarelli. Reprinted by permission of The Sheep Meadow Press.

Jaime Sabines, "Pieces of Shadow," translated by W. S. Merwin, from *Pieces of Shadow*. © W. S. Merwin, reprinted by permission of The Wylie Agency LLC.

Nelly Sachs, "Chorus of the Rescued" from *O the Chimneys* by Nelly Sachs, translated by Michael Roloff. Translation © 1967, renewed 1995 by Farrar, Straus & Giroux, Inc. Reprinted by permission of Farrar, Straus and Giroux, LLC.

Tomaž Šalamun, *"Pour un jeune Chalamoun qui se vend dans la rue,"* translated by Michael Biggins, from *The Four Questions of Melancholy: New and Selected Poems.* © 1997 by Tomaž Šalamun. Translation © 2007 by Michael Biggins. Reprinted by permission of White Pine Press, www.whitepine.org. "The Field of Ptuj," translated by Christopher Merrill, from *The Selected Poems of Tomaž Šalamun.* © 1991. Reprinted by permission of HarperCollins Publishers.

George Seferis, from "Mythistorema, #4" and "Interlude to Joy," translated by Edmund Keeley and Philip Sherrard, from *George Seferis: Collected Poems.* © 1967 Princeton University Press, 1995 renewed PUP/revised edition. Reprinted by permission of Princeton University Press.

Léopold Sédar Senghor, "Taga for Mbaye Dyôb" and "To New York, #3," translated by Melvin Dixon, from *The Collected Poetry.* © 1991 University of Virginia Press. Reprinted by permission of University of Virginia Press.

Aharon Shabtai, "Rosh HaShanah," translated by Peter Cole, from *J'Accuse.* © 1998, 1999, 2000, 2001, 2002 by Aharon Shabtai. Translation © 2001, 2002, 2003 by Peter Cole. Reprinted by permission of New Directions Publishing Corp. "My heart's so full of shit" and "When You Were Twenty," translated by Peter Cole. Reprinted by permission of the translator.

Malka Shaked, "Shame," translated by Shirley Kaufman. Reprinted by permission of Hakibutz Hameuchad Publishing House.

Ahmad Shamlou, "Existence," translated by Zara Houshmand. © 2003 by Zara Houshmand. Published in *Words Without Borders* July/August 2003. Reprinted by permission of *Words Without Borders.*

Shin Shifra, "Moonstruck" and from "A Woman Who Practices How to Live," translated by Tsipi Keller. Reprinted by permission of the translator.

Kazuko Shiraishi, "The Donkey Speculates," translated by Samuel Grolmes and Yumiko Tsumura, from *Let Those Who Appear.* © 1984,

1986, 1992, 1996, 2000, 2001, 2002 by Kazuko Shiraishi. Translation © Samuel Grolmes and Yumiko Tsumura. Reprinted by permission of New Directions Publishing Corp.

Elena Shvarts, "Remembrance of Strange Hospitality," translated by Michael Molnar, from *Paradise*. Bloodaxe Books, 1993. © 1993 Bloodaxe Books. Reprinted by permission of Bloodaxe Books.

Leonardo Sinisgalli, "Dog Flies," translated by Jamie McKendrick. Reprinted by permission of the translator. "Old Grief" and "Via Velasca," translated by W. S. Di Piero. Reprinted by permission of the translator.

Sǒ Chǒngju, "Self-portrait," translated by Peter H. Lee. In *An Anthology of Korean Poetry*, John Day Publishers. "Elephants of Thailand," translated by David McCann, from *Selected Poems of Sǒ Chǒngju*. © 1989. Reprinted by permission of Columbia University Press.

Edith Södergran, "On Foot I Wandered Through the Solar Systems" and "The Trees of My Childhood," translated by Malena Mörling and Jonas Ellerström. By permission of the translators.

Piotr Sommer, "Transportist," translated by Jarosław Anders and W. Martin, from *Continued*. © 2005 Piotr Sommer. Reprinted by permission of Wesleyan University Press.

Marin Sorescu, "Destiny," from *The Biggest Egg in the World*, translated by Ioana Russell-Gebbett et al (Bloodaxe Books, 1987). "With a Green Scarf," from *Selected Poems*, translated by Michael Hamburger. Bloodaxe Books, 1983. Reprinted by permission of Bloodaxe Books.

Marcin Świetlicki, "Six Times Coltrane" and "M—Black Monday," © Marcin Świetlicki. Translation © Elżbieta Wójcik-Leese. Reprinted by permission of the author and translator.

Anna Swir, "She Does Not Remember," "The First Madrigal," "The Second Madrigal," and "A Woman Talks to Her Thigh." From *Talking to My Body*. © 1996 Czesław Miłosz and Leonard Nathan, translation.

Reprinted by permission of Copper Canyon Press. "Conversation Through the Door," "Building the Barricade," "He Steals Furs," "A Woman Said to Her Neighbor," "Two Hunchbacks," "He Was Lucky," translated by Magnus Jan Krynski and Robert A. Maguire. By permission of Princeton University Press.

Wisława Szymborska, "I Am Too Near," "A Great Number," "Letters of the Dead," and "The Joy of Writing," translated by Czesław Miłosz. © 1965, 1983 Czesław Miłosz. Reprinted by permission of The Wylie Agency, Inc. "In Praise of My Sister," "Homecoming," "The Terrorist, He Watches," translated by Adam Czerniawski. Reprinted by permission of the translator. "Pietà" and "Under a Certain Little Star," translated by Magnus Jan Krynski and Robert A. Maguire, from *Sounds, Feelings, Thoughts*. © 1981 by Princeton University Press. Reprinted by permission of Princeton University Press. "Children of the Epoch" and "Hunger Camp at Jaslo," translated by Grazyna Drabik and Austin Flint. Reprinted by permission of the translators.

Novica Tadić, "The Cats' Strike," translated by Michael March and Dusan Puvacic, from *Child of Europe: A New Anthology of East European Poetry* (Penguin, 1991). © 1991 by Michael March. Reprinted by permission of the translators.

Rabindranath Tagore, "On My Birthday," translated by William Radice, from *Selected Poems: Rabindranath Tagore*. © 1985, 1987 William Radice. Reprinted by permission of the translator.

Shuntaro Tanikawa, "Growth," "Twenty Billion Light Years of Loneliness," "'Porno-Bach,'" and "Landscape with Yellow Birds," translated by Harold Wright. Reprinted by permission of the author and translator.

Jorge Teillier, "End of the World," translated by Miller Williams. Reprinted by permission of Miller Williams.

Georg Trakl, "A Romance to Night" and "Grodek," from *Autumn Sonata: Selected Poems of Georg Trakl*. Translation © 1989, 1998 by Daniel Simko. Reprinted by permission of the estate of Daniel Simko.

Tomas Tranströmer, "Grief Gondola, #2," translated by Malena Mörling. By permission of the translator. "Track" and "Vermeer," translated by Robert Bly. By permission of the translator.

Marina Tsvetaeva, from "Poems for Moscow," from "Poems to Czechia," from "Poems for Blok," and from "Poems for Akhmatova," translated by Jean Valentine and Ilya Kaminsky. © 2009 by Jean Valentine and Ilya Kaminsky. "To Kiss a Forehead," translated by Ilya Kaminsky. © 2007 by Ilya Kaminsky. By permission of the translators.

Tristan Tzara, "Metal Coughdrops," from *Writing Through*, translated and edited by Jerome Rothenberg (Wesleyan University Press, 1984). © 1984 by Jerome Rothenberg and reprinted by permission of Wesleyan University Press.

Giuseppe Ungaretti, "In Memoriam," translated by Patrick Creagh, published in *Penguin European Modern Poets*, 1971.

Paul Valéry, "The Angel Handed Me a Book," translated by Carolyn Forché, from *Angel of History*, published by HarperCollins Publishers, 1994. Copyright © 1994 by Carolyn Forché. Reprinted by permission of the translator.

César Vallejo, "The Black Riders," "The Anger That Breaks a Man Down into Boys," "Masses," and "Black Stone Lying on a White Stone," translated by Robert Bly. Reprinted by permission of the translator. "There are days, there comes to me an exuberant, political hunger," "A man walks by with a baguette on his shoulder," "The Nine Monsters," and "Today I like life much less," from *César Vallejo: The Complete Poetry: A Bilingual Edition,* edited and translated by Clayton Eshleman. Copyright 2007 by The Regents of the University of California. Reprinted by permission of the University of California Press and the translator.

Miriam Van hee, "Evening in Dún Laoghaire" and "Sycamores at Nîmes Station," translated by Judith Wilkinson. Reprinted by permission and with the support of the Flemish Literature Fund.

Orhan Veli Kanik, "Rumors," "My Gold-Toothed Beauty," "Quantitative," and "Poem with a Tail," translated by Murat Nemet-Nejat, from *I, Orhan Veli*. Reprinted by permission of Hanging Loose Press.

Veronica Volkow, "The Washerwoman." Translated by Forrest Gander. From *Mouth to Mouth: Poems by 12 Mexican Women*, edited by Forrest Gander. Published by Milkweed Press, 1993. By permission of the translator.

Andrei Voznesensky, "Darkmotherscream," translated by Robert Bly and Vera Dunham, from *News of the Universe: Poems of Twofold Consiousness*. Published by Sierra Club Books. © 1980 by Robert Bly. Reprinted by permission of Robert Bly.

Aleksander Wat, "Before Breughel the Elder," translated by Czesław Miłosz, from *Postwar Polish Poetry, Third Edition*. © 1965, 1983 by Czesław Miłosz, reprinted by permission of The Wylie Agency.

Wen I-To, "Perhaps," translated by Arthur Sze, from *The Silk Dragon: Translations from the Chinese*. © 2001 Arthur Sze. Reprinted by permission of Copper Canyon Press, www.coppercanyonpress.org.

Meir Wieseltier, "Abraham." From *The Flower of Anarchy: Selected Poems*. © 2003 University of California Press. Reprinted by permission of University of California Press.

Xi Chuan, "After Wang Ximeng's Blue and Green Horizontal Landscape Scroll, *A Thousand Miles of Rivers and Mountains*," translated by Arthur Sze. By permission of Xi Chuan and Arthur Sze.

Yen Chen, "The Plum Hint," translated by Arthur Sze, from *The Silk Dragon: Translations from the Chinese*. © 2001 by Arthur Sze. Reprinted by permission of Copper Canyon Press, www.coppercanyonpress.org.

Ghirmai Yohannes, "Unjust Praise," translated by Charles Cantalupo and Ghirmai Negash. Published in *Words Without Borders*, August 2005. Reprinted by permission of *Words Without Borders*.

Yu Jian, "Opus 39," translated by Fang Dai, Dennis Ding, and Edward Morin, from *The Red Azalea: Chinese Poetry Since the Cultural Revolution*. © 1990 University of Hawaii Press. Reprinted by permission of University of Hawaii Press.

Oksana Zabuzhko, "Letter from the Summer House," translated by Douglas Smith. Reprinted by permission of the author.

Adam Zagajewski, "To Go to Lvov" and "Late Beethoven" from *Tremor: Selected Poems* by Adam Zagajewski. Translation © 1985 by Farrar, Straus and Giroux. Reprinted by permission. "Try to Praise the Mutilated World," from *Without End* by Adam Zagajewski. Translation © 2003 by Farrar, Straus and Giroux. "A Talk with Friedrich Nietzsche," from *Canvas* by Adam Zagajewski. Translation © 1991 by Farrar, Straus and Giroux. All reprinted by permission of of Farrar, Straus and Giroux, LLC. "Music Heard with You," translated by Clare Cavanagh. Translation © 2005 by Clare Cavanagh. Published in *Words Without Borders*, September 2005. Reprinted by permission of *Words Without Borders*.

Zahrad, "Cleaning Lentils," translated by Diana Der-Hovanessian. Reprinted by permission of the translator.

Zelda, "A Woman Who's Arrived at a Ripe Old Age," translated by Miriyam Glazer. Reprinted by permission of the translator.

Zhai Yongming, from "Fourteen Plainsongs," translated by Andrea Lingenfelter. By permission of the author and translator.

Zhang Er, "Cross River . Pick Lotus," translated by Rachel Levitsky. Reprinted by permission of the author.

INDEX OF POETS